REASON & WRITING

Custom Edition of Essay Essentials

Fanshawe College

NELSON / EDUCATION

NELSON EDUCATION

ISBN-13: 978-0-17-649562-6
ISBN-10: 0-17-649562-2

Consists of Selections from:

Essay Essentials with Readings,
Fourth Edition
Norton, Green
ISBN 10: 0-17-640704-9, © 2006

Steps to Writing Well with
Additional Readings
Wyrick, Bose
ISBN 10: 0-17-644048-8, © 2010

Perspectives on Contemporary
Issues: Readings Across
the Disciplines,
First Canadian Edition
Ackley, Blank, Hume
ISBN 10: 0-17-610328-7, © 2008

Copyright Acknowledgements

Dallaire, Roméo. (2003). "Introduction to *Shake Hands with the Devil: The Failure of Humanity in Rwanda.*" Excerpted from *Shake Hands with the Devil: The Failure of Humanity in Rwanda* by LGen Roméo Dallaire. Copyright © 2003 Roméo Dallaire, LGen (ret) Inc. Reprinted by permission of Random House Canada.

Friedman, Thomas L. (2004). "30 Little Turtles." From *The New York Times*, © 2004 *The New York Times*. All rights reserved. Used by permission and protected by the Copyright Laws of the United States. The printing, copying, redistribution, or retransmission of the Material without express written permission is prohibited.

Geddes, Carol. (1990). "Growing Up Native." Reprinted by permission of the author, 2009.

LaFraniere, Sharon. (2006). "Africa's World of Forced Labour in a 6-Year-Old's Eyes." From *The New York Times*, © 2006 *The New York Times*. All rights reserved. Used by permission and protected by the Copyright Laws of the United States. The printing, copying, redistribution, or retransmission of the Material without express written permission is prohibited.

Russell, Bertrand. (1967). "What I Have Lived For." Prologue. *The Autobiography of Bertrand Russell*. By Russell. Boston: Little, Brown, 1967, 3-4.

Sontag, Susan. (2001). "A Century of Cinema" from WHERE THE STRESS FALLS by Susan Sontag. Copyright © 2001 by Susan Sontag. Reprinted by permission of Farrar, Straus and Giroux, LLC.

The Wadsworth Essential Reference Card to the MLA Handbook for Writers of Research Papers 7th Edition. (2009). From WADSWORTH. *The Wadsworth Essential Reference Card to the MLA Handbook for Writers of Research Papers*, 4E. © 2010 Heinle/Arts & Sciences, a part of Cengage Learning, Inc. Reproduced by permission. www.cengage.com/permissions

Contents

....

Introduction

Chapter 1   Your Audience and You .... *page 7*

Chapter 2   Choosing the Right Words .... *page 22*

Chapter 3   Selecting a Subject .... *page 37*

Chapter 4   Managing the Main Points .... *page 42*

Chapter 5   Writing the Thesis Statement .... *page 59*

Chapter 6   Preparing an Outline .... *page 69*

Part 2

Chapter 7   Understanding Paragraph Form and Function .... *page 79*

Chapter 8   Keeping Your Readers with You .... *page 96*

Chapter 9   Writing Introductions and Conclusions .... *page 108*

Part 3

Chapter 10   The Three Steps to Revision .... *page 123*

Part 4

Chapter 17   Argument and Persuasion .... *page 141*

Chapter 15   Comparison and Contrast .... *page 162*

Part 5

Chapter 18   Researching Your Subject .... *page 178*

Chapter 19   Summarizing, Paraphrasing, and Quoting .... *page 190*

Chapter 20   Documenting Your Sources .... *page 209*
                 The Wadsworth Essential Reference Card to the MLA
                 Handbook for Writers of Research Papers .... *page 213*

Chapter 21   Formatting a Research Paper .... *page 228*

Part 6

Sentence Structure

Chapter 22   Cracking the Sentence Code .... *page 249*

Chapter 23   Solving Sentence-Fragment Problems .... *page 261*

Chapter 24   Solving Run-On Problems .... *page 269*

Chapter 25   Solving Modifier Problems .... *page 274*

Chapter 26   The Parallelism Principle .... *page 283*

Chapter 27   Refining by Combining .... *page 289*

Grammar

Chapter 28   Mastering Subject-Verb Agreement .... *page 294*

Chapter 29   Using Verbs Effectively .... *page 304*

Chapter 30   Solving Pronoun Problems .... *page 318*

Punctuation

Chapter 31   The Comma .... *page 338*

Chapter 32   The Semicolon .... *page 349*

Chapter 33   The Colon .... *page 354*

Chapter 34   Quotation Marks .... *page 359*

Chapter 35   Question and Exclamation Marks .... *page 362*

Chapter 36   Dashes and Parentheses .... *page 366*

Spelling

Chapter 37   Hazardous Homonyms .... *page 372*

Chapter 38   The Apostrophe .... *page 385*

Chapter 39   The Hyphen .... *page 393*

Chapter 40   Capital Letters .... *page 397*

Chapter 41   Numbers .... *page 404*

Essay Essentials

Introduction to Shake Hands with the Devil:
The Failure of Humanity In Rwanda .... *page 413*
Lt.-Gen. Roméo Dallaire (With Brent Beardsley)

A Century of Cinema .... *page 418*
Susan Sontag

Africa's World of Forced Labor, In a 6-Year-Old's Eyes
Sharon Lafraniere

30 Little Turtles
Thomas L. Friedman

Don't Let Stereotypes Warp your Judgment .... *page 431*
Robert L. Heilbro

The Holocaust .... *page 436*
Bruno Bettelheim

New World Daughters:
How Parents Raise Boys and Girls Differently and Why It's Wrong .... *page 442*
Judy Mann

Kids in the Mall: Growing up Controlled .... *page 447*
William Severini Kowinski

Why We Crave Horror Movies .... *page 454*
Stephen King

Why I stopped Being a Vegetarian .... *page 459*
Laura Fraser

It's Later Than You Think .... *page 464*
Mark Lynas

Why Schools Don't Educate .... *page 471*
John Taylor Gatto

"My Son Doesn't Act Like a Boy":
What It's Like to Have a Child Who Challenges Gender Stereotypes .... *page 476*
Nancy Kalish

Girls Will Be Girls. Unfortunately. .... *page 483*
Ellen Goodman

Growing Up Native .... *page 487*
Carol Geddes

Appendix

APA Format .... *page 493*

PART 1

Introduction: Why, What, and How to Learn to Write

Few people enjoy writing; after all, it's hard work. Writing is a complex process, a learned skill that requires patience, concentration, and persistence. Unlike most of the skills you acquire in a career program, however, writing is not job-specific. **The skills you learn from this book will be useful to you in all your college courses** and **in every job you hold throughout your working life.** If you have graduated from college or university, your prospective employer will assume that you are able to communicate in writing frequently, correctly, and in a manner that will do credit to the company. The higher you climb on the organizational ladder, the more you will write and the more complex your writing tasks will become. Furthermore, evaluations of your performance in any job will be based at least in part on your communication skills.

Essay Essentials will teach you to write essays of various kinds. The word "essay" comes from the French *essayer*, to try or attempt. **An essay is an attempt to communicate information, opinion, or emotion.** In the context of a college or university, an essay is an exercise that gives students an opportunity to explore and explain their own and others' thoughts about a subject. In the larger world, essays appear in newspapers and magazines as editorials, reviews, opinion pieces, and commentaries on news and public affairs.

If at times the essay form seems artificial or unrelated to the kinds of writing you expect to do in your profession, remember that thinking, organizing, and researching are basic to all practical writing tasks. **In this book, you will learn how to find and organize thoughts, to develop ideas in coherent paragraphs, and to express yourself clearly, correctly, and concisely.** Once you've mastered these basics, you can develop any job-specific writing styles that may be required of you. If you can write well-organized, convincing, and error-free essays of five or more paragraphs, you will have no difficulty adapting your skills to business or technical reports, instructions, proposals, memoranda, sales presentations, commercial scripts, or legal briefs.

The fact that literacy is in decline does not make the ability to write less important; rather, it means that those who can write competently are in high demand. **You can learn to write well if you are willing to work at it.** We have designed this text to enable you to master the theory of good writing and to practise it successfully. Because it is more fun and more efficient to learn with others than it is to struggle alone, we have included many group-based exercises. To make the process less onerous, we have also introduced a few humorous essays, and, in Part 6, as many entertaining exercises as we could think of. If you follow the guidelines in this book, you will produce effective essays in college and creditable communications in your career.

THE WEBSITE

In addition to the material in this book, you will find useful information and helpful exercises on our website. Go to http://www.essayessentials4e. nelson.com and click on "Student Resources" to find the menu of options available to you. Under "More Information" you will find helpful supplements to the book, and under "More Practice" you will find additional exercises for the chapters in Part 6. The answers to these exercises are marked automatically, so you will know instantly whether or not you have understood the material.

Also on the website are practice tests, reference links, and an "Ask the Authors" button that enables you to send us any questions you have about *Essay Essentials* or about your writing. We take your questions seriously and will answer as soon as we get your message. Purchase of this book also entitles you to free access to InfoTrac®, an easy-to-use online library of source materials you can use for your research in this and other courses. You will learn more about InfoTrac® and other databases in Chapter 18.

WHAT THE SYMBOLS MEAN

This symbol in the margin beside an exercise means the exercise is designed to be done by two or more students working together. Carefully read the directions that introduce the exercise to find out how many students should participate and what task is to be performed. Often you are instructed to begin work in a pair or group, then to work individually on a writing task, and finally to regroup and review your writing with your partner(s).

This symbol means "note this." We've used it to highlight writing tips, helpful hints, hard-to-remember points, and information that you should apply whenever you write, not just when you are dealing with the specific principle covered in the paragraph marked by the icon.

This icon attached to an exercise means that the exercise is a mastery test designed to check your understanding of the chapter you have just completed. The answers to these exercises are not in the back of the book; your instructor will provide them.

GO TO WEB

EXERCISE

This symbol means that the *Essay Essentials* website has information or exercises to supplement the chapter you are working on. Log on to the website, click on the "More Practice" button, and then click on "Web Exercises." The information and exercises are arranged by chapter, so to get to the exercises for the apostrophe, for example, click on Chapter 38, and do the numbered exercises listed below the icon.

THE PROCESS OF WRITING

Writing is a three-step process consisting of
1. planning or prewriting
2. drafting
3. revising and editing

This book explains and illustrates two approaches to the process of writing: top-down and bottom-up. The **top-down approach** assumes that you know what you have to say before you begin to write. You identify your subject and main points, draft your thesis statement (the statement that orients your readers to the content of the paper), and plan your topic sentences (those sentences that identify the content of each paragraph). Research papers, business reports, and essay questions on exams are examples of writing that require a "top-down" approach.

The **bottom-up approach** is useful when you do not know ahead of time what you want to say. You discover your meaning through the act of writing. With this approach, you rely on prewriting strategies such as brainstorming and freewriting to get into the process of writing.

You will probably need to use both approaches. Sometimes you will discover your subject through writing; at other times, using "top-down" strategies will help you to express clearly what you already know. You should experiment with both approaches so that you can comfortably use whichever is more appropriate for a particular writing task.

WHAT YOUR READERS EXPECT

Whichever approach you use, your goal is to make your finished essay easy for your readers to read and understand. To achieve that goal, you must meet your readers' expectations.

Readers have five unconscious expectations when they begin to read a piece of extended prose. They expect to find

- paragraphs
- a sentence (usually the first) in each paragraph that identifies the topic
- unified paragraphs, each of which explores a single topic
- connections (transitions) within and between paragraphs
- a preview (in the introduction) of the content and organization of the paper

Keep in mind that readers want to obtain information quickly and easily, without backtracking. They rely on the writer—you—to make efficient reading possible.

Your readers will read more easily and remember more of what they read if you include a thesis statement to introduce them to the content and organization of the piece, and if you begin each paragraph with a topic sentence. If you do not organize and develop your paper and its paragraphs in a clearly identifiable way, readers will impose their own organization on the paper. The result will be longer reading time, or difficulty in understanding and remembering the content, or, worse, the assumption that a paragraph or even the whole paper has a meaning other than the one you intended. You can help your readers to read efficiently if you follow the old adage: "Tell them what you're going to tell them; tell them; then tell them what you've told them."

HOW TO BEGIN

Having a conversation with someone who never seems to get to the point is a tiresome and frustrating experience. Similarly, an essay—or any other form of written communication—that has no point and that rambles on will turn readers off.

How can you avoid boring, confusing, or annoying your readers? To begin with, you need to have something to say and a reason for saying it. Very few people can write an essay straight through from start to finish without spending a considerable amount of time thinking and planning. Some prewriting will help you to develop the structure more easily; freewriting and brainstorming (Chapter 3 will explain these) stimulate thinking.

Once you've determined what it is you want to say, you need to arrange your main points in the most effective order possible. If you organize your ideas carefully, you won't ramble. Writing an essay is like building a house. If you have a clear plan or blueprint, you can construct the house without the frustration of having to double back or even to start all over again from the beginning. A good plan saves time.

As a general rule, the more time you spend on prewriting and planning, the less time you'll need to spend on drafting and revising. Careful planning will enable you to produce papers that your readers will find clear and understandable.

THE PARTS OF AN ESSAY

An essay has a beginning, a middle, and an end. The most basic form is the five-paragraph essay, which teaches you everything you need to know about writing nonfiction prose. Think of this highly structured form of prose not as a straitjacket that stifles your creativity, but rather as a pattern to follow while you develop the skills and abilities you need to build other, more complex prose structures.

The beginning, or **introduction**, tells your reader the point, the purpose, and the scope of your essay. If your introduction is well crafted, its **thesis statement** will identify the main points you will discuss in the paragraphs that follow.

The middle, or **body**, of an essay consists of paragraphs that discuss in detail the points that have been identified in the introduction. In a short essay, each paragraph develops a separate main point. Each paragraph should contain three essential components:

- a **topic sentence**, which identifies the point of the paragraph
- development, or **support**, of the topic sentence. Supporting sentences provide the detailed information the reader needs in order to understand the point.
- a **concluding sentence** that either brings the discussion of the topic to a close or provides a transition to the next paragraph

The end, or **conclusion**, is a brief final paragraph. Unless your essay is very short, you summarize the main points to reinforce them for the reader, then say goodbye with a statement that will give your readers something to think about after they have finished reading your essay.

Bertrand Russell's "What I Have Lived For" is a good example of a well-structured essay. The introduction contains a clear thesis statement. Each paragraph of the body consists of a clearly identifiable topic sentence, development sufficient to explain it, and a concluding sentence. The conclusion is brief, pointed, and memorable.

WHAT I HAVE LIVED FOR
Bertrand Russell

INTRODUCTION

Thesis statement

Three passions, simple but overwhelmingly strong, have governed my life: the longing for love, the search for knowledge, and unbearable pity for the suffering of mankind. These passions, like great winds, have blown me hither and thither, in a wayward course, over a deep ocean of anguish, reaching to the very verge of despair.

BODY

Topic sentence

I have sought love, first, because it brings ecstasy—ecstasy so great that I would often have sacrificed all the rest of life for a few hours of this joy. I have sought it, next, because it relieves loneliness—that terrible loneliness in which one shivering consciousness looks over the rim of the world into the cold unfathomable lifeless abyss. I have sought it, finally, because in the union of love I have seen, in a mystic miniature, the prefiguring vision of the heaven that saints and poets have imagined. This is what I sought, and though it might seem too good for human life, this is what—at last—I have found.

Support

Concluding sentence

Topic sentence

With equal passion I have sought knowledge. I have wished to understand the hearts of men. I have wished to know why the stars shine. And I have tried to apprehend the Pythagorean power by which number holds sway above the flux. A little of this, but not much, I have achieved.

Support

Concluding sentence

Love and knowledge, so far as they were possible, led upward toward the heavens. But always pity brought me back to earth. Echoes of cries of pain reverberate in my heart. Children in famine, victims tortured by oppressors, helpless old people a hated burden to their sons, and the whole world of loneliness, poverty, and pain make a mockery of what human life should be. I long to alleviate the evil, but I cannot, and I too suffer.

Topic sentence

Support

Concluding sentence

CONCLUSION

This has been my life. I have found it worth living, and would gladly live it again if the chance were offered me.

Russell, Bertrand. "What I Have Lived For." Prologue. *The Autobiography of Bertrand Russell.* By Russell. Boston: Little, Brown, 1967. 3–4.

1

Your Audience and You

Before you begin to write anything—an essay, a report, an e-mail message, or a set of instructions—you must have something to write about (your subject) and someone to write for (your audience). Writing is communication, and for communication to take place, you (the writer) must be able to make your ideas or message clear to your readers.

Addressing Your Readers

As you plan, draft, and revise your paper, ask yourself the following questions:

- How old are your readers?
- What is their level of education?
- What do they do for a living?
- What is their income?
- What is their cultural background?
- Are they male or female?

While you must be careful to avoid generalizing or stereotyping, the answers to these questions do influence most people's views, and you would be wise to consider them before you begin to write.

Before you begin to plan an essay, write at the top of the page the specific audience for whom your message is intended.

Naturally, your instructor will be reading your early (and your late) assignments, but, for your first draft, you should write at the top of the page the name of someone other than your instructor whom you might expect to be interested in your subject. Be creative: your high-school principal, a recent immigrant, a union official, a member of the Liberal Party, a religious leader, the CEO of a polluting company, someone receiving social assistance income. Keeping this reader in mind will help you to plan, develop, and write your assignment in a tone and style appropriate to your message.

Spend a little time thinking about your subject in relation to your audience. Consider carefully the following three questions when you are deciding what to include in your essay.

1. What does my reader know about my subject?
2. What is my reader's attitude toward my subject?
3. What are my reader's needs in regard to my subject?

READERS' KNOWLEDGE

The first question will help you choose the kind and amount of information that should be included. Are you writing for someone who knows little about your subject, or for someone with fairly detailed knowledge? Do you have to cover all the basics, or can you take it for granted your audience is familiar with them? You don't want to bore your readers by telling them things they already know. On the other hand, if you fail to provide information they need in order to understand your message, you'll turn them off or lose them entirely.

READERS' ATTITUDES

The second question helps you decide how to approach your subject. Will your readers be sympathetic to what you have to say? If so, you will aim to reinforce their agreement. You will probably state your opinion up front, to show you're on their side. If, however, you think they may be hostile to what you have to say, you might lessen their resistance by providing reasons and support for your ideas before revealing your point of view. Gentle persuasion is usually more effective than confrontation in writing, as it is in life.

READERS' NEEDS

The third question helps you to decide whether to persuade or instruct, to compare or classify, to describe or analyze. Which approach will give your readers the information they need about your subject? The answers to this question will determine whether your remarks should be fairly general or quite specific. Do you intend to add to or reinforce your audience's general knowledge, or do you want your readers to apply your information only in specific situations?

Reflecting Yourself

Once you are clear about who your readers are, what they know, and what they need to know, you should spend a little time considering your role in the communication process. Any time you speak or write, you present yourself in a particular way to your audience. We all play a variety of roles. We choose a role, often unconsciously, that we hope will suit the expectations of the people we are communicating with. These roles are not false or hypocritical; they are simply facets of our personality that we try to match to the needs of each situation. Choosing and maintaining an appropriate role is essential in successful communication.

Each day, for example, you meet a variety of people. Some of them you know well—parents, siblings, friends, classmates, teachers, coworkers, supervisors. Others you know only casually—the cashier in the restaurant, the police officer at the radar trap, the enumerator for the upcoming election, the checkout person in the grocery store. With each of these people, whether the contact is casual or intense, you consciously or unconsciously adjust your language in order to communicate. If you speak to your spouse as you might to your dog, you'll be sleeping on the couch. If you speak to a salesperson as you would to a love interest, you'll get arrested.

Consider the following three questions when you are deciding what role would be most appropriate in a particular communication situation.

1. What is my purpose in writing?
2. What is my attitude toward my subject?
3. What are my readers' expectations of me in this communication?

YOUR PURPOSE

The most common purposes of writing are to inform, to persuade, and to entertain. Your purpose will depend largely on the needs and expectations of your readers. It will influence your choice of supporting details to develop your points and will affect your tone. How you say something often has more impact on your audience than what you say.

YOUR ATTITUDE

The second question requires you to clarify your attitude to the subject of your paper. This involves more than simply asking, "Am I for or against it?" You should consider how strongly you feel about the subject because your attitude will influence your tone as well as the kinds of evidence you present. You should also think about how personal you want to be in presenting your ideas, or how balanced and objective you wish (or are able) to be. In answering these questions, consider how closely your attitude toward the subject aligns with your audience's attitude. If your views coincide, then a fairly informal approach may be appropriate; if they differ, then an impersonal, objective approach is preferable.

YOUR ROLE

The third question requires you to think about what role your audience is likely to expect of you. If you write as an authority, will you be credible? If you write as a peer or friend, will you be effective? What are your readers likely to expect from someone in your position writing to them on this subject? Taking the time to think about your readers' expectations will help you to make appropriate choices with respect to the point of view you take, the examples and support you provide for your ideas, and the level of language you use.

Levels of Standard English Writing

Good writing involves more than the meaning of words and sentences. It also requires the choice of appropriate language. No one would submit a book review that began, "This is an awesome book with, like, ideas that sort of make you think, you know?" You know instantly that the language is inappropriate. Similarly, if you were discussing the book with friends over coffee and announced, "This book contains provocative and stimulating ideas that engage and challenge the reader," your language would be equally inappropriate.

Written English (e-mail notwithstanding) is usually more formal than spoken English. Because writers have time to consider what they want to say and how best to say it, they can choose their words carefully, arrange them in meaningful sentences, and organize ideas into logical paragraphs. An appropriate level of language is an essential part of effective writing.

Choose a level that suits both your topic and your reader. There will be times when you need to compromise; for example, when you send one message to several people. In such cases, the safe bet is to aim at the highest level of receiver and trust that the others will understand.

NEL

Sometimes it isn't clear what level you should be using. At such times, your reader's preference should determine your choice. Many colleges and universities expect students to write academic papers in formal English, which requires, among other things, third-person pronouns (*he, she, one, they*). Informal writing, with its first- and second-person pronouns (*I, me, you*), may not be acceptable. (See page 496 for an explanation of pronoun "person.") Ask your instructor about your school's policy and follow it.

Similarly, because employers tend to favour formal letters of application over casual ones, if you want to get the job, you will write a formal letter. For a talk you give to your class, an informal, conversational style may be appropriate. Most of what you read and write falls somewhere in the middle. Business documents, for example, are usually written in general-level Standard English.

There are no fixed divisions of language use; the three levels we've identified often overlap. To help you choose the most appropriate level for your message and audience, the table below outlines the basic features of informal, general, and formal written English.

	Informal	**General**	**Formal**
Vocabulary and Style	Casual, everyday; usually concrete; some slang, colloquial expressions, contractions. Written in 1st and 2nd persons.	The language of educated persons; nonspecialized; balance of abstract and concrete; readily understood. Can use 1st, 2nd, and 3rd persons.	Often abstract, technical, or specialized; no contractions or colloquialisms. Written in 3rd person.
Sentence and Paragraph Structure	Sentences short, simple; some sentence fragments; paragraphs short.	Complete sentences of varying length; paragraphs vary, but are often fairly short.	Complete sentences, usually long, complex; paragraphs fully developed, often at length.
Tone	Conversational, casual; sounds like ordinary speech.	Varies to suit message and purpose of writer.	Impersonal, serious, often instructional.
Typical Uses	Personal letters, some fiction, some newspapers, much advertising.	Most of what we read: newspapers, magazines, novels, business correspondence.	Academic writing, some textbooks, scientific reports, journal articles, legal documents.

No one level is "better" than another. Each has its place and function. Your message, your audience, and your purpose in writing are what should determine the level you choose.

Read the following selections and consider each writer's purpose, the audience for whom the message is intended, and why the writer's level of language is appropriate to the readers, the subject, and the purpose.

INFORMAL

Love him or hate him, Michael Moore has turned the world of documentary film on its ear. Documentaries are stuffy and boring, aren't they? They certainly aren't supposed to be wildly popular or turn their directors into media stars. But starting with *Roger and Me* back in 1989, Moore has almost single-handedly made the documentary fun, personal, and popular. Like most film students, I began thinking I wanted someday to make blockbuster Hollywood hits like the movies Canadians Norman Jewison and James Cameron are famous for, but now I'm a convert to documentaries and that other Canadian production star: the NFB.

Who is the intended audience? This paragraph is intended for general readers, not people who are looking for a scholarly discussion of film. The writer assumes some interest in and knowledge of Michael Moore and his films.

What is the writer's role? The writer wants to inform readers in a personal way about his point of view. He plays the role not of expert or teacher, but rather of a friend or acquaintance supplying the information for discussion in a casual way.

Why is the level of language appropriate? The use of contractions and colloquialisms ("the world . . . on its ear," "stuffy and boring") and especially the use of first and second persons in direct address clearly mark this as an informal and friendly communication. Short sentences and a conversational style add to the informal tone.

GENERAL

What is a documentary film? The so-called father of documentary film, John Grierson, called it "the creative treatment of reality," but that definition is uncomfortably broad. For example, is *Alexander* a documentary? What about *Troy* or *Amadeus* or *Lawrence of Arabia*? All are about real people and contain a version of historical events, but few would classify them as documentaries. The purpose of these films is to entertain (if you discount their real purpose: to make money), and perhaps purpose lies at the heart of the definition. The primary purpose of a documentary film is to inform.

Who is the intended audience? Readers of this paragraph will be knowledgeable enough about films to have seen at least one of the three major releases mentioned, and interested enough in film to want to know more about the documentary genre.

What is the writer's role? The writer is providing information from an expert point of view, but in a friendly way rather than as a lecture or formal instruction. The use of humour and casual language makes the information easy to absorb, and the direct address and use of questions add a friendly tone to the paragraph.

Why is the level of language appropriate? The vocabulary and writing style are easily understood by general readers. The use of second person ("if you discount their real purpose") adds to the personal nature of the language, as do the questions directed to the reader. This message is designed to appeal to the widest audience possible.

FORMAL

John Grierson, best known as "the father of documentary film" and the founder of the National Film Board of Canada, called documentary "the creative treatment of reality." Since its inception in 1939, the NFB has been presenting reality to Canadians and the rest of the world in creative ways. While it has earned recognition in other cinematic fields (notably animation), the NFB has achieved most of its international acclaim from more than 60 years of producing first-class documentary films, many of them Academy Award winners.

Who is the intended audience? The readers of this passage are literate and well read. They are people whose education and experience have enabled them to appreciate that good films can be informative as well as entertaining.

What is the writer's role? The writer's purpose is to highlight the achievements of the NFB to an audience of educated peers who share his aesthetic interests. The writer presents himself not as an expert addressing nonexperts, but rather as an enthusiast who wants to share knowledge with a receptive audience.

Why is the level of language appropriate? The vocabulary is fairly sophisticated, and the sentences are fairly long and complex. There are no contractions or colloquialisms, no first- or second-person pronouns. The writer addresses his audience as peers—fellow film enthusiasts—but not as close friends. The objective tone would be suitable for an article in a professional magazine.

Exercise 1.1*

Read the excerpts below and discuss the intended audience, the author's role, and the appropriateness of the language. Answers for this chapter begin on page 512.

1.   One of the most frequent complaints about Wal-Mart, which employs 1.4 million people worldwide, is its failure to pay workers a living wage. Store employees are paid 20–30 percent less than the industry average, making many of them eligible for social assistance. It is estimated that American taxpayers fork out $2.5 billion a year in welfare payments to Wal-Mart employees (Head, 2004). Because the retailer hires hard-to-place workers, like recent immigrants, seniors, and single mothers, its employees are often afraid they will not find work elsewhere. The kind of work Wal-Mart does offer is gruelling: stores are intentionally understaffed—the strategy behind the company's legendary productivity gains—so that existing employees will work harder (Head, 2004). It is alleged that systemic discrimination against women within the corporation has denied the majority of Wal-Mart workers the chance at promotion, a charge that is now the subject of the largest civil-rights suit in US history.

Parmar, Deenu. "Labouring the Wal-Mart Way." 224.

Who is the intended audience? _____

_____

_____

_____

_____

What is the writer's role? _____

_____

_____

_____

_____

Why is the level of language appropriate? _____

_____

_____

_____

_____

2.   The "inletting" or "butt mortise" plane is designed to cut precise mortises for butt hinges, lock fronts, and strike plates, or to repair jambs, doors, furniture, and millwork, wherever the ability to do inletting is important. The plane has a completely open throat so that you can watch what you are doing. The 3/4" wide cutter is set at a 40 degree pitch for general work. This can be increased to 70 degrees (plus or minus) for difficult grain simply by inserting the blade bevel-up. For inletting, such as hinges, you set the blade extension at the hinge leaf thickness, score the outline and plane to depth, using overlapping strokes for a smooth bottom. The same technique would be used for a veneer repair on solid wood.

Lee Valley Catalogue. Tenth Anniversary Issue, 1987–88. 23.

Who is the intended audience? _____

_____

_____

_____

_____

What is the writer's role? _____

_____

_____

_____

_____

Why is the level of language appropriate? _____

_____

_____

_____

_____

3.   Doing business with the Chinese is an enterprise fraught with peril for the unwary Western business person. While in the West most business is ultimately conducted face to face between the principals, negotiations seldom if ever achieve this intimacy in the Orient. It is common for gatherings of ten or more to take part in the early stages of agenda-setting and prioritizing, and the hapless Westerner who has not engaged the services of a Chinese guide will have to sort out the Party overseers from the ineffectual hangers-on and try to hone in on the power brokers who often remain in the background to assess and evaluate before making themselves known. Often the early stages of business relationships are conducted in the very formal atmosphere of banquets, with hierarchical seating arrangements and ritual toasts. Coping with the exotic atmosphere, the oblique method of negotiation, the recondite formality, and the unidentifiable food is a formidable challenge: one that should be undertaken without assistance by only the most intrepid and experienced of Western entrepreneurs.

Czereczovich, Katlin. "Business Abroad." *Canadian Women Entrepreneurs* Spring 2002: 91.

Who is the intended audience? _____

_____

_____

_____

_____

What is the writer's role? _____

_____

_____

_____

_____

Why is the level of language appropriate? _____

_____

_____

_____

_____

4.   A parent quickly learns that no matter how much money you have, you will never be able to buy your kids everything they want. You can take a second mortgage on your house and buy what you think is the entire

Snoopy line: Snoopy pajamas, Snoopy underpants, Snoopy linen, Snoopy shoelaces, Snoopy cologne, and Snoopy soap, but you will never have it all. And if Snoopy doesn't send you to the poorhouse, Calvin Klein will direct the trip. Calvin is the slick operator who sells your kids things for eighty-five dollars that cost seven at Sears. He has created millions of tiny snobs, children who look disdainfully at you and say, "Nothing from Sears." However, Dad-Can-I fought back: I got some Calvin Klein labels and sewed them into Sears undershorts for my high fashion junkies.

Cosby, Bill. *Fatherhood*. New York: Doubleday, 1994. 41–42.

Who is the intended audience? _____

_____

_____

_____

_____

What is the writer's role? _____

_____

_____

_____

_____

Why is the level of language appropriate? _____

_____

_____

_____

_____

5.   The conclusion of *Jane Eyre* has Jane and Rochester married at last. Jane no longer needs to compromise herself in order to be with him, and his first wife is not the only obstacle that has been removed. The man who insisted that she abandon her conscience to live in sin has changed significantly. Rochester now complements Jane as never before. His mutilation has been referred to as a "symbolic castration" by Richard Chase (qtd. in Gilbert and Gubar 368), but it is his spirit rather than his masculinity that seems to have been honed. Rochester has been humbled, and the taste of humility has taught him wisdom. He is able to admit to Jane, "I did wrong: I would have sullied my innocent flower—breathed guilt on its purity"

(Brönte 495; ch. 37). During their first engagement, Jane was unsure and often uncomfortable about her place in Rochester's life. In her description of their marriage, however, she says that "we are precisely suited in character—perfect concord is the result" (Brönte 500; ch. 38). Such a perfect fit is only made possible by Rochester's movement away from his earlier extreme. He has become a close match for Jane on every level, and therefore becomes her ideal mate.

Friedland, Jess. "The Evolution of Moral Balance in Charlotte Brönte's *Jane Eyre*." 322–23.

Who is the intended audience? _____

_____

_____

_____

_____

What is the writer's role? _____

_____

_____

_____

_____

Why is the level of language appropriate? _____

_____

_____

_____

_____

Exercise 1.2

As a class, select one of the five paragraphs found on pages 16–20. First, be sure you all agree on the intended audience and purpose of the paragraph. Your objective is to "translate" the paragraph for a different audience. The purpose of your revision will be the same as that of the original, but the language and tone will be adapted to suit the audience for whom the new message is intended.

Next, in groups of three, choose an audience for your revision from the following list. (Each group must select a different audience.)

elementary-school children	very hip, very cool grade 12 students
your family	your English instructor
a close friend	*Globe and Mail* readers
an elderly relative	your college newspaper

Once all groups have completed their translations, compare the results by reading the newly translated paragraphs aloud. Try to guess who each other's intended audience is. How do you know? How does the language work to meet the needs of the new audience?

The following exercise will give you practice in communicating effectively by adjusting your level of language to suit your purpose, your message, and your audience.

Exercise 1.3

Imagine, in each of the following situations, that you must deal with three different audiences face to face. Before you begin, analyze each audience in terms of knowledge, attitudes, and needs; then clarify the purpose of your message, your attitude toward your subject, and your audience's expectations of you.

1. You prepared your company's sales presentation in PowerPoint and stored it on the hard drive of your notebook computer. On your way to a meeting with clients in Detroit, your notebook was handled roughly by customs inspectors at the airport. When you got to the sales meeting, your computer would not open PowerPoint.

   You made the sales presentation as well as you could, but the clients were not impressed, and your company did not get the contract. Explain these circumstances to

   - your supervisor in the sales department
   - the U.S. Customs complaint bureau
   - a representative of the computer company, which claims its notebook computers are practically indestructible

2. At 8:30 this morning, your friend Jaron phones you from a police station. He has been arrested because, according to the arresting officer, he has 37 unpaid parking tickets outstanding. He claims he's innocent; he's never had a parking ticket. He has called to ask you to come down and bail him out. If you do so, you will be very late for work. Jaron refuses to call his parents for help. Tell this story to

- your parents
- your boss
- Jaron's parents

3. You recently bought a pair of silk pants from Bottom Drawers Pants Company. They ripped in the crotch the first time you bent over. You were dancing enthusiastically with a very attractive partner and were deeply embarrassed. Before you could recover your composure, the owner of the club asked you to leave immediately. Tell your story to

- Bottom Drawers
- the owner of the club
- your dancing partner

4. After only three weeks at your new job, you felt you had to tell someone that your fellow employees were routinely stealing office supplies, sales samples, and even tools and equipment. After speaking to your union steward and your manager, you were laid off without any explanation or warning, and as a probational employee you have no protection. Explain your situation to

- the president of your union
- a longtime employee of the company who doesn't know why you were let go
- an employment counsellor

5. You are short of money—so short you can't even buy gas for your car. If you can't get gas money, you will be late for work, and your boss is annoyed because you've been late twice this week already. Ask for money from

- your parents
- a friend
- someone who owes you money

6. Turn one of the 15 role-playing situations above into a written assignment.

Exercise 1.4

This exercise is designed to reinforce your understanding of the importance of knowing your reader. An effective communicator figures out ahead of time not only what his or her readers need to know, but also what they do not need to know. Some information is necessary and some is superfluous, with the mix varying widely from audience to audience. With this in mind, describe one of the following topics to three different audiences: choose one from each of the three groups listed below.

Topics: a favourite musician or group, a favourite standup comic or other performer

Group A: a grandparent, a teacher, an employer

Group B: a coworker, a classmate, an old friend you haven't seen in years

Group C: The president of your college or university or the Student Council Social Committee, whom you are trying to persuade to support a fundraising event featuring your topic.

Choosing the Right Words

In this chapter, we provide a brief introduction to language that is accurate and appropriate for your message and your audience. Our assumption is that you are writing for readers in academic and professional environments. Our goals are to help you convey your message clearly and in a way that will leave your readers with a positive impression of you and your ideas.

Before you get started, you need to equip yourself with a few essential resources and some basic knowledge of what kinds of language are inappropriate when you write.

The Writer's Toolkit

In addition to basic skills, all workers need tools. As a general rule, the better their tools, the better their work. Every writer comes equipped with a set of language skills acquired from birth. In most cases, however, these skills are not sufficiently developed to handle the complex task of producing clear, error-free prose in a professional style. Fortunately, tools are available to assist writers in bringing their language skills up to the standards required by professional environments. Collectively, we call these indispensable aids the Writer's Toolkit.

No one expects a writer to write without assistance. In fact, our first recommendation to beginning writers is to GET HELP! Every writer needs three basic tools and to know how to use them.

1. Buy and use a good dictionary.

A dictionary is a writer's best friend. You will need to use it every time you write, so if you don't already own a good dictionary, you need to buy one. For Canadian writers, a good dictionary is one that is Canadian, current, comprehensive (contains at least 75,000 entries), and reliable (published by an established, well-known firm).

A convenient reference is the *Gage Canadian Dictionary*, available in an inexpensive paperback edition. It is the dictionary on which we have based the examples and exercises in this chapter. Also recommended are the *ITP Nelson Canadian Dictionary of the English Language*, the *Canadian Oxford Dictionary* (2nd ed., 2004), and, for those whose native language is not English, the *Oxford Advanced Learner's Dictionary*. Unfortunately, no comprehensive Canadian dictionary is available on the Internet.

Begin by reading the "Guide to the Dictionary" in the front matter. The information in the Guide may not be very entertaining, but it is essential if you want to understand how to read your dictionary accurately. No two dictionaries are alike. In order to use your dictionary efficiently, you need to be familiar with its symbols, abbreviations, and the format of its entries.

Knowing what is in the dictionary guide will also save you time. For example, you may not need to memorize long lists of irregular plurals. Good dictionaries include irregular plurals in their entries. They also include irregular forms of verbs, adjectives, and adverbs. And if you've forgotten how regular plurals, verbs, adjectives, and adverbs are formed, you'll find that information in the guide as well.

2. Use spelling and grammar checkers responsibly.

Good spell-check programs can find typing errors and common spelling mistakes that distract your readers and make you look careless. They do have limitations, however. As we'll see, they can't tell if you meant to write "your" or "you're" and will not flag either word, even if it's used incorrectly. (You'll learn more about such words in Chapter 37, "Hazardous Homonyms.")

Also, since we use Canadian English, our spelling is frequently different from American spelling, which is the standard on which most word-processing programs are based. Set your program to Canadian spelling if the option exists. If it does not, be aware that words such as *colour*, *honour*, and *metre*—all correct Canadian spellings—will be flagged as errors.

Another useful tool is a hand-held spell checker. Conveniently pocket-sized and not expensive, these devices contain a large bank of words and can provide the correct spelling if the "guess" you type in is not too far off. Some checkers even pronounce the word for you. Ask your instructor if you can use this device (sound turned off, please) when you are writing in class and during exams.

The best advice we can give you about grammar checkers (they announce their presence by producing wavy green lines under words or sentences as you write on your word processor) is to use them with caution. So far, no grammar checker has been able to account for even most, let alone all, of the subtleties of English grammar. A grammar program is as likely to flag a perfectly good sentence, even to suggest a "fix" that is incorrect, as it is to ignore a sentence full of errors. "I done real good on my grammar test," for example, escapes the dreaded wavy green line.

3. Buy and use a good thesaurus.

If you repeat yourself, using the same words again and again, you won't communicate your thoughts interestingly, let alone memorably. Worse, you will bore your reader. A thesaurus is a dictionary of synonyms—words with similar meanings. For any word you need to use repeatedly in a document, a good thesaurus will provide a list of alternatives.

Synonyms are *not* identical in meaning. Your dictionary will help you decide which of the words listed in your thesaurus are suitable for your message and which are not. We do not recommend that you rely on the thesaurus in your word-processing program. For any given word, a word-processing thesaurus provides a list, in alphabetical order, of more-or-less synonyms, with no usage labels or examples. "More-or-less" is not good enough. At the very least, you need to know whether the synonyms offered are nouns or verbs and whether they are in general use or are informal, technical, derogatory, or even obsolete. For this information, buy a good book-form thesaurus and use it in conjunction with your dictionary. Two thesauruses are available in inexpensive paperback editions: the *Oxford Thesaurus of Current English* (2003) and *Roget's 21st Century Thesaurus in Dictionary Form* (3rd ed., 2005).

Use the information you find in a thesaurus with caution. Inexperienced writers sometimes assume that long, obscure words will impress their readers. In fact, most readers are irritated by unnecessarily "fancy" language. For more information on this topic, see the "Pretentious Language" section on pages 31–32.

NEVER use a word whose meaning you do not know. When you find a potential but unfamiliar synonym, look it up in your dictionary to be sure it's the word you need.

So far, we've introduced you to the tools you'll need as a writer and to the levels of language you can choose from when writing a message for a particular audience. Let's turn now to the writing errors you must not commit, no matter what message you're sending or the audience to which you're sending it: wordiness, slang and jargon, pretentious language, clichés, sexist language, offensive language, and "abusages."

The Seven Deadly Sins of Writing

1. WORDINESS

Wordiness—words and phrases that are not essential to the communication of your message—is annoying to readers, no matter what topic you are writing about. Good writing communicates a message as concisely as possible. Wordy messages take up your readers' time and try their patience. If you want to please your audience, be brief.

Sometimes wordiness results from a failure to revise carefully. In the editing stage of writing, you should be looking for the best words to express your meaning. Wordy expressions and awkward phrasing often pop into your mind when you are struggling to express an idea, and they often make their way into a first draft. There is no excuse for them to survive a careful edit and make their way into the second draft, however.

Here's an example of what can happen when a writer fails to prune his or her prose:

> In my personal opinion, the government of this country of ours needs an additional amount of meaningful input from the people of Canada right now.

This wordy sentence could be nicely condensed into "In my opinion, our government needs to hear more from the people." The writer has chosen impressive-sounding phrases (*meaningful input, this country of ours*) and has slipped in unnecessary and meaningless words that should have been caught during editing (*personal opinion, an additional amount*). The result is a sentence that is so hard to read that it isn't worth the effort to decipher.

As you can see from the above example, one of the symptoms of wordiness is redundancy, or saying the same thing twice. Another is using several words where one or two would do.

The following list contains some of the worst offenders we've collected from student writing, corporate memoranda, form letters, and advertisements.

Wordy	Concise
a large number of	many
absolutely nothing/everything/ complete/perfect	nothing/everything/ complete/perfect
actual (*or* true) fact	fact
almost always	usually
at that point in time	then
at the present time	now
consensus of opinion	consensus
continue on	continue
could possibly (*or* may possibly, might possibly)	could (*or* may, might)
crisis (*or* emergency) situation	crisis (*or* emergency)
due to the fact that	because
end result	result
equally as good	as good
few and far between	rare
final conclusion	conclusion
for the reason that	because
free gift	gift
I myself (*or* you yourself, *etc.*)	I (*or* you, *etc.*)
I personally think/feel	I think/feel
in actual fact	in fact
in every instance	always
in my opinion, I think	I think
in the near future	soon
in today's society/in this day and age	now (*or* today)
is able to	can
many different kinds	many kinds
mutual agreement/cooperation	agreement/cooperation
my personal opinion	my opinion
no other alternative	no alternative
personal friend	friend
real, genuine leather (*or* real antique, *etc.*)	leather (*or* antique, *etc.*)
red in colour (*or* large in size, *etc.*)	red (*or* large, *etc.*)
repeat again	repeat
return back	return (*or* go back)
really, very	*These words add nothing to your meaning. Leave them out.*
8:00 a.m. in the morning	8:00 a.m.
such as, for example	such as

Wordy	Concise
take active steps	take steps
totally destroyed	destroyed
truly remarkable	remarkable
very (most, quite, almost, rather) unique	unique

Exercise 2.1*

Working with a partner, revise these sentences to make them as concise and clear as possible. Then compare your answers with our suggestions on page 513.

1. I myself personally feel that there is absolutely no basis in fact for the idea that UFOs exist.
2. Basically, I myself prefer modern contemporary furniture to old antiques.
3. I personally think Alison is faking her illness and pretending to be sick so she can stay at home and not have to go to work.
4. It has come to my attention that our competitor's products, though not equally as good as ours are, are nevertheless, at this point in time, selling better than those which we produce.
5. In my opinion, I believe that my essay is equally as good as Jill's and deserves equally as good a mark, which it would have got if it weren't for the fact that the professor hates me.
6. In my opinion, I doubt that this particular new innovation will succeed in winning much in the way of market share.
7. In my view, I feel that an English course that teaches the basic fundamentals is an essential prerequisite before a person can succeed in college, the business world, and the community at large.
8. "As a new beginning teacher," we told our English instructor, "you should try to understand the utter impossibility of gaining and holding the respect of us students so long as you are so completely and totally devoted to insisting that we follow grammar rules and regulations that totally inhibit the creativity in our writing."
9. I myself believe that, in all probability, this trend can be turned right around if we return back to basic fundamentals in our design process and introduce a few new innovations in our manufacturing process.
10. Due to the fact that the law, not to mention our company's policy, rules, and regulations, absolutely prohibits any mention of race, age, sex, religion, or marital status in official documents such as personnel documents, we have made sure that all such descriptors are entirely eliminated from our files, resulting in the fact that all our personnel documents are now almost virtually identical.

2. SLANG AND JARGON

Slang is "street talk": nonstandard words and phrases used by members of a group—people who share a culture, interest, or lifestyle. The group may be as large as a generation or as small as a high-school clique. Do you know what "amped," "badload," "busting," and "hodger" mean? Probably not. The whole point of slang is its exclusivity. It's a private language and thus not appropriate for a message aimed at a general reader.

Another characteristic of slang is that it changes quickly. Terms that were "in" last month are "out" today. Except for a few expressions that manage to sneak across the line that separates private language from mainstream English, most slang expressions are quickly outdated and sound silly. And finally, slang is an oral language. It is colloquial—that is, characteristic of casual speech—and not appropriate for use in professional or academic writing.

When you aren't sure if a word is appropriate for a written message, consult your print dictionary. The notation *sl.* or *slang* appears after words that are slang or have a slang meaning. (Some words, such as *house*, *cool*, and *bombed*, have both a general and a slang meaning.) If the word you're looking for isn't listed, chances are it's a recent slang term, and you should avoid using it in writing. Taking the time to choose words that are appropriate to written English increases your chances both of communicating clearly and of winning your readers' respect.

Exercise 2.2

- Working in groups of three or four, identify five current slang expressions.
- Now list five slang expressions that are no longer in use among your peers.
- Finally, define each current slang term in language appropriate to a general reader. (If you don't have a clear picture of a "general reader," write each definition in words your parents and teachers would understand.)

Jargon is similar to slang because it, too, is the private language of a subgroup; however, whereas the subgroups for slang are formed by culture or lifestyle, the subgroups who speak jargon are formed by profession or trade. The jargon of some professions is so highly technical and specialized it amounts almost to a private language.

Although jargon is useful, even necessary, in the context of some jobs, it is inappropriate in most writing because it does not communicate to a general reader. Our vocabulary and even the content of our writing are influenced by the contexts within which we work and live. In the following paragraph, D. E. Miller explains the extent to which our individual perceptions are influenced by our life experience.

A group of people witness a car accident. What each person sees, and how he or she describes it, is determined to a large extent by the language each one normally uses. A doctor or nurse would see and describe contusions, lacerations, and hemorrhages. A lawyer would think in terms of civil liabilities and criminal negligence. A mechanic would see crushed fenders, bent axles, and damaged chassis. A psychologist would be concerned about stress reactions, trauma, and guilt. You or I might see and describe the pain and injury caused by a driver's error in judgement or lapse of skill.

Miller, D. E. *The Book of Jargon.* New York: Collier, 1981. 26.

Jargon restricts your audience to those who share your specialized vocabulary and limits or destroys your ability to reach a wider audience. The cure for jargon is simple: unless your readers share your technical background, use nonspecialized language.

Exercise 2.3

Working in small groups, list as many examples of technical jargon as you can for each of the following occupations.

1. police officer (e.g., perpetrator, murder two)
2. nurse (e.g., bug, elopement risk)
3. car enthusiast (e.g., shift throw, stance)
4. financial analyst (e.g., beauty contest, fallen angel)
5. filmmaker (e.g., sync sound, M.O.S.)

Choose five technical terms from your own career field and write a general-level equivalent for each one.

3. PRETENTIOUS LANGUAGE

One of the challenges writers face when trying to adapt their style from the familiar to the formal level is a tendency to overcompensate. Many beginning writers try so hard to impress their readers that they forget that the purpose of writing is to communicate. Writing filled with abstract nouns, multi-syllable words, and long, complicated sentences is **pretentious**. All readers hate pretentious writing because they have to take the time to "translate" it into language they can understand. (Most teachers and supervisors won't bother. They'll just return the piece to the student or employee for revision.)

Sometimes called "gobbledygook," pretentious language has sound but no meaning:

> Our aspirational consumer strategy must position the brand's appeal to women shoppers who are seeking emblematic brands that are positively identified with health-oriented and fitness-centred lifestyles, so they can align their personal images with those lifestyle indicators.

This sentence, part of a marketing presentation to senior management, was written by a middle manager for a major yogurt company. What the poor writer is trying to say is that the company's customers want to be seen as people interested in fitness and health, so the company should advertise its yogurt accordingly.[1]

One symptom of pretentious writing is "buzzwords." These are words and phrases that become popular because they reflect the latest academic or psychological fad. They are often nouns with *-ize* added to them to make them into verbs: *utilize, verbalize, conceptualize*. What's wrong with *use, say,* and *think*? Every teacher knows this annoying trick; so do most managers. Instead of impressing readers, pretentious writing makes readers impatient and causes them to lose respect for the writer. If you really want to get your message across, write plainly and clearly in language your readers can understand.

Exercise 2.4*

Rewrite the following sentences, expressing the ideas in a way that allows the reader to grasp your meaning clearly, easily, and quickly. Then compare your answers to our suggestions on page 513.

1. We were forced to utilize the moisture-removing apparatus in our motorized personal conveyance when precipitate liquid impacted our windshield.
2. The chronologically less advanced generation sometimes achieves a communication deficit with authority figures and parental units.
3. The witness was ethically disoriented truthwise when she claimed that her interface with the accused resulted in his verbalization of an admission of guilt.
4. The parameters of our study vis-à-vis the totality of research in the field demonstrate that surveywise our validity is on a par with that of other instruments.

---

[1] This anecdote is paraphrased from Doug Saunders, "Aspiration Nation: Life Is but a Brand-name Dream," *Globe and Mail* 3 Jul. 2004: F3.

5. The cancellation of IMF funds to the Pacific Rim countries could lead to negative distortion of mutual interrelationships between developed and developing nations.

---

4. CLICHÉS

Unless you're a career civil servant or a longtime bureaucrat, writing pretentious language is a time-consuming and tiring task. You have to look up practically every word in a thesaurus to find a polysyllabic equivalent. Clichés, on the other hand, are easy to produce: they represent language without thought.

A **cliché** is a phrase that has been used so often it has lost its ability to communicate a meaningful idea to a reader.

> In this day and age, it seems that anything goes in our private lives. But in our professional lives, the name of the game is what it has always been: the bottom line.

In this day and age, anything goes, the name of the game, and *the bottom line* are clichés. Readers know what these phrases are supposed to mean, but they have been used so often they no longer communicate effectively. Cliché-filled writing will not only bore readers, but also affect their reaction to your message: "There's nothing new here. It's all been said before."

Spoken English is full of clichés. In the rush to express an idea, we often take the easy way and use ready-made expressions to put our thoughts into words. There is less excuse to use clichés in writing. Writers have time to think through what they want to say. They also have the opportunity to revise and edit. Writers are expected to communicate with more care, more precision, and more originality than speakers.

Clichés are easy to recognize if you are a native speaker. When you can read the first few words of an expression and automatically fill in the rest, the phrase is a cliché: free as a _____; a pain in the _____; last but not_____; it goes without _____. It is difficult to get rid of *all* clichés in your writing, but you can be aware of them and use them as seldom as possible.

The solution to a cliché problem involves time and thought. Think carefully about what you want to say; then say it in your own words, not everyone else's.

As you read through Exercise 2.5, notice how hard it is to form a mental picture of what the sentences mean and how hard it is to remember what you've read—even when you've just read it!

Exercise 2.5

Working with a partner, rewrite these sentences, expressing the ideas in your own words. When you're finished, exchange papers with another team and compare your results.

1. The boardroom was so quiet you could hear a pin drop.
2. It was raining cats and dogs, but we slept like logs through the storm.
3. When you are playing poker, you should keep your cool; otherwise, you could lose your shirt.
4. The CEO could not find a way to stay afloat, so she threw in the towel.
5. I burned the midnight oil and managed to finish the assignment at the crack of dawn.
6. Is this concept a flash in the pan or an idea whose time has come?
7. If we can nip this problem in the bud, there will be light at the end of the tunnel!
8. She stopped dead in her tracks. Lying on the floor was her son, crying his eyes out.
9. Your proposal is as good as they come; however, until the deal is signed, sealed, and delivered, we had better not count our chickens.
10. Even though I sweated it out night after night and kept my nose to the grindstone, I didn't meet my sales quota. As a result, I am sadder but wiser.

5. SEXIST LANGUAGE

Any writing that distracts your readers from your meaning is weak writing. Whether the distraction is caused by grammatical errors, spelling mistakes, slang, or the use of sexist language, your readers' concentration on your message is broken, and communication fails. **Sexist** (or gender-biased) **language** includes the use of words that signify gender (e.g., *waitress, sculptress, actress*) and the use of the pronouns *he, his, him* to refer to singular antecedents such as *everybody, anyone, no one*. Some readers object to terms that draw attention to gender differences, such as *man and wife* or *host and hostess*, preferring instead gender-neutral, inclusive terms such as *married couple* and *hosts*.

It is easy to dismiss nonsexist writing as "politically correct," but the language we use is a powerful force that influences the way we think. If we consistently refer to a *chairman* or *businessman*, we are perpetuating the idea that only men qualify for these positions. Far from being a politically correct fad, the use of inclusive or neutral words is both accurate and evenhanded.

Here are three tips to help you steer clear of sexist writing.

- Avoid using the word *woman* as an adjective. There is an implied condescension to phrases such as *woman athlete* and *woman writer* and *woman engineer*.
- Be conscious of the dangers of stereotyping. Physical descriptions of women are appropriate only where you would offer a similar description if the subject were a man. Just as some men can be excellent cooks, some women can be ruthless, power-hungry executives. It is possible for men to be scatterbrained and gossipy, while women can be decisive, tough, even violent.
- When making pronouns agree with singular antecedents, be careful that your pronouns do not imply bias. For example, "A teacher who discovers plagiarism must report it to *his* supervisor." Either use masculine and feminine pronouns interchangeably, or switch to a plural noun and avoid the problem: "Teachers who discover plagiarism must report it to their supervisors."

Exercise 2.6*

Correct the use of sexist or gender-biased language in the following sentences. Exchange papers with a partner and compare revisions. Then turn to pages 513–14 and compare your answers with our suggestions.

1. The well-known female producer Elaine May often regrets that she cannot go out in public without attracting the attention of fans and photographers.
2. Amy King, an attractive, blonde mother of two, first joined the company as a saleswoman; 10 years later, she was promoted to president.
3. A businessman sitting in the first-class cabin rang for the stewardess, a friendly gal who quickly arrived to assist him.
4. The list of ingredients on food packages contains information that may be important to the housewife, especially if she is the mother of young children.
5. The typical working man with a wife and two children is often hard-pressed to find time for recreation with his bride and the kids.

---

6. OFFENSIVE LANGUAGE

The last thing you want to do when you write is to offend your reader, even if you are writing a complaint. As we've seen above, some words occasionally used in speech are always inappropriate in writing. Swear words, for example, are unacceptable in a written message. So are obscene words, even "mild" ones. Offensive language appears much stronger in print than in speech and can provoke, shock, or even outrage a reader. Racist language and blasphemy (the use of names or objects that are sacred to any religion) are deeply offensive and always unacceptable.

Many writers have experienced the acute embarrassment of having a message read by people for whom it was not intended. What might have seemed at the time of composition to be an innocent joke may prove hateful to the unintended audience and mortifying to the writer.

It is wise to avoid all questionable, let alone unacceptable, expressions in your writing. Language has power: as many linguists have observed, our language actually shapes as well as reflects our attitudes and values. Those who use racist, blasphemous, sexist, or profane terms not only reinforce the attitudes contained in those terms, but also project a profoundly negative image of themselves to their readers.

7. ABUSAGES

Some words and phrases, even ones we hear in everyday speech, are *always* incorrect in written English. Technically, they are also incorrect in speech, but most people tolerate them in informal conversation. If these expressions appear in your writing, your reader will assume you are uneducated, ignorant, or worse. Even in some conversations, particularly in academic and professional environments, these expressions make a poor impression on your listeners.

Carefully read through the following list and highlight any words or phrases that sound all right to you. These are the ones you need to find and fix when you revise.

allready	A common misspelling of *already*.
alot	There is no such word. Use *much* or *many*. (*A lot* is acceptable in informal usage.)
anyways (anywheres)	There is no *s* in these words.
between you and I	The correct expression is *between you and me*.
can't hardly **couldn't hardly**	Use *can hardly* or *could hardly*.
could of (would of, **should of)**	The helping verb needed is *have*, not *of*. Write *could have, would have, should have*.

didn't do nothing	All double negatives ("couldn't see nothing," "couldn't get nowhere," "wouldn't talk to nobody") are wrong. Write *didn't do anything, couldn't see anything, couldn't get anywhere, wouldn't talk to anyone.*
for free	Use *free* or *at no cost.* (Also "free gift." Is there any other kind of gift?)
in regards to	Use *in* (or *with*) regard to.
irregardless	There is no such word. Use *regardless.*
***media* used as singular**	The word *media* is plural. The singular is *medium.* Newspapers and television are mass *media.* Radio is an electronic *medium.*
most all	Use *most* or *almost all.*
off of	Use *off* alone: "I fell *off* the wagon."
***prejudice* used as an adjective**	It is wrong to write "She is *prejudice* against blondes." Use *prejudiced.*
prejudism	There is no such word. Use *prejudice.* "A judge should show no *prejudice* to either side."
***real* used as an adverb**	"Real good," "real bad," and "real nice" are wrong. You could use *really* or *very,* but such filler words add nothing to your meaning.
reason is because	Use *the reason is that*: "The reason is that my printer blew up."
suppose to	This expression, like *use to,* is nonstandard. Use *supposed to* and *used to.*
themself	Also "theirself," "ourselfs," "yourselfs," and "themselfs." These are all nonstandard words. The plural of *self* is *selves: themselves, ourselves,* and so on. Don't use "theirselves"; it's another nonstandard word.
try and	Use *try to.*
youse	There is no such word. *You* is the singular and plural form of the pronoun.

Exercise 2.7*

Correct the following sentences where necessary. Suggested answers are on page 514.

1. Irregardless of what you think, the problem between her and I has nothing to do with you.
2. If you want to be in the office pool, I need $5.00 off of you today because there will be no spots left by tomorrow.
3. Because they didn't finish the job theirself the way they should of, we will have to work real late to get it done.
4. I didn't feel like seeing nobody, so I went home, turned on the TV, and didn't do nothing for the rest of the night.
5. This use to be a real good place to work, but now we are suppose to work a full shift every day, or a penalty is deducted off of our pay.
6. Alot of young people today fight against prejudism not only in society but also within themselfs.
7. I'm suppose to ask youse if the reason for the delay is because there has been another bomb threat.
8. It's unresponsible of us to blame television or any other media for causing violence.
9. Television is partly responsible, however, for the fact that alot of ungrammatical expressions sound alright to us.
10. Between you and I, the reason I didn't speak to no one about Elmo's cheating is because he would of broke my arm.

3

Selecting a Subject

Approximately one-third of the time you devote to an essay should be spent on the planning stage (and the remainder to drafting and revising.) If you take the time to analyze your audience, find a good subject, and identify interesting main points to make about that subject, you will find that the mechanics of writing will fall into place much more easily than if you try to sweat your way through the paper the night before it's due. After you have considered your readers' background, needs, and expectations, the next step is to choose a satisfactory subject to write about.

Even when you are assigned a topic for an essay, you need to examine it, focus it, and consider different ways of approaching it. Depending on your knowledge of the topic and the readers you are writing for, the range of specific subjects for any broad topic is almost endless. For example, given the broad topic "Research sources," here are some of the approaches from which you might choose.

Can you trust Internet sources?
Interviewing to develop original source material
Books: still the best "random access device"
Journal indexes: an underused source of mountains of material
How to do an effective Internet search

Your first task, then, is to choose a satisfactory subject, one that satisfies the basic principles of the **4-S test**:

A satisfactory subject is significant, single, specific, and supportable.

If it passes the 4-S test, your subject is the basis of a good essay.

MAKE YOUR SUBJECT SIGNIFICANT

Your subject must be worthy of the time and attention you expect your readers to give to your paper. Can you imagine an essay on "How to buy movie tickets" or "Why I hate pants with button flies," for example, as being meaningful to your readers?

Exercise 3.1*

From the list below, choose those subjects that would be significant to a typical reader. Revise the others to make them significant, if possible. If not, suggest another, related subject that is significant. When you have finished this exercise, compare your answers with those provided on page 514.

1. Tips for travelling with small children
2. Using the reference library
3. Page-turning techniques
4. The perfect vacation spot
5. How to use the number pad on a calculator
6. Television is a threat to Canadian independence
7. Why you should write on one side of the page only

MAKE YOUR SUBJECT SINGLE

Don't try to crowd too much into one paper. Be careful that your subject is not actually two or three related subjects masquerading as one. If you attempt to write about a multiple subject, your readers will get a superficial and possibly confusing overview instead of the interesting and satisfying detail they expect to find in a well-planned paper. A subject such as "The problem of league expansion in basketball and other sports" is too broad to be dealt with satisfactorily in one essay. More manageable alternatives are "The problems of league expansion in the NBA" or "Why Montreal can't get an NBA franchise."

Exercise 3.2*

From the following list, choose the subjects that are single and could be satisfactorily explored in a short essay. Revise the others to make them single.

1. Causes of unemployment among college students and new graduates
2. Pub night at different colleges
3. How to change a tire and adjust the timing
4. The importance of accuracy in newspaper and television reporting
5. Methods of preventing the spread of STDs

6. Causes of injury in industry and professional sports
7. Nursing and engineering: rewarding careers

MAKE YOUR SUBJECT SPECIFIC

Given a choice between a broad, general topic and a narrow, specific one, always choose the specific one. Most readers find concrete, specific details more interesting than broad generalizations. It would be difficult to say anything very detailed about a huge subject such as "The roles of women in history," for example. But with some research, you could write an interesting paper on "The roles of 19th-century prairie women" or "Famous female pilots."

You can narrow a broad subject and make it more specific by applying one or more *limiting factors* to it. Try thinking of your subject in terms of a specific *kind*, *time*, *place*, *number*, or *person* associated with it. By applying this technique to the last potential subject above, you might come up with "Amelia Earhart's last flight."

Exercise 3.3*

In the list below, identify the subjects that are specific and could be explained satisfactorily in a short essay. Revise the others to make them specific by applying one or more of the limiting factors to each one.

1. Summer employment opportunities in my home town
2. Modern heroes
3. How to enjoy winter weather
4. The effects of government cutbacks on low-income families
5. The problems of urban living
6. How to repair your home appliances
7. Binge drinking among college women

MAKE YOUR SUBJECT SUPPORTABLE

You must know something about your subject (preferably more than your readers know), or you must be able to find out about it. Remember, your readers want information that is new, interesting, and thought provoking—not obvious observations familiar to everyone. You must be able to include *specific examples, facts, figures, quotations, anecdotes,* or other *supporting details.* Supporting information can be gathered from your own experience, from the experience of other people, or from both. If you don't know enough about your topic to write anything but the obvious, be prepared to do some research.

Exercise 3.4*

From the subjects given below, choose those that are clearly supportable in a short essay. Revise the others to make them supportable.

1. My career as a student
2. Movie review: *Star Wars: Episode III—Revenge of the Sith*
3. Crisis in the Canadian airline industry
4. The Chinese secret service
5. Space travel in the year 2100
6. Art through the ages
7. The hazards of working in a fast-food outlet

Exercise 3.5*

Together with a partner, discuss the acceptability of the potential subjects listed below. Indicate with check marks (✔) whether each subject below passes the 4-S test by being significant, single, specific, and supportable. Revise each unsatisfactory subject (fewer than four check marks) to make it a satisfactory subject for a short essay.

The 4-S Test

Subject	significant	single	specific	supportable	Revision
1. Computers	☐	☐	☐	☐	_____
2. Insomnia and other stress-related disorders	☐	☐	☐	☐	_____
3. The Arctic 200 years from now	☐	☐	☐	☐	_____
4. Dressing for an interview	☐	☐	☐	☐	_____
5. Architecture	☐	☐	☐	☐	_____

GO TO WEB

EXERCISE 3.1

Exercise 3.6

Write down three subjects that you think pass the 4-S test. When you've finished, exchange papers with another student and carefully check each other's work.

Once you have selected an appropriate subject, it's time to move on to the next stage: identifying solid main points to support that subject.

4

Managing the Main Points

While you were selecting subjects and testing them against the four principles presented in Chapter 3, you were thinking, consciously or unconsciously, about what you could say about them. **Main points** are the two or three or four most important things you have to say about your subject. Selecting them carefully is a vitally important part of the writing process.

Generating Main Points: The Bottom-Up Approach

If you are feeling intimidated by your task and unsure about how to present your subject, some prewriting activities can be helpful. Writers use several methods to stimulate thinking and prepare for a productive first draft. Two techniques are especially effective: freewriting and brainstorming. Either will get your creative juices flowing; we recommend that you try both to see which works best for you in particular situations.

Understand that you employ these techniques when you already have the necessary material in your head. Either you are writing from personal experience or you've done some research. (You'll learn about research in Part 5.) Freewriting and brainstorming are designed to get your ideas on the page in any order, shape, or form. Don't worry about making a mess. You can clean it up later.

FREEWRITING

Freewriting does what its name implies. It sets you free to write without worrying about any of the possible writing errors you might make that block the flow of your ideas. Forget about grammar, spelling, word choice, and so on, for a while, until you get some ideas down on the page. Here's how to go about freewriting:

1. Put your watch and a pad of paper on your desk. If you can type faster than you can write, open a new document on your computer. (Some writers find it helpful to turn the monitor off.) Write your subject at the top of the page or tape it to the top of your computer monitor. Ideally, your subject will have passed the 4-S test, but if you're really stuck, you can begin with just a word or a phrase.
2. Make a note of the time and start writing. Don't stop until you have written for three, five, or even ten minutes straight. Write anything that comes to mind, even if it seems boring or silly. If you get stuck for words, write your subject or even the last phrase you've written over and over until something new comes to mind. (Don't worry, it will!)
3. Write as quickly as you can. Don't pause to analyze or evaluate your ideas, and don't scratch out or delete anything. This technique is designed to get thoughts into words as quickly as possible without self-consciousness.
4. When the time is up, stop and stretch. Then read over what you've written. Underline anything that is related to your subject. Much of your freewriting will be irrelevant nonsense that you can delete. But what you have underlined will be useful in the next step: identifying the main points you will focus on to explain your subject.
5. Turn the phrases, fragments, and sentences you have underlined into clear, understandable points. If you don't end up with at least 10 points, continue freewriting for another few minutes and see what new ideas you can discover.
6. On a separate piece of paper, list the points you have identified. Study the possible relationships among these points and cluster them under two or three headings. These are your main points. Now you can move on to the next step: testing each main point to be sure it is satisfactory for your essay.

Here is an example of the freewriting technique. The assigned topic, for a course in law enforcement fundamentals, was "Crime and Punishment." Victor Chen was interested in the difference between crime as it is portrayed in the media and the reality of Canada's justice system. After doing some research and finding statistics that he thought might be useful, he drafted the following on his computer in 15 minutes.

What's really happening in our system in terms of crime and punishment is really different from what we see in the media. Look at TV crime shows. It used to be that all the courtroom shows were about defence lawyers trying to prove their clients' innocence. The prosecutors were the bad guys doing everything they could to put the defence attorney's client in jail or worse. There has been a big shift in the last five years or so and now we seem to have developed a taste for law and order. Now it's the prosecutors who are the good guys and the defence attorneys are trying to prevent their sleazy clients from escaping justice. The sad thing is that we form opinions about what goes on in real courtrooms based on stories like these. Almost all of the courtroom dramas on TV are American, and what goes on in American courtrooms is different from Canada's court procedures, so we are definitely not very aware of how our justice system really works.

To prove this, look at the study that was done by Roberts and Doob. They took a group of people and gave them the newspaper articles about a trial. When they had read the stories, they were asked about the trial. Most of them thought the criminal had gotten a sentence that was too light and only 15 percent thought the sentence was too tough. Then they took another group and gave them the court documents and transcripts of what actually went on in the trial. This group was reversed, more than half of them thought the sentence was too tough. Less than 20 percent agreed with the majority in the other group that the criminal should have got a longer sentence. This shows that we are getting a distorted impression of reality when we read about violent crime in the papers or on TV. It's like we're living in two worlds, the imaginary media one and the real one we don't know about. Also the news distorts violence. Reading the papers or watching TV, you'd think there was an epidemic of crime and that our streets are unsafe and murder was a common occurrence. This is so they can sell more papers and attract more viewers. In fact crime rates are falling. About half the crime reported in the news is violent while violent crime is actually less than 12 percent of cases that are reported. Murders are less than 1 percent of violent crimes but they are 25 percent of crime stories. If all you did was read the papers and watch TV you'd think that violence and murder were very common but actually they are quite rare. It's easy to see how we get the idea that violence in our society is a real problem. So it's really important that the people who make the laws don't rely on the media, because it is very distorted information.

After completing this freewriting exercise, Victor underlined all the points that he considered significant, supportable, and related to the subject. He quickly realized that the paper would be too long, and that one of his points was based on personal observation rather than provable facts. He crossed out everything related to television shows and then rearranged the other information into a rough outline of an essay with two main points.

Intro: the reality of the justice system and the media accounts of it are two different things. Take two examples: violence and court proceedings.

1. Crime
   • murders in reality vs. murders in the media
   • violent crime in reality vs. violent crime in the media
2. Courts—the Roberts and Doob study
   • opinions of group that read newspaper accounts of a trial
   • opinions of group that read court documents of a trial

Conclusion: lawmakers need to base decisions on reality and not on the media or public opinion.

Working from this rough outline, Victor developed a first draft. In reading it over, he noted where he needed to add more support to make the contrast clearer and more emphatic. After two more revisions and a careful edit, he submitted "Justice and Journalism," which you will find on pages 209–10.

Exercise 4.1

Choose a subject, or work with an assigned subject. Follow the six steps outlined on page 45 to see what main points you can come up with. Don't worry if your work is messy. Freewriting is a record of your thoughts, and thinking is messy.

BRAINSTORMING

In **brainstorming**, you write down a list of every idea you can think of about a specific subject. You can brainstorm alone, with a partner, or—best of all—in a group. If you run out of ideas too quickly, then try the age-old journalist's technique: ask the questions *who, what, why, when, where,* and *how* about your subject. Here's how to proceed. (The first three steps below assume you are working with a partner or in a small group. You can also do them by yourself, but you'll have less fun.)

1. Write your topic at the top of the page. Again, you will save time if you've checked your subject against the 4-S test. Decide how much time you will spend on this exercise: three, five, or more minutes. As in freewriting, working against the clock can bring surprising results.
2. Write down in short form—words or phrases—every idea you can think of that is even vaguely related to your subject. Choose the fastest writer in your group to be the recorder. Work quickly. Don't slow yourselves down by worrying about grammar or repetition.

3. When the time is up, relax for a minute, then go over the list carefully. Underline the points that seem most clearly related to your subject and scratch out any duplicates or any ideas that are vague, trivial, or irrelevant. If you don't end up with at least three or four points that are meaningful to you, brainstorm again for a few minutes, using the six journalist's questions to generate more ideas.
4. Working alone now, take your three or four most significant points and rephrase them in clear sentences on a new sheet of paper. Now you're ready to move on to the next step: testing your main points to ensure that they are suitable for use in your essay.

The following example demonstrates how brainstorming can be used to overcome the most frustrating inertia. The subject was "Your college English course." As you might expect, the class groaned when the subject was assigned, but one group's quick brainstorming produced some unique and interesting approaches to the topic. The time limit given for this exercise was four minutes. After brainstorming, at least one student was convinced that her career opportunities would improve if she learned how to communicate better.

Your College English Course

- have to take it
- should like it but I don't
- writing is important
- speaking's easier than writing
- bosses will hire you if you can write
- you can get a job
- letter of application
- have to write on the job
- have to write to the boss, other departments
- have to write to customers
- embarrassed about my writing
- people don't respect a poor writer
- writing helps you think
- writing helps you read better
- have to write reports
- need to know how to write a good report
- have to prepare slides for presentations
- need to write to get promoted

This list contains several significant points along with some irrelevant and trivial ones, which the group deleted. Then they talked about possible relationships among the remaining items on the list.

At this point, each student began working alone. After one student had underlined the points she felt were most important, she noticed that these points could be divided into two related ideas: what college English teaches and why it is useful. She then combined these two ideas into a thesis (a point of view about a subject). Here is her list of revised points.

College English is useful because
- it improves writing and thinking skills
- you will communicate better on the job
- you will get promoted

Exercise 4.2

In groups of four or five, brainstorm as many topics as you can in five minutes. Do not censor or cut any ideas. You should end up with at least 20 topics. Then exchange papers with another group, and edit that group's topics, crossing out any that are too broad or too narrow. Switch papers again, with a different group, and choose four topics that pass the 4-S test. Finally, select the best of the four topics and present it to the rest of the class, explaining why it's a good choice for an essay.

Exercise 4.3

Choose one of the two prewriting techniques presented in this chapter: freewriting or brainstorming. Generate as much information as you can in five minutes about one of the topics presented to the class in Exercise 4.2. Then narrow your information down to three main points, decide how to present them, and write a brief outline (no longer than the example given at the top of this page) for a short essay.

Generating Main Points: The Top-Down Approach

Another way to find out what you have to say about a subject is to ask specific questions of it. Questioning lets you "walk around" your subject, looking at it from different angles, taking it apart and putting it back together again. Each question is a probe that enables you to dig below the surface and find out what you know. The top-down approach is more structured than the strategies we have discussed so far, but it has the advantage of producing clear main points with few or no off-topic responses. It also identifies for you the kinds of development you can use in your essay.

Questioning your subject works best if you know it well or have done some research but are not sure how to approach it. Any subject can be approached in a number of ways. The needs of your audience and your purpose in writing should determine the approach you choose.

Here's how to use the questioning technique to generate ideas:

1. Begin by writing your proposed subject at the top of the page, or tape it to your monitor.
2. Now apply the 12 questions listed below, one at a time, to your subject to see which ones "fit" best. That is, find the questions that call up in your mind answers that could be used as points to develop your subject. As you go down the list, you will probably find more than one question for which you can think up answers. Do not stop with the first question that produces answers. The purpose of this idea-generating technique is to discover the *best* approach for your target audience and writing purpose.
3. Go through the entire list and record your answers to any questions that apply to your subject. Ignore the questions that make no sense in relation to the subject.
4. Finally, study the questions that produced answers and choose the one that generated the ideas that are closest to what your reader needs to know and what you want to say.

The questions listed in the left-hand column lead to the kinds of essay development listed in the column on the right. Don't worry about these now. We'll discuss them in detail in Part 4.

The Answers to This Question	Produce This Kind of Paper
1. What does your subject *look, feel, sound, smell*, and/or *taste* like?	*Description*
2. How did your subject *happen*?	*Narration*
3. How is your subject *made* or *done*? 4. How does your subject work?	*Process*
5. What are the main *kinds* of your subject? 6. What are the component *parts* of your subject? 7. What are the significant *features, characteristics,* or *functions* of your subject?	*Classification/ Division*
8. What are the *causes* of your subject? 9. What are the *effects* or *consequences* of your subject?	*Cause/Effect*
10. What are the *similarities* and/or *differences* between your subject and *X*?	*Comparison/ Contrast*
11. What are the main *advantages/disadvantages* of your subject? 12. What are the reasons *in favour of/against* your subject?	*Argument/ Persuasion*

NEL

Here is an example of how the process works. Alice Tam, a recent college graduate, has decided to write about her first job as a management trainee. Her target audience is general readers, not experts in her field. The subject passes the 4-S test: it is significant, single, specific, and supportable.

1. What does my job feel like?
   At first glance, this question doesn't make much sense. A *job* can't feel; the *employee* does. However, by interpreting the question loosely, Alice could describe her nervousness, her desire to do well, the pressures she felt, and the rewards of the job.

2. How did my job happen?
   This question doesn't sound promising. How Alice landed her job would be of interest to her family and friends, but probably would not appeal to a broader audience unless her experience was highly unusual or could be instructive to others.

3. How is my job done?
   The answer to this question is basically a job description, which would be of little interest to anyone other than Alice's close friends, her supervisor, or the person hired to replace her. Let's move on.

4. How does my first job work?
   All jobs are different; this question doesn't take us anywhere.

5. What are the main kinds of first jobs?
   This question might lead to an acceptable topic for a research paper on the kinds of entry-level jobs graduates from specific programs can expect to get, but the answers won't produce the sort of personal experience essay Alice wants to write.

6. What are the component parts (i.e., main requirements) of my job?
   Our writer might use this question as a starting point for a discussion of her main job functions, but this information would be of interest only to those in her career field, not to a broad, general audience.

7. What are the significant features of my job?
   This question has possibilities. Alice could tell her readers about those aspects of her job that apply to all first-time employees, perhaps limiting her focus to the aspects of the working world that she hadn't expected, that in fact surprised her.

8. What were the causes of my first job?
   This question doesn't produce useful answers. Most people work because they have to support themselves. The answer is self-evident.

9. What are the effects of my first job?
   This question raises some interesting answers. What effect has full-time employment had on Alice's life? She might discuss the self-esteem that

replaced her earlier insecurity and fear of the job search; she might discuss her new independence, both financial and social.

10. What are the similarities (or differences) between my first job and . . . what? A second or third job?
   Our writer is still on her first job and so can't really comment on this question.

11. What are the main advantages (or disadvantages) of my first job?
   This question produces answers that are easy to explain—and that's the problem with it. Unless Alice has a very unusual first job, the answers to this question are predictable and therefore of little interest to a broad audience.

12. What are the reasons in favour of (or against) my first job?
   This question leads to answers that overlap with those produced by question 11. It would lead to an average essay, but not to anything outstanding or memorable.

After patiently going through the list, our writer found two questions, 7 and 9, that produced answers she felt she could work with. She especially liked the possibilities suggested by question 7. As Alice focused her thoughts, she realized that what she wanted to write about was the unexpected challenges she confronted when she joined the world of work. So she refined the question to capture what she wanted to write about ("What are the most significant challenges I faced in my first job?") and came up with three solid answers: the expectations of my boss, my coworkers, and myself. The essay that resulted from this process, "On-the-Job Training," appears on pages 188–89.

Generating main points is a time-consuming but worthwhile process. The more time you spend at this stage, the less time it will take you to draft your essay. To sharpen your skills, study the examples given below. Each consists of a 4-S test–approved subject, a question about that subject, and some answers the question produces that would form solid main points to support, explain, or prove the subject of the essay.

Subject	Selected Question	Main Points
Hockey violence	What are the reasons in favour of violence in hockey?	• releases aggression • keeps players alert • attracts fans
Law enforcement officers	What are the main functions of law enforcement officers?	• preventing crime • apprehending criminals • enforcing the law • acting as role models

Subject	Selected Question	Main Points
Job interviews	How do you make a negative impression in a job interview?	• be late • be inappropriately dressed • be ignorant about the company • complain about former employers
Essay topics	What are the characteristics of a satisfactory essay topic?	• single • significant • specific • supportable

Exercise 4.4

Working in pairs, apply the questions on pages 51–52 to each of the subjects listed below. Select the question that produces the answers you both like best, and list three or four of these answers as main points.

Subject	Selected Question	Main Points
1. Procrastination		• • • •
2. E-mail		• • • •
3. SUVs		• • • •

4. Business dress
   codes

   -
   -
   -
   -

5. Ice cream

   -
   -
   -
   -

In pairs, choose two subjects that you think would be suitable for short essays. Be sure all are significant, single, specific, and supportable. For each subject, list at least three strong main points. Use the questions on pages 51–52 to help you identify main points. When you've finished, exchange your ideas with another team, critique each other's main points, and make suggestions.

Subject　　　　　　　＿＿＿＿＿＿＿＿＿＿＿＿＿＿＿＿＿＿＿＿＿＿

Selected Question　　＿＿＿＿＿＿＿＿＿＿＿＿＿＿＿＿＿＿＿＿＿＿

Main Points
-
-
-

Subject　　　　　　　＿＿＿＿＿＿＿＿＿＿＿＿＿＿＿＿＿＿＿＿＿＿

Selected Question　　＿＿＿＿＿＿＿＿＿＿＿＿＿＿＿＿＿＿＿＿＿＿

Main Points
-
-
-

Testing Your Main Points

Now that you've practised identifying main points using freewriting, brainstorming, and the questioning approach, the next step is to examine the points you've come up with to make sure each is going to work as a major component in your essay. Some may be too minor to bother with; some may overlap in meaning; some may even be unrelated to your subject. Here's how to test your main points to be sure they are satisfactory. Whether you've arrived at your main points through freewriting, brainstorming, or questioning, the test is the same.

> Main points must be significant, distinct, and relevant.

ARE YOUR MAIN POINTS SIGNIFICANT?

Each main point should be worth writing and reading about. If you can't write at least one interesting and informative paragraph about a point, it is probably not significant enough to bother with. Don't waste your readers' time with trivial matters. In the following example, one of the main points does not have the same importance as the others; it should be eliminated or replaced. Which one would you discard?

Reasons for attending college
- to learn career skills
- to improve one's general knowledge of the world
- to enjoy the social life
- to participate in student government

ARE YOUR MAIN POINTS DISTINCT?

Each of the main points you choose must be different from all the others; there must be no overlap in meaning. Check to be sure you haven't given two different labels to what is really only one aspect of your subject. Eliminate or replace any main points that duplicate other points or that can easily be covered under another point. Here's an example of a list that contains a redundant main point. Which point would you eliminate?

Advantages of cycling
- improves fitness
- stimulates enjoyment of surroundings
- keeps one in shape
- doesn't damage the environment

ARE YOUR MAIN POINTS RELEVANT?

The main points you choose must be clearly and directly related to your subject. They all must be aspects of that subject and must add to the development of your readers' information on the subject. In this example, the third main point listed should be eliminated because it does not relate to the stated topic.

The miseries of winter
- numbing cold
- layers of uncomfortable clothes
- Christmas presents
- dangerous driving conditions

Exercise 4.6*

At least one main point in each item below is unsatisfactory. Identify each faulty point and explain why it should be deleted. When you have finished, compare your answers with those on page 515.

1. Business communication devices
- telephone
- e-mail
- fax
- mail
- cell

2. Advantages of locating a business outside the city
- cheaper cost of living
- calmer pace
- distance from suppliers and markets
- government subsidies and tax benefits

3. Kinds of television commercials
- boring
- clever
- misleading
- puzzling
- repetitive

4. Causes of college failure	• lack of preparation in high school
	• procrastination
	• poor study habits
	• irregular attendance
5. How to choose a place to live	• determine your needs
	• determine your budget
	• find a reliable real-estate agent
	• seek expert advice
6. Reasons for high staff turnover	• salary lower than industry standard
	• no chance for advancement
	• uncomfortable work environment
	• competitors offer better pay

Organizing Your Main Points

After you've identified the main points for your essay and checked to make sure they are satisfactory, your final task in the planning process is to list them in order. (This list of points is sometimes called a plan of development or a path statement.) Main points are like menu items on a website: the more logically they are arranged, the easier it is to navigate your way through them.

> There are four ways to order your main points:
> chronological, climactic, logical, and random.

CHRONOLOGICAL ORDER

When you present your points in order of time from first to last, you are using **chronological order**. You will find it most appropriate in process essays, but it can be used in other essays as well. Here are two examples.

Subject	Main Points
The process of writing a paper	• select an appropriate subject • list and edit the main points • write a thesis statement • write an outline for the paper • write a first draft • revise, edit, and proofread
The evolution of a relationship	• meeting • attraction • discovery • intimacy • disillusionment

CLIMACTIC ORDER

Persuasion most often uses a climactic arrangement, but climactic order is also common in papers based on examples, comparison or contrast, and classification or division. In **climactic order**, you save your strongest or most convincing point for last (the climax of your argument). You lead off your essay with your second-strongest point, and arrange your other points in between, as in this example.

Subject	Main Points
Advantages of a college education	• development of skills and knowledge • friendships and contacts with compatible people • potential for higher income • discovery of one's own potential

LOGICAL ORDER

Cause-and-effect essays, or any writing in which one point must be explained before the next point can be understood, are based on **logical order**. Your main points have a logical relationship, and you cannot take them out of order without confusing your readers. Consider the following sequence.

Subject	Main Points
Main causes of youth crime	• lack of opportunity or motivation for work • lack of recreational facilities • boredom • quest for "kicks"

NEL

The logical links here are clear: because of unemployment, recreational facilities are needed. Because of both unemployment and inadequate recreational facilities, boredom and the quest for "kicks" become problems. Readers must grasp each point before the next can be explained and understood.

RANDOM ORDER

On the rare occasions when your points can be explained in any order without affecting your readers' understanding, you can use **random order**. A random arrangement is possible only if all your main points are of equal significance and if they are not linked together logically or chronologically. In this example, all three points have equal weight.

Subject	Main Points
The garbage disposal crisis	• disposal sites are hard to find • cartage costs are high • new technologies are not yet fully developed

---

Exercise 4.7*

Choose the type of order—chronological, climactic, logical, or random—you think is most appropriate for each of the following subjects. Arrange the main points in that order by numbering them in the spaces provided.

Subject	Order	Main Points
1. How to impress a client	_____	_____ firm handshake _____ friendly closing _____ well-prepared sales presentation _____ knowledge of client's needs _____ appropriate business attire
2. How to handle tax preparation	_____	_____ do your own _____ don't bother to file a return _____ go to a franchise tax-preparation company _____ hire an accountant

3. Reasons for   _____   _____ it offers informative
    listening to   programs
    the CBC   _____ your taxes are paying for it
                                                             _____ it provides a sense of
                                                                Canadian unity

4. Methods of   _____   _____ nicotine patch
    quitting smoking   _____ cold turkey
                                                               _____ gradual withdrawal

5. Causes of   _____   _____ incompetent or unfriendly
    dissatisfaction   supervisor
    with employment   _____ incompatible coworkers
                                                               _____ inappropriate pay for skills
                                                              and effort
                                                               _____ unfulfilling work
                                                              assignments

GO TO WEB

EXERCISE **4.1**

Exercise 4.8

Now go back to the subjects and main points that you developed in Exercise 4.5. First, reconsider your main points: are they all significant, distinct, and related to the subject? Next, put the main points in the order that is most appropriate for the subject to which they belong.

When you've finished this task, exchange papers with another student and check each other's work. Can your partner identify the order of points you have chosen? Does he or she agree with your choice?

In this chapter, you've learned how to identify main points, how to test them for suitability, and how to arrange them in the most appropriate order. You're ready now to go on to the next step: writing the thesis statement—probably the most important sentence in your paper.

5

Writing the Thesis Statement

The key to clear organization in any paper is a thesis statement near the beginning that announces the paper's subject and scope. The thesis statement not only helps a reader to see how you are going to approach the subject, but also serves to keep you, the writer, on track.

A **thesis statement** is one or more sentences that clearly and concisely indicate the subject of your paper, the main points you will discuss, and the order in which you will discuss them.

In business communication, technical writing, and some academic writing (e.g., research papers and dissertations) it is important to indicate the subject and scope of your paper at the outset. Readers expect this sort of preview.[1]

The number of sentences in a thesis statement depends on what the subject is, how best to phrase it, how many points there are, and how complex they are. A thesis statement in a short paper is usually a single sentence at the end of the first paragraph, but in a lengthy paper on complicated issues, it might be several sentences or even a paragraph long. Occasionally (in a technical description, for example), a writer will choose a short thesis and omit the main points from the thesis statement.

To write a thesis statement, you combine your subject and your main points. Here is a simple formula for constructing a thesis statement:

---

[1]In less formal writing, such as newspaper or magazine articles and informal essays—including some of the essays in this book—a thesis statement is unnecessary.

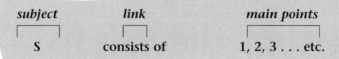

subject	link	main points
S	consists of	1, 2, 3 . . . etc.

These three elements can be combined in various ways. For example:

The most prolific producers of unnecessary jargon are politicians, sports writers, advertising copy writers, and educators. (Subject and main points are linked by *are*.)

Because the United States influences Canada's foreign policy, dominates its culture, and controls its economy, Canada is little more than an American satellite. (Main points precede subject and are linked to the subject by *because*.)

Fad diets are not the quick fix to weight problems that they may appear to be. On the contrary, they are often costly, ineffective, and even dangerous. (Subject is one sentence. Main points are in second sentence, linked to the first by *On the contrary*.)

Two cheers for democracy: one because it admits variety, and two because it permits criticism. (E. M. Forster) (Subject and main points are linked by a colon.)

Once you have mastered the basic formula, you can experiment with creative ways of expressing a thesis statement. Just be sure that it is appropriate in form, language, and tone to the kind of paper you are writing. The thesis statements in the exercise below range from short to long, formal to informal, and serious to flippant.

Exercise 5.1*

In each of the following thesis statements, underline the subject with a double line and the main points with a single line. When you have finished all seven, compare your answers with those on page 516.

1. Students who try to combine a full-time job with a full-time program face problems at school, at work, and at home.
2. To be successful in a broadcasting career, you must be talented, motivated, and hardworking.
3. The ideal notebook computer for business applications is reliable, lightweight, powerful, and flexible.
4. Establishing a local area network would increase efficiency and flexibility in the office.

5. The chairperson's job calls for a responsible and sensitive person, someone who is knowledgeable about company policy, sensitive to personnel issues, and a creative problem solver. It wouldn't hurt if he or she could also walk on water.

6. The business traveller can learn much from the turtle. Carry everything you need with you. Move slowly but with purpose and consistency. Keep your head down until you are sure you know what's going on.

7. Large energy producers and some provincial governments say we cannot afford to live up to the terms of the Kyoto Accord, which seeks to reduce the production of greenhouse gases. But can we afford not to comply with this international agreement? Can we afford to compromise the health of Canadians by continuing to pollute? Can we afford to risk the effects of global warming on our environment? Can we afford to fall behind the rest of the world in research and development leading to a solution to the problem of greenhouse gases?

Exercise 5.2

Each of the five introductions below contains a thesis statement. Working with a partner or in groups of three or four, identify the thesis statement in each paragraph.

1. What does an interviewer look for in a new job applicant? Good credentials, good preparation, good grooming, and good communication skills are essential features for anyone who wants a job. No interviewer would seriously consider an applicant who comes to an interview without the required educational background and work experience, without information about the job and the company, without appropriate clothing, and without the ability to present ideas clearly in the interview.

2. In the traditional manufacturing sectors, sales growth has stagnated in Canada over the past five years. Our products and services have secured as large a market share as we can expect, and we can anticipate further decline over the next 10 years as a result of increased competition. For these reasons, we have undertaken a study to determine where our best expansion opportunities lie. The following report outlines growth opportunities in the emerging markets of China and India.

3. Suddenly a man steps into the road in front of me. He's wearing a uniform and he's waving his hand for me to pull over to the side. My heart pounds and my pores prickle with anxiety. I feel guilty, but I don't know what I've done wrong—maybe speeding 10 kilometres over the limit, but no more. Anyone who has been caught in a radar trap knows this momentary feeling of panic, guilt, and resentment. We fear that the police officer will be brusque and blaming, but we are often surprised. There are as many kinds of police officers as there are people. Four kinds, however, dominate the profession: the confident veteran, the arrogant authoritarian, the cocky

novice, and the friendly professional. As I roll down my window, I wonder which kind of police officer has stopped me.

4.   After a hard day's work, do you relax with two or three stiff drinks? Do you enjoy a few beers while watching a game on TV? Do you believe mixed drinks make a party more fun? Do you cool off with gin fizzes on a hot afternoon? If you answered "yes" to most of these questions, you are probably abusing alcohol. The line between excessive social drinking and a serious addictive habit is a blurry one. Most alcoholics don't know they are hooked until they try to stop drinking. What are the signs that a drinker is no longer drinking for pleasure only? If a person "needs" a drink, or drinks alone, or can fall asleep only after a few drinks, or can find enjoyment only when drinking, that person is probably in trouble.

5.   Ours is a transient society. Most of us travel more kilometres in a year than our grandparents travelled in a lifetime. We move from one city to another, one province to another, and one country to another. In the course of moving, we inhabit many homes. The family home of the past might have been inhabited by several generations, consecutively or concurrently. Today's average Canadians will probably have 10 or more addresses during their adult lives. Our restlessness is particularly hard on the children in our migrating families: they have to leave familiar surroundings and friends, and they must adjust to a new environment, new habits, and sometimes a new language. These children pay a heavy price for the mobility of modern impermanence.

Phrasing Your Statement of Subject

The first part of a thesis statement is the statement of subject. It identifies *your idea about* or *your approach to* your subject. It states a viewpoint that must be explained or proved. (The main points provide the explanation or proof.)

Your statement of subject should be as clear and concise as you can make it. It must not be boring, however.

Beginning writers often fall into the trap of stating the obvious: "In this paper, I am going to discuss . . ." or "The subject of this memo is . . ." Your readers *know* it's your paper; you needn't hit them over the head by pointing out the fact that the paper contains your ideas. Here are three examples of faulty subject statements and their revisions.

Poor	Better
In this essay, I am going to discuss violence in hockey. (What about it?)	Violence in hockey is misunderstood by the nonplaying public.

This paper is about Canada's multiculturalism policy. (What about it?)	Canada's multiculturalism policy is neither practical nor desirable.
I am going to examine the influence of Wal-Mart in Canada. (What about it?)	With over 200 stores in Canada and plans for expansion, Wal-Mart's effects on labour are worth considering.

As soon as you write, "In this essay . . ." or "I am going to discuss (write about, explore) . . . ," you trap yourself into simply announcing your subject, not stating your idea or opinion about it. Avoid these traps. Always let your reader know *what it is about your subject* that your paper will explain or prove.

Phrasing the Main Points

When you combine your statement of subject with your main points to form your thesis statement, be sure that all your main points are phrased in the same way, in grammatically parallel form. If point 1 is a single word, then points 2, 3, and so on must also be single words. If point 1 is a phrase, then all the points following it must be phrases. If point 1 is a clause or a sentence, then the succeeding points must also be in clause or sentence form.

The following sentence contains a main point that is not parallel with the others.

Of the many qualities that combine to make a good nurse the three most important are strength, intelligence, and she must be compassionate.

Here is the sentence rewritten to be grammatically parallel:

Of the many qualities that combine to make a good nurse the three most important are strength, intelligence, and compassion.

Or, the sentence could be rewritten this way:

Of the many qualities that combine to make a good nurse the three most important are that she or he be strong, intelligent, and compassionate.

If you have trouble with grammatical parallelism, turn to Chapter 26 before you try the exercise below.

Exercise 5.3

In each of the following lists, one point is not parallel with the others. Rephrase the incorrect item so that all are in grammatically parallel form.

1. Our employees are
   a. motivated
   b. good training
   c. knowledgeable
2. Our doctor is
   a. full of compassion
   b. competent
   c. hard-working
3. I've noticed that my friends are increasingly
   a. concerned about smoking
   b. interested in fitness
   c. environmental awareness
4. To upgrade our educational system, we need
   a. more effective teacher training
   b. better liaison between levels of education
   c. students must be motivated to learn
5. An investment strategy must be
   a. based on current information
   b. appropriately diversified
   c. the client has to be tolerant of the degree of risk

Exercise 5.4

Work in pairs to develop two thesis statements for potential essays. Phrase the two thesis statements so that one has a poor statement of subject and the other lacks parallelism. Switch your creations with another team and identify each other's problems. Then correct the sentences. Exchange papers again. Did the other team identify and correct the problems you thought you'd created? If not, revise your own team's faulty sentences.

Exercise 5.5

Working with a partner, combine each of the following subjects with its main points to form a clear thesis statement that is expressed in grammatically parallel form.

1. Causes of stress
- change of employment
- financial problems
- death of family member

Thesis statement: _____

_____

_____

_____

_____

2. Steps in finding a job
- conduct an Internet job search
- prepare a letter of application
- perform well in the interview

Thesis statement: _____

_____

_____

_____

_____

3. How to save money
- automatic payroll deductions
- keep a record of expenditures
- reduce impulse buying
- establish and maintain a budget

Thesis statement: _____

_____

_____

_____

_____

4. Evolution of a recession
- unemployment causes general economic slowdown
- consumer buying decreases, resulting in inflation
- inflation causes fear and further decrease in consumer demand

Thesis statement: _____

_____

_____

_____

_____

Exercise 5.6*

Working independently, combine each of the following subjects with its main points to form a grammatically parallel thesis statement. Then compare your answers to our suggestions on page 516.

1. Comparison between McDonald's and Wendy's (or any other two fast-food restaurants)
   - food
   - atmosphere
   - service
   - price

   Thesis statement: _____

   _____

   _____

   _____

   _____

2. Effects of urban overcrowding
   - traffic jams
   - too much air pollution
   - high rate of homelessness
   - violence on the streets

   Thesis statement: _____

   _____

   _____

   _____

   _____

3. Characteristics of a successful small business
   - adequate capital
   - marketable product
   - personnel that are dedicated
   - workable business plan

Thesis statement: _____

_____

_____

_____

_____

In groups of three or four, share the thesis statements you developed for Exercise 5.6 and discuss your decisions. As a group, revise each statement until you are all satisfied they meet the criteria for satisfactory thesis statements.

You have now covered all the steps leading to the construction of a good thesis statement. The exercises above have given you practice in the skills you need to phrase subjects and main points correctly and effectively.

Exercise 5.8 will walk you through the process of developing a thesis statement for a subject of your own choice. As you fill in the blanks in this exercise, you will be reviewing the first five chapters of this book and also testing your mastery of the writing skills they presented.

1. Select a subject.

   _____

   _____

2. Test whether your subject is significant, single, specific, and supportable.

3. Using either a bottom-up or a top-down approach to generate ideas, identify three to five main points in support of your subject.

   _____

   _____

   _____

   _____

   _____

4. Test whether your main points are all significant, distinct, and clearly related to your subject.

5. Arrange your main points in the order that is most likely to guarantee your readers' understanding of your subject: chronological, climactic, logical, or random.

_____

_____

_____

_____

_____

6. Rewrite your main points so that they are grammatically parallel: all single words, all phrases, or all clauses.

_____

_____

_____

_____

_____

7. Combine your statement of subject with your main points to produce your thesis statement.

_____

_____

_____

_____

_____

The seven points listed in Exercise 5.8 summarize the steps to follow in planning an essay. Keep this outline handy and refer to it when you start your next paper or research report.

6

Preparing an Outline

Writing a paper is like building a house: you save much time and frustration if you start with a plan. For anything longer than about 250 words, writers need a plan or outline to guide them as they begin to build words into sentences, sentences into paragraphs, and paragraphs into the final product, whether it's a term paper, a research report, a business plan, or a market analysis.

Wise writers treat an outline as tentative, not something chiselled in stone. As you draft your paper, you may discover new ideas or a new structure that better suits your purpose. If so, change your thesis statement and outline to accommodate it. (It's a good idea to make these changes in pencil or in a new file because you may decide at the end of the draft that these new ideas weren't so great after all.)

If you have access to a word-processing program with an outline feature, try it out. These programs can be a great help to an inexperienced writer with little knowledge of how to plan a writing assignment.

As we have seen, all written messages consist of an introduction, a body, and a conclusion, but each of these may vary from one to several paragraphs in length, and from simple to sophisticated in style. The model format on the next page is a basic outline for a five-paragraph essay. Once you've mastered this basic structure, you can modify, expand, and develop it to suit any of the kinds of writing you'll be called upon to do.

Outline Format

Title _____

INTRODUCTION _____

*Attention-getter** _____
_____
_____

Thesis statement <u>Subject consists of 1, 2, and 3.</u>

BODY <u>Topic sentence introducing main point 1 goes here.</u>

*Support
for first
main point*
_____
_____
_____
_____
_____

<u>Concluding (or transition) sentence goes here.</u>
<u>(Transition or) Topic sentence introducing main point
2 goes here.</u>

*Support
for second
main point*
_____
_____
_____
_____

<u>Concluding (or transition) sentence goes here.</u>
<u>(Transition or) Topic sentence introducing main point
3 goes here.</u>

*Support
for third
main point*
_____
_____
_____
_____

<u>Concluding (or transition) sentence goes here.</u>

CONCLUSION _____

Summary _____
_____

*Memorable
statement** _____.

Note: Occasionally, a writer will begin a body paragraph with a transitional phrase or sentence. Variety adds interest to writing style. You will see examples of this technique in Part 4.

*Terms marked with an asterisk are explained and illustrated in Chapter 8.

The outline below follows the format on page 72. The final version of "Ready, Willing . . . and Employable" appears after the outline.

Ready, Willing . . . and Employable	*Essay title*
What are employers looking for today?	*Attention-getter*
Employers are looking for a new breed of employee: one who has knowledge, flexibility, and the right attitude.	*Thesis statement*
Knowledge is still first on the list.	*1. Topic sentence*
• colleges offer a broad range of programs to meet employers' needs • graduates must know current trends as well as theory • some employers test for knowledge • some rely on college's reputation plus recommendations of professors and recruiters	*Support for first main point*
Adaptability is essential for a prospective employee.	*2. Topic sentence*
• today's jobs require multitasking • flexible workers are more cost-effective and better problem solvers • flexible workers can adapt to change • students need to broaden their education and learn a variety of skills	*Support for second main point*
Employers complain about graduates' poor attitude.	*3. Topic sentence*
• graduates lack the ability to take direction, use team skills, communicate well, and motivate themselves • similar problems show up in class —chronic lateness —lack of cooperation —laziness • students need to correct these attitude problems on their own	*Support for third main point*
Students must be ready, able, and willing to work.	*Summary of main points*
With these skills, a good résumé, and professional contacts, graduates can enter the workforce with confidence.	*Memorable statement*

READY, WILLING . . . AND EMPLOYABLE

Attention-getter

What are employers looking for in today's job market? Several recent surveys point to a subtle shift in the requirements of businesses looking to hire college and university graduates. Only a few years ago, knowledge was the prerequisite to employment in most industries. Employers needed workers with the highly specialized skills of an emerging high-tech workplace. Now many of

Thesis statement those skills are taken for granted, and other characteristics have become increasingly important. Employers are seeking a new breed of employee: one who has the knowledge required to do the job, the flexibility to adapt, and—most important—the attitude to succeed.

Topic sentence

Knowledge of how to do the job is, understandably, still first on the shopping list that employers bring to job fairs. Colleges across the country have responded to marketplace requirements with an array of programs designed to prepare students to meet the needs of industries from broadcasting to photonics, from microelectronics to winemaking. Graduates are expected to have up-to-the-minute information on current trends in their fields, as well as solid

Support for first main point grounding in the theory and practice of their specialty. Some employers test applicants for this knowledge; others rely on the reputation of the institution, the recommendation of professors with whom they have professional connections, and the insights of recruiters. As valuable as knowledge is to the employer,

Concluding statement (transition) however, an employee's flexibility is quickly becoming just as important.

"Multitasking" is a buzz word often used to describe the ability to move quickly and easily between projects and work environments, bringing a wide range of skills to bear on a variety of situations. Adaptability is an essential char-

Topic sentence acteristic of any prospective employee. Workers who can use their expertise simultaneously on several different tasks within a project are valuable not only because they are more cost-effective than several single-task specialists, but also because they tend to see projects holistically and are better problem solvers as

Support for second main point a result. In addition, flexible workers are those who most quickly and easily adapt to changes in technology or work practice, and such changes are a way of life in today's work environment. Students must prepare themselves to be flexible workers by broadening their education and by learning as many skills as possible. Unlike their parents, workers in the current generation have little hope of finding a job that will require only one skill set over the course of a career. Adaptability is a critical skill, but even when combined with knowledge,

Concluding statement it is not enough to ensure employability. Increasingly, attitude is the determining factor in who gets hired (and promoted!).

Transition

Employers continually complain to colleges and universities that students on placement and graduates in their first position fail to impress, not from lack of knowledge, skill, or preparation, but from a broad range of inadequacies best summed up as "poor attitude." Among the faults cited under this broad heading are inability to take direction, failure to work well with colleagues, inability to communicate effectively, and lack of enthusiasm and initiative. How can such problems be corrected before graduates reach the workplace? Colleges do not offer courses in attitude adjustment, but perhaps they should. Most of these problems have surfaced in classes long before graduation. Students who are chronically late, frequently uncooperative, constantly complaining, or visibly lazy are those who, with all the skills and ability in the world, will not succeed in any job worth having. Even highly motivated and ambitious graduates have sometimes had difficulty adjusting to entry-level positions when they find themselves working under the supervision of people they consider less talented or skilled. It is up to students themselves to correct their attitudinal deficiencies. They need to pay attention to the criticisms of teachers, classmates, even family members, and make an honest evaluation of consistently noticed faults. Only when such attitude faults have been identified and acknowledged can they be corrected, and only when they have been corrected will the student be an asset to an employer.

Topic sentence

Support for third main point

Concluding statement

As graduation draws near, most students view their coming transformation into workers with eagerness liberally mixed with anxiety. Statistics tell us that most college and university graduates find employment in their fields within a year of graduation. Armed with this encouraging information, together with a good résumé, professional contacts, and the knowledge, flexibility, and attitude to succeed, graduates can face employers and the workplace with confidence.

Summary and Memorable statement

Exercise 6.1

Read "Of Men and Machines in the 21st Century" (pages 189–91) and "Lightweight Lit." (pages 218–19). Identify in each essay the sentences that correspond to the major structural items in the outline formats that follow. If you're working through this textbook in order, you may not have studied some of the terms mentioned, but you should be able to make a good guess at identifying the attention-getter and the memorable statement. To make your task easier, the sentences in each essay have been numbered.

OF MEN AND MACHINES IN THE 21ST CENTURY

INTRODUCTION

Attention-getter   Sentence(s)   _____

Thesis statement   Sentence(s)   _____

BODY PARAGRAPH #1

Topic sentence   Sentence(s)   _____

Support for first main point   Sentence(s)   _____

Conclusion/Transition   Sentence(s)   _____

BODY PARAGRAPH #2

Topic sentence   Sentence(s)   _____

Support for second main point   Sentence(s)   _____

Conclusion/Transition   Sentence(s)   _____

BODY PARAGRAPH #3

Topic sentence   Sentence(s)   _____

Support for third main point   Sentence(s)   _____

Conclusion/Transition   Sentence(s)   _____

CONCLUSION

Summary/Reinforcement   Sentence(s)   _____

Memorable statement   Sentence(s)   _____

LIGHTWEIGHT LIT.

INTRODUCTION

Attention-getter   Sentence(s)   _____

Thesis statement   Sentence(s)   _____

BODY PARAGRAPH #1

Topic sentence   Sentence(s)   _____

Support for first main point   Sentence(s)   _____

Conclusion/Transition   Sentence(s)   _____

BODY PARAGRAPH #2

Topic sentence   Sentence(s)   _____

Support for second main point Sentence(s)   _____

Conclusion/Transition   Sentence(s)   _____

BODY PARAGRAPH #3

Topic sentence   Sentence(s)   _____

Support for third main point   Sentence(s)   _____

Conclusion/Transition   Sentence(s)   _____

CONCLUSION

Summary/Reinforcement   Sentence(s)   _____

Memorable statement   Sentence(s)   _____

Exercise 6.2

1. With a partner, choose either "The Train Ride" (pages 160–61), "A Slender Trap" (pages 221–23), or "A City for Students" (pages 242–43). Read the essay carefully and create an outline for it, following the format on page 72.

2. Compare outlines with another team that selected the same reading. Are there significant differences between the two outlines? If so, which outline best reflects the components of the introduction, body, and conclusion of the essay?

PART 2

7

Understanding Paragraph Form and Function

What Does a Paragraph Look Like?

Essays are divided into paragraphs. **Paragraphs** are sentence groups that are separated from each other in their physical presentation and in their content. They usually have an indentation at the beginning (on a typed page, the first word begins five spaces in from the left margin) and some white space at the end (the last line is left blank following the paragraph's last word). Between the indentation and the final period comes the paragraph—a group of sentences that explains a single idea or topic.

If you were to draw a blueprint for a single paragraph, it would look like this:

A sentence that introduces the **topic** (or main idea) of the paragraph goes here.

Three or more sentences that specifically support or explain the topic go in here.

A sentence that concludes your explanation of the topic (or provides a transition to the next paragraph) goes here.

How Does a Paragraph Function?

Readers expect a paragraph to present a unit of thought or a single, developed idea. The white space at the beginning and end of each paragraph defines your thought units and also serves two other functions.

1. Paragraphs provide visual cues that make your writing "reader friendly." Imagine how intimidating the page you are now reading would be if were one continuous block of print: no headings, no indentations, no paragraphs.
2. Paragraphs divide your writing into linked but separate sections. Without paragraphs, ideas would blur and blend one into another. Readers would find it difficult to identify them, let alone follow the organization and development of the writer's thoughts.

In a typical essay, an introductory paragraph is followed by paragraphs that add details and depth to the ideas set out in the introduction. A concluding paragraph brings all the ideas together again and leaves the reader with a complete understanding of the writer's thinking.

Readers can tell a great deal about your thinking just by glancing at a page of your paper. A number of short paragraphs indicates a series of ideas, briefly (and perhaps superficially) explained. Long paragraphs—half a page or longer—suggest complex ideas that require explanation and details. They signal serious thought but are more difficult to read because they require close attention.

As a general rule, you explore one major idea or main point in each paragraph. When you have finished exploring one topic and wish to move on to another, you signal this shift to your readers by beginning a new paragraph.

How Long Should a Paragraph Be?

The answer to this question depends on the topic, your readers' familiarity with it, and your purpose in writing. If your topic is complex, your readers' knowledge is limited, and your purpose is to persuade readers who do not share your point of view, then you'll probably need a fairly long paragraph to accomplish your goal. On the other hand, if you're writing about a topic your readers are likely familiar with, and your purpose is simply to share with them your understanding of that topic, you may be able to accomplish your task in a few sentences.

Work in groups of five or six. Each group will take one of the paragraphs below to read and analyze by answering the following questions. Share your analysis with the class.

- What is the topic of the paragraph, stated in a few words?
- How much knowledge of the topic does the writer assume the readers have?
- What is the writer's purpose in this paragraph?

1.   Violence as a way of achieving racial justice is both impractical and immoral. It is impractical because it is a descending spiral ending in destruction for all. The old law of an eye for an eye leaves everybody blind. It is immoral because it seeks to humiliate the opponent rather than win his understanding; it seeks to annihilate rather than to convert. Violence is immoral because it thrives on hatred rather than love. It destroys community and makes brotherhood impossible. It leaves society in monologue rather than dialogue. Violence ends by defeating itself. It creates bitterness in the survivors and brutality in the destroyers. A voice echoes through time saying to every potential Peter, "Put up your sword." History is cluttered with the wreckage of nations that failed to follow this command.

King, Martin Luther, Jr. "Three Types of Resistance to Oppression." *Stride Toward Freedom*. New York: Harper & Row, 1958. 215.

2.   Take William Lyon Mackenzie King, our prime minister through the war and, so it seemed, for all time until Pierre Trudeau came along and seemed to be prime minister for all time. King held power longer than any other Western politician in this century. How did such a pudgy, mundane little man do it? The truth is, he did it deliberately. He was shrewd and self-effacing, and he told his friends that he made every speech as boring as possible because then no one would ever remember what he said and hold it against him. Twenty-two years in power, droning on and on over the airwaves, and meanwhile, he was as crazy as a loon.

Callaghan, Barry. "Canadian Wry." *Canadian Content*. Ed. Sarah Norton and Nell Waldman. 2nd ed. Toronto: Harcourt, 1992. 92.

3.   *Vinaya* means humility; it is the complete surrendering of the self on the part of the *shishya* [the disciple] to the *guru*. The ideal disciple feels love, adoration, reverence, and even fear toward his *guru*, and he accepts equally praise or scoldings. Talent, sincerity, and the willingness to practise faithfully are essential qualities of the serious student. The *guru*, as the giver in this relationship, seems to be all-powerful. Often, he may be unreasonable, harsh, or haughty, though the ideal *guru* is none of these. Ideally, he should

respond to the efforts of the disciple and love him almost as his own child. In India, a Hindu child, from his earliest years, is taught to feel humble toward anyone older than he or superior in any way. From the simplest gesture of the *namaskar*, or greeting (putting the hands palm to palm in front of the forehead and bowing), or the *pranam* (a respectful greeting consisting of touching the greeted person's feet, then one's own eyes and forehead with the hands held palm to palm) to the practice of *vinaya* or humility tempered with a feeling of love and worship, the Hindu devotee's vanity and pretension are worn away.

Shankar, Ravi. "Studying Music in India." *My Music, My Life.* Delhi: Vikas Publications, 1968. 11–12.

4.   When I found [the snakeskin], it was whole and tied in a knot. Now there have been stories told, even by reputable scientists, of snakes that have deliberately tied themselves in a knot to prevent larger snakes from trying to swallow them—but I couldn't imagine any way that throwing itself into a half hitch would help a snake trying to escape its skin. Still, ever cautious, I figured that one of the neighborhood boys could possibly have tied it in a knot in the fall, for some whimsical boyish reason, and left it there, where it dried and gathered dust. So I carried the skin along thoughtlessly as I walked, snagging it sure enough on a low branch and ripping it in two. . . . I saw that thick ice still lay on the quarry pond and that the skunk cabbage was already out in the clearings, and then I came home and looked at the skin and its knot.

Dillard, Annie. *Pilgrim at Tinker Creek.* New York: Harper's Magazine Press, 1974. 73.

5.   [T]here needs to be a thorough revision of the maximum-penalty structure to remove the incongruities that riddle the current Criminal Code. Should forgery or certain kinds of fraud really have the same maximum penalty as sexual assault with a weapon? The maximum penalties are also much too high; most were created many decades ago, when our perceptions of the seriousness of various crimes differed from those today. The maximum penalty for breaking and entering is life imprisonment, for example, but in practice the average sentence is well under one year. This is called "bite and bark" sentencing; the system barks more loudly than it bites, and creates false expectations among the public.

Roberts, Julian V. "Three Steps to Make the Punishment Fit the Crime." *Globe and Mail* 7 Dec. 1993: A25.

Exercise 7.2

Write a short paragraph (five to seven sentences) that demonstrates your understanding of paragraph form and function. Choose any topic you like. When you have finished, exchange papers with another student and check each other's paragraph for

- Form: Is there a clear introduction to and conclusion of the topic?
- Function: Is the paragraph sufficiently developed for the reader to understand the topic clearly? The reader should have no questions left unanswered.

Crafting the Topic Sentence

The **topic sentence** in each paragraph is the sentence that clearly identifies what the paragraph is about—its main idea. The topic sentence focuses the paragraph, helps to unify it, and keeps you and your readers on track. In professional writing, the topic sentence is not always the first sentence of the paragraph. Sometimes it is more effective to announce the topic in the second, third, or even the last sentence. But professional writers, through years of practice, have earned the right to break the rules. Beginning writers should remember this: *most readers assume that the first sentence of a paragraph identifies the topic of that paragraph.* If your first sentence doesn't do this, then your readers may go through your paragraph assuming the topic is something other than what you intended. Miscommunication frustrates readers and wastes their time. To be absolutely clear, identify your topic up front.

A good topic sentence does three things:

1. It introduces the topic of the paragraph.
2. It makes a point about the topic.
3. It makes a statement that is neither too broad nor too narrow.

Readers appreciate writers who get to the point quickly, make the point clearly, and support or explain it adequately. They also appreciate writers who can make their points in an interesting way. Take the time to write topic sentences that are something more than straightforward, flat announcements of your main idea. Compare the following pairs of topic sentences.

Weak	Strong
I am going to explain why I love "trash."	I'm ashamed to confess my secret vice, but because we're friends, I can tell you: I love "trash."
This paragraph is about violence.	Violence as a way of achieving social justice is both impractical and immoral (Martin Luther King, Jr.).

A good way to introduce the topic so that it is both interesting and effective is to make a point about it. You save your readers' time and eliminate the risk of confusion if you make clear at the outset your idea about or your attitude toward your topic. Consider these examples.

Weak	**Strong**
Many people around the world enjoy music.	Nothing bridges gaps between cultures like music.
Canadians are different from Americans.	Canadians should be thankful for their differences from Americans.

Finally, the topic you choose must be "the right size"—neither so broad that you cannot support it adequately in a single paragraph, nor so narrow that it doesn't require support. The 4-S test that you used to determine whether a subject was suitable for a paper can also be applied to potential paragraph topics. If your topic is single, significant, specific, and supportable, it should form the basis for a solid paragraph. Take a look at these topic sentences.

Weak	**Strong**
The legal system in Canada discriminates against men. (too broad)	Single fathers who seek custody of their children are often treated unfairly in family court.
My children won't eat peas, broccoli, or spinach. (too narrow)	Getting young children to eat a balanced diet is not an easy task.
Cars should be banned from city streets. (too broad)	Cars should be banned from the downtown core from 7:00 a.m. to 7:00 p.m.

Exercise 7.3*

Read through each of the following paragraphs, then underline the topic sentence.

1.   The third consideration is perhaps the most important. Canada makes no economic sense. There may be excellent reasons for Canada's existence historically, socially, culturally, and even geographically, but the lines of trade and commerce flow north–south. If a government's chief concern is the economy, that government will naturally draw the country closer and closer to the United States, cinching in those belts of commerce that bind Canada to her southern partner. Only governments whose major goals are cultural or social will loosen the longitudinal ties and seek east–west bonds.

2.   Winston Churchill said, "Golf is a game whose aim it is to hit a very small ball into an even smaller hole with weapons singularly ill-designed for the purpose." It has been said that baseball is an activity where 14 men stand idly by while two play catch. In fact, all sports can be made ridiculous because the essence of sport is rules. If you really want to put a ball into a hole in the ground, it's very easy to do: pick it up, carry it to the hole, and drop it in. The fun in golf, as in all sports, is that the task is made challenging by very rigid and complex regulations. Reduced to its essential, sport is the attempt by one person or group to win dominance over another while encumbered by complicated rules. The rules in a game like hockey or baseball are enormously complex, while those in soccer or bowling are less so; however, the objective of all games is the same as the objective of war. Luckily, civilized humans have a love of rules and laws, and can take out their aggressions within the very rigid confines of the rule book.

3.   Seen by scanning electron microscope, our taste buds look as huge as volcanoes on Mars, while those of a shark are beautiful mounds of pastel-colored tissue paper—until we remember what they're used for. In reality, taste buds are exceedingly small. Adults have about 10,000, grouped by theme (salt, sour, sweet, bitter), at various sites in the mouth. Inside each one, about fifty taste cells busily relay information to a neuron, which will alert the brain. Not much tasting happens in the center of the tongue, but there are also incidental taste buds on the palate, pharynx, and tonsils, which cling like bats to the damp, slimy walls of a cave. Rabbits have 17,000 taste buds, parrots only about 400, and cows 25,000. What are they tasting? Maybe a cow needs that many to enjoy a relentless diet of grass.

Ackerman, Diane. *A Natural History of the Senses*. New York: Vintage-Random House, 1991. 138.

4.   Scholarly explanations of humor fall into three major categories. According to superiority theories, we laugh at the henpecked husband and the woman hit with a banana cream pie because the misfortunes of others make us feel better about our own lot. The 17th century philosopher Thomas Hobbes, for example, described laughter as a result of the "sudden glory" of increased self-esteem at the expense of others. Incongruity theories . . . stress the cognitive jolt of bringing together unrelated ideas. Thus the infant who chuckles when Mommy eats the baby food is savoring the incongruity of a grown woman making a fool of herself. Finally, tension-relief theories attribute our laughter to a sudden release from strain. Freud argued that our jokes, like our dreams, allow pent-up sexual and aggressive images to suddenly leap into consciousness, albeit in a disguised form.

"What's So Funny?" *Psychology Today* June 1978: 101.

5.   "Why do you want it?" This should be the first question a good computer salesperson asks a prospective customer. With the huge variety of computers now on the market, the determining factor in a purchase should be the job the machine will be expected to do. While a network card, premium audio system, and 21-inch VDT are great for watching movies, a user who wants a basic word processor would be throwing away money to buy them. Home users and small businesses often get carried away with the desire for gigantic memory capacity, lightning speed, and high resolution capability, but these are advertising gimmicks rather than useful purchases for most small users. On the other hand, it can be a costly error for a buyer to underestimate long-term computer needs and buy a machine that must be upgraded or replaced in a year.

Now compare your answers with ours on page 516.

GO TO WEB

EXERCISE 7.1

Exercise 7.4

Each of the following thesis statements contains a subject and main points. Working with a partner or in a small group, develop the main points of each thesis statement into effective topic sentences.

1. Volunteering is a valuable addition to a college education because it provides work experience, develops professional contacts, and enhances self-esteem.
2. Unemployment, poverty, and loneliness are factors that may lead to depression.
3. Canadians emigrate to other countries for three main reasons: a warmer climate, better job opportunities, and new cultural experiences.

Exercise 7.5

For each of the thesis statements below, develop the main points into effective topic sentences. Make sure each topic sentence you write introduces the topic clearly, makes a point about the topic, and is neither too broad nor too narrow.

1. The driver who caused your accident last weekend was probably one of four types: a road hog, a tailgater, a speed demon, or a Sunday driver.

NEL

2. There are three types of supervisor in this world: the good, the bad, and mine.
3. The thought of moving to the country is attractive to many city dwellers because of the slower pace, the healthier environment, and the closer-knit communities.

Developing the Topic

Once you've written your topic sentence, the next step is to develop it. An adequately developed paragraph gives enough supporting information to make the topic completely clear to the readers. Unless you are writing from a detailed outline listing all the supporting material you need, it's time to focus once again on your intended audience. Put yourself in your readers' place.

- How much information do your readers already have about your topic?
- Are they inclined to agree or disagree with you?
- What do your readers need to know to understand your point clearly?

There are seven ways to develop a topic. Not all will be appropriate in every case, and some will be more effective than others. Let your topic and your audience guide you in choosing the most appropriate kind(s) of development.

1. Tell a story. Everyone loves to read a story if it's relevant and well told. An anecdote can be an effective way to help your readers not only understand your idea but also remember it. Below are two examples that illustrate the use of narration to develop a topic.

I first experienced culture shock when I travelled to Egypt. I was walking down the main street on the day of my arrival when it suddenly struck me that the crowds on the street were stepping aside to make way for me. It was 1980, and my height, blond hair, and blue eyes were so unusual to the Egyptians that I was an object of intense curiosity. The staring and pointing followed me everywhere. Finally, unable to cope any longer with being constantly on display, I took refuge in the Canadian Embassy and spent a couple of hours quietly leafing through back issues of *Maclean's* magazine.

Imagine that two accountants do similar jobs for similar companies. One day they make the same discovery: with almost no chance of getting caught, they can embezzle a large sum from their employers. They can both use the money to pay off debts or buy a new car. The first accountant right away says to himself, "It's wrong to steal," and never considers the matter again. But the second accountant is torn. She, too, knows that stealing is wrong, but she's tempted and at first decides to go ahead. Then she decides she won't, and then that she will. Finally, after weeks of agonizing, she decides not to embezzle. Who is the morally better person?

Hurka, Thomas. "Should Morality Be a Struggle? Ancient vs. Modern Ideas about Ethics." *Principles: Short Essays about Ethics.* Toronto: Harcourt Brace, 1994. 83.

Exercise 7.6

Using a story to develop your topic, write a paragraph on one of following, or choose a topic of your own.

1. A road-rage experience
2. The day I became an adult
3. The customer is not always right
4. How not to treat employees
5. Defusing a tense situation

2. Define your topic. A definition paragraph explains and clarifies the meaning of a word or idea. Use the definition paragraph to explain a term that may be unfamiliar to your readers. (Write your own definition, please. Quoting from a dictionary is an overused and boring way to start a paragraph.) Below are definitions of two terms that the authors wanted to be sure their readers would understand from the *writers'* point of view.

Culture shock is the inability to understand or cope with experiences one has never encountered before. It commonly affects travellers who journey to lands whose climate, food, language, and customs are alien to the traveller. In addition to confusion and anxiety, culture shock may even produce physical symptoms: chills, fever, trembling, and faintness.

A hybrid is a cross between two established varieties of plant, animal, . . . or technology. The hybrid bicycle, for example, combines the features of a road bike with those of an off-road bike to produce a comfortable and efficient bicycle for short distance cycling. For most people, however, the word "hybrid" signifies a fuel-efficient, low-emission automobile. Hybrid car technology combines a gasoline or diesel internal combustion engine with a battery-powered electric motor. Its objective is to maximize the best properties of both the gas engine and the electric motor.

Howerth, Sara R. "The Gas-Electric Hybrid Demystified." 207.

You should include a definition, too, if you're using a familiar term in an unusual way. Here Martin Luther King defines what he means by "the length of life":

> Now let us notice first the length of life. I have said this is the dimension of life in which the individual is concerned with developing his inner powers. It is that dimension of life in which the individual pursues personal ends and ambitions. This is perhaps the selfish dimension of life, and there is such a thing as moral and rational self-interest. If one is not concerned about himself he cannot be totally concerned about other selves.

King, Martin Luther, Jr. "The Dimensions of a Complete Life." *The Measure of a Man.* 1959. Philadelphia: Pilgrim Press, 1969.

Exercise 7.7

Choose one of the following topics (or select one of your own) and write a paragraph in which you develop the topic by defining it.

1. Burnout
2. A good boss (employee, customer, colleague)
3. An extrovert (introvert)
4. A great artist (musician, actor, writer, etc.)
5. A bad habit

3. Use examples. Giving examples is probably the most common method of developing an idea and supporting a statement. Readers can become confused or suspicious when they read unsupported statements of "fact," opinion, or ideas. One of the best ways to support your topic is by providing clear, relevant examples.

Sometimes, as in the paragraph below, one extended example is enough to allow your readers to see clearly what you mean.

> Culture shock can affect anyone, even a person who never leaves home. My grandfather was perfectly content to be an accountant until he retired, and was confident that his company would need his services for the foreseeable future. Computers were "silly toys" and modern business practices just "jargon" and "a new fad." When he was laid off four years before his retirement, he went into shock. It wasn't just the layoff; it was the speed of change—the idea that he was stranded in a new and unfamiliar culture for which he was unprepared, and in which he had no useful role.

Sometimes a number of examples may be necessary to develop a point, as in this paragraph.

All sports may be reduced to a few basic skills, which, if learned properly at the outset and drilled until they are instinctive, lead to success. Tennis is no exception; however, few people seem willing to spend the time needed to master the basics. Having been shown the proper grip and swing for a forehand, backhand, and serve, my students seem to feel they can qualify for Wimbledon. The basics are not learned that easily. Many tennis schools are now using a system first developed in Spain that is very successful in establishing the correct stroke in new players: for the first month of lessons, they aren't allowed to use a tennis ball. For that first month, correct positioning, proper swing, footwork, and technique are drilled without any of the distractions of keeping score, winning or losing, or chasing errant balls. That's how important the basics are to winning tennis.

Green, Brian. "How to Play Winning Tennis." 173.

Exercise 7.8

Using examples to develop your topic, write a paragraph on one of following, or choose a topic of your own.

1. Parents and privacy
2. Computers: the biggest time-wasters of modern life
3. Childless by choice
4. Adjusting to life away from home
5. The incompetence (incomprehensibility) of men (women)

4. Use a quotation or paraphrase. Occasionally you will find that someone else—an expert in a particular field, a well-known author, or a respected public figure—has said what you want to say better than you could ever hope to say it. Relevant and authoritative quotations, as long as they are kept short and are not used too frequently, are useful in developing your topic. Two sources of quotations on practically any subject are *John Robert Colombo's Famous Lasting Words: Great Canadian Quotations* (Vancouver: Douglas & McIntyre, 2000) and *Bartlett's Familiar Quotations* (http://www.bartleby.com/101/). **Never forget to acknowledge the source of your quotation!** In the paragraph below, the writer introduces his topic with a thought-provoking quotation.

"Although one can experience real pain from culture shock, it is also an opportunity for redefining one's life objectives. Culture shock can make one develop a better understanding of oneself and stimulate personal creativity." As with any experience that forces us out of our comfort zone and shatters our complacency, culture shock can be an opportunity for growth and development, as this quotation from the College of Education at San Diego State University makes clear. The trick is to recognize this unpleasant experience as a starting point for personal change. Here's an opportunity to re-examine our preconceptions about our place in society, about our interactions with others, even about the path we have chosen to take in life: has it become a rut?

A **paraphrase** is a summary in your own words of someone else's idea. Remember to indicate whose idea you are paraphrasing, the way the author of "The Myth of Canadian Diversity" does in the following paragraph.

... [O]ur much-discussed ethnic differences are overstated. Although Canada is an immigrant nation and Canadians spring from a variety of backgrounds, a recent study from the C.D. Howe Institute says that the idea of a "Canadian mosaic"—as distinct from the American "melting pot"—is a fallacy. In *The Illusion of Difference*, University of Toronto sociologists Jeffrey Reitz and Raymond Breton show that immigrants to Canada assimilate as quickly into the mainstream society as immigrants to the United States do. In fact, Canadians are less likely than Americans to favour holding on to cultural differences based on ethnic background. If you don't believe Mr. Reitz and Mr. Breton, visit any big-city high school, where the speech and behaviour of immigrant students just a few years in Canada is indistinguishable from that of any fifth-generation classmate. (321–22)

Exercise 7.9

Choose one of the following topics (or select one of your own) and write a paragraph in which you develop the topic by using quotations and/or paraphrase.

1. The most inspiring (uninspiring) teacher you have known
2. Everything I know I learned from my mother (father, brother, etc.)
3. A favourite book (movie, website)
4. The wisdom of children
5. Father knows (does not know) best

5. Use a comparison. A comparison shows similarities between things; it shows how two different things are alike in a particular way or ways. If you have a difficult or abstract topic to explain, try comparing it to something that is familiar to your readers, as this writer does.

Being left on your own in a foreign land is a bit like being forced to play a card game when you're the only one who doesn't know the rules. As the stakes get higher and the other players' excitement and enjoyment increase, you get correspondingly more frustrated and miserable. Finally, in desperation, you want to throw your cards on the table, absorb your losses, and go home.

In this next paragraph, the writer uses an **analogy**—an extended comparison—between a date and a car to make the point both clear and interesting.

The economy-model date features cramped conditions and a lack of power. The econo-date thinks that his personality can make up for the fact that you never go anywhere except for walks and never do anything that costs money. He tends to be shy, quiet, and about as much fun as an oil leak. It's not that he doesn't have money to spend; it's that he doesn't use any imagination or creativity to compensate for his lack of cash.

Exercise 7.10

Choose one of the following topics (or select one of your own) and write a paragraph in which you develop the topic by using comparison.

1. The modern workplace
2. E-mail
3. Two consumer products
4. Type A (Type B) personalities
5. Engineering (or computer science, arts, or nursing) students

---

6. Explain steps or stages in a process. Sometimes the most effective way to develop the main idea of your paragraph is by explaining how something occurs or is done—that is, by relating the series of steps involved. Make sure you break the process down into its component parts and detail the steps logically and precisely.

The first sign of culture shock is usually anxiety. The traveller feels uncomfortable and ill at ease; nothing looks, smells, sounds, or tastes familiar. Next, he may become resentful, even angry, and withdraw from his new surroundings, seeking isolation in safe, familiar territory—his room. Unfortunately, solitude reinforces anxiety and makes the situation worse. Over time, the victim of culture shock may begin to perceive the environment not as "strange but neutral" but as "strange and hostile." Friendly interaction with others and positive experiences in the new culture are the cure, but one is not likely to encounter either while cocooned in a small boarding house or hotel room. Fortunately, most travellers find that culture shock diminishes with rest. As anxiety lessens, curiosity grows, and they begin to venture out to participate in the life of the new country. In extreme cases, however, travellers suffering from culture shock can develop flu-like symptoms: fever, chills, sleeplessness, and a debilitating loss of energy. When these symptoms strike, it's time to call home for moral support and encouragement to get out and enjoy the sights and scenes one has travelled so far to experience.

In writing a process paragraph, you need to pay particular attention to transitions, which are discussed in the next chapter, or you'll leave your readers gasping in the dust as you gallop through your explanation. The paragraph below illustrates a simple yet effective use of transitions.

In 1983, a Harvard Medical School team led by Dr. Howard Green found a revolutionary way to repair burned skin. Here is how it is done. Doctors cut up a small patch of skin donated by a patient, treat it with enzymes, then spread it thinly onto a culture medium. After only ten days, colonies of skin cells begin linking up into sheets, which can then be chopped up and used to make further sheets. In twenty-four days, enough skin will be produced to cover an entire human body. About ten days later, the gauze is removed, and the skin soon grows into a surface much smoother and more natural-looking than the rough one a normal skin-graft usually leaves.

Ackerman, Diane. *A Natural History of the Senses.* New York: Vintage-Random House, 1990. 69–70.

Exercise 7.11

Choose one of the following topics (or select one of your own) and write a paragraph in which you develop the topic by describing the series of steps or stages involved in the process.

1. Career planning
2. Buying a used car
3. Understanding women (men)
4. Writing a business report
5. Getting out of debt

7. Provide specific details. Concrete, specific, descriptive details can be an effective way to develop your main idea. In the paragraph below, the writer uses specific detail to describe treatment for culture shock.

Culture shock can be alleviated by taking action to reduce the impact of the cause, and then treating each of the symptoms separately. Prevention is the best cure: introduce yourself gradually to a new environment. Explore in small stages, while keeping contact with safe and familiar surroundings. Don't plunge into the bazaar within an hour of your arrival in Marrakesh, but begin your exploration in the Western quarter and gradually expose yourself to the sights, sounds, and smells of areas that seem threateningly foreign. If you should come down with symptoms of shock, go to bed, stay warm, drink lots of bottled water, and sleep as much as you can. When you begin to feel better, take things slowly and avoid stressful situations where you have to make decisions or confront the unexpected. A guided bus tour of the city is a good way to begin familiarizing yourself with a new physical and cultural environment, and discovering what's available that you want to explore.

In some paragraphs, numerical facts or statistics can be used to support your point effectively. However, in keeping with Benjamin Disraeli's immortal comment ("There are three kinds of lies: lies, damned lies, and statistics"), critical readers tend to be suspicious of statistics. Be very sure that your facts are correct and that your statistics are current.

Canadians are great travellers. We not only travel around our own country, exploring every nook and cranny from Beaver Creek in the Yukon Territory to Bay Bulls in Newfoundland, but we also can be found touring around every other country on Earth. Statistics Canada reports that we take about 150 million overnight trips a year within our own borders. Abroad, we favour our next door neighbour by a wide margin above other destinations, averaging around 15 million overnight trips a year to the United States. The United Kingdom is our second favourite destination, with over 800,000 visits, followed by Mexico (over 600,000) and France (over 400,000). Of the Caribbean islands, Cuba is our favourite winter escape. Cuba ranks fifth overall, with 350,000 annual visits by Canadians. Of the Asian nations, Hong Kong, in tenth place, tops the list with 115,000 visits. Australia, in fourteenth place with about 90,000 visits, ranks just ahead of Japan. Rounding Canada's population off to about 30 million, we can use these figures to deduce that, on average, a Canadian travels within Canada five times every year and takes a trip abroad twice in three years.

Exercise 7.12

Using specific details to develop your topic, write a paragraph on one of following, or choose a topic of your own.

1. A web page
2. A migraine headache

3. The myth of the shorter work week
4. The best team in basketball (baseball, football, soccer, lacrosse)
5. Money can't buy happiness

In writing your own paragraphs, you will often need to use more than one method of development to explain your point. The seven methods described in this chapter can be used in any combination you choose.

How Do You End a Paragraph?

A good paragraph doesn't just end; like a door, it should close firmly, with a "click." Finish your paragraph with a statement that serves either as a **clincher**—an unmistakable and appropriate conclusion—or a **transition** to the new idea that will be developed in the next paragraph.

Exercise 7.13

Turn back to the paragraphs in Exercise 7.1 (pages 83–84). Reread each one and decide whether it ends with a clincher or a transition sentence.

Exercise 7.14

To stretch your imagination and improve your mastery of the kinds of support you can choose from to develop a topic, write a paragraph on one of the following topics, using two or more methods of development. Your target audience is your instructor and your classmates.

1. Getting along with coworkers
2. Performance appraisal
3. Training a new employee
4. Life is like a game of _____
5. Canadians don't appreciate how lucky they are

8

Keeping Your Readers with You

As you write, remember that it is your responsibility to make it as easy as possible for your readers to follow you through your essay. Unity, coherence, and tone can make the difference between a paper that confuses or annoys your readers and one that enlightens and pleases them.

Unity

Unity means "oneness." The contents of a paragraph must relate to a single main idea. All supporting sentences in the paragraph must clearly and directly relate to the topic sentence of that paragraph.

Achieving unity requires care. Your job is to develop the points that you have set out to make, not other points that may occur to you as you write. (The time to set down whatever happens to come to mind is in the prewriting stage, not the paragraph development stage.) Any material that does not clearly support the topic sentence should be deleted or moved to another paragraph in the essay—assuming, of course, that it is directly relevant there.

Take a look at the following paragraph. It contains several sentences that spoil the unity of the paragraph because they do not clearly relate to the topic.

(1) I knew I wanted to return to school, but did I want to be a full-time or a part-time student? (2) The major consideration was, not surprisingly, money. (3) If I chose to go to college full-time, then I would have to give up my full-time job. (4) The resulting loss of income would reduce my buying power to zero. (5) Even the tuition fees would be beyond my reach. (6) Also, my choice of program would be a difficult decision, because I still wasn't sure which career path to follow. (7) My other option was part-time education. (8) If I kept my full-time job,

I could at least pay for food, rent, and a modest amount of clothing. (9) Also, I could afford the tuition fees. (10) Going to school part-time costs less per year because the expenditure is spread over a longer period of time than it is in the full-time program. (11) Therefore, I chose to educate myself part-time, through continuing education courses. (12) While working, I could learn new skills in my spare time. (13) My career choice would still be in doubt, but I would have a longer time in which to make up my mind. (14) Money is scarce for a full-time, self-supporting student, but as a part-time student I could have the best of both worlds: a steady income and a college education.

Draw a line through the sentences that do not logically and directly support the topic of the paragraph: the writer's decision whether to be a full-time or part-time student.[1]

Exercise 8.1[*]

The paragraphs below contain some irrelevant sentences that disrupt unity. Read each paragraph and then, with a partner, find and cross out the sentences that don't belong. Answers for exercises in this chapter begin on page 517.

1. (1) A good pizza consists of a combination of succulent ingredients. (2) First, you prepare the foundation, the crust, which may be thick or thin, depending on your preference. (3) I like my crusts thick and chewy. (4) The crust is spread with a layer of basil- and oregano-flavoured tomato sauce. (5) Next, a rich smorgasbord of toppings—pepperoni, mushrooms, green peppers, bacon, anchovies—should be scattered over the tomato sauce. (6) *Smorgasbord* is a Swedish word meaning a buffet meal; *pizza* is Italian in origin. (7) Last of all, a double-thick blanket of grated mozzarella cheese should be spread over all. (8) Pizza is simple to make—all you need is dough, tomato sauce, vegetables, sausage, herbs, and cheese—but the combination has an unbeatable taste.

2. (1) Keeping a job is not easy in a tight market in which well-educated job-seekers are plentiful. (2) Here are a couple of hints you will find helpful in maintaining your "employed" status. (3) First, you should not only apply your specialized knowledge on the job every day, but also continually update it by taking seminars and evening courses to enhance your skills. (4) Doing your job effectively is difficult without becoming burned out. (5) Second, good communication—with the public, your fellow workers, and your supervisor—is perhaps the most important factor in keeping you on the payroll. (6) Upgrading your education and improving your communication skills are your best defences against the pink slip.

---

[1]The sentences that you should have crossed out because they do not belong in this paragraph and detract from its unity are 6, 12, and 13.

3.	(1) Comedies are my favourite way to relax. (2) Horror films terrify me, and adventures become tedious after the tenth chase, but comedies entertain and refresh me after a long shift at work. (3) Woody Allen pictures, especially the early farces, help me to take my mind off the stress of the day. (4) For example, *Bananas*, a satire about American politics in the 1960s, is more relaxing for me than a double martini. (5) It's also less fattening, and I've been trying to give up drinking. (6) *Sleeper*, a futuristic spoof, has me laughing, on average, twice a minute. (7) Perhaps my favourite, however, is *Annie Hall*. (8) After viewing it, I am so weak with laughter that I can go to sleep within minutes. (9) Now that all of Allen's comedies are available on DVD, I never need to feel tense and worn out for longer than it takes to insert a disc.

4.	(1) My department's job is to produce reports. (2) We research and prepare year-end reports, stockholders' reports, reports on the competition, on the customers, on the suppliers, and on just about everything else. (3) We think of ourselves as creative rather than technical writers because there is no future in our company for anyone who is critical or who dares to tell the truth if truth isn't what the senior managers want to hear. (4) Instead of fixing the problem, they punish the person who tells them what's wrong; that is, they "shoot the messenger." (5) I believe this saying originated in ancient days, long before there were guns, so presumably the original idea was "knife the messenger" or "behead the messenger." (6) If employees understand this management practice, however, they can protect themselves. (7) For example, our department has developed three rules to help us produce reports that are guaranteed a favourable reception. (8) First, teamwork is essential; without it, you have no one else to blame. (9) Second, when you don't know what you're doing, do it neatly. (10) Third, if at first you don't succeed, destroy all evidence that you ever tried. (11) With these rules to guide us, our department has survived three new managers in the past two and a half years.

5.	(1) The office manager who demands that all employees not only arrive on time but actually get in early to demonstrate their enthusiasm and drive is actually damaging productivity. (2) Such a manager is, of course, always in the office at least an hour early herself, and because she attributes her success to this habit, she demands it of others. (3) Not everyone is suited to an early start. (4) Individual biorhythms vary widely, and some employees may be better suited to demonstrating their keenness by staying late at night. (5) The old adage "The early bird gets the worm" is based on some truth, but there are many exceptions. (6) Besides, what office worker wants a worm, anyway? (7) For that matter, there are lots of other sayings and aphorisms that can apply just as readily to the situation. (8) If your manager cites this tired old phrase as her justification for demanding unreasonably early hours, you may want to point out that another saying is equally true: "The second mouse gets the cheese."

Coherence

Coherence means "sticking together." The sentences within each paragraph need to cohere, as do the paragraphs within an essay. If your sentences and paragraphs are not coherent, your reader will have great difficulty trying to fit together your bits of information to make sense of the whole. Sorting out sentences as if they were pieces of a puzzle is not the reader's job. It is the writer's responsibility to put the pieces together to form a complete and clear picture.

Coherence is achieved in two ways.

1. First, you need to arrange the sentences in each paragraph according to an organizational principle. Remember the options you chose from to arrange ideas in Chapter 4, "Managing the Main Points"? You should arrange your development within paragraphs in the same ways: chronological, climactic, logical, or, infrequently, random order. (Turn to pages 57–59 to review these.)
2. Second, you achieve coherence by providing **transitions**. Transitions are connections between one idea and the next within a paragraph, and between one paragraph and the next within an essay. Why are transitions needed? Read the paragraph below and you'll see clearly that something is missing. The paragraph has adequate development, but no transitions.

We were bored one day. We didn't know what to do. It was Friday. We thought about going to the library. No one really wanted to do schoolwork. We went to the mall. For a short time we window-shopped. We discussed what to do. It was agreed that we would drive to the American side of the border. We would do our shopping. It was a short drive. We went to a discount mall. The bargains were great. We spent much more money than we intended to. We went home. We discovered that with the American exchange, prices were better at home. We should have gone to the library.

Not very easy to read, is it? Readers are jerked abruptly from point to point until, battered and bruised, they finally reach the end. This kind of writing is unfair to readers. It makes them do too much of the work. The ideas may all be there, but the readers have to figure out for themselves how the ideas fit together. After a couple of paragraphs like the one above, even the most patient readers can become annoyed.

Now read the same paragraph, rewritten with transitions.

Last Friday we were so bored we didn't know what to do. We thought about going to the library, but no one really wanted to study, so we went to the mall and window-shopped for a while. After a long discussion about what to do next, we agreed to drive to the American side of the border for some serious shopping. A short drive later, we arrived at a discount mall, where the bargains were so great that we spent much more money than we had intended. Finally, we returned home, where we discovered that, with the American exchange, prices were better at home after all. We should have gone to the library.

In this paragraph, readers are gently guided from one point to the next. By the time they reach the conclusion, they know not only what ideas the writer had in mind, but also how the ideas fit together to form a unit. The transitions make the reader's job easy and rewarding.

You can choose from an array of strategies to improve the coherence of your writing. There are five techniques to master. Be sure to use a variety of these techniques every time you write. Nothing improves the polish of your prose more than the use of coherence strategies.

1. Repetition. Repetition focuses the reader's attention on an idea and creates a thread of meaning that runs through a paragraph or a paper, tying the whole thing together. Don't overdo it, though.

2. Synonyms. Frequent repetition of a key word can become monotonous after a while. You can keep the reader focused on the idea by using synonyms—different words that convey the same meaning.

3. Pronoun references. Another way of maintaining the focus but varying the wording is to use appropriate pronouns to refer to a key noun. (This technique involves pronoun–antecedent agreement, a topic covered in Chapter 32.)

4. Parallel structure. Phrasing your sentences in parallel form helps to maintain focus, reinforces the unity of your thoughts, and adds emphasis. Parallelism adds "punch" to your writing. (More punch is served in Chapter 26.)

5. Transitional words and phrases. Transitional words and phrases show the relationships between points in a paragraph as well as between paragraphs in an essay. They act like tape, sticking together the elements of a paragraph or a paper so your reader does not fall between the cracks. Use them the way you use turn signals on a car: to tell the person following you where you're going.

Here are some transitional phrases that will help make your writing read smoothly.

Transitional Function	Words/Phrases Used
1. To show a time relationship between points	• first, second, third • now, simultaneously, concurrently, at this point, while • before, to begin, previously • after, following this, then, later, next • finally, last, subsequently • during, meanwhile, presently, from time to time, sometimes
2. To add an idea or example to the previous point	• and, in addition, also, furthermore, besides, moreover, for the same reason • another, similarly, equally important, likewise • for example, for instance, in fact
3. To show contrast between points	• although, nevertheless, on the other hand, whereas, while • but, however, instead, nonetheless • in contrast, on the contrary, in spite of, despite
4. To show a cause-and-effect relationship between points	• since, because, thus, therefore, hence • as a result, consequently, accordingly
5. To emphasize or repeat a significant point	• in fact, indeed, certainly, undoubtedly • in other words, as I have said, that is to say
6. To summarize or conclude	• in brief, on the whole, in summary, in short • therefore, as a result, last, finally

The paragraph below illustrates the use of all five coherence strategies to achieve unity. As you read, pay particular attention to the writer's use of repetition and parallelism.

While the Internet can be a useful tool for some businesses, studies have shown that in most workplaces it is a time-wasting drain on resources. As a result of one such study, Deloitte and Touche have issued a report pointing out the "five G's": risks of allowing employees unsupervised Internet activity during business hours. A company risks Giving, handing trade or business secrets over to the competition or the general public. A company risks Gawking, time-wasting employee fascination with particular sites, including pornography. A company risks Gambling, an increasingly common and potentially addictive lure for surfers. A company risks Goofing off, the pointless surfing of sites that are unrelated to the task at hand. A company risks Grabbing, the downloading of virus-infected material and copyrighted software. To counter the five G's, Deloitte and Touche recommend that companies establish clear policy on Internet use.

Owner Manager Advisor newsletter. *Globe and Mail* 25 Jan. 1998: B15.

Exercise 8.2*

Working with a partner, identify the transitional words and phrases that create coherence in each of the sentence groups below.

1. The spruce budworm threatens B.C.'s forests, killing trees that have resisted all other predators. Therefore, governments at both the local and provincial levels have begun a controlled burn program.
2. The two women spent the whole day tramping from car dealer to car dealer. Finally, they found a used Toyota they could live with, but the price was higher than they had hoped to pay.
3. There are many jokes about cats. Unfortunately, however, in most of them the cat is either very unhappy or dead.
4. There are those who think Quebec would thrive as a separate state. On the other hand, some feel that its economic viability depends on a close relationship with the rest of Canada.
5. Although we fear the size and power of our big banks, we must admit that they serve us well when compared with the banking institutions of other countries. For example, Canadian banks are second only to Japanese banks, and ahead of those in the United States and Germany, in the number of ATMs per person they provide. In addition, they lead all three of these countries in the number of full-service branches per capita.

Exercise 8.3

In each of the following sentences, supply transitional words or phrases that help the meaning become clearer and make the sentence more coherent. When you've finished, exchange exercises with another student and check each other's answers. If you disagree with any of your partner's choices, explain why.

1. My first impression of my supervisor was that he was aloof and arrogant; _____, I discovered I was wrong. He was painfully shy.

2. Many bestsellers have become pathetic movies, now long forgotten. _____ many poor novels have been turned into movie classics, such as *Gone with the Wind*, that last forever.

3. Many sports were discovered by accident. _____, one day at Rugby school in the 1830s, an English schoolboy, during a game of rugby, threw the ball overhand down the field. Football (as we call it in North America) was born.

4. Architecture in the 20th century has become more streamlined, geometrical, and uniform. _____, it has become monotonous.

5. The Bush administration believes that an expensive and unproven missile defence system is needed to protect North American from a non-existent threat. _____, Canadians disagree.

Exercise 8.4*

Read the paragraphs below and identify the transitional strategies that contribute to coherence. Both paragraphs contain examples of all five techniques listed on page 102.

1.   Finally, developing the proper attitude is the true key to winning tennis. I define winning tennis as playing the game to the best of your ability, hitting the ball as well as you know you can, and enjoying the feeling of practised expertise. Winning tennis has nothing to do with beating an opponent. Naturally, if you play winning tennis by learning the basics, practising sufficiently, and concentrating, you'll win many matches, but that is the reward of playing well, not the reason for playing well. People who swear and throw their racquets when they lose are very useful; they are the most satisfying players to trounce. But I don't understand why they play a game that causes them such pain. Tennis players who enjoy the feel of a well hit ball and the satisfaction of a long, skilfully played rally are winners, regardless of the score.

2.   Travel abroad offers you the best education you can get. For one thing, travel is a course in communication skills. In order to function in a foreign language, you must practise every aspect of the communication process from body language to pronunciation. In fact, just making yourself understood is

a lesson in creativity, a seminar in sign language, and a lab in communication theory. Another educational aspect of travel is the history, geography, and culture that you learn about almost unconsciously. Everywhere you go, you encounter memorable evidence of historical events you may dimly recall from school, and you are continually confronted by the practical realities of geography as you try to find your way around. As for culture, no book or course of study could provide you with the understanding and appreciation of another society that living in it can. A third way in which travel educates is through teaching you about yourself. Your ability—or inability—to cope with unfamiliar customs, with language difficulties, and with the inevitable problems of finding transportation and accommodation will tell you more than you might want to know about yourself. Without the safety net of family and friends, perhaps without even the security of knowing where you'll spend the night, you develop self-reliance or you go home. Either way, you learn valuable lessons. While you may not get a diploma from Travel U., you'll learn more about the world, about people, and about yourself than you will in any classroom.

Now compare your answers to ours on pages 517–18.

Exercise 8.5

Now consider the ways coherence strategies can be used to promote the smooth flow of ideas throughout an essay. Identify the transitional techniques used in Bertrand Russell's "What I Have Lived For," on page 6.

Tone

As you write the paragraphs of your paper, be conscious of your **tone**. Your audience, purpose, and subject will all influence the tone you choose, which must be appropriate to all three. The words you use, the examples, quotations, and other supporting materials you choose to help explain your main points—all these contribute to your tone.

When you are trying to explain something to someone, particularly if it's something you feel strongly about, you may be tempted to be highly emotional in your discussion. If you allow yourself to get emotional, chances are you won't be convincing. What will be communicated is the strength of your feelings, not the depth of your understanding or the validity of your opinion. To be clear and credible, you need to restrain your enthusiasm or anger and present your points in a calm, reasonable way.

Here are a few suggestions to help you find and maintain the right tone:

- Be tactful. Avoid phrases such as "Any idiot can see," "No sane person could believe," and "It is obvious that...." What is obvious to you isn't necessarily obvious to someone who has a limited understanding of your subject or who disagrees with your opinion.

- Don't talk down to your readers as though they were children or hopelessly ignorant. Never use sarcasm, profanity, or slang.

- Don't apologize for your interpretation of your subject. Have confidence in yourself. You've thought long and hard about your subject, you've found good supporting material to help explain it, and you believe in its significance. Present your subject in a positive manner. If you hang back, using phrases such as "I may be wrong, but ... " or "I tend to feel that ... ", your reader won't be inclined to give your points the consideration they deserve. Keep your reader in mind as you write, and your writing will be both clear and convincing.

The following paragraph is an example of inappropriate tone. The writer is enthusiastic about the topic, but the tone is arrogant, bossy, and tactless rather than persuasive.

It is time that governments at all levels did something completely out of character: take action. We need laws requiring the addition of 10 percent ethanol to gasoline. Ethanol burns cleaner than gas and also boosts octane, so it's completely obvious that the oil companies don't have to put so many poisonous additives in the gas to make our already too powerful cars go even faster. For another thing, anybody who has done any reading knows that ethanol is made out of corn, which is grown on farms and is a renewable resource. Growing it will make farmers happy, and drivers should also be cheerful because it can be produced for less than the outrageous prices we pay for straight gasoline. Adding 10 percent of the cheaper fuel should bring pump prices down, although I'm sure the oil companies will find a way to gouge the consumer. Obviously, the government is going to have to pass laws forcing the oil companies to add ethanol because there's no way these corporate creeps are going to do what is good for the environment and the economy at the expense of lining their own pockets. However, relying on government to do the right thing is just as precarious a proposition; I wouldn't hold my breath.

Now read the paragraph below, which argues the same point but in a courteous, tactful way.

Legislation requiring the addition of ethanol to gasoline is both sensible and overdue. The addition of 10 percent ethanol to the gasoline that is sold at the pump is sensible for two reasons. First, it makes the fuel that is burned in our cars and trucks cleaner. Ethanol burns hotter than gasoline and burns up more of the pollutants, rather than sending them out of the tailpipe. Because it provides a higher octane fuel, ethanol also eliminates the need for some of the toxic additives currently used to boost octane. Second, ethanol is a renewable source of energy that will provide jobs in rural Canada because it is made from corn. At current oil prices, ethanol is cheaper than gasoline, so its addition to our fuel will help to reduce costs for consumers. Why should governments have to legislate such a sensible course of action? The petroleum industry, from exploration to retail, is not about to voluntarily dilute its product—or, more important, its profits—by any amount, let alone 10 percent!

Exercise 8.6*

The following paragraph is a draft written for a general reader. The writer's purpose is to persuade her audience that city dwellers should be more aware of the labour that lies behind every packaged product we eat. Revise the paragraph to make it appropriate to its audience and purpose by deleting or rewording any lapses in tone. Then compare your answer with ours on page 518.

I'm from the city, so I may not know much about the subject, but it seems to me that we urbanites have lost touch with the food we eat. By this I mean, obviously, that we no longer appreciate the farmers and farm workers who supply the food that we enjoy every day. Anyone with half a brain should realize that most of the food we buy is prepackaged in Styrofoam, wrapped in plastic, or precooked and frozen by huge corporations whose goal is to make humongous profits by selling us the packaging, not the contents. Do any urban consumers understand that their ketchup is made from farm-grown tomatoes? Do any advertising-driven supermarket shoppers really think about the fact that those overpackaged frozen pork chops, so irresistible with their sprig of parsley, were once a pig, raised by a farmer? Not only are we ignorant, but also we could care less about the journey our food makes from farm to fridge. My guess is that if you asked most city kids where their food comes from, they'd say, "the food factory."

Revise the following paragraph, adding transitions and moderating its tone.

The armed forces of most nations are trained to be psychopaths. Canada's military personnel face a greater challenge: they need to be schizophrenics. The boot-camp training that recruits undergo, together with instruction in combat and weaponry, produces efficient and remorseless killers—psychopaths. The role of Canada's armed forces over the past 50 years has been to keep the peace. When the Nobel Peace Prize was awarded to the United Nations peacekeeping forces, Canada, as the only nation to have participated in every mission, considered the prize largely hers. Canada's elite forces played a traditional military role as hunters and killers in Afghanistan. Is Canada's military adequately trained for these two contradictory roles? Our country needs highly trained units of efficient psychopaths. The majority of armed forces personnel need training in mediation, conflict resolution, cultural sensitivity, basic medical treatment, and infrastructure repair. This is a hard concept for fans of the military to get through their thick skulls: soldiers trained to prevent violence. Peacekeeping is still the Canadian military's primary function. Canada's armed forces have two roles. Both must be prepared for.

9

Writing Introductions and Conclusions

All of the concepts you have studied so far can be applied to any paragraph. Two paragraphs, however—the first and the last—serve special purposes and need extra care. All too often, the introduction and the conclusion of a paper are dull or clumsy and detract from its effectiveness. But they needn't be dull or clumsy. Here's how to write good ones.

The Introductory Paragraph

The introduction is worth special attention because that's where your readers either sit up and take notice of your paper or sigh and pitch it into the wastebasket.

There are two parts to an introductory paragraph:
1. an attention-getter
2. a thesis statement

Getting and Holding Your Readers' Attention

Your readers must be attracted to your writing or there's no point in putting pen to paper or fingers to keyboard. The attention-getter must be appropriate to the content of your essay and to your intended readers. If your audience is known for a solemn approach to life and your topic is serious (environmental ethics, for instance, or equal opportunity policies in the workplace), then there is no point in leading off with a pun or joke, no matter how witty. Such an opening would be inappropriate and probably offensive to your readers.

Your attention-getter does not have to be a single sentence; in fact, good ones are often several sentences long. Your readers will be committing varying amounts of personal time to reading your writing. You owe it to them to make your opening sentences clear, interesting, and creative.

An effective attention-getter should be followed by an equally effective thesis statement, one that slides smoothly and easily into place. Your readers should be aware only of a unified paragraph, not of two separate parts in your introduction.

Below are eight different kinds of openings you can choose from to get your readers' attention and lead up to your thesis statement. In each of the example paragraphs, note how the attention-getter and the thesis statement are solidly linked to form a unified whole. To demonstrate that you can take many different approaches to a subject, depending on your purpose and your audience, we have used the same subject—physical fitness—in all of the introductions.

1. Spell out the significance of your subject. If your subject's significance can catch your readers' interest, they will want to know more about it, especially if it is a subject that affects them directly.

More and more young people are dying of heart disease. Despite the statistics that say most people in our society are living longer thanks to advances in medicine and surgery, the figures can be misleading. It is a fact that people in their thirties and forties are dying from coronary problems that once threatened people in their fifties and sixties. What has caused this change? Certainly, the increase in stress, the fatigue of overwork, the rise in obesity, and the decline in physical activity are all contributing factors. To combat the risk of cardiovascular disease, we need physical activity. Regular exercise can forestall the ravages of heart disease and promote longevity.

2. Begin with a well-phrased quotation. You might choose a famous statement, a popular slogan, or a common saying. Use a quotation when it sums up your point of view more succinctly and effectively than your own words could. As a rule, you should identify the source of the quotation.

"Who can be bothered?" "I'm much too busy." "I get all the exercise I need at the office." We've all heard excuses like these, excuses for avoiding regular exercise. Modern life, with its distractions and conveniences, tends to make people sedentary and lazy, but the human organism cannot tolerate inactivity and stress indefinitely. Eventually, it begins to break down. Those who want to keep in shape for the challenges of modern life should consider the benefits of working out a few times a week. Regular exercise can rejuvenate the body, refresh the mind, and improve self-confidence.

3. Use a startling statement. Sometimes a surprising remark (not an insult or a false exaggeration) is effective in getting readers' attention. A little-known or striking fact will have the same effect.

After the age of 30, the average North American puts on 10 to 20 kilo-grams of fat. Presumably, the cause for this startling increase in avoirdupois is a combination of metabolic changes, decreased physical activity, and hundreds of kilos of junk food ingested since childhood. It's difficult to stop the spread of middle-aged corpulence, but experts tell us we *can* resist the rise in flab by reducing our caloric intake and increasing our physical activity. Regular exercise can rejuvenate the body, refresh the mind, and improve self-confidence.

4. Ask a question or two. Questions are often an effective way to encourage interest because your readers will find themselves thinking of answers. Some questions are rhetorical; that is, they will not have specific answers. Others might be answered in your essay.

Have you been feeling sluggish and exhausted lately? Has your blood pressure increased along with your waistline in the past few years? Are you stalled in front of the television set every night with potato chips and a beer? If so, you are probably suffering from a common middle-aged ailment called *flabitis*. This malady strikes most people over 30: they put on weight, have trouble concentrating, tire easily, and prefer watching sports to participating in them. Fortunately, there is a cure for flabitis: a three-times-weekly dose of exercise. With regular exercise, you can rejuvenate your body, refresh your mind, and improve your self-confidence.

5. Begin with a generalization related to your subject. Generalizations can be useful for suggesting the context and scope of your subject. They must, however, be narrowed down carefully to a focused thesis statement.

Until the 20th century, physical exercise was part of the normal workday. Our ancestors were farmers, pioneers, sailors, and so on. Few of our parents, however, made their living by ploughing the land or chopping down trees. Since the early 1900s, the trend in work has been away from physical exertion and toward automation. Today's generation uses technology to reduce physical activity even further: they pick up the phone, ride the elevator, and take the car to the corner store. Modern inactivity has negative consequences that only physical exercise can counter. To sustain good health, sharpen your mental edge, and have fun, you should take up aerobics or sports and use your body in the way it was intended—actively.

6. Challenge a common opinion. Perhaps your readers have also doubted a popular belief. Your thesis statement can assert that an opinion is false, and the body of your paper can contain evidence to support your opposing view.

Physical activity is for kids. Adults don't have time to hit a baseball or run around a field chasing after one, or to do aerobics and lift weights in a gym. They have to earn a living, raise families, and save money for retirement. They can leave exercise to their children. I firmly believed this until one morning when, late for work, I ran after a bus. My heart pounded; my lungs gasped; my head swam. It had been some years since my last stint of exercise, and I realized I wouldn't be around to do my job, support my family, or enjoy retirement unless I got into the habit of doing something physical to maintain my health. Regular exercise can rejuvenate the body, refresh the mind, and broaden one's interests.

7. Begin with a definition. A definition is a good way to begin if you are introducing a key term that you suspect may be unfamiliar to your readers. If the subject of your essay depends on a personal meaning of a term that most people understand in a different way, a definition is essential.

Myocardial infarction: the very term is frightening. It occurs when a person's muscles slacken from disuse, the veins clog up with sticky fats, and the heart has to work too hard to sustain even minor exertion such as raking leaves or shovelling snow. The muscles of the heart become strained to exhaustion or balloon outward because the veins cannot pass blood quickly enough. In plain English, a myocardial infarction is a heart attack. If the victim is lucky enough to survive, physicians prescribe a regimen of less stress, low fat intake, and regular exercise.

8. Describe an interesting incident or tell an anecdote related to your subject. Readers like stories. Keep yours short and to the point by narrating only the highlights. The incident or anecdote you select might be a story from the media, an event involving family or friends, or a personal experience.

Last year, I got a free invitation in the mail to a fitness club. I responded, out of curiosity, but I needed to be convinced. After all, I was 35, had grown a little paunch, and was a bit short of breath on the stairs; 10 years had passed since I had last played sports. My first workout was a nightmare. My joints ached, my muscles throbbed, and my head spun. I was in worse shape than I thought. After a few weeks, those symptoms disappeared, and I began to enjoy myself. My paunch vanished and my muscles toned up. My capacity for concentration increased. Also, I met some new people who have become friends. Obviously, 10 years is too long between workouts, given that exercise not only rejuvenates the body and refreshes the mind but also improves one's social life.

Exercise 9.1

In small groups (four or five people), consider five movies you have all seen within the past year. How did each of these movies begin so that the audience was "locked in"? How do these movie "grabbers" relate to the kinds of attention-getters you have just read?

Exercise 9.2

Each of the following paragraphs is the introductory paragraph of an essay. Work in pairs and, using the strategy given in parentheses, write an appropriate attention-getter for each paragraph.

1. (significance of subject) _____

_____

TV commercials that portray unrealistic and unattainable lifestyles should be banned. Although I do not support censorship, I believe there is sufficient evidence of the damage done by these advertisements to justify eliminating them in the name of public interest. The objectionable commercials promote sexual stereotyping, set up unrealistic and dangerous expectations, and encourage irresponsible consumerism.

2. (quotation) _____

_____

Every sport has its strange expressions, just as every sport has its devoted fans, its famous teams, and its legendary heroes. A sport that gets very little attention in Canada but is very popular in many parts of the world, especially Commonwealth countries, is cricket. Like the sports that millions of Canadians follow enthusiastically, cricket is an exciting and fascinating game once you become familiar with its rules and style. In fact, it compares very favourably with baseball in skill, pace, and strategy.

3. (startling statement) _____

_____

Canadian roads are overrun by drivers who are a danger to themselves, their passengers, and others on the road. Inept drivers demonstrate their inadequacies in so many ways that it would be impossible to list them all in one short paper. Nevertheless, bad drivers can be broadly categorized as traumatized turtles, careening cowboys, and daydreaming dodos.

4. (question) _____

_____

Arranged marriages are a very important part of my culture. When my family moved to Canada, we left behind many of the traditions and customs that were as natural to us as breathing. However, my parents retained their right to choose a wife for me, even though they are aware that this custom is at odds with the Canadian way of life. Although their decision was at first difficult to accept, I believe there are good reasons that an arranged marriage may be best for me. The decision will be made by mature people in a thoughtful manner, uninfluenced by the enthusiasms of youth; the decision will be made by people who have at heart the best interests of our family, the bride's family, and me; and the decision will be made in accordance with a centuries-old tradition that has proven its success generation after generation.

5. (generalization) _____

_____

My first project manager was the sort of person that nightmares are made of. It's been a year since she was finally transferred to another department, but I still shudder when I recall our six months together. Denise was rude, bossy, and, worst of all, thoughtless.

6. (opinion you challenge) _____

_____

The evidence strongly suggests that overexposure to the sun can cause several forms of cancer at worst and premature aging at best. We can't completely avoid the sun's rays, but there are several measures we can take to prevent the damage that normal outdoor activity might cause. To enjoy the summer without fear, use an effective sun block, cover sensitive skin completely, and limit your time in the sun.

7. (definition) _____

_____

The choice of corrective lenses is an individual matter, but many people go through a tough decision-making process when confronting the issue. In deciding whether contact lenses or eyeglasses are more suitable, one should examine factors such as comfort, convenience, and appearance.

8. (anecdote or incident) _____

_____

Black flies are just one of the pests that make life less than comfortable in Canada during the spring, but they tend to be the most irritating. No method of combatting the pests is foolproof, but there are several methods that can be employed, either singly or together, to repel most of them. The campaign against the black fly begins with protective clothing, follows up with an effective repellent, and goes over the top with the secret weapon: garlic.

Exercise 9.3

With the class divided into four or five teams, consider the following essay topics. Each team will take one of the topics and develop the first sentence of an introductory paragraph for it. The sentence will then be passed in sequence to the next group, who will add a sentence to the paragraph. Continue this exercise until each paragraph contains both an attention-getter and a thesis statement. When each team gets back the paragraph it initiated, it will revise and polish the paragraph, identify the kind of attention-getter that has been developed, and underline the thesis statement. Share the results with the rest of the class. (Keep these paragraphs; you will need them later.)

1. Why I want to be a _____ (fill in your career choice)
2. Why I chose _____ (fill in your school)
3. How not to treat a coworker
4. My favourite TV show
5. The trouble with customers (parents, teachers, etc.)

The Concluding Paragraph

Like the introduction, the conclusion of your paper has a special form. Think of your favourite television sitcom. The last section of the show wraps up the plot, explains any details that might still be unresolved, and leaves you with a satisfying sense that all is well, at least until next week. A concluding paragraph works in a similar way.

The last paragraph of your paper has two functions.
1. It summarizes or reinforces the main points of your paper.
2. It ends with an appropriate memorable statement.

Your **summary statement** should be as concise as you can make it, and must be phrased in such a way that it does not repeat word for word the portion of your thesis statement that identifies the main points. (Note that a summary is not needed in a very short essay.)

A **memorable statement** is a sentence designed to leave your readers feeling satisfied with your essay and perhaps taking away with them something for further thought. Never end without a clincher. Don't just quit writing when your main points are covered, or you'll leave your readers hanging, wondering what to make of it all.

Six strategies you can choose from when you write a concluding paragraph are listed below. Each strategy is illustrated by an example paragraph. Identify the summary and the memorable statement in each conclusion.

1. End with a relevant or thought-provoking quotation. You can use this type of ending in two ways: repeat an earlier quotation but give it a new meaning, or place your subject in a larger context by supplying a new quotation from a recognized authority in the field.

Since I began lifting weights every second day, I have lowered my blood pressure, improved my productivity at work, and made some new friends at the fitness club. I will never be Arnold Schwarzenegger, but that isn't my goal. My muscles are pleasantly sore after a good workout, but as Arnold says, "No pain, no gain." As long as the pain is so little and the gain is so great, I will continue to enjoy my regular workouts.

2. Offer a solution to a problem discussed in your paper. You can plan an organization for your paper that will allow you to resolve a problem or neutralize negative consequences in your conclusion.

I've got the best intentions in the world. I know that exercise benefits me physically, mentally, and emotionally—but I still don't have the time. I didn't, that is, until last month, when I was home from work for a week because I sprained my ankle while walking the dog. That never would have happened if I had been in shape. Since then, I have forced myself to manage my time to allow for a fitness program. Four hours of exercise a week is not a very big investment of time compared with four days of lying on the couch with a painfully swollen foot.

3. End with one or more relevant or thought-provoking questions. The advantage of clinching with a question is that readers tend automatically to pause and consider it: questions stimulate thought. Before they know it, readers will begin to formulate answers to your question—and that activity will make them remember your points. Be sure your question relates directly to your subject.

My life has improved considerably since I took up jogging three times a week: I enjoy better health, less brain-fog, and more confidence. And I'm inspired to continue jogging by the fact that coronary disease runs in my family. My father and grandfather both suffered heart attacks in their fifties. If they had done regular exercise, could they have reduced their chances of coronaries? Would they still be alive today?

4. Point out the value or significance of your subject to your readers. If you emphasize your subject matter at the end of your paper, you can stamp its importance on your readers' memory.

Regular exercise is the best way to stay in shape, be sharp, and feel strong; it is the best way to reduce the risk of arthritis, arterial decay, and heart dysfunction. In a country where the most common cause of mortality is coronary collapse, everyone needs to consider the value of consistent exercise. It is a small daily inconvenience that pays large and long-term rewards.

5. Make a connection to a statement made in your introduction. This strategy provides your readers with a sense of closure. They will recall your earlier statement and feel satisfied that the loose ends have been tied up.

Having exercised now for six months, I can run for the bus without losing my breath, sweating profusely, or feeling dizzy. My body is in better trim; my endurance and confidence on the job have grown. After a lapse of 20 years, I have even taken up bicycling again: I go riding along local bike trails with friends. And now, when my children are playing baseball in the yard, I don't think, "Baseball is for kids." I'm first at the plate. Batter up!

6. End with a suggestion for change or a prediction about the future. Your suggestion for change will influence your readers if they have been persuaded by your arguments. Your predictions of events that might occur should not be misleading or exaggerated, or your readers will be skeptical. Make predictions that are possible and plausible.

If those of us who still prefer junk food, overwork, and television don't shape up, then the incidence of coronary disease will continue to rise. Moderate exercise will benefit body, mind, and spirit. If we follow common sense and change our habits of self-pollution and self-destruction, all of us can lead long, active, and healthy lives.

Exercise 9.4

Each of the following is the concluding paragraph of an essay. Working in pairs, underline the summary statement and write a memorable conclusion. See if you can use a different kind in each paragraph.

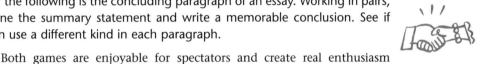

1.   Both games are enjoyable for spectators and create real enthusiasm among fans. High schools that have chosen soccer have seen no reduction in school spirit or fan support. For educational institutions to make the switch from football is really a "no-lose" proposition because soccer provides dramatic advantages in reducing player injury, increasing player fitness, and shaving thousands of dollars from school expenses.

_____

_____

_____

_____

2.   In retrospect, the NHL lockout was completely avoidable. It had been predicted and discussed for two years prior to the date of the lockout, yet neither side made a meaningful move to prevent it. Only when the 2004–05 season was on the edge of cancellation did the players and owners begin to make concessions that moved them closer to a settlement. Had these moves been made a year or even half a year earlier, the lockout need never have happened. But both sides engaged in brinksmanship in the hope that the other would cave in, and we are all living with the results.

_____

_____

_____

_____

3.   Although the causes of dropout among first-year students are as individual as the students themselves, the effects are easier to categorize. Conflict with parents and others whose expectations have not been met

comes first, followed by a loss of self-esteem. The determination to succeed despite this unfair setback is common, but statistics show that low-paying, dead-end jobs are the norm for the college dropout. The situation is much worse, of course, for those who don't complete high school.

_____

_____

_____

_____

4.   Employers who need to replace retiring workers with skilled young people must take into account the major differences between the generation of retiring boomers and the generation that is replacing them. Unlike their parents, who were raised to respect age and authority, members of Generation Y (broadly defined as anyone born after 1980), are used to calling their teachers and their parents' friends by their first names; they think of themselves as less experienced equals. They believe that their opinions count, that their feelings matter, and that they should be heard. While they lack the relentless career ambition and drive of their parents, they seek career satisfaction in enjoyable work, opportunities for growth, and more leisure time. They see "the good life" not as their parents did, as a matter of accumulating wealth, but as a satisfying balance between their professional and personal lives.

_____

_____

_____

_____

5.   Drinking and driving must be stopped. To stop it will require substantial commitment from all levels of government, both in terms of money and in terms of political will. The penalties for driving while under the influence of alcohol must be increased, and more money must be spent for education and publicity. But, more than these measures, it will take the individual will of every Canadian to make the promise not to drive after drinking. Nothing will bring my sister back, but there are lots of other sisters out there—and brothers and mothers and fathers—who can be saved.

_____

_____

_____

_____

With the class divided into the same teams as in Exercise 9.3, write concluding paragraphs to complement the introductions you developed. Here's how to proceed:

- Review the paragraph you developed for Exercise 9.3.
- Write the first sentence of a concluding paragraph for this same topic.
- Pass your sentence, together with your introductory paragraph, along to the next team, who will write a second sentence for the conclusion.
- Continue this process until the conclusion contains both a summary or reinforcement and a memorable statement.
- Return the paragraph to the team that initiated it for revising and polishing.
- Share the results with the rest of the class.

PART 3

The Three Steps to Revision

No one can write in a single draft an essay that is perfectly organized and developed, let alone one that is free of errors. The purpose of the first draft is to get down on paper something you can work with until it meets your reader's needs and expectations. Planning and drafting should take about half the time you devote to writing a paper. The rest should be devoted to revision.

Revision is the process of refining your message until

- it says what you want it to say,
- your reader(s) will understand it, and
- your reader(s) will receive it favourably.

These three goals are the essentials of good communication. You can achieve them only if you keep your readers in mind as you revise. Because a first draft reflects the contents of the writer's mind, it often seems all right to the writer. But in order to transfer an idea as clearly as possible from the mind of the writer to the mind of the reader, revision is necessary. The idea needs to be honed and refined until it is as clear to your reader as it is to you. By revising from your reader's point of view, you can avoid misunderstandings before they happen.

What Is Revision?

Revision means "re-seeing." It does *not* mean recopying.

The aim of revision is to improve your writing's organization, accuracy, and style. Revising is a three-stage process. Each step requires that you read through your entire essay. The goal of your first reading is to ensure that your reader's information needs are met. In your second reading, you focus on paragraph and sentence structure. Your third reading concentrates on correctness. Here are the steps to follow in revising a paper:

1. Improve the whole paper by revising its content and organization.
2. Refine paragraph and sentence structure, and correct any errors in grammar.
3. Edit and proofread to catch errors in word choice, spelling, and punctuation.

Inexperienced writers often skip the first two stages and concentrate on the third, thinking they will save time. In fact, they waste time—both theirs and their readers'—because the result is writing that doesn't communicate clearly and won't make a positive impression.

The best way to begin revising is to let as much time as possible pass between completing your first draft and rereading it. Ten minutes, or even half a day, is not enough. The danger in rereading too soon is that you're likely to "read" what you think you've written—what exists only in your head, not on the paper.

If you haven't allowed enough time for this cooling-off period, there are two other things you can do to help you get some distance from your draft. If your first draft is handwritten, type it out. Reading your essay in a different form helps you to "re-see" its content. Alternatively, read your paper aloud and try to hear it from the point of view of your reader. Listen to how your explanation unfolds, and mark every place you find something unclear, irrelevant, inadequately developed, or out of order.

Step 1
Revise Content and Organization

As you reread your paper, keep in mind the three kinds of changes you can (and probably should) make at this stage:

1. You can rearrange information. This is the kind of revision that is most often needed but least often done. Consider the order in which you've arranged your paragraphs. From your reader's point of view, is this the most effective order in which to present your ideas?

2. You can add information. Adding new main ideas or more development is often necessary to make your message interesting and convincing as well as clear. It's a good idea to ask a friend to read your draft and identify what needs to be expanded or clarified. (Be sure to return the favour; you can learn a great deal by critiquing other people's writing.)

3. You can delete information. Now is the time to cut out anything that is repetitious, insignificant, or irrelevant to your subject and reader.

Your outline is the best place to begin checking the adequacy and organization of your information. Keep it beside you and change it as your revise your essay. In most cases, your paper will be improved by rearranging, adding, and subtracting ideas.

The thesis statement is your contract with your reader, so it should be the guiding principle of your paper. It should contain nothing that is not developed in the body of the essay, and there should be nothing in the essay that is not directly related to your thesis statement. When you find a mismatch between the thesis statement and the paper, change one or the other or both until the two agree. Using a word processor to move blocks of text around is as easy as shuffling a deck of cards.

If you are not already using a word-processing program, now is the time to begin. Before you start to revise, change the computer's settings to meet the format requirements of your paper: set the spacing, margins, font style and size, etc. (See Chapter 21 for instructions and examples.) Most people find it easier to revise from a paper copy, so print out your draft double- or triple-spaced. Read it through carefully, making notes for changes in the margins or in the spaces between the lines; then go back to the computer to make the changes.

Remember to save your work frequently. It takes only a split second to click on the Save icon, but that split second could save you hours—even days—in the event of a computer disaster. Learn to save your work in a systematic and easy-to-find filing system. Calling a paper "draft" or "essay" will cause frustration later when you want to reopen the file to revise it but can't remember the name of the file you were working on. Give each file a distinctive name (or name and number), and save each draft separately just in case you want to go back and use material from a previous version of your document.

Use the checklist that follows to guide you as you review your paper's form and content.

CONTENT AND ORGANIZATION CHECKLIST

ACCURACY
- Is your information consistent with your own experience and observations or with what you have discovered through research?
- Are all your facts and evidence up to date?

COMPLETENESS
Have you included enough main ideas and development to explain your subject and convince your reader? Remember that "enough" means from the reader's point of view, not the writer's.

SUBJECT
Is your subject
- significant? Does it avoid the trivial or the obvious?
- single? Does it avoid double or combined subjects?
- specific? Is it focused and precise?
- supportable? Have you provided enough evidence to make your meaning clear?

MAIN POINTS
Are your main points
- significant? Have you deleted any unimportant ones?
- distinct? Are they all different from one another, or is there an overlap in content?
- relevant? Do all points relate directly to your subject?
- arranged in the most appropriate order? Again, "appropriate" means from the reader's perspective. Choose chronological, climactic, logical, or random order, depending on which is most likely to help the reader make sense of your information.

INTRODUCTION
Does your introduction
- catch the reader's attention and make him or her want to read on?
- contain a clearly identifiable thesis statement?
- identify the main points that your paper will explain?

CONCLUSION
Does your conclusion
- contain a summary or reinforcement of your main points, rephrased to avoid word-for-word repetition?
- contain a statement that effectively clinches your argument and leaves the reader with something to think about?

Read the following draft outline for a short essay on how to write effective e-mail in a business environment. Working with a partner, rearrange the main points in chronological order, delete any unnecessary supporting points, and write a thesis statement to produce a working outline for the essay. Then compare your answer with our suggestion. Answers for exercises in this chapter begin on page 519.

E-Mail Excellence

Attention-getter: As the recipient of approximately 1,000 business-related e-mail messages every month, I am something of an expert on what is effective and what is not in e-mail correspondence.

Thesis statement: _____

_____

_____

_____

Main points:

I. Subject line

    A. always include one

    B. make sure it states clearly what the message is about

    C. never use vague subject lines such as "hello," or "message," or "are you there?"

    D. never leave the subject line blank

II. Attachments

    A. use sparingly

    B. may carry viruses

    C. take time to transfer and to open

    D. attach text-only files unless a graphic is absolutely necessary

    E. use only if necessary

III. Message

    A. Content

        1. be concise and to the point

        2. tell the reader what action is needed, by whom, and when

        3. don't be a novelist or a "Chatty Cathy"

        4. use plain English, not "cyberspeak"

        5. use an appropriate level of language in your message as well as in your salutation and signature

    B. Format

        1. use bullets to identify points you want to emphasize

        2. leave white space between points

        3. avoid sending your message in uppercase letters (shouting)

        4. avoid smilies and other "cute" computer shorthand symbols

Summary: If you follow my recommendations on these three points whenever you write an e-mail, you will make the recipient of your message very happy.

Memorable statement: Especially if you're writing to me.

Step 2
Revise Paragraphs and Sentences

Here, too, you should allow time—at least a couple of days—between your first revision and your second. Read your draft aloud, and use this list of questions to help you improve it.

PARAGRAPH AND SENTENCE CHECKLIST

PARAGRAPHS

Does each paragraph

- begin with a clear, identifiable topic sentence?
- develop one—and only one—main idea?
- employ one or more kinds of development appropriate to the main idea?
- contain clear and effective transitions to signal the relationship between sentences? Between paragraphs?

SENTENCES

Sentence Structure

1. Is each sentence clear and complete?
   - Are there any fragments or run-ons?
   - Are there any misplaced or dangling modifiers?
   - Are all lists (whether words, phrases, or clauses) expressed in parallel form?
2. Are your sentences varied in length? Could some be combined to improve the clarity and impact of your message?

Grammar

1. Have you used verbs correctly?
   - Are all verbs in the correct form?
   - Do all verbs agree with their subjects?
   - Are all verbs in the correct tense?
   - Are there any confusing shifts in verb tense within a paragraph?
2. Have you used pronouns correctly?
   - Are all pronouns in the correct form?
   - Do all pronouns agree with their antecedents?
   - Have any vague pronoun references been eliminated?

When you're sure you've answered these questions satisfactorily, go to the third and last stage of the revision process.

Exercise 10.2*

Here is the first draft of the essay on e-mail. Revise it to correct errors in paragraph structure, sentence structure, and grammar. Then compare your answer with our suggestion on pages 519–20.

1   As the recipient of approximately 1,000 business-related e-mail messages every month, I am something of an expert on what is effective and what is not in e-mail correspondence. The three areas that need attention in most e-mail messages are the subject line, the content, and format of the message and the use of attachments.

2   Some people leave the subject line blank, this is a mistake. I want to know what the message is about before I open it so I can decide if it needs my immediate attention. Or can wait until later. A message with no subject line or with a line that didn't tell me nothing about the content of the e-mail get sent to the bottom of my "to-do" list. There are lots of readers like me busy people who receive tons of e-mail, much of it unsolicited advertising that clutter up their in-boxes. For this reason the subject line should always clearly state the subject of the message and should never be vague or cute like "hello" or "message" or "are you there?"

3   As for the message itself, it's function should be to tell the reader what action one wants, you need to be clear about this and be as brief as possible. What is it that you want the recipient to do. Who else needs to be involved. By when does the action need to take place. Communicate your message in plain English, not in "cyberspeak" Not everyone knows Net lingo, and even some who are famliar with it find it irritating not charming. Use an appropriate level of language (general level Standard English will always be appropriate) to convey you're message. Use the same level of language in you're salutation and closing or "signature." One should definitely not sign off a message to you're client or you're boss with "love and kisses." Format you're message so that the recipient will be able to read it quickly and understanding it easily. Use bullets to identify points you want to emphasize, separate the bullets with white space so they can be read at a glance and

reviewed individually if necessary. There are some important points of e-mail etiquette that you should observe. Don't type you're message in upper case letters, that's considered "shouting." Do avoid "smilies" and other "cute" computer shorthand symbols. Some of you're readers won't understand them others will have seen them so often they will be turned off.

4   Attachments should be included only if they are really necessary, for one thing, they may carry virruses and some people won't open them. Another disadvantage is that they take time to send download and open. Unless I am sure that an attachment is both urgent and vitally important—the agenda of tomorrow's meeting, for example—I don't bother to open it, for all I know, it might contain not only a virus but also footage of the sender's toddler doing her latest photogenic trick. As a general rule attach only what you must and attach text-only files. Try to include everything you need to say in the message itself and use attachments only as a last resort. Think of them as equivalent to footnotes supplementary to the message not an essential part of it.

5   If you follow my recommendations on these three points whenever you write an e-mail, you will make the recipient of your message very happy, especially if you're writing to me.

Step 3
Edit and Proofread

By now you're probably so tired of refining your paper that you may be tempted to skip **editing**—correcting errors in word choice, spelling, and punctuation—and **proofreading**—correcting errors in typing or writing that appear in the final draft. But these final tasks are essential if you want your paper to make a positive impression.

Misspellings, faulty punctuation, and messiness don't always create misunderstandings, but they do cause the reader to form a lower opinion of you and your work. Careful editing and proofreading are necessary if you want your writing to be favourably received.

Most word-processing programs include a grammar checker and a spell checker. The newer programs have some useful features. For example, they will question (but not correct) your use of apostrophes; they will sometimes catch errors in subject–verb agreement; and they will catch obvious misspellings and typos. But don't make the mistake of assuming these programs will do all your editing for you. Many errors slip past them. Only you or a knowledgeable and patient friend can find and correct all errors.

If spelling is a particular problem for you, you should first run your paper through a spell checker. After that, you're on your own. Read your paper backward word by word, from the end to the beginning. Reading backward forces you to look at each word by itself and helps you to spot those that look suspicious. Whenever you're in doubt about the spelling of a word, look it up! If you find this task too tedious to bear, ask a good speller to read through your paper for you and identify any errors.

Here are the questions to ask yourself when you are editing.

EDITING CHECKLIST
WORDS

Usage
Have you used words to "mean" rather than to "impress"?
- Have you eliminated any slang, pretentious language, or offensive language?
- Have you cut out any unnecessary words?
- Have you corrected any "abusages"?

Tone
- Is your tone consistent, reasonable, courteous, and confident throughout your essay?

Spelling
Are all words spelled correctly?
- Have you double-checked any homonyms?
- Have you used capital letters where they are needed?
- Have you used apostrophes correctly for possessives and omitted them from plurals?

PUNCTUATION

Within Sentences
- Have you eliminated any unnecessary commas and included commas where needed? (Refer to the comma rules on pages 417–22 as you consider this question.)
- Have you used colons and semicolons where appropriate?
- Are all quotations appropriately marked?

Beginnings and Endings
- Does each sentence begin with a capital letter?
- Do all questions—and only questions—end with a question mark?
- Are all quotation marks correctly placed?

Exercise 10.3*

Read the following sentences carefully and edit them to correct any errors in usage, spelling, and punctuation. Then compare your answers to our suggestions on pages 520–21. (Our thanks to *Fortune* magazine for collecting these howlers from real résumés and cover letters.)

1. I demand a salary commiserate with my qualifications and extensive experience.

2. I have lurnt Microsoft Word and Excel computor and spreasheet progroms.

3. I received a plague for being salesperson of the year.

4. Reason for leaving last job; maturity leave.

5. You will want me to be Head Honcho in no time.

6. I am a perfectionist and rarely if if ever forget details.

7. Marital status: single. Unmarried. Unengaged. Uninvolved. No commitments.

8. In my previous job I became completely paranoid, trusting completely no one and absolutely nothing.

9. As indicted, I have over five years of analyzing investments.

10. I was responsible for ruining the entire operation for a Western chain store.

TIPS FOR EFFECTIVE PROOFREADING

By the time you have finished editing, you will have gone over your paper so many times you may have practically memorized it. When you are very familiar with a piece of writing, it's hard to spot the small mistakes that may have crept in as you produced your final copy. Here are some tips to help you find those tiny, elusive errors:

1. Read through your essay line by line, using a ruler to guide you.
2. If you've been keeping a list of your most frequent errors in this course, scan your essay for the mistakes you are most likely to make.
3. Use the "Quick Revision Guide" on the inside front cover of this book to make a final check of all aspects of your paper.
4. Use the list of correction marks on the inside back cover to check for errors your instructor has identified in your writing.

Your "last" draft may need further revision after your proofreading review. If so, take the time to rewrite the paper so that the version you hand in is clean and easy to read. If a word processor is available to you, use it. Computers make editing and proofreading almost painless, since errors are so easy to correct.

At long last, you're ready to submit your paper. If you've followed the three steps to revision conscientiously, you can hand it in with confidence that it says what you want it to say. One last word of advice:

DON'T FORGET TO KEEP A COPY FOR YOUR FILES!

Exercise 10.4*

Now go through the revised first draft of the e-mail essay that you produced in Exercise 10.2. This is your last chance to make this essay error-free. Use the Editing Checklist and the Tips for Effective Proofreading to guide you as you make your final pass through this document. Then compare your answer with our suggestion on pages 521–22.

GO TO WEB

EXERCISE 10.1

Is the following essay ready for submission? Go over it carefully, correcting any errors. Then get together with another student and compare your proofreading skills. (There are 20 errors in this exercise.)

According to a recent survey in Maclean's magazine, only 43 percent of Canadians are satisfied with their jobs. What can you do to ensure that you will not be one of the 57 percent who are unhappy with the work they do. There are three questions to consider when seeking employment that will provide satisfaction as well as a paycheque.

First are you suited to the kind of work you are applying for. If you enjoy the outdoors, for example, and like to be active, your not going to be happy with a nine to five office job, no matter how much it pays.

Second is the job based in a location compatible with your prefered lifestyle. No matter how much you like your work, if you go home every night to an enviorment you are miserable in, it will not be long before you start transfering your disatisfaction to your job. If you like the amenities and conviences of the city, you probably will not enjoy working in a small town. If, on the other hand, you prefer the quiet and security of small town life, you may find the city a stressful place in which to live.

Finally, is it one that you want to work for. Do you need the security of generous benifits, a good pension plan, and incentives to stay and grow with one company? Or are you an ambitous person who is looking for variety, quick advancement, and a high salary. If so, you may have to forego security in favour of commissions or cash incentives and be willing to move as quickly and as often as opportunities occur. Some carful self-analysis now, before you start out on your career path, will help you chose a direction that will put you in the 43 percent minority of satisfied Canadian workers.

This exercise will serve as a review of the three stages of the revision process. Below is a first draft of an essay. Applying all the principles you have learned in Chapter 10, revise this essay to make it a model of good communication: complete, correct, concise, and courteous. When you have finished, exchange papers with another student and compare your results. What errors did you miss? If this assignment were worth 20 percent of your final grade, would you hand it in now, or would you revise it again?

We are having a garbage crisis. There is so much waste being produced in North America, we no longer have any idea of were to put it. Toronto's garbage problem is so great that they are trucking thousands of tonnes of it to Michigan every year. But how long will that last? We must act now, and we must act as individuals. We cannot wait for the Government to save us from this crisis. We produce the garbage; we must solve the problem. In very practical, down to earth, concrete terms, here are some things we can do to reduce, recycle, and reuse.

First we must reduce the amount of garbage we produce. We can do this be refusing to buy products that are over packaged, like fast food that comes in styrafoam containers and chocolates that have a paper wrapping, a box, lining paper, a plastic tray for the candies, and foil wrap around each chocolate. By not purchasing such wasteful items, we say to the manufacturer, Either reduce the packaging in your product or lose business to your competition. We can also be less wastful in our own habits by carpooling, for example, or by using cloth diapers or biodegradable disposables.

We must recycle everything we can instead of sending it to the dump. Old cloths can be sent to the Salvation Army, the Scott mission, or other charitable organizations. As can furniture, appliances, books, and most other household items. There are dozens of ways to make useful items from packaging that would otherwise be thrown away, such as bird feeders from plastic jugs, braided rugs from old rags, and fire logs from newspapers. We don't need to consume as much as we do, and it won't hurt us to use things longer instead of buying new items before the old ones are completely worn out. Many companies now manufacture products from recycled goods, and we should be on the lookout for their products to support their efforts and to reduce the waste that is dumped into landfills.

Third, we can reuse most things. Composting vegetable garbage is a good way to put waste to valuable use. Or we can offer the things we no longer want to others through lawn sales and flea markets.

This is an absolute necessity. If we do not stop producing so much waste, we will inevitibly destroy our own enviornment. Unlike most efforts to improve things, the move to recycle, reuse, and reduce has one other advantage: it doesn't cost any money. In fact, it can save every household that practices it hundreds of dollars a year.

PART 4

PART 4

17

Argument and Persuasion

How many times have you won an argument? If you're like most of us, not very often. Getting people to understand what you say is hard enough; getting them to agree with you is the most difficult task any writer faces.

In the context of writing, the terms *argument* and *persuasion* have specific meanings, slightly different from their meanings in general conversation.

- An **argument** is a piece of writing that is intended to convince readers that the writer's opinion about an issue is reasonable and valid. An **issue** is an opinion or belief, something that not all people agree on; it is *controversial*, a word that literally means "having two sides."

  Factual reports, memos, and analyses are not likely to be arguments, although some writing intended primarily to inform may also be intended to influence the reader's thinking: "Pucker Up"(page 195), "The Slender Trap" (page 221), and "Justice and Journalism" (page 209) are just three examples.
- **Persuasion** is intended to change the way readers think or feel about an issue, perhaps even to act in some way that supports the writer's point of view (e.g., buy a product, donate to a charity, vote for a particular candidate).

Drafting, revising, and editing argument and persuasion are much the same as for other kinds of writing. Planning, however, requires a slightly different approach.

Choose Your Issue Carefully

Assuming that you have not been assigned a topic, you will need to choose one. Your choice is even more critical for an argument or a persuasive paper than it is for a factual analysis. You can argue only matters of opinion, not fact. Facts can be interpreted in different ways—that's what an argument is: an interpretation of a set of facts. No one can dispute the fact that Canada has ten provinces and three territories. An appropriate subject for your paper is one that can be disputed. Someone has to be able to say, "No. You are not right. That's not what these facts mean." For example, "Canada should be reorganized into five regional provinces and one territory."

You cannot argue matters of taste, either. Taste is personal preference: there is no point in arguing that Thai food is better than pizza, or that green is more flattering than blue. Even if you could argue these assertions, they are not significant enough to bother with. Choose your subject carefully. It must pass the 4-S test (see page 39), and it should be one you know and care about. Ideally, it should be one your reader cares about, too.

GO TO WEB

EXERCISE 17.1

Next, consider the scope of your subject. How much time do you have to prepare? How long is your paper expected to be? Throughout this book, we have recommended that when you choose a subject, you should limit your focus. This recommendation is even more important when you are preparing an argument than when you are proposing to explain something. Even subjects that look narrowly focused can require surprising amounts of development when you are composing an argument for or against them.

Avoid large, controversial issues: abortion, for example, or capital punishment, or religious faith. There are two reasons for this caution. First, they are hugely complex issues; and, second, they are issues on which virtually everyone already has an opinion. It is difficult enough to convince readers about an issue on which they have not already formed an opinion; it's practically impossible to get them to change their minds when they hold an entrenched belief.

Consider Your Audience

When you are trying to get readers to agree with you, you must know (or be able to make an educated guess about) what opinions they already hold and how likely they are to disagree with your views. If, for example, you want to convince your readers that music broadcasters should be required to adhere strictly to Canadian content regulations, the approach you take will depend on your readers' level of knowledge, their interest in the subject, even their age. What do they think about the issue? Do they care about it, one way or the other? What beliefs do they hold that would make them inclined to agree or disagree with you? If you know the answers to these questions, you'll know how to approach your subject: what points to argue, which to emphasize, and which to downplay.

Identify Your Purpose

Do you want your readers simply to understand and respect your opinion on an issue? Or do you want to change their thinking or their behaviour in some way? If your primary purpose is to get them to agree with you, your argument will rely on solid evidence and sound, logical reasoning.

If your primary purpose is to get your readers to do something, to act in some way, your argument will need to appeal not only to their sense of what is reasonable, but also to their feelings, loyalties, ambitions, or desires.

State Your Thesis

Before you begin your first draft, write out your opinion in the form of a proposition (opinion statement). You may or may not use this statement in your paper, but you need it in front of you as you (1) identify your reasons for holding the opinion you do, (2) list the evidence you intend to use, and (3) decide on the order of presentation. If you have ever heard a formal debate, you know what a proposition is. It is the statement of opinion that one side argues in favour of and the other side argues against. Here are three examples:

> Few cities in the world offer the affordable living, student amenities, and cultural dynamism that Montreal does. (thesis of "A City for Students," pages 242–43)

> . . . I cannot deny that by catching a fish, I am in a sense torturing it for my pleasure. (thesis of "Of Pain, Predators, and Pleasure," pages 246–47)

> A liberal arts education is a sound investment of time and money. (thesis of "Arts Education Does Pay Off," pages 248–49)

The test of a satisfactory proposition is that it is arguable—i.e., someone could defend the contrary point of view. (A statement that includes the

NEL

word *should* or *must* is likely to be a proposition.) You could argue that fishing is a cruel, unjustifiable sport, or that a liberal arts education is a waste of time and money, or that to anglophone students, Montreal offers decrepit housing, poor amenities, and few cultural opportunities.

Once you have a clear statement of a specific opinion, you are ready to identify your reasons for holding it and evidence to support your reasons. It is possible to support an argument entirely from personal experience, but you are more likely to convince your readers if you provide a variety of kinds of evidence (see Chapters 7 and 18).

Identify Your Reasons and Evidence

Readers are not likely to be convinced of anything unless the concept is first clearly explained to them. Whether your purpose is to argue or to persuade, you need to provide reasons for believing your opinion. Your reasons, which are your main points, must be significant, distinct, and relevant (see Chapter 4). To support each reason, you need to provide lots of accurate evidence: facts, concrete details, statistics, events or experiences your readers are familiar with or can relate to, authorities you can refer to or quote. To engage your readers' hearts as well as their minds, at least some of your evidence should be emotionally "loaded"; that is, it should arouse the readers' compassion, or anger, or sense of justice, or any other feeling that supports your side of the issue.

Decide on an Approach: Direct or Indirect?

If you think your readers are likely to argue with your view or even slightly inclined to oppose it, it is best to build your case with definitions, examples, and other evidence before stating your own opinion. Readers who are confronted early by a statement they disagree with are often not open to argument or persuasion. Instead, they are inclined to read the rest of the paper trying to pick holes in your argument and thinking of rebuttals. A potentially hostile audience would respond best to an indirect, or inductive, approach:

> Before we decide how to vote, we should consider the candidates' records, their platforms, and their characters.

On the other hand, if your readers are sympathetic to your point of view, you can state your opinion up front and then identify your reasons and the evidence that supports those reasons. This is called the direct, or deductive, approach:

> Based on her record, her platform, and her character, Julie Kovac is the candidate who deserves your vote.

For an explanation of inductive and deductive reasoning, together with some of the common logical fallacies that can damage your argument, see "Making the Argument" on the *Essay Essentials* website (http://www.essayessentials4e.nelson.com).

Arrange Your Reasons and Evidence

An argument or a persuasive paper can be developed in several ways. It is possible, as you will see in the readings for this chapter, to use a number of different structural patterns to convince your readers. A cause–effect analysis might be an effective way to urge action to lower the carbon monoxide and carbon dioxide emissions that contribute to global warming. You might choose comparison to discuss the efficiency of Canada's regulated airline industry as opposed to the deregulated industry in the United States and to argue in favour of one approach over the other.

Two patterns are specific to argument and persuasion. One is the classic "their side–my side" strategy, which is particularly useful when you are arguing a controversial position that may provoke serious dispute. This pattern involves your presenting the "con" (or "against") points of an argument, then refuting them with the "pro" (or "for") side of the argument. For instance, if a writer were to argue that women in the Canadian Armed Forces should participate in combat, she might choose to present the opposing position and then counter each point with well-reasoned arguments of her own.

Like a comparison, the "their side–my side" strategy can be presented either in block form or in point-by-point form, depending on how many points there are to discuss. Be sure to arrange your points in the order in which they will be most effective (see the list of possible arrangements discussed in Chapter 4).

If you are a skilled debater, you can often dismiss the opposing side's argument by identifying and exposing flaws in their reasoning or evidence. If you are an inexperienced writer, however, you will probably find it easier to use one or more of the following techniques:

- Identify any irrelevant or trivial points.
- Show that a point covers only part of the issue.
- Show that a point is valid only some of the time.
- Show that a point may have immediate advantages, but that its long-term results will be negative.
- Acknowledge the validity of the opposition's point(s), but provide a better alternative.

Carefully presented, the "their side–my side" pattern impresses readers with its fairness and tends to neutralize opposition.

The second structural pattern specific to argument and persuasion makes use of the familiar thesis statement. Add carefully worded reasons to your proposition, and you have a thesis statement that can appear near the beginning of your paper, in a direct approach, or near the end, if you are treating your subject indirectly. Be sure you have arranged your reasons in the most effective order. Usually, writers present their reasons in climactic order, saving their most compelling reason for the end of the paper.

The keys to good argumentation and persuasion are to think carefully about your opinion and to present fairly your reasons for believing it—*after* you have analyzed your reader's possible biases or prejudices and degree of commitment to one side or the other.

To argue or persuade successfully, you need to be not only well organized, informative, and thorough, but also honest and tactful, especially if your readers are not already inclined to agree with you.

Tips on Writing Argument and Persuasion

1. Choose an issue that you know and care about and can present with enthusiasm.
2. Select your reasons and evidence with your audience in mind. You are already convinced; your task is to convince your readers.
3. Decide whether your audience can be approached directly or if they should be approached indirectly—gently and with plenty of evidence before receiving your "pitch."
4. Arrange your argument in whatever structural pattern is most appropriate for your issue and your audience.
5. Remember that there is another side to the issue. You can help your own cause by presenting the opposing viewpoint and refuting it. Present the other side tactfully and fairly. You will only antagonize readers by unfairly stating or belittling the case for the other side. Opinions are as sensitive as toes: tread carefully to avoid causing pain.

Argumentation

Consider using Rogerian techniques, if they are appropriate. In some cases, especially those involving tense situations or highly sensitive issues, you may wish to incorporate some techniques of the noted psychologist Carl Rogers, who developed a procedure for presenting what he called the non-threatening argument. Rogers believed that people involved in a debate should strive for clear, honest communication so that the problem under discussion could be resolved. Instead of going on the defensive and trying to "win" the argument, each side should try to recognize common ground and then develop a solution that will address the needs of both parties.

A Rogerian argument uses these techniques:

1. A clear, objective statement of the problem or issue
2. A clear, objective summary of the opposition's position that shows you understand its point of view and goals
3. A clear, objective summary of your point of view, stated in non-threatening language
4. A discussion that emphasizes the beliefs, values, and goals that you and your opposition have in common
5. A description of any of your points that you are willing to concede or compromise
6. An explanation of a plan or proposed solution that meets the needs of both sides

By showing your opposition that you thoroughly understand its position and that you are sincerely trying to effect a solution that is in everyone's—not just your—best interests, you may succeed in some situations that might otherwise be hopeless because of their highly emotional nature. Remember, too, that you can use some of these Rogerian techniques in any kind of argument paper you are writing if you think they would be effective.

Problems to Avoid

Writers of argumentative essays must appear logical or their readers will reject their point of view. Here is a short list of some of the most common *logical fallacies*—that is, errors in reasoning. Check your rough drafts carefully to avoid these problems.

Students sometimes ask, "If a logical fallacy works, why not use it? Isn't all fair in love, war, and argumentative essays?" The honest answer is maybe. It's quite true that speakers and writers do use faulty logic and irrational emotional appeals to persuade people every day (one needs only to look at television or a newspaper to see example after example). Uncritical or inattentive audiences seem to accept arguments based on logical fallacies. But the cost of the risk is high: if you do try to slide one by your readers and they see through your trick, you will lose your credibility instantly. Your college and university audiences will be experienced readers who will not be impressed by fallacious reasoning. Deliberate use of faulty reasoning is also unethical. On the whole, it's far more effective to use logical reasoning and strong evidence to convince your readers to accept your point of view.

■ Common Logical Fallacies

Hasty generalization: The writer bases the argument on insufficient or unrepresentative evidence. Suppose, for example, you have owned two poodles and they have both attacked you. If you declare that all poodles are vicious dogs, you are making a hasty generalization. There are, of course, thousands of poodles who have not attacked anyone. Similarly, you're in error if you interview only campus athletes and then declare, "Students favour a new stadium." What about the opinions of the students who aren't athletes? In other words, when the generalization is drawn from a sample that is too small or select, your conclusion isn't valid.

Non sequitur ("it doesn't follow"): The writer's conclusion is not necessarily a logical result of the facts. An example of a *non sequitur* occurs when you conclude, "Professor Smith is a famous chemist, so he will be a brilliant chemistry teacher." As you may have realized by now, the fact that someone knows a subject well does not automatically mean that he or she can communicate the information clearly in a classroom; hence, the conclusion is not necessarily valid.

Begging the question: The writer presents as truth what is not proven by the argument. For example, in the statement "All useless laws such as Reform Bill 13 should be repealed," the writer has already pronounced the bill useless without assuming responsibility for proving that accusation. Similarly, the statement "Professors on our campus who are using their classroom solely for preaching their political ideas should be banned" begs the question (that is, tries like a beggar to get something for nothing from the reader), because the writer gives no evidence for what must first be argued, not merely asserted—that there are in fact professors on that particular campus using class time solely for spreading their political beliefs.

Red herring: The writer introduces an irrelevant point to divert the readers' attention from the main issue. This term originates from the old tactic used by escaped prisoners, of dragging a smoked herring, a strong-smelling fish, across their trail to confuse tracking dogs by making them follow the wrong scent. For example, roommate A might be criticizing roommate B for his repeated failure to do the dishes when it was his turn. To escape facing the charges, roommate B brings up times in the past when the other roommate failed to repay some money he borrowed. Although roommate A may indeed have a problem with remembering his debts, that discussion isn't relevant to the original argument about sharing the responsibility for the dishes. (By the way, you might have run across a well-known newspaper photograph of a California environmentalist group demonstrating for more protection of dolphins, whales, and other marine life; look closely to see, over in the left corner, almost hidden by the host of placards and banners, a fellow slyly holding up a sign that reads "Save the Red Herring!" Now, who says rhetoricians don't have a good sense of humour?)

Argument *ad hominem* ("to the man"): The writer attacks the opponent's character rather than the opponent's argument. The statement "Dr. Bloom can't be a competent marriage counsellor because she's been divorced" may not be valid. Bloom's advice to her clients may be excellent regardless of her own marital status.

Faulty use of authority: The writer relies on "authorities" who are not convincing sources. Although someone may be well known in a particular field, he or she may not be qualified to testify in a different area. A baseball player in an advertisement for laser surgery may stress his need for correct vision, but he may be no more knowledgeable about eye care than anyone else on the street. In other words, name recognition is not enough. For their testimony to count with readers, authorities must have expertise, credentials, or relevant experience in the area under discussion. (See also "transfer of virtue" in the discussion of "bandwagon appeal" on this page.)

Argument *ad populum* ("to the people"): The writer evades the issues by appealing to readers' emotional reactions to certain subjects. For example, instead of arguing the facts of an issue, a writer might play on the readers' negative response to such words as "communism," "fascism," or "radicalism," and their positive response to words like "God," "country," "liberty," or "patriotism." In the statement "If you are a true Canadian, you will vote against the referendum on a two-tiered health care system," the writer avoids any discussion of the merits or weaknesses of the bill and merely substitutes an emotional appeal. Other popular "virtue words" include "duty," "common sense," "courage," and "healthy." (Advertisers, of course, also play on consumers' emotions by filling their advertisements with pictures of babies, animals, status objects, and sexually attractive men and women.)

Either/or: The writer tries to convince the readers that there are only two sides to an issue—one right, one wrong. The statement "If you don't go to war against Iceland, you don't love your country" is irrational because it doesn't consider the other possibilities, such as patriotic people's right to oppose war as an expression of love for their country. A classic example of this sort of oversimplification was illustrated in the bumper sticker that was popular in America in the 1960s during the debate over the Vietnam War: "America: Love It or Leave It." Obviously, there are other choices ("Change It or Lose It," for instance, to quote another either/or bumper sticker of that era).

Hypostatization: The writer uses an abstract concept as if it were a concrete reality. Always be suspicious of a writer who frequently relies on statements beginning "History has always taught us . . ." or "Science has proven . . ." or "Research shows. . . ." The implication in each case is that history or science (or any other discipline) has only one voice, one opinion. On the contrary, "history" is written by a multitude of historians who hold a variety of opinions; doctors and scientists also frequently disagree. Instead of generalizing about a particular field, it is best to quote a specific, respected authority or to at least qualify your initial general statement by referring to "many" or "some" scientists, historians, or other professionals. You should be prepared to back up your general assertions and qualifications with specific evidence.

Bandwagon appeal: The writer tries to validate a point by intimating that "everyone else believes in this." Such a tactic evades discussion of the issue itself. Advertising often uses this technique: "Everyone who demands real taste smokes Phooey cigarettes"; "Discriminating women use Candy-Gloss lipstick." (The ultimate in "bandwagon" humour may have appeared on a recent Colorado bumper sticker: "Eat lamb—could 1000s of coyotes be wrong?") A variation of the "bandwagon" fallacy is sometimes referred to as "transfer of virtue," the sharing of light from someone else's sparkle. Advertisers often use this technique by paying attractive models or media stars to endorse their product. The underlying premise is this:

Popular/beautiful/"cool"/rich people use/buy/wear "X"; if you use "X," you too will be popular/beautiful/and so on.

Intelligent readers and consumers know, of course, to suspect such doubtful causal relationships.

Straw man: The writer selects the opposition's weakest or most insignificant point to argue against, to divert the readers' attention from the real issues. Instead of addressing the opposition's best arguments and defeating them, the writer "sets up a straw man"—that is, the writer picks out a trivial (or irrelevant) argument against his or her own position and easily knocks it down, just as one might easily push over a figure made of straw. Perhaps the most famous example of the "straw man" occurred in 1952 when, during the American vice-presidential campaign, Richard Nixon was accused of misappropriating campaign funds for his personal use. Addressing the nation on television, Nixon described how his six-year-old daughter, Tricia, had received a little cocker spaniel named Checkers from a Texas supporter. Nixon went on about how much his children loved the dog and how, regardless of what anyone thought, by gosh, he was going to keep that cute dog for little Tricia. Of course, no one was asking Nixon to return the dog; they were asking about the $18,000 in missing campaign funds. But Nixon's canine gift was much easier for him to defend, and the "Checkers" speech is now famous as one of the most notorious "straw man" diversions.

Faulty analogy: The writer uses an extended comparison as proof of a point. Look closely at all extended comparisons and metaphors to see if the two things being compared are really similar. For example, in a recent editorial a woman protested the new laws requiring parents to use car seats for small children, arguing that if the province could require the seats, they could just as easily require mothers to breastfeed instead of using formula. Are the two situations alike? Car accidents are the leading cause of death of children under four; is formula deadly? Or perhaps you've read that putting teenagers in sex education classes is like taking an alcoholic to a bar. Is it? If readers don't see the similarity, the analogy may not be persuasive. Moreover, remember that even though a compelling analogy might suggest similarities, it alone cannot *prove* anything.

Quick fix: The writer leans too heavily on catchy phrases or empty slogans. A clever turn-of-phrase may grab one's attention, but it may lose its persuasiveness when scrutinized closely. For instance, a banner at a rally to protest gun registration read, "When guns are outlawed, only outlaws will have guns." Although the sentence had nice balance, it oversimplified the issue. The legislation in question was not trying to outlaw all guns, just to make the acquisition of guns more difficult for those with criminal records. Other slogans sound good but are simply irrelevant: a particular soft drink, for example, may be "the real thing," but what drink isn't? Look closely at clever lines substituted for reasoned argument; always demand clear terms and logical explanations.*

---

* Sometimes advertisers get more for their slogans than they bargained for. According to one news source, a popular soft-drink company had to spend millions to revise its slogan after introducing its product into parts of China. Apparently the slogan "Come alive! Join the Blah-Blah-Cola Generation!" translated into some dialects as "Blah-Blah Cola Brings Your Ancestors Back from the Dead"!

A. Imagine that you are writing an argumentative essay addressing the controversial question "Should home-schooled students be allowed to play on public school athletic teams?" You have investigated the topic and have noted the variety of opinions listed here. Arrange the statements into two lists: A "Pro" list (those statements that argue for allowing home schoolers to play) and a "Con" list (those statements that are against allowing home schoolers to play). Cross off any inappropriate or illogical statements you find; combine any opinions that overlap.

1. Parents of home schoolers pay the same taxes as public school parents.

2. Public school kids must meet grade requirements to be eligible.

3. School rules prohibit non-enrolled youth on school property.

4. Home schoolers shouldn't get the benefits of a school they've rejected.

5. Public school kids are bad influences on home schoolers.

6. Home schoolers need the social interaction.

7. Public school teams can always use more good athletes.

8. More students will overburden athletic facilities.

9. Home schoolers miss their public school friends, and vice versa.

10. Home schoolers will displace public school students on teams.

11. Public school students have to meet attendance rules to be eligible.

12. Athletic competition is good for everybody.

13. Home schoolers often have controversial political beliefs that will cause fights.

14. Team members need to share the same community on a daily basis.

15. Home schoolers aren't as invested in school pride.

Once you have your two lists, decide your own position on this topic. Then select two points you might use to argue your position and one opposing criticism you might refute. Put your working thesis into an "although–because" format.
Compare your choices to those of your classmates.

B. Errors in reasoning can cause your reader to doubt your credibility. In the following mock essay, for example, the writer includes a variety of fallacies that undermine his argument; see if you can identify all his errors.

The five essays that follow illustrate a variety of approaches to argument and persuasion. Read the essays and answer the questions that follow each one.

A CITY FOR STUDENTS

Aliki Tryphonopoulos

1   It is hard to think of a city more exhilarating for a student to live in than Montreal. Where else can you hear a conversation shift between two or even three languages with ease and playfulness at the local coffee shop? Cosmopolitan and cultured, *la belle ville* is unique in North America for its intersection of two historically established language groups with a large and growing immigrant population. Montrealers have translated this rich cultural diversity into a vibrant civic life with world-renowned festivals, a well-established art scene, lively café culture, and acclaimed international cuisine and fashion. Few cities in the world offer the affordable living, student amenities, and cultural dynamism that Montreal does.

2   Long-standing socioeconomic factors make Montreal an affordable city for students—no small consideration given that Canadian undergraduate tuition has risen by 111 percent since 1990 ("Bottom Line," 2004). Naysayers point out that although Quebec has the lowest tuition rates in Canada (frozen since 1994), out-of-province students must pay roughly twice as much as Quebec residents, placing them in the higher bracket of national tuition payers. Some students get around this disadvantage by working and taking part-time classes for a year in order to qualify for the in-province tuition rates. For those who are required to pay the higher rates, however, the financial burden is more than offset by the relatively low cost of rental housing in Montreal (Canada Mortgage, 2004, table 2). One of the best ways for students to economize is by living close to the university. Montreal is a walking city, so it is possible for students to conduct all of their business within a five-block radius.

3   Pedestrian-friendly urban planning plays a large part in Montreal's reputation as a festival city that hosts over 40 events annually. In the sultry summer months, streets shut down for the Jazz Festival, the Montreal Grand Prix, and Just for Laughs, while the Fête des Neiges and the Montreal High Lights Festival provide outdoor activities and culinary delights in the winter. Students find plenty of ways to keep active—cycling, jogging, skating, skiing, dancing and drumming at Montreal's sexy Tam-Tams in Mount Royal Park—and gain

an appreciation of the city's vibrant arts scene, from the numerous galleries in Old Montreal to fine art cinemas such as Cinema du Parc and Ex-Centris. Students can argue the merits of the latest Denys Arcand film in one of the many cafés along St. Denis frequented by their compatriots from Concordia, McGill, Université de Montréal, and Université du Québec à Montréal. As for ambience, the eclectic mix of old European limestone mansions and North American glass towers lends this oldest of Canadian cities a unique architectural allure.

4 Montreal's cultural dynamism, whose historic roots draw comparisons to such international cities as Barcelona and Brussels, is not only the city's most attractive attribute, but sadly, what scares many students away. Bill 101, meant to protect the French language in Quebec, contributed to the exodus of nonfrancophones from Montreal during the 1980s and 1990s. That trend is slowly reversing (DeWolf, 2003). A recent study reveals what Montrealers already know: the unique interaction of francophone, anglophone, and allophone (languages other than French or English) cultures in Montreal is characterized by mutual respect, accommodation, and even a sense of fun (Lamarre, 2002). Students can absorb and appreciate the international flavour of the various boroughs and contribute to the daily cultural exchange. With the city's high rates of bilingualism and trilingualism, anglophone students do not need to know French in order to function, but their social and cultural life will be far richer if they do. And what better place to learn *la langue française* than in the second-largest French-speaking city in the world!

5 Education is as much about what goes on outside the classroom as in it. Those students who are willing to embrace Montreal's vibrant cultural milieu will find their worldviews challenged and broadened. In a global environment fraught with the dangers of intercultural miscommunication and ignorance, that kind of education is vital.

References

The bottom line. (2004, November 15). *Maclean's*, p. 72.

Canada Mortgage and Housing Corporation. (2004, December 1). *Average rents in privately initiated apartment structures of three units and over in metropolitan areas* (table 2). Retrieved December 22, 2004, from http://www.cmhc.ca/en/News/nere/2004/2004-12-21-0715.cfm

DeWolf, C. (2003, May 25). The road to Montreal. *The Gazette* [Montreal]. Retrieved December 20, 2004, from http://maisonneuve.org/about_media.php?press_media_id=21

Lamarre, P. (2002). Multilingual Montreal: Listening in on the language practices of young Montrealers. *Canadian Ethnic Studies, 34*(3), 47–75.

Questions for Discussion

1. This essay's introduction establishes the author's thesis and previews her main points. What other purposes does it serve?
2. In an argument, it is often necessary to address the opposition's point of view. The writer can choose either to turn a negative into a positive, or to present the opposition's arguments and then refute them. Find examples of both techniques in this essay.
3. The acknowledgment of source material is a standard feature of academic research papers. Why do you think the author of this general-interest essay uses and documents source material?
4. Use InfoTrac to do a keyword search of "Montreal." How many hits did you get? Narrow your search to find information that supports the key points of this essay. What keyword gave you the best results?

"HIRE" LEARNING
Editorial[1]

1   Ideally, at the core of our education system lies the desire to inculcate those talents and attitudes that prepare the young for the obligations of citizenship and open them to greater intellectual and spiritual life. What, then, should we make of suggestions that children be paid to get good grades? "Kids are growing up in a lean and mean environment," says psychologist Robert Butterworth, president of Los Angeles-based International Trauma Associates. "If adults don't work for free, why should kids?" Mr. Butterworth says governments should consider rewarding students with a $50 cheque for every A grade.

2   Right off the bat, we're flunking Mr. Butterworth—for promoting even more government interference in our lives (with the extra taxation that implies). But his cash for grades idea should also be condemned for its reductionist view of education and human psychology.

3   Don't get us wrong. Rewarding children for getting good grades with money is a common practice in many families, and there's nothing wrong with it as long as the money is not an end in itself. But that is precisely what Mr. Butterworth is proposing. He effectively makes money the "end" of education by saying, implicitly at least, that the only reason to get good grades is for cash. To our mind, that's the same as saying that money is the only standard by which people's accomplishments are to be judged, that without the money they have accomplished nothing. In short, money becomes the cause, not the effect. It becomes the only measure of human worth.

---

[1]*Ottawa Citizen*, August 13, 1999.

4   It is a measure. Certainly, many people go to school—particularly college and university—so that they'll be able to get good jobs. But that is not the deepest purpose of education. A good education may be essential to job success, but at the same time, it is also the best route for availing us of those spiritual satisfactions that give our practical success wider significance. Education, ultimately, opens our psyche to the possibility of being better than we might otherwise be.

5   Consider the student who spends weeks on some project and wins the plaudits of his teacher and classmates. Sure, a bit of cash might be nice; heck, the plaudits are nice. But the real reward is psychological. It comes from knowing that you have done something, accomplished something, learned something, that wasn't yours yesterday. Such recognition reinforces those talents that push a student to greater achievements in a cycle that, hopefully, leads to a modicum of wisdom. In that sense, intellectual endeavour is its own reward.

6   Mr. Butterworth's proposals, if instituted, would forego this spiritual dimension of education, turning a child's schooling into a "job." Indeed, his prescription would reduce education to the functional task of gaining "competitive advantage" or "enhancing productivity" (this sounds a bit like the debate over teaching liberal arts in universities).

7   But what about the school years as a time of playfulness, discovery, risks, and failures? In a world where your "income" depends on your grades, who'd want to waste time on some difficult intellectual effort? Why savour Shakespeare if a scan of Coles Notes will win the paycheque?

8   Yes, parents reward their children for good performance. Sometimes that includes a bit of cash. But, first, we hope, it includes sharing the excitement of learning. Mr. Butterworth gets an F.

Questions for Discussion

1. Is this editorial intended to be an argument or a persuasive piece? Support your answer with evidence from the piece.
2. Review the discussion of the "their side–my side strategy" and "the proposition + supporting reasons" structures on pages 240–41. Which of these structural patterns does the author use in this piece?
3. Paragraph 7 contains three rhetorical questions (questions to which no answer is expected). Why do you think the writer chose rhetorical questions rather than declarative sentences? Rewrite the three questions as statements and then describe the different effects the two versions have on the reader.
4. As a postsecondary student, do you think that education should be exclusively about learning how to earn a living? Or do you believe

that contribute to your learning how to live the life that you earn? Did reading this editorial influence your opinion in any way? How?

5. It is said that most newspapers are aimed at a grade 8 reading level. Cite evidence that suggests " 'Hire' Learning" was written for a higher-level reader. Why do you think this editorial is aimed at a more-educated audience than the newspaper norm?

6. Use InfoTrac to find another article by or about California child psychologist Robert R. Butterworth. (Be careful! The database contains articles by several Robert Butterworths.) Read the article and then, using both the article and " 'Hire' Learning" for support, summarize your opinion of Mr. Butterworth's ideas about child psychology.

OF PAIN, PREDATORS, AND PLEASURE
Walter Isaacs

1 The issue of whether fish feel pain when hooked by an angler has been widely debated in a number of publications recently. Scientific studies arguing that the fish's mouth does or does not have pain receptors have supported both sides of this debate. It seems to me that this squabble is as irrelevant as the medieval debates about how many angels can dance on the head of a pin. Of course we cause the fish distress, mortal distress! Like any animal, the fish is programmed to survive and procreate. Any predatory threat to that primal function—from a bear, an osprey, a bigger fish, or an angler—must cause extreme stress; whether that stress can be called "pain" through anthropomorphism, it's certainly more dire to the fish than the prick of a hook in its jaw (felt as "pain" or not). To argue that we aren't distressing a fish by catching it is to hand opponents of fishing proof that fishers are either in denial or just plain stupid.

2 I admit that I love tricking fish. I take as much pleasure as anyone in catching them, and my pleasure is increased when I've been especially clever or skillful in fooling the creature into taking my fly. I do everything that I can to minimize the pain and stress on any fish I catch, but I cannot deny that by catching the fish, I am in a sense torturing it for my pleasure. How can I justify my actions?

3 First, I acknowledge that I am a predator and something somewhere in me loves the idea of taking a wild animal through stealth or guile, even when (as I almost always do) I release it unharmed. Whether this instinct comes from a gene somewhere in my DNA or a gland buried in the folds of my brain, there's no denying that it's there. Just as I enjoy sex, laughter, anchovies on pizza, warm fall days, a Bach concerto, and a good Riesling, I enjoy catching fish on

a fly. Some pleasures are instinctive, some are learned, but the fact that they are pleasures cannot be denied. Yes, I could give up any of these pleasures if the motivation were sufficient, but so far I haven't had sufficient motivation to relinquish any of them.

4   Second, let's acknowledge that, as predators go, anglers are relatively benign. When you compare the millions of fish that are hatched to the number that live long enough to be the prey of anglers, it's clear that other predators are more efficient and more dangerous than fly fishers. I suppose the case could be made that for every salmon killed by an angler, thousands of eels and other sea creatures are saved. If we can anthropomorphize the fish's pain, let's go another step and ask the fish which predator it would rather be caught by: that female osprey gliding over the river, or Walter Isaac. Both predators will cause it the immediate fear/stress/pain of being caught, but in the first case, the osprey will feed its catch alive to its chicks; in the second, the fish will survive to procreate.

5   Finally, because of my love of fishing, I contribute both time and money to support such activities as the restoration and maintenance of stream habitat, stocking programs, and the development of a cleaner, wilder environment in which fish can thrive. In other words, my conservation efforts help to produce more and healthier fish at the end of each season than there would be if I didn't love tricking them.

6   If I could fish without harming the creatures in any way, I'd do it in a heartbeat. But since I must hurt the fish somewhat to pursue an activity that gives me such pleasure, these justifications serve to let me do it in good conscience, while recognizing and respecting the stress I cause. I know that what I've said won't convince those who are fundamentally opposed to angling, and I understand their viewpoint. But such people just don't seem to have that gene or gland that makes fishing such a pleasure for me. Heck, I even know people who don't like sex.

Questions for Discussion

1. The argument that is the basis for this essay is supported by three points. What are they? In what order has the author arranged his supporting evidence?
2. This essay was first published in a fly-fishing magazine. Identify clues that indicate the piece was written for a sympathetic audience.
3. How would the essay differ if it had been written for an audience of animal-rights activists? Draft a rough outline for such an essay.
4. The essay's concluding sentence seems to have been tossed off for the purpose of ending on a light note. What more serious purpose does it serve in supporting the author's argument?

5. This essay is, among other things, the author's response to contradictory findings about whether or not fish feel pain the way humans do. Use InfoTrac to find articles on this subject. Be sure to choose articles that reflect both sides of the argument. After reading a few of these articles, decide which side of the debate you support. In a sentence or two, summarize your opinion and identify three or four reasons that support it.

ARTS EDUCATION DOES PAY OFF
Livio Di Matteo

1   Canada's universities—particularly the humanities and social sciences—face a major challenge. The current approach to education emphasizes immediate tangible benefits. This has led to government funding initiatives in science and technology that fail to recognize the importance of a liberal arts education. Yet supporting a humanities and social science education is justified on sound economic grounds, not just on the civic and academic grounds usually used.

2   The humanities and social sciences provide social benefits that private market mechanisms do not count. Just as a vaccination benefits people other than those inoculated by reducing disease transmission, the humanities and social sciences have spill-over benefits by transmitting wisdom to society. The inability to attach a market price to a literate and civil society of educated citizens does not make this type of education valueless.

3   The humanities and social sciences complement scientific and technical training, and provide innovative strategies for meeting future challenges. While science graduates can provide technical solutions to problems, only individuals trained in human science can deal with the economic, ethical, cultural and social implications of these solutions. For example, we are told that advances in genetics are making a vastly extended human lifespan possible in the not-so-distant future. How will this affect the distribution of income and employment, and the quality of life in our society? Is this type of analysis not of economic benefit to society?

4   Market benefits to humanities and social science graduates translate into jobs, as economist Robert Allen of the University of British Columbia recently demonstrated in a study. Prof. Allen found that unemployment rates for humanities and social science graduates did not substantially differ from those of graduates in other fields. Moreover, these graduates' age–income profiles can actually be steeper than those in the sciences or technical programs, where the latest technical knowledge depreciates quickly. Like fine wine, humanities and social science graduates appreciate with age as their skills

versities, such as Dalhousie, are beginning to [issue transcripts that list] skills such as collaborative work, oral communication, and analytical work to their liberal arts graduates. This communicates what was once obvious, but now has to be marketed: Liberal arts graduates are prized because of their ability to think creatively and laterally, using skills acquired in analysis, synthesis, research and communication.

5   Having reduced their market intervention on the grounds that private forces work best, governments are now replicating that interventionist role in post-secondary education by targeting funding increases to programs in science and technology. These programs are worthy of funding, but for universities to function according to a private-sector model, governments should provide universities with block increases in funding and allow them to pursue those programs they are best at. Targeted funding distorts resource allocation decisions by inducing universities to expand government-favoured programs. This leaves governments selecting educational winners and losers when the economy's future needs are uncertain.

6   Other issues present themselves, too. What about the long-run cost structure of universities, given that the per-student cost of producing science and engineering graduates is higher than in other fields? Who is responsible if such funding generates a graduate glut in any one discipline? Will government be accountable, or will the buck be passed to the universities for once again "failing" in their role to society?

7   Humanities and social sciences students make up approximately half of university enrolments. If you believe that "voting with your feet" is a test of market demand, this enrolment share should be sending a clear message to educational policy-makers as to how the public values these programs. Humanities and social science students should be entitled to adequate research and teaching facilities, and to professors who conduct leading-edge research. When it comes to resource allocation, why should half of university students be placed on a path to second-rate treatment when they are indeed "paying customers"?

8   It is time to restore some balance. The current targeted funding approach ignores the obvious demand for humanities and social science training. Governments can best serve the university system by ensuring adequate general funding and allowing universities, in consultation with government and the public, to make the resource allocation decisions. In neglecting the humanities and social sciences, governments have not fully consulted all constituencies, and their funding decisions implicitly attach a negative value to these disciplines. Canadian society will pay huge economic and cultural costs if such myopic policies are continued.

Di Matteo, Livio. "Arts Education Does Pay Off." *Financial Post* 31 May 1999: 3.

Questions for Discussion

1. Does the author approach his argument directly or indirectly? Where is the thesis statement? Identify the reasons the author cites to support his opinion.
2. Who is the target audience for this essay? How do you know?
3. What is the author's purpose: to win his readers' agreement, or to move them to action? What sort of action could they take to support the author on this issue?
4. Identify the various kinds of evidence the author uses in this essay.
5. The author uses a number of rhetorical questions (questions to which no answer is expected). Are they effective in supporting his argument? Why?
6. In your own words, explain why the author thinks targeted funding is a poor idea. (See paragraphs 5 and 6.)
7. Do you agree with the author? Why or why not?

STUPID JOBS ARE GOOD TO RELAX WITH
Hal Niedzviecki

1 Springsteen kicked off his world tour at Toronto's Massey Hall a while back. Along with record company execs and those who could afford the exorbitant prices scalpers wanted for tickets, I was in attendance. As Bruce rambled on about the plight of the itinerant Mexican workers, I lolled in the back, my job, as always, to make myself as unapproachable as possible—no easy feat, trapped as I was in paisley vest and bow-tie combo. Nonetheless, the concert was of such soporific proportions and the crowd so dulled into pseudo-reverence, I was able to achieve the ultimate in ushering—a drooping catatonia as close as you can get to being asleep while on your feet at a rock concert.

2 But this ushering nirvana wouldn't last long. For an usher, danger takes many forms, including vomiting teens and the usher's nemesis: the disruptive patron. And yes, to my semi-conscious horror, there she was: well-dressed, blond, drunk and doped up, swaying in her seat and . . . clapping. Clapping. In the middle of Springsteen's solo dirge about Pancho or Pedro or Luisa, she was clapping.

3 Sweat beaded on my forehead. The worst was happening. She was in my section. Her clapping echoed through the hall, renowned for its acoustics. The Boss glared from the stage, his finger-picking folksiness no match for the drunken rhythm of this fan. Then, miracle of miracles, the song ended. The woman slumped back into her seat. Bruce muttered something about how he didn't need a rhythm section. Placated by the adoring silence of the well-to-

do, he launched into an even quieter song about an even more desperate migrant worker.

4   I lurked in the shadows, relaxed the grip I had on my flashlight (the usher's only weapon). Springsteen crooned. His guitar twanged. It was so quiet you could hear the rats squirrelling around the ushers' subterranean change rooms. The woman roused herself from her slumber. She leaned forward in her seat, as if suddenly appreciating the import of her hero's message. I wiped the sweat off my brow, relieved. But slowly, almost imperceptibly, she brought her arms up above her head. I stared, disbelieving. Her hands waved around in the air until . . . boom! Another song ruined, New York record execs and L.A. journalists distracted from their calculations of Bruce's net worth, the faint cry of someone calling, "Usher! Do something!"

5   For several years now, I have relied on stupid jobs to pay my way through the world. This isn't because I am a stupid person. On the contrary, stupid jobs are a way to avoid the brain-numbing idiocy of full-time employment. They are the next best thing to having no job at all. They will keep you sane, and smart.

6   I'm lazy sometimes. I don't always feel like working. On the stupid job, you're allowed to be lazy. All you have to do is show up. Hey, that's as much of an imposition on my life as I'm ready to accept. Does The Boss go to work every day? I don't think so. He's The Boss.

7   Understanding the stupid job is the key to wading your way through the muck of the working week and dealing with such portentous concepts as The Youth Unemployment Crisis and The Transformation of the Workplace. So sit back and let me explain. Or, as I used to say behind the scowl of my shining grin: "Hi, how are you this evening? Please follow me and I will show you to your seat."

8   "Out of Work: Is There Hope for Canada's Youth?" blurted the October 1997 issue of *Canadian Living*. My answer? There is more hope than ever. I'm not talking about ineffectual governments and their well-intentioned "partners," the beneficent corporations, all banding together to "create" jobs. After all, what kind of jobs do you think these corporations are going to create? Jobs that are interesting, challenging and resplendent with possibilities? Hardly. These are going to be stupid jobs. Bring me your college graduates, your aspiring business mavens, your literature lovers and we will find them rote employment where servility and docility are the best things they could have learned at university.

9   But hope, hope is something altogether different. Hope is the process whereby entire generations learn to undervalue their work, squirm out of the trap of meaningless employment, work less, consume less and actually figure out how to enjoy life.

10   I hope I'm right about this, because the reality of the underemployed, overeducated young people of Canada is that the stupid job is their future. As the middle-aged population continues to occupy all the "real" jobs, as the universities continue to hike tuition prices (forcing students to work and study part time), as the government continues to shore up employment numbers with make-work and "retraining," there will be more stupid jobs than ever. And these stupid jobs won't be reserved for the uneducated and poor. The fertile growth of the stupid job is already reaping a crop of middle-class youngsters whose education and upbringing have, somehow, given way to (supposedly) stalled prospects and uncertain incomes.

11   These are your grandchildren, your children, your sisters, your cousins, your neighbours. Hey, that might very well be a multicoloured bow-tie wrapped around your neck.

12   I took a few tenuous steps down the aisle. All around me, luxurious people hissed in annoyance and extended their claws. Clapping woman was bouncing in her seat. She was smiling. Her face was flushed and joyous. The sound of her hands coming together was deafening. I longed for the floor captain, the front-of-house manager, the head of security, somebody to come and take this problem away from me. I hit her with a burst of flashlight. Taking advantage of her momentary blindness, I leaned in: "Excuse me Miss," I said. "You can't do that." "What?" she said. "That clapping," I said. "Listen," she slurred. "I paid $300 to see this. I can do what I want."

13   My flashlight hand wavered. Correctly interpreting my silence for defeat, she resumed her clapping. Springsteen strummed louder, unsuccessful in his attempt to drown out the beat of luxury, the truth of indulgence. I faded away, the darkness swallowing me up. For a blissful moment, I was invisible.

14   A lot of young people think their stupid jobs are only temporary. Most of them are right, in a way. Many will move on from being, as I have been, an usher, a security guard, a delivery boy, a data co-ordinator, a publishing intern. They will get marginally better jobs, but what they have learned from their stupid jobs will stay with them forever. Hopefully.

15   If I'm right, they will learn that the stupid job—and by extension, all jobs—must be approached with willing stupidity. Set your mind free. It isn't neces-sary, and it can be an impediment. While your body runs the maze and finds the cheese, let your mind go where it will.

16   Look at it this way: you're trading material wealth and luxury for freedom and creativity. To simplify this is to say that while you may have less money to buy things, you will have a lot more time to think up ways to achieve your goals without buying things. It is remarkable how quickly one comes to value time to just sit and think. Oddly, many of us seem quite proud of having

absolutely no time to think about anything. The words "I'm so busy" are chanted over and over again like a mantra, an incantation against some horrible moment when we realize we're not so busy. In the stupid job universe, time isn't quantifiable. You're making so many dollars an hour, but the on-job perks include daydreams, poems scribbled on napkins, novels read in utility closets and long conversations about the sexual stamina of Barney Rubble. How much is an idea worth? An image? A moment of tranquillity? A bad joke? The key here is to embrace the culture of anti-work.

17   Sometime after the Springsteen debacle, I was on a delivery job dropping off newspapers at various locales. I started arguing with my co-worker, the van driver, about work ethic. I suggested we skip a drop-off or two, claiming that no one would notice and even if they did, we could deny it and no one would care. He responded by telling me that no matter what job he was doing, if he accepted the work, he was compelled to do it right. I disagreed. Cut corners, I argued. Do less for the same amount of pay. That's what they expect us to do, I said. Why else would they pay us so little? Not that day, but some weeks later, he came to see things my way.

18   What am I trying to tell you? To be lazy? To set fire to the corporation?

19   Maybe. Our options might be limited, but they are still options. Somewhere in the bowels of Massey Hall it has probably been noted in my permanent record that I have a bad attitude. That was a mistake. I wasn't trying to have a bad attitude. I was trying to have no attitude. . . .

20   What I should have told my friend in the delivery van was that when working the stupid job, passivity is the difference between near slavery and partial freedom. It's a mental distinction. Your body is still in the same place for the same amount of time (unless you're unsupervised), but your mind is figuring things out. Figuring out how many days you need to work to afford things like hard-to-get tickets to concerts by famous American icons. Or figuring out why it is that at the end of the week, most people are too busy or too tired to do anything other than spend their hard-earned dollars on fleeting moments of cotton candy ecstasy as ephemeral as lunch hour. Personally, I'd take low-level servitude over a promotion that means I'll be working late the rest of my life. You want me to work weekends? You better give me the rest of the week off. . . .

21   Montreal has one of the highest unemployment rates of any city in Canada. Young people in that city are as likely to have full-time jobs as they are to spend their nights arguing about Quebec separation. Not coincidentally, some of the best Canadian writers, comic artists and underground periodicals are from that city. We're talking about the spoken-word capital of North America here. Creativity plus unemployment equals art.

22　The burgeoning stupid job aesthetic is well documented in another youth culture phenomenon, the vaunted 'zine (photocopied periodicals published by individuals for fun, not money). Again, it doesn't take a genius to make the connection between the youth culture of stupid jobs and the urgency and creativity 'zine publishers display when writing about their lives. "So why was I dishonest and subversive?" asks Brendan Bartholomew in an article in the popular Wisconsin 'zine *Temp Slave*. "Well, I've been sabotaging employers for so long, it's become second nature. It's in my blood. I couldn't stop if I wanted to."

23　Slacking off, doing as little as possible, relishing my lack of responsibility, this is what the workplace has taught me to do. This is the stupid job mantra. It isn't about being poor. The stupid job aesthetic is not about going hungry. Canada is a country of excess. You cannot have a stupid job culture when people are genuinely, truly, worried that they are going to starve in the streets.

24　Nevertheless, the tenets of the stupid job revolution are universal: work is mainly pointless; if you can think of something better to do, you shouldn't have to work; it's better to have a low-paying job and freedom than a high-paying job and a 60-hour workweek. It was Bruce's drunken fan who highlighted the most important aspect of what will one day be known as the stupid job revolution: with money, you think you can do whatever you want, but you rarely can; without money, you can be like Bartholomew—a postmodern rat, a stowaway writing his diaries from the comfort of his berth at the bottom of the sinking ship.

25　My father's plight is a familiar one. He started his working life at 13 in Montreal. He's 55 now. His employer of 12 years forced him to take early retirement. The terms were great, and if he didn't own so much stuff (and want more stuff) he could live comfortably without ever working again. But he feels used, meaningless, rejected.

26　On his last day, I helped him clean out his office. The sight of him stealing staplers, blank disks and Post-it note pads was something I'll never forget. It was a memo he was writing to his own soul (note: they owe me).

27　But the acquisition of more stuff is not what he needs to put a life of hard work behind him. I wish that he could look back on his years of labour and think fondly of all the hours he decided not to work, those hours he spent reading a good book behind the closed door of his office, or skipping off early to take the piano lessons he never got around to. Instead of stealing office supplies, he should have given his boss the finger as he walked out the door. Ha ha. I don't care what you think of me. And by the way, I never did.

28　Despite his decades of labour and my years of being barely employed (and the five degrees we have between us), we have both ended up at the same place. He feels cheated. I don't.

Questions for Discussion

1. Which paragraph states the thesis of the essay?
2. What strategy does the author use in his conclusion (see paragraphs 25 to 28)? Do you think it's effective? Why?
3. What were your expectations of the author when you read the title of the essay? Were you surprised to find words such as "exorbitant," "soporific," and "catatonia" in the first paragraph? What other elements of style and structure tell us that the author is far from "stupid"?
4. Is this essay primarily argument or persuasion?
5. What is the basis of the author's argument with the van driver as they're dropping off newspapers? (See paragraphs 17 to 20.) Whom do you agree with? Who has the right attitude toward the job?
6. What proof does the author offer to support his point that art and creativity are likely to flourish among people who are unemployed or have "stupid jobs"?
7. What is the author's attitude toward consumerism? Does he think we buy too much or not enough? Where in the essay is his attitude most clearly revealed? Do you agree with him? Why?

Exercise 17.1

Read through the following list of propositions. With a partner, select one that you are both interested in, but do not discuss it. Working individually, write down two or three points both for and against the issue. Then exchange papers and read each other's work. Which points appear on both lists? Why? Can you judge from the points presented whether your partner is for or against the issue?

> Canada should (should not) increase its level of immigration.
> The salaries of professional athletes should (should not) be capped.
> Music lyrics should (should not) be monitored and censored.
> Technology is (is not) improving the workplace.
> Courses in physical education should (should not) be required throughout high school.
> Smokers should (should not) receive the same medical coverage as non-smokers.

Exercise 17.2

Most people have firm convictions, yet few are willing to take action to uphold them. Everyone agrees, for example, that a cure for cancer should be found, but not everyone participates in fundraising events or supports the Cancer Society. With a partner, choose a charitable cause in which you believe and list all the reasons why people should give money to support it. Then list all the reasons people might give for not donating.

Decide which of you will take the "pro" side and which the "con," and write a short essay arguing your position. You will know from your discussion whether your partner is sympathetic or hostile, so you will know whether you should approach your subject directly or indirectly. Then exchange papers and critique each other's work.

Exercise 17.3

Together with a partner, select a *small*, controversial, local issue (one involving your community, college, or profession, for example). Choose sides, and write an argument using the "their side–my side" pattern of organization.

Exercise 17.4

With a partner, develop a questionnaire and survey at least 20 students in your college, from different programs and different years, to determine their attitude toward one of the following:

food services
class sizes
professors' teaching ability
required (or general education) courses
tutorial (or counselling) services

Both of you should take notes during these interviews.

When you and your partner have gathered enough information, it's time to work independently. Compose an indirect argument that arrives at a conclusion about the issue and makes a recommendation based on the evidence you have gathered. Compare your paper with your partner's. What are the main similarities and differences between your two compositions? What conclusions can you draw from your comparative analysis?

Exercise 17.5

Choose an issue with which you are familiar and about which you feel strongly. If you don't feel strongly about anything, choose a proposition from the list below. Draft a statement of thesis and outline your reasons and evidence. Then write a persuasive paper, making sure that your points are well supported and that the paper is clearly structured. Assume that your reader is not hostile, but is not enthusiastically supportive, either.

Forty percent of the college curriculum should/should not be devoted to liberal arts (general education) courses.
Marijuana should/should not be available for sale through government-controlled retail outlets.
Grades in college courses should/should not take effort into consideration, not just results.
Parents of underage youth should/should not be financially responsible

Comparison and Contrast

If you are focusing on the similarities between two things (or ideas or concepts or points of view), you are writing a **comparison**. If you are focusing on the differences, you are writing a **contrast**. Most people, however, use the term "comparison" to cover both (as in "comparison shopping"), and similarities *and* differences are often discussed together in a paper.

You can choose from two approaches when you are organizing a comparison. In the first option, you discuss one item fully and then turn to the other item. This approach is called the **block method** of organizing. The alternative option is to compare your two items **point by point**. For example, suppose you decided to compare Russell Crowe and Brad Pitt. You might identify the following three points:

- physical appearance
- acting technique
- on-camera heroics

Using the block method, you would first consider Crowe in terms of these three points; then you would do the same for Pitt. You would need to outline only four paragraphs for your essay:

1. Introduction
2. Crowe's physical appearance, acting technique, and on-camera heroics
3. Pitt's physical appearance, acting technique, and on-camera heroics
4. Conclusion

The block method works best in short papers, where the points of comparison are easy to understand and remember. As comparisons get more complex, your readers will be able to understand your points better if you present them point by point. You would then need to write an outline of five paragraphs for your essay:

1. Introduction
2. Physical appearance of Crowe and Pitt
3. Acting technique of Crowe and Pitt
4. On-camera heroics of Crowe and Pitt
5. Conclusion

The introductory paragraph in the comparison essay usually tells readers what two things are to be assessed and what criteria will be used to assess them. The concluding paragraph may (or may not) reveal a preference for one over the other.

Tips on Writing a Comparison or Contrast

1. Make sure that the two items you have chosen are appropriately paired; to make a satisfactory comparison, they must have something in common. Both might be baseball teams or world leaders; but to compare the Toronto Blue Jays and the Calgary Stampeders or to contrast Queen Elizabeth and your Aunt Agatha would be futile and meaningless.
2. Your main points must apply equally to both items. Reject main points that apply to one and have only limited application to the other. For example, in a comparison of digital and analog instruments, a category for dial configuration would be pointless.
3. Your thesis statement should clearly present the two items to be compared and the basis for their comparison. Consider these examples.

   E-mail and interoffice memos differ not only in format but also in style and purpose.

   The major points of comparison in automobiles are performance, comfort, and economy, so I applied these factors to the two cars in the running for my dollars: the Saturn and the Mazda 3.

4. Use transitional words and phrases within and between paragraphs to provide coherence. (See pages 102–04.)

The following four examples demonstrate different approaches to writing comparisons and contrasts. After reading each essay, answer the questions that follow it.

THE CANADIAN CLIMATE

D'Arcy McHale

1   The student who comes to Canada from a tropical country is usually pre-pared for cold Canadian winters, a sharp contrast to our hot northern sum-mers. What the student may not be prepared for is the fact that Canadian personalities reflect the country's temperature range but are less extreme. Canadian personalities fall into two categories: warm and cool. The two groups share the Canadian traits of restraint and willingness to compromise, but they are dissimilar in their attitudes both to their own country and to the foreign student's country of origin.

2   Warm Canadians are, first of all, warm about Canada and will, at the first sound of a foreign accent, describe with rapture the magnificence of the country from the Maritimes to the West Coast, praising the beauty of the Prairies, the Rockies, and even the "unique climate of the Far North." Canadian leisure activities are enthusiastically described with a special place reserved for hockey. "So you've never skated? You'll learn. Come with us; you'll have a great time." The Warm Canadian wants the newcomer to share in the pleasures of life in Canada. When she turns her attention to the foreign student's homeland, she seeks enlightenment, asking questions about its geography, social and economic conditions, and other concerns not usually addressed in travel and tourism brochures. The Warm Canadian understands that the residents of tropical countries are not exotic flower children who sing and dance with natural rhythm but are individuals who, like Canadians, face the problems of earning a living and raising a family.

3   Compared to the Warm Canadian, who exudes a springlike optimism, the Cool Canadian is like November. Conditions may not be unbearable for the moment, but they are bound to get much colder before there is any sign of a thaw. The Cool Canadian's first words on hearing that the foreign student is from a warm country are, "How could you leave such a lovely climate to come to a place like this?" Not from him will one hear of Banff, or Niagara Falls, or anything except how cold and dark and dreary it gets in the winter. It some-times seems that the Cool Canadian's description of his own country is designed to encourage foreign students to pack their bags and return home at once. As for the foreign student's country of origin, the Cool Canadian is not really interested, although he may declare, "I hear it's beautiful. I'd love to go there." Beyond that, however, he has no interest in information that may shake the foundations of his collection of myths, half-truths, and geo-graphic inaccuracies. This type of Canadian, if he does travel to a tropical country, will ensure that he remains at all times within the safe confines of his hotel and that he returns to Canada with all his preconceived ideas intact.

4   Foreign students should not be upset by the Cool Canadian; they should

can occur and create extraordinary warmth. Likewise, a Warm Canadian may become a little frosty sometimes, but, like a cold spell in June, this condition won't last. And when the weather changes, foreign students will find an opportunity to display their own qualities of understanding, tolerance, and acceptance of others as they are.

Reprinted by permission of the author.

Questions for Discussion

1. What are the main points of contrast in "The Canadian Climate"?
2. Which method of contrast has the author chosen for the subject, block or point by point?
3. Why did the author choose this approach? Would the essay work as well if it were organized the other way? Outline the main points of contrast as they would look in the other format.
4. What other points of contrast between the two kinds of Canadians can you think of?
5. What audience does the author have in mind? How do you think Canadians would respond to this essay? Foreign students?

SHOPPING AROUND

Aniko Hencz

1   The word "shopping" inspires visions of crowded, airless malls, aggressive salespeople, whining children, and weary feet. Some consumers embrace the ritual chaos while others recoil in horror. For the mall-weary shopper, help has arrived in the form of the Internet. Online shopping has exploded in recent years and now offers a viable alternative to the bricks-and-mortar experience. However, as my partner and I discovered recently, when it comes to selection, service, pricing, and convenience, there are significant differences between the two options. Which should you choose? It depends on your priorities.

2   Sometimes too much choice leads to confusion, but having a wide selection to choose from is generally considered a good thing. Online shopping makes available millions of products at the click of a mouse. When we explored dozens of sites in our search for a digital video camera, national borders didn't limit us, and we found models with all the latest features and functions. In contrast, when we visited a number of electronics stores—after wasting half an hour looking for a parking space—we found a limited selection of models and options in our price range.

3   While we are not exactly Luddites, we needed the intricacies and features of the latest generation of video cameras explained to us. Most electronics

stores are staffed with knowledgeable salespeople who are only too happy to explain technical jargon, demonstrate a product's features, and offer an opinion on its relative merits. On the other hand, if you are willing to spend time on your computer, online information may well serve your needs. You can do all your research and decision-making electronically by visiting manufacturers' and retail outlets' websites, and even by consulting the opinions of other consumers at product comparison and review sites.

4   "Where can I get the best deal?" is something every consumer wants to know. Ask happy customers the reason for their satisfaction, and the answer invariably involves price. Online merchants can often offer lower prices because they can avoid the overhead (rent, inventory, heat and light, wages, etc.) of conventional stores. Not surprisingly, we found that in-store prices for digital video cameras were routinely higher than those posted by online merchants. Electronics stores have responded to the online competition by routinely offering coupons and special discounts.

5   Shopping online is undoubtedly convenient. As long as you have a credit card, you can shop anywhere, anytime. There are no salespeople to pressure you, and you never have to deal with parking or crowds. However, these advantages are countered by the major inconvenience of returning a damaged or unsatisfactory product, especially if you have to repackage the item and ship it across borders. We were disconcerted by the possibility that we would have to return our video camera, a fragile item that could be easily damaged during shipping. Offsetting the limitations of the bricks-and-mortar experience is the relative speed with which items can be returned or exchanged.

6   So where did we buy our camera? We weighed the pros and cons of the alternative selections, services, prices, and convenience of the two shopping environments, and decided that service—both before and after our purchase—was more important to us than saving money and time by shopping online. While we chose the local electronics store as the supplier that best met our needs, other consumers have different priorities, as the increasing popularity of online shopping demonstrates. Bricks and mortar or mouse and monitor? North Americans should consider themselves fortunate to enjoy the advantages of both—for now.

Questions for Discussion

1. Draft a rough outline for this essay. How is the information organized: in blocks or point by point? Why do you think the author chose this organizational pattern?
2. In your own words, combine the thesis and the main points of this essay in a single sentence. Is it an effective thesis statement? Why?

3. This piece is told from the first-person plural point of view. Consider how the effect on the reader would change if it had been written from either the first-person singular point of view (personal) or from the third-person point of view (impersonal). Did the author choose her point of view wisely? Why?

4. Identify three or four transitional techniques the author has employed to enhance her essay's coherence. (See pages 102–04 for a review of transition strategies.)

5. Early in the essay, the author provides clues as to which shopping option she and her partner chose. Do these hints spoil the conclusion for the reader? Why?

6. Search InfoTrac to find two or three articles that present evidence of the rapid growth of online shopping and its negative effects on the profitability of bricks-and-mortar stores.

7. Does it matter to you who wins the battle of the shopping options? Why?

THE GAS-ELECTRIC HYBRID DEMYSTIFIED
Sara R. Howerth

1   A hybrid is a cross between two established varieties of plant, animal, . . . or technology. The hybrid bicycle, for example, combines the features of a road bike with those of an off-road bike to produce a comfortable and efficient bicycle for short distance cycling. For most people today, the word "hybrid" signifies a fuel-efficient, low-emission automobile. Hybrid car technology combines a gasoline or diesel internal combustion engine with a battery-powered electric motor. Its objective is to maximize the best properties of both the gas engine and the electric motor.

2   A gasoline engine is powerful enough for the pickup, torque, and speed any driver requires. Because of the petroleum infrastructure that has developed over the past 100 years, gas-powered vehicles are also easy to refuel and can travel 400 km to 800 km between fill-ups. On the other hand, they are expensive to operate and are becoming even more so as fuel prices rise. More importantly, they are a major cause of the pollution that contributes to smog, environmental degradation, and global warming.

3   Battery-powered electric motors are quiet, efficient, and relatively clean—depending, of course, on how the electricity that charges them is produced. However, they cannot yet travel very far on a charge (some can go 200 km), and most need to be recharged 12 hours or overnight. The technology is evolving rapidly, however, and these limitations of distance and time will probably be significantly reduced in the coming years.

4   The hybrid vehicle uses both types of motors and exploits the advantages of each. A gasoline engine provides the power and torque, while an electric engine adds power and thus reduces the amount of gasoline required. There are two types of hybrid vehicle; the difference between them consists of their approach to the twinning of the two engines.

5   The "mild hybrid" uses a small electric motor that boosts the capability of the gas engine, thus enabling a smaller gas engine to get the same performance as a larger power plant. Small engines consume less gas and produce fewer emissions, so the smaller the gas engine, the more cost and environmental benefit, so long as the electric motor can deliver the performance equivalent of a more powerful engine. Another way the mild hybrid saves fuel is by allowing the gas engine to shut down when the vehicle is stopped, even for a few seconds at a stoplight. The electric engine starts instantly when the accelerator is touched, and it acts as a starter for the gas motor.

6   The "full hybrid" uses the two motors quite differently. Like the mild hybrid, the full hybrid allows the gas engine to shut down when the vehicle is stopped, but it stays off at low speeds (under about 40 km/h), since the vehicle is powered only by the electric motor until more power is required. As speed increases, the gas or diesel motor kicks in automatically and the two work in tandem to provide the power needed for highway driving, acceleration, and climbing. This arrangement means that cars equipped with full-hybrid engines get better mileage in stop-and-start city driving than they do in long-distance highway conditions.

7   Both hybrid models use the power produced by the gas engine to recharge the onboard batteries, so they never need to be recharged by plugging the vehicle into an outlet. In addition, both models use the electric motor as a generator during deceleration; therefore, power that is normally lost as heat when a conventional car brakes is recaptured and sent to the batteries, keeping them charged. This process is called "regenerative braking."

8   Each year, the marketplace offers more hybrid technology models to cost-conscious and environmentally aware consumers. This trend will continue so long as gas prices rise, and so long as people are concerned about the pollution caused by petroleum-powered vehicles. Perhaps the hybrid will be a stepping stone to even more efficient, less polluting technologies, such as hydrogen fuel-cell powered cars. But for now and into the foreseeable future, the hybrid automobile is a technology whose time has arrived.

Questions for Discussion

1. "The Gas-Electric Hybrid Demystified" has a more complex structure than the first two essays in this chapter. To understand how the piece is put together, write an outline for it.

2. What audience did the author have in mind as she wrote this essay? Are her intended readers car enthusiasts? Auto mechanics? Use examples from the essay to support your answer.

3. What methods of paragraph development does Howerth use to help her readers understand her explanation of her subject? Support your answer with specific examples.

4. Search InfoTrac to find another article that discusses the differences between the "full hybrid" and the "mild hybrid." Compare that article to Howerth's essay. Consider level of language, target audience, and the purpose of the two pieces. Which was easier for you to understand? Why?

5. In the last decade, the word "hybrid" has come to signify the type of car that is the subject of this essay. Using the resources of InfoTrac, identify five applications of the word "hybrid" that have nothing to do with automobiles. List the meanings in order of your familiarity with them, from most to least.

JUSTICE AND JOURNALISM
Victor Chen

1   "Justice must not only be done, it must be seen to be done." This principle, in part, accounts for the news media's appetite for stories about our justice system. It is the principle that news organizations always cite when their access to information about the courts, criminals, or police is limited, or when they are prevented from distributing that information. Given the media's apparent concern for the public's knowledge about Canadian justice, it is troubling to learn that what we read, hear, and see is often distorted. The reality of our justice system and what we learn about it from our media are, all too often, two different things. Two aspects of our justice system will serve to illustrate this contrast: the incidence of violent crime and the sentencing of criminals.

2   Occurrences of violent crime have declined steadily in Canada over the past decade. While this fact has occasionally been reported, it doesn't sell newspapers or advertising nearly as well as juicy stories about murder, mayhem, assault, or aggression. The news media are in business to attract an audience, and the pressure to sensationalize is relentless. Hence, while murders constitute about 1% of violent crime committed in Canada, in our news media more than 25% of crime stories are about killings. Since virtually all of our information about crime comes to us from newspapers and news broadcasts, is it any wonder that we have the impression that murders are far more common than they really are? Furthermore, violent crime itself represents about 12% of all crime that is dealt with by our police and courts. Yet, in the media, 50% of

the coverage of criminal activity is devoted to violent crime. We have two societies: an imaginary one, created by the news media, that most of us live in, and the real, less violent one that few of us know about.

3   As well as a distorted view of violent crime, the media give us false impressions about proceedings in the criminal courts. Except in a few notable cases, reporters are not assigned to cover an entire trial; instead, they attend the courtroom only for the sensational opening addresses and for the verdict and sentencing. Very little of what goes on for most of the trial—the evidence, the arguments, the painstaking detail, and the finer points of courtroom procedure—ever appears in the news. What effect does this omission have on our understanding of law and order? In a recent study, J. Roberts and A. Doob demonstrate that the public's understanding of the justice system is distorted. Half of the participants in the study read the newspaper accounts of a trial. The other half read the court documents—transcripts of what had actually taken place during the trial. Of those who read the newspapers, the vast majority (over 60%) thought that the sentence handed down by the judge was too lenient. Less than 15% felt the sentence was too harsh. However, of those who read the court proceedings without the slant provided by reporters and editors, the majority felt the punishment was too harsh. Less than 20% believed that a more severe sentence was warranted, while more than 50% thought the sentence given for the crime was too long (508–12). What does this experiment tell us about how Canadians form their often strongly held opinions about the justice system?

4   The contrast between what our news media tell us about our justice system and the reality of what is going on in the police departments and courtrooms of the nation is an indictment of the sensationalist media. Even more important, this contrast is a sobering reminder that our opinions can be based on a superficial understanding of the issues. The news media will not change; the pressures for sensational reporting are too great. Public opinion will, therefore, be based on distorted impressions. We can only hope that our lawmakers will form their opinions and base their decisions not on media reports and not on the popular opinion which those reports create, but on a careful, researched study of the reality behind the headlines.

Work Cited

Roberts, J., and A. Doob. "Sentencing and Public Opinion: Taking False Shadows for True Substances." *Osgoode Hall Law Journal* 27.3 (1989): 491–515.

Questions for Discussion

1. Which method of contrast has Chen used to organize this essay? Using the information given in the essay, write a point-form outline for an essay organized according to the alternate method. Which organization do you think is more effective? Why?
2. What purpose—other than contrasting the image and reality of our justice system—does the author of this piece have in mind? Does he achieve his purpose?
3. Statistics do not often make very interesting reading. How has the author tried to make the statistics in this essay readable as well as meaningful? Is he successful?
4. So long as they are not overused, rhetorical questions (questions asked for effect rather than to elicit an answer) can be effective in capturing and holding readers' attention. Identify two rhetorical questions in this essay and rephrase them as statements. Which version—question or statement—has more impact on the reader? Why?
5. Parallelism (see Chapter 26) is often used by writers to reinforce the seriousness of a subject or the weight of an argument. Identify four examples of parallel structure that you think contribute effectively to the solemn tone of this essay.

FOR MINORITIES, TIMING IS EVERYTHING
Olive Johnson

1   Left-handedness and homosexuality both tend to run in families. As my husband's family and mine have some of each, it is not surprising that one of our children is left-handed and another homosexual. Both my left-handed daughter and my homosexual son turned out to be bright, funny, talented people with loving friends and family. But their experience of growing up in different minority groups was a striking contrast and an interesting illustration of how societal attitudes change as sufficient knowledge accumulates to make old beliefs untenable.

2   By the time my daughter was growing up, left-handedness was no longer regarded as a sign of immorality or mental deficiency. Almost everybody knew "openly" left-handed friends, teachers and relatives and viewed them as normal people who wrote differently. Except for a little awkwardness in learning to write at school, my daughter's hand preference was simply never an issue. If people noticed it at all, they did so with a shrug. Nobody called her nasty names or banned school library books about left-handed families, as

school trustees in Surrey, B.C., recently banned books about gay families. Nobody criticized her left-handed "lifestyle" or suggested that she might be an unfit role model for young children. Nobody claimed that she *chose* to be left-handed and should suffer the consequences.

3   My gay son did not choose to be different either, but when he was growing up, homosexuality was still too misunderstood to be accepted as just another variant of human sexuality. Because gay people still felt unsafe revealing their sexual orientation, he was deprived of the opportunity of knowing openly gay teachers, friends and relatives. He grew up hearing crude jokes and nasty names for people like him, and he entered adulthood knowing that being openly gay could prevent you from getting a job or renting an apartment. It could also get you assaulted.

4   Bigotry has never been reserved for homosexuality, of course. I am old enough to remember the time when bigotry directed toward other minorities in Canada was similar to that which is still sometimes aimed at homosexuals. In my Vancouver childhood, Chinese were regularly called "Chinks" (the boys in my high school wore black denim "Chink pants" tailored for them in Chinatown). Black people were "niggers," prohibited from staying in most Vancouver hotels. Kids in the special class were "retards" or "morons." Jews were suspected of all sorts of crazy things, and physically disabled people were often regarded as mental defectives.

5   Left-handed children were still being punished for writing with their left hand, particularly in the more religious parts of Canada. (When I was a graduate psychology student in Newfoundland doing research on handed-ness, I discovered that several of my "right-handed" subjects were actually left-handers; at school their left hands had been tied behind their backs by zealous nuns.)

6   The gay children and teachers of my childhood were simply invisible. Two female teachers could live together without raising eyebrows, chiefly because women in those days (especially women *teachers*) were not generally thought of as sexual persons. Two male "bachelors" living together did tend to be sus-pect, and so gay men brave enough to live together usually kept their living arrangements quiet. "Sissy" boys and "boyish" girls took a lot of teasing, but most people knew too little about homosexuality to draw any conclusions. These boys and girls were expected to grow up and marry people of the oppo-site sex. Some of them did, divorcing years later to live with one of their own.

7   Many of the teachers and parents of my childhood who tried to convert left-handed children into right-handers probably believed they were helping children avoid the stigma of being left-handed, just as many misguided ther-apists tried to "cure" patients of their homosexuality to enable them to avoid the stigma of being gay in a heterosexual world.

8   Thanks to advances in our understanding, left-handedness gradually came to be seen as a natural and innate trait. We know now that people do not

choose to be more skillful with one hand than the other; they simply are. While researchers are still debating the precise mechanisms that determine hand preference, there is general agreement that left- and right-handedness are just two different (and valid) ways of being. Left-handers are a minority in their own right, not "deviants" from normal right-handedness.

9   The same is true for sexual orientation. Although we do not yet clearly understand the mechanisms that determine sexual orientation, all indicators point to the conclusion that it results from interactions between genetic, hormonal and possibly other factors, all beyond the individual's control. Like left-handedness, sexual orientation is an innate trait, not a choice or "lifestyle." Like left-handedness, homosexuality is a valid alternative sexuality, not a deviance from "normal" heterosexuality.

10   As with other minorities, attitudes toward homosexuality are inevitably becoming more liberal, at least in Canada. A recent poll, commissioned by the B.C. Teachers' Federation, found that almost 70 per cent of B.C. residents think students should be taught in school to accept homosexuals and treat them as they would other people. (Twenty per cent said homosexuality should be discouraged, 9 per cent said they didn't know and 3 per cent refused to answer.) These results indicate that overt bigotry toward homosexuality is increasingly limited to religious extremists. The Surrey school trustees who voted against having gay and lesbian resource materials in schools are probably at about the same stage of cultural evolution as were the Newfoundland nuns who tied children's left hands behind their backs 40 years ago.

11   Even so, I'm grateful that they're further along the path of enlightenment than their predecessors in medieval Europe, who burned many left-handers and homosexuals at the stake. Being born in the late 20th century was a wise move on the part of my son and daughter. In some things, timing is everything.

Johnson, Olive. "For Minorities, Timing Is Everything." *Globe and Mail* 7 July 1997: A14.

Questions for Discussion

1. To develop the main points of this essay, the author uses her own children as examples. Would the essay have been more effective had she supported her argument with less personal examples? Why?
2. Under what points does the author compare the treatment of left-handedness and homosexuality in Canada in the last century?
3. Comparing two groups is not the purpose of this essay; it is the means the author has chosen to accomplish her purpose. What is the main purpose of this piece? How effective do you think the author is in achieving it?

4. What is the topic sentence of paragraph 10? How is the topic developed? Do you agree with the statement the author makes in the fourth sentence of that paragraph? Why?

5. Consider the final paragraph of this essay. What function does it serve, other than to conclude the piece? What is its effect on readers?

Exercise 15.1

List eight to ten characteristics of two people, or jobs, or courses. Examine your lists and choose characteristics of each that would make a basis for a comparison between the two. Then go back over the lists and choose characteristics that would make a basis for contrast.

Exercise 15.2

Write a comparison or contrast essay on one of the following subjects. Be sure to follow the guidelines for essay development, from selecting a subject, through managing your main points, to outlining your paper and writing your paragraphs.

Two fast-food restaurants
Two magazines with the same target audience (e.g., *Maclean's* and *Time*, *People* and *Us*, *Shift* and *Wired*)
Two approaches to child-rearing
College and university
Two political leaders
Two management styles
Your generation and that of your parents (or grandparents)

Exercise 15.3

 Contrast papers often turn persuasive, but they don't have to. When you are presenting a contrast, try not to be influenced by your own opinion. List the arguments on both sides of three of these controversial issues.

Single-sex schools
Gay marriage
The use of animals in medical research
Nuclear power
Physician-assisted suicide

For one of the topics you worked on in Exercise 15.3, write an essay contrasting the views held by the two sides. Some research may be necessary to find out exactly what the opposing arguments are and to explain those arguments to your reader.

Construct a comparison essay or a contrast essay, using one of the suggestions given below. Develop a thesis statement that reflects the relationship of the two subjects. Before you begin, write an outline of your thoughts, using either the block or the point-by-point method.

Quebec and TROC (the rest of Canada)

Your spouse and the fantasy you had of a spouse before you were married

Two newspapers' coverage of a news event

Your life now with your life five (or ten or twenty) years ago

Working in an office and working at home

Television advertisements for one of these pairs of consumer products: new cars and beer; home-care and personal-care products; financial services and travel services, a fast-food chain and muffler repairs

PART 5

18

Researching Your Subject

Your first step in writing a research paper is the same as your first step in any writing task: select a suitable subject, preferably one you are curious about. Whether you are assigned a topic or choose your own, don't rush off to the library or log onto the Internet right away. A little preparation up front will save you a lot of time and possibly much grief later on.

First of all, if you're not sure what your instructor expects, clarify what is required of you. Next, even if your subject is tentative, check it with the 4-S test: is it significant, single, specific, and supportable (researchable)? If not, refine it by using the techniques discussed in Chapter 3. Finally, consider what approach you might take in presenting your subject. Does it lend itself to a comparison? Process? Cause or effect? If the topic is assigned, often the wording of the assignment will suggest how your instructor wants you to develop it. Deciding up front what kind of paper you are going to write will save you hours of time, both in the library and at your desk.

Exercise 18.1

In the workplace, people rarely have the opportunity to select a research topic without consultation. In some cases, the subject is assigned or approved by a board of directors; in others, a committee is responsible for ensuring that a research project meets the company's needs.

Before you start your own research project, take some time to ensure that your proposed subject is appropriate for the time and space you have been given. The class should be divided into "committees" of four or five people. Each committee should be given four or five pieces of coloured paper, a different colour for each group.

- Each committee identifies a chairperson and a note-taker. At the direction of the chair, each member of the committee presents an idea for a research paper. After each presentation, discuss the subject in terms of its significance to the target audience (the whole class, including the instructor). If the committee feels a subject requires revision to be significant, make these revisions as a group. It is important that the committee come to a consensus regarding any revisions.
- Once each subject is agreed upon as significant, record it on a slip of the coloured paper assigned to your committee.
- Repeat this procedure until your committee has identified at least one significant subject for each of its members.
- Toss your committee's subjects into the company's think tank (a container), along with the subjects submitted by the other committees in the class.
- The chair of each committee draws out of the think tank four or five proposed research subjects. Be sure to draw a representative sampling of colours from other committees.
- As a committee, discuss each subject that has been drawn from the think tank. Since each has already been approved as significant by another committee, your task is to determine whether each proposed subject is single and specific.
- For each subject, record any revisions that the committee deems necessary and briefly explain why.
- Return the revised subjects to their appropriate committees according to the corresponding coloured paper.
- When every committee has received its original proposed research subjects, each group discusses the suggested revisions until everyone understands them.
- Next, as a committee, discuss whether each proposed subject is supportable. What sorts of research materials would you look for to help you explain and defend each subject?
- Record the final version of the proposed research subjects on a flip chart, ready to present to a board of directors. (You should have one subject for each member of the committee.)
- Present your committee's proposed research subjects before the board of directors (the whole class). Discuss the revisions and decide whether each proposal now meets the criteria of the 4-S test.

When you're sure your subject is appropriate and you've decided, at least tentatively, on the approach you're going to take, you are ready to focus on the kind of information you need to look for in your research. For example, if you've been asked to apply four theories of conflict to a case study, you won't waste time discussing the major schools of conflict theory or their

NEL

development over the last few decades. You can restrict your investigation to sources that contain information relevant to your specific subject.

Once you have an idea of the kind of information you need in order to develop your topic, it's time to find the best sources you can. But how will you know if what you've found is "good" information?

Selecting Your Sources

Not all sources are created equal. There's no point in wasting time making notes on a source unless the information is relevant, current, and reliable. Evaluating the quality of source material before you use it is a key step in the research process.

To evaluate a print source, first check it over closely. Scan the table of contents, the headings, and chapters or articles to ensure the book or periodical contains information relevant to your topic. ("Periodicals" are publications that are produced at regular "periods," such as daily newspapers or monthly magazines.) Then check to see where the information comes from: its author, the date it was published, and the organization or company that published it. Most traditional print sources—newspapers, magazines, and scholarly journals—have fact-checkers and editorial boards to ensure that the information they publish is reliable.

Print sources are easier to assess for reliability than electronic sources. Yet the Internet and the World Wide Web have vastly increased the amount of potential research material, and it is essential to learn how to evaluate it. For example, if you are doing a report on a recent business venture or medical breakthrough, the most current information will be online. How do you decide, given the millions of pieces of information out there in cyberspace, what is useful for your specific purpose? Of course, when you use online editions of traditional print sources (e.g., electronic versions of newspapers, magazines, and books), you can assume the same standards of credibility and reliability. The CD-ROM full-text versions of *The Globe and Mail* or the *Financial Times* are no less (and no more) accurate than the printed versions.

With electronic sources that have no hard-copy equivalent, the domain name is one place to begin your evaluation. Does the source's URL end with .com (commercial), .gov (government), or .edu (educational institution)? Sites from these different sources will present data on a topic in different ways. A commercial site will probably attempt to influence consumers as well as to inform them. A .edu suffix suggests the credibility of a recognized college or university, but offbeat student web pages or the informal musings of faculty members at the institution may share the suffix as well.

Another difference between print and electronic sources is authorship. There is seldom any doubt about who wrote a particular book or article. In online material, however, often no author (or date) is identified. Sometimes the person who compiles ("comp") or maintains ("maint") the website is the only one named. For academic research, it's wise to be cautious of "no-name" sources. If you wish to use information from one of these sources, be sure the organization or institution where it originated is reliable. You wouldn't want to be researching the history of discrimination in Canada, for example, and find yourself quoting from the disguised website of a hate organization.

Recognizing that much online work is collaborative and that several writers may have contributed to a potential source, it is a good idea to check out the people who are involved in producing it. Powerful online search engines such as Google make checking the author's reliability easier for electronic sources than it is for print sources. Simply key the author's name into the search engine and then evaluate the results to see if he or she is a credible person in the field. Often you'll be able to check the author's biography, credentials, other publications, and business or academic affiliation. If no author's name is given, you can check out the company, organization, or institution in the same way. Cyber-sleuthing is a useful skill to learn!

In the end, however, with both print and electronic sources, you must apply your own critical intelligence. Is the information timely, accurate, and reliable? Is there evidence of any inherent bias? How can you best make use of the findings to support and enhance your own ideas? The answers to these questions are critical to producing a good research paper.

Taking Good Research Notes

Once you've found a useful source, record the information you need. You'll save time and money by taking notes directly from your sources rather than photocopying everything. Most often, you will need a summary of the information. Follow the instructions on summarizing given on pages 272–75. Alternatively, you can paraphrase (see pages 277–79). Sometimes a quotation is appropriate; when this is the case, it's wise to make a copy of your source. Whenever you take notes—in any form—from a source, be sure to record the information you will need about the source itself. For each published source that you use in your paper, you should write down the following information.

For Books

1. Author(s)' or editor(s)' full name
2. Full title and edition number (if any)
3. City of publication
4. Name of publisher
5. Year of publication
(You will find all this information on the front and back of the title page.)
6. Page(s) from which you took notes

For Internet Sources

1. Author(s)' full name
2. Title of the document
3. Title of the database, periodical, or site
4. Name of the editor (if any)
5. Date of publication or last update
6. Name of the institution or organization sponsoring the site (if any)
7. Network address, or URL
8. Date you accessed the source

For Journal Articles

1. Author(s)' full name
2. Title of the article
3. Name of the journal
4. Volume number of the journal
5. Year of publication
6. Inclusive page numbers of the article
7. Page(s) from which you took notes

For Newspaper or Magazine Articles

1. Author(s)' full name
2. Title of the article
3. Title of the newspaper or magazine
4. Date of publication
5. Inclusive page numbers of the article
6. Page(s) from which you took notes

Some researchers record each piece of information on a separate index card. Others write their notes on sheets of paper, being careful to keep their own ideas separate from the ideas and words taken from sources. (Using a highlighter or a different colour of ink will help you to tell at a glance which ideas you have taken from a source.) Use the technology available to help you record, sort, and file your notes. You can record and file information by creating a database, and you can use a photocopier (usually available in the library) to copy relevant pages of sources for later use. Whatever system you use, be sure to keep a separate record for each source and to include the documentation information. If you don't, you'll easily get your sources confused. The result of this confusion could be inaccurate documentation, which could lead your reader to suspect you of plagiarizing.

Avoiding Plagiarism

Plagiarism is presenting someone else's ideas as your own. It's a form of stealing (the word comes from the Latin word *plagiarius*, which means "kidnapper.") There have been famous cases of respected journalists and academics who have been accused of plagiarizing the articles or books they have written. Suspected plagiarists who are found guilty often lose their jobs. Sometimes the accusation alone is enough to compromise an author's reputation and thus prevent him or her from continuing to work as a scholar or writer.

Students who copy essays or parts of essays from source material, download them from the Internet, or pay someone else to write them are cheating. And, in so doing, they commit a serious academic offence. Sometimes, however, academic plagiarism is accidental. It can result from careless note-taking or an incomplete understanding of the conventions of documentation. It is not necessary to identify the sources of common knowledge (e.g., *The solstice occurs twice a year; B.C. is Canada's westernmost province*) or proverbial sayings (e.g., *Love is blind*), but when you are not sure whether to cite a source, it's wise to err on the side of caution and provide documentation. Statistics should always be cited because the meaning of numbers tends to change, depending on who is using them and for what purpose.

If, after you have finished your first draft, you are not sure which ideas need documenting and which don't, take your research notes and your outline to your instructor and ask. It's better to ask before submitting a paper than to try to explain a problem afterward. Asking saves you potential embarrassment as well as time.

Using the Library

The electronic age has transformed the library—traditionally a warehouse of information contained within print sources—into a Learning Resource Centre: a portal to sources of information such as databases, e-books, e-journals, and the Internet, together with the traditional print and audio-visual resources. With new technology, information retrieval is faster, easier, and more efficient than ever before. However, this fact does not make the library any less intimidating to inexperienced users. Many students are overwhelmed by what at first appears to be a vast and confusing array of collections. Using the library becomes a less daunting prospect when you realize that all of its contents are organized and classified in such a way as to make finding information easy, if not simple. First, you need to know the organizational system used by your library. In this section, we will describe the collections found in most academic libraries, give you tips on how to access them, and summarize their strengths and weaknesses as sources. We will also decode some of the terminology used by library staff to describe and arrange collections.

THE ONLINE CATALOGUE (OPAC)

All but the smallest libraries today use automated catalogue systems to access collections. These online catalogues are commonly called OPACs (Online Public Access Catalogues). They may be stand-alone computer terminals within the library or accessible via the library's website. OPAC search options usually include title, author, subject, or keyword. How you search the catalogue will depend on what you are looking for and on what you already know.

Along with books, the OPAC may list other resources available in the library, such as periodical titles. If a periodical title is available in full-text format from one of the library's subscription databases, there may be a link to the title and, possibly, the text from the OPAC. Many of today's OPACs allow the library to link to several useful online sources of information. Your library's OPAC should be the first place you check for resources when beginning your research paper.

BOOKS

Book collections are represented in the online catalogue and may be searched in a variety of ways: by author, title, subject, keyword, and sometimes call number.

If you know of a particular book by title, choose that option and enter the **title**—*English Online*, for example. If your search is successful, write down the call number of the book. Alternatively, if you know that Eric Crump wrote a book on using the Internet, but you aren't sure of the title, do an **author** search, using the last name first: Crump, Eric. If you don't know of any books or authors in your field of research, begin by doing a **subject** or **subject keyword** search, such as "online English composition instruction." Most systems will respond by identifying relevant holdings and listing instructions to follow at the bottom of the computer screen. One of the biggest advantages of automated systems is that they identify the **status** of the book, letting you know if the book is in or when it is due back. Many systems allow you to place a **hold** on a book that is out. This means that when the book is returned to the library, it will be set aside for a period of time to allow you to go in and pick it up.

In order to find a book on the shelves, you must match the **call number** as it appears on the screen or catalogue card with the number taped on the spine of the book. Every book has a unique call number, and books are arranged on the shelves according to their call numbers. Guide signs are usually posted on the ends of shelving units (sometimes called **stacks**). Most colleges and universities use the **Library of Congress** (**LC**) system of classification, which uses a letter or combination of letters to begin the call number. The LC system is generally more suitable to academic collections than the Dewey decimal system used by public and smaller libraries.

A title keyword search is often the fastest way of retrieving books on your topic. If the library carries a book on your subject of research, chances are the topic will appear somewhere in the title.

Strengths	Weaknesses
• Author may be an authority on the subject	• Information cannot be as current as other sources
• Information is usually reliable (if published by a respected publisher)	
• Several aspects of the topic may be covered in the book	

PERIODICALS

Your library's collection of **periodicals**—publications that are issued at regular intervals, such as magazines, newspapers, and scholarly or technical journals—may contain useful articles on the subject you are researching.

To locate specific articles, you need to use one or more of the databases and periodical indexes available from your library. Before you begin, read the description of the database to determine if it includes periodicals on your topic. Each database has specific strengths and will allow you to search a subject in a wide variety of periodicals. From the selection offered in your library, you may be able to search databases such as EBSCOhost, ProQuest, LexisNexis, or InfoTrac.[1] These databases are delivered using the Internet, but are paid for by the library; their use is limited by licence agreements to students and staff of the institution that pays for them. It may be possible to access them from home, but you will need a log-in or other means of identifying yourself as a student. Check with the library staff at your institution to find out more about access from your Internet service provider.

Databases have been created with users in mind; they have search interfaces that make finding information relatively simple. Once you have found the database you wish to use, you will be presented with a search box similar to those found on Internet search engines. Here you type in a word or phrase that relates to your research topic. For example, if you were researching the art movement known as Impressionism, you would enter this word in the text box. The search mechanism of the database would look for this term, and all articles containing the word "Impressionism"

---

[1]Your purchase of *Essay Essentials,* Fourth Edition, entitles you to free access to InfoTrac.

would be displayed on the screen. From the list, you would select those you think may be useful to you.

Most databases allow you to e-mail the results of your search. If you are pressed for time, do a quick search, e-mail the results to yourself, and check them later for relevancy. You can always delete them and start over.

Increasingly, full-text articles are included with each new release of these databases. This means you can print or download the text of an article without having to retrieve the actual magazine or journal. If you find a reference to a magazine article for which the full text is not available, be sure to note the title and date of the periodical in which it appeared; then check to see if your library subscribes to this periodical.

Strengths

- Contain current information
- Articles in databases are easy to retrieve
- Databases are accessible 24/7

Weaknesses

- Some articles may be opinion pieces but presented as factual

ENCYCLOPEDIAS

A useful source of general information on a topic is an encyclopedia; it is often a good place to begin your research. There are many types of encyclopedias, and several are now available online or on CD-ROM. Information is easy to find, usually through a user-friendly search screen, and CD versions of encyclopedias often include sound or video clips to enhance the text. You might begin your search with a general encyclopedia such as *Britannica*, *Colliers*, or the *World Book* and then move on to a specialized encyclopedia related to your subject. Look in the reference collection for a call number area that matches the one in which you found books on your topic (for example, medical encyclopedias are in the R section), or ask the reference librarian if a specialized encyclopedia exists on your subject.

Strengths

- Provide a good overview of a subject
- Often list titles of major books on the subject
- Online editions are convenient, easy to use, and updated regularly

Weaknesses

- Information in print versions may be dated

THE INTERNET

Most students today have grown up with the Internet and are accustomed to using it to meet their information needs. They turn to the Net for news reports, weather updates, and maps to destinations near and far; to find phone numbers and addresses, purchase theatre tickets, shop online, and plan vacations. They use search engines to locate information about topics ranging from medical disorders to building a deck. Canada is one of the world's leaders in per capita Internet use.

When you are gathering material to write a research paper, however, you should keep in mind that the Internet is not necessarily a reliable source of information. (Some instructors will not accept websites as legitimate resources for research papers, so be sure you have permission to use them before you spend hours on Google or Yahoo.) Evaluating Internet information for reliability is not a simple matter. We've already mentioned checking the domain name as one place to begin. A good guide to evaluating websites can be found at http://www.lib.berkeley.edu/TeachingLib/Guides/Internet/Evaluate.html.

The number of results called up by a keyword search can be overwhelming. All search engines offer advice on effective searching from the home page. Here are four ways you can limit and focus the results of an initial query:

- Use one or more of the shortcuts available on most search engines.
- Use an Advanced Search screen that allows you to combine concepts. For example, the Advanced Search screen at Google allows you to search for an exact phrase such as "breast cancer" and include the word "treatment" without the word "chemotherapy." You can also limit the type of domain you'd like returned (.edu) as an example, choose the language you'd like for your results, and decide where you'd like the search engine to look for your terms (in the title only, for example).
- Put quotation marks around your search term(s). Doing so turns your keyword search into a search for a phrase ("breast cancer treatment," for example).
- Use the tilde sign (~) or plus and minus signs to add or eliminate concepts. Plus and minus signs add or subtract words from your search word or phrase ("breast cancer" + treatment – chemotherapy). Google interprets the tilde as a signal to search for variations of a word. For example, "~treatment" would include the plural, "treatments," in your results list.

Get in the habit of using more than one search engine to vary results. A subject directory search engine, such as Yahoo, may be a better starting point for your topic than a general keyword search.

Librarians regularly scour the Internet for exceptional websites as good sources of information. Look for these recommendations on your library's website, or look for links to government websites or sources such as the Internet Public Library (http://www.ipl.org) from your library's OPAC.

Strengths	Weaknesses
• Fast and convenient	• Number of results can be daunting
• Excellent resource for directory-type information	• Reliability and authority can be difficult to determine
• Websites of leading experts are sometimes available	• Amount of information is staggering (most users will not browse past the first two or three pages of results, so valuable information may be missed)
• Increasingly, authoritative information sources are posted on the Net (e.g., government documents, databases of scholarly journals)	• Questionable content may appear to be valid

OTHER SOURCES

Most libraries contain other collections that may help you in your research. Don't overlook the possibility of finding useful information in the **audio-visual collection**, which normally includes videotapes, films, audiotapes, DVDs, and slide presentations. **Government publications** are another good source of information. The government, as one of the country's largest publishers, may have produced documents related to your topic. Many of these documents are available on the Internet.

Finally, the library is not the only source of information you can use. Interviews with people familiar with your subject are excellent sources because they provide a personal view, and they ensure that your paper will contain information not found in any other paper the instructor will read. It is perfectly acceptable to e-mail a question or set of questions to an expert in a field of study. **Original research**, such as surveys or questionnaires that you design, distribute, and analyze can also enhance your paper. Doing your own research is time-consuming and requires some knowledge of survey design and interpretation, but it has the advantage of being original and current.

A good research paper will contain references to material from a variety of sources. Some instructors require a minimum number of references from several types of sources: books, periodicals, encyclopedias, interviews, etc. Most, but not all, institutions will allow you to use Internet sources, but use them with caution. Be mindful that anyone can place information, reliable or not, on any subject at a website. For this reason, it is best to use research gathered from reliable sources such as books, encyclopedias, scholarly journals, and reputable magazines.

As you conduct your research and think about your paper, keep your reader in mind. Every teacher faced with a pile of papers hopes to find some that are not simply a rehash of known facts. Before anything else, teachers are learners; they like nothing better than discovering something new. If you cannot find new information about your subject, be sure to provide an original interpretation of the evidence you find.

Exercise 18.2

This exercise will quickly familiarize you with your school's library: the variety and extent of its holdings; the different ways you and your library can communicate with each other; and basic library policies you should know about.

1. Does your library provide handouts or other documents on how to conduct research? On how to format electronic source citations?
2. Check your library's OPAC (online catalogue) for a video that deals with study skills. Make a note of the title and call number.
3. How many newspapers does the library subscribe to? Name two and note how long the library keeps them.
4. What is the URL for the library's website? Find two unique resources or services listed there.
5. Is it possible to contact the library staff by e-mail? If yes, note the e-mail address.
6. What is the loan period for books? What is the fine charged for an overdue video?
7. What does it mean when a book is "on reserve"?
8. Using one of your library's subscription databases, search for an article on smoking-cessation programs. Give the title of the article, the author's name, and the name and date of the publication in which it appeared.
9. Using a different database from the one you searched in question 8, find a Canadian newspaper article that deals with genetically modified (GM) foods. Provide the article title and the name of the newspaper it appeared in.
10. Can you access your library's databases from your home Internet service provider? If so, what procedure do you follow?

19

Summarizing, Paraphrasing, and Quoting

Once you have identified and evaluated your research sources, you must make accurate notes of the information you think you might use in your paper. There are many ways to take notes, ranging from jotting down single words or phrases to photocopying entire articles. You will save time if you remember that there are three ways of incorporating source information into your own writing: **summary**, **paraphrase**, and **direct quotation**. When you summarize or paraphrase, you restate in your own words the idea(s) of another speaker or writer. When you quote, you reproduce the exact words of another speaker or writer. Before we examine those three techniques, it is worthwhile to review what plagiarism is and how to avoid it.

PREVENTING PLAGIARISM

You can avoid plagiarism—the single biggest problem faced by students writing research papers and the instructors who mark them—by acknowledging (citing) all information you found in the sources you used for your paper. Cite your sources in an approved documentation style (usually MLA or APA).

Here are some guidelines to follow:

- Facts or sayings that are common knowledge do not have to be attributed; that is, you need not give sources for them. Examples: "Quebec City is the capital of Quebec"; "Sir John A. Macdonald was Canada's first prime minister"; "Beauty is in the eye of the beholder."

- Any passage, long or short, taken word for word from a source must be marked as a quotation, and you must cite its source. (See below, pages 280–86, and Chapter 20.)
- Facts, opinions, or ideas that you discovered on the Internet, found in a book or article, or learned from any other source—even if you express the information in your own words—must be acknowledged. (See below, pages 280–86, and Chapter 20.)
- Facts, opinions, or ideas that you remember reading or hearing somewhere cannot be presented as your own. If you cannot find and acknowledge the source, you should not use the information.
- If you are not sure whether a fact, opinion, or idea should be acknowledged, err on the side of caution and cite it. It's better to be safe than sorry.

Summarizing

When you summarize information, you find the main ideas in an article, essay, report, or other document, and rephrase them. You shorten (condense) the most important idea or ideas in the source material and express your understanding of them in your own words. The purpose of summarizing is to give the reader an overview of the article, report, or chapter. If the reader is interested in the details, he or she will read the original.

It's hard to overstate how valuable the ability to summarize is. Note-taking in college is one form of summarizing. Abstracts of articles, executive summaries of reports, market surveys, legal decisions, research findings, and records (called "minutes") of meetings, to name only a few kinds of formal documents, are all summaries. Thesis statements and topic sentences are essentially summaries; so, often, are conclusions. In committee, group, or teamwork, imagination and creativity are valuable, but the ability to summarize is even more so. There is no communication skill that you will need or use more than summarizing.

As a matter of fact, you summarize for yourself and others in every conversation you have. With friends, you may summarize the plot of a movie you've just seen or what happened in class this morning. When your mother calls, you'll summarize the events of the past week that you want her to know about. But most of us are not very good at summarizing effectively, especially in writing. It is a skill that doesn't come naturally. *You need to practise it.* You'll improve very quickly, however, if you think about what you're doing—that is, if you are conscious rather than unconscious of the times and the circumstances in which you call upon your summarizing skills. The following exercise will get you started.

Exercise 19.1

1. In groups of three or four, choose a movie you have all seen, a course you have all taken, a party or concert you have all attended, or a book you have all read. Then, without discussing your topic first, spend five minutes each writing a one-paragraph summary. After you have written your summary, use a highlighter to accent your main points.
2. Read and compare your summaries. What similarities and differences do you notice? Can you all agree that one summary is both complete and accurate? If not, spend another five or ten minutes discussing which are the main ideas and which are secondary to a discussion of your topic.
3. Now revise your one-paragraph summary to include all the main ideas and no secondary details.
4. Once again, read and compare each other's paragraphs. Which paragraph summarizes the topic best? What features does this paragraph have that the others lack?

HOW TO WRITE A SUMMARY

The work you summarize can be as short as a paragraph or as long as a book, as the following passage demonstrates:

> One of Edward de Bono's books is called *Six Thinking Hats*. [In it] he proposes that you adopt six different mind sets by mentally putting on six different coloured hats. Each hat stands for a certain way of thinking about a problem. By "putting on the hat" and adopting a certain role, we can think more clearly about the issues at hand. Because we're only "playing a role," there is little ego riding on what we say, so we are more free to say what we really want to say. De Bono likens the process of putting on the six hats one at a time to that of printing on a multicoloured map. Each colour is not a complete picture in itself. The map must go through the printing press six times, each time receiving a new colour, until we have the total picture.

Perrin, Timothy. "Positive Invention." *Better Writing for Lawyers*. Toronto: Law Society of Upper Canada, 1990. 51.

Notice that Perrin is careful to tell his readers the source of the ideas he is summarizing: both the author and the book are identified up front.

Before you can summarize anything, you need to *read* and *understand* it. The material you need to summarize is usually an article, essay, or chapter (or some portion of it). Depending on how much of the piece you need, your summary will range from a few sentences to one or two paragraphs.[1] Here's how to proceed:

1. Read through the piece carefully, looking up any words you don't understand. Write their meanings between the lines, above the words they apply to.
2. Now read the article or essay again. Keep rereading it until you have grasped the main ideas and formed a mental picture of their arrangement. Highlight the title, subtitle, and headings (if there are any). The title often identifies the subject of the piece, and a subtitle usually indicates its focus. If the article is long, the writer will often divide it into a number of smaller sections, each with its own heading. These headings usually identify the main points. If there are no headings, pay particular attention to the introduction—you should find an overview of the subject and a statement of the thesis—and the conclusion, which often summarizes the information and points to the significance of the topic.
3. In point form, and in your own words, write out a bare-bones outline of the piece. Your outline should consist of the controlling idea (thesis) of the article and the main ideas, in the order in which they appear. Do not include any supporting details (statistics, specific facts, examples, etc.).
4. Working from your outline, draft the summary. In the first sentence, identify the article or essay you are summarizing (by title, enclosed in quotation marks) and the author (by name, if known). Complete the sentence by stating the author's controlling idea. Here's an example:

In his essay "The Canadian Climate," D'Arcy McHale divides Canadians into two types: warm and cool.

Then state, in order, the author's main points. After each sentence in which you identify a main point, include any necessary explanation or clarification of that point. (The author, remember, developed each idea in the supporting details.) Try to resist going back to the article for your explanation. If you have truly understood the article, you should be

---

[1]This restriction applies only to the kind of research paper we are discussing in this part: one prepared for a college course. Other kinds of summary are longer. A précis, for example, is one-third the length of the source document. An abstract, which is a summary of a dissertation, academic paper, or public presentation, can be several paragraphs long.

able to explain each point from memory. If the author's conclusion contains any new information (i.e., is more than a summary and memorable statement), briefly state that information in your conclusion.

5. Revise your draft until it is coherent, concise, and makes sense to someone who is unfamiliar with the original work. It's a good idea to get someone to read through your summary to check it for clarity and completeness.

6. Don't forget to acknowledge your source. (Chapter 20 will show you how.)

The paragraph below summarizes the essay found on pages 204–05. Read it first, before you read the summary that follows.

In his essay "The Canadian Climate," D'Arcy McHale divides Canadians into two types: "warm" and "cool." The first category includes people who are enthusiastic about Canada's scenery, climate, and recreational activities, which they encourage newcomers to enjoy. Warm Canadians are also sincerely interested in learning about what life is like in the visitor's country of origin. In contrast, Cool Canadians are negative about their country and find it hard to believe that anyone from a warm climate would choose to endure the cold, bleak Canadian winters. Cool Canadians are not interested in detailed information about the visitor's country of origin, either; they are comfortable with their stereotypes. Finally, McHale acknowledges that the two types are mixed: each can at times behave like the other. Canadians, like the weather, are unpredictable, and newcomers are encouraged to accept them as they are and for themselves.

This seven-sentence paragraph (140 words) captures the gist of McHale's 600-word essay. Admittedly, it isn't very interesting. It lacks the flavour of the original. Summaries are useful for conveying an outline or a brief overview of someone else's ideas, but by themselves they are not very memorable. Details and specifics are what stick in a reader's mind; these are what your own writing should provide.

A summary should be entirely in your own words. Your ability to identify and interpret the author's meaning is evidence of your understanding of the article or essay. If you must include a short phrase from the source because there is no other way to word it, enclose the quoted material in quotation marks.

When writing a summary, do not

- introduce any ideas not found in the original
- change the proportion or emphasis of the original
- introduce your own opinion of the material

Following the first five steps of the process outlined above, summarize "Ready, Willing . . . and Employable," which appears on pages 74–75. When you have completed your work, exchange papers with a partner. Use the following checklist to critique each other's summary.

	Good	Adequate	Try Again
1. The first sentence gives the title and the author's name.			
2. The essay's thesis is clearly and concisely reworded.			
3. Each main point (topic sentence) is restated in a single sentence.			
4. Each main point is briefly explained.			
5. The summary includes no secondary details that could be eliminated without diminishing the reader's understanding.			
6. The summary is balanced and objective.			
7. The paragraph flows smoothly; there are no obvious errors in sentence structure, grammar, spelling, or punctuation.			

Exercise 19.3

Select an article from a professional journal in your field. Summarize it by following the six steps given on pages 274–75. Assume your reader is a professional in the field.

Exercise 19.4

Choose an article that interests you from one of the regular sections (e.g., business, medicine, education, music, art) of a general news magazine such as *Maclean's*, *Time*, *Newsweek*, or the *Economist*. Summarize the article for a friend who is not an expert in the field and who has not read it. Do not evaluate the article or give your opinion about it. In a paragraph of approximately 150 to 200 words, simply inform your friend of its contents. Don't forget to cite your source!

Paraphrasing

When you paraphrase, you restate someone else's ideas in your own words. Unlike a summary, a paraphrase includes both the main and supporting ideas of your source. The usual purpose of a paraphrase is to express someone else's ideas more clearly and more simply—to translate what may be complex in the original into easily understandable prose. A paraphrase may be longer than the original, it may be about the same length, or it may be shorter. Whatever its length, a good paraphrase satisfies three criteria:

1. It is clear, concise, and easy to understand.
2. It communicates the idea(s) of the original passage.
3. It doesn't contain any idea(s) not found in the original passage.

Occasionally, you may need to clarify technical language or explain an aphorism, a proverb, or other saying that states a principle, offers an insight, or teaches a point. Statements that pack a lot of meaning into few words can be explained only at greater length. For example, one of the principal tenets of modern biology is "ontogeny recapitulates phylogeny." It simply isn't possible to paraphrase this principle in three words. (It means that as an embryo grows, it follows the same pattern of development that the animal did in the evolutionary process.)

Exercise 19.5

Working with a partner or a small group, discuss the meaning of the following expressions. When you are sure you understand them, write a paraphrase of each one.

1. A picture is worth a thousand words.
2. Money talks.
3. More haste, less speed.
4. Birds of a feather flock together.
5. Too many cooks spoil the broth.

To paraphrase a passage, you need to dig down through your source's words to the underlying ideas and then reword those ideas as clearly and simply as you can. Like summarizing, the ability to paraphrase is not an inborn talent; it takes patience and much practice to perfect it. But the rewards are worth your time and effort. First, paraphrasing improves your reading skill as well as your writing skill. Second, it improves your memory. In order to paraphrase accurately, you must thoroughly understand what you've read—and once you understand something, you're not likely to forget it.

First, let's look at how *not* to paraphrase. Assume we are writing an essay on designing an energy-efficient home, and we want to use the information given in the following paragraph.

> The site and how the building relates to it is a critical determinant in the calculation of energy consumption. The most profound effects, and the ones the individual has least control over, are the macro-climatic (regional) factors of degree days, design temperature, wind, hours of bright sunshine, and the total solar insolation. Other factors which can have an enormous effect on the energy consumption of a house are micro-climatic. These include the topography of a site, the sun path, specific wind regime, vegetation, soil, and the placement of other buildings.

Argue, Robert. *The Well-Tempered House: Energy-Efficient Building for Cold Climates*. Toronto: Renewable Energy, 1980. 14.

There are two pieces of information in this paragraph that we want to include in our essay:

1. Some of the factors influencing energy consumption relate to the climate and weather patterns of the region (macro-climatic factors).
2. Some of the factors influencing energy consumption relate to the specific characteristics of the building site (micro-climatic factors).

If we are not careful, or if we don't have much experience with paraphrasing, our paragraph might look something like this:

> In *The Well-Tempered House*, Robert Argue explains that a designer must consider two critical determinants in building an energy-efficient home. The most important factors, and the ones the individual has least control over, are the macro-climatic (regional) factors of degree days, design temperature, wind, hours of sunshine, and the total solar insolation. The other significant factors are the micro-climatic ones, which include the topography of the site, the sun path, wind regime, vegetation, soil, and the location of other buildings on or near the site.

This is plagiarism. Although we have indicated the source of the information, we have not indicated that the wording is almost identical to that of the original. Of the total 90 words, 50 come from the source. There are no visual or verbal cues to alert the reader that these are Argue's words, not ours. Let's try again.

In *The Well-Tempered House*, Robert Argue identifies two significant influences the cost-conscious home builder must consider in designing an energy-efficient house. The first and strongest influence is the typical weather of the region. The designer must be familiar with such "macro-climatic factors" as "degree days" (the difference between the indoor comfort temperature and the average daily outdoor temperature), "design temperature" (the lowest temperature to be expected during the heating season), wind, and the total effect of the sun. The other influences are called "micro-climatic factors" and include the site's topography (elevation and slope of the land), sun path, prevailing wind pattern, and the presence or absence of vegetation and nearby buildings.

Although this draft is technically a paraphrase rather than plagiarism, it doesn't demonstrate very much work on our part. We have replaced the source's words with synonyms and added explanations where the original is too technical to be easily understood by a general reader, but our paragraph still follows the original too closely. A paraphrase should not be used to pass off someone else's ideas as your own by changing a few words and sentences. A good paraphrase goes further. It uses source information but rearranges it, rephrases it, and combines it with the writer's own ideas to create something new. Let's try once more:

The cost-conscious home builder must consider a number of factors that will affect the energy consumption of his or her new home. The exterior design of the house should take advantage of the natural slope of the land, the presence of sheltering vegetation, prevailing wind patterns, the path of the sun, and other characteristics of the building site (Argue 14). In addition to sufficient insulation, the interior should feature appropriate heating and cooling devices to keep the family comfortable during the coldest winter days and the hottest summer days. To keep costs down, these devices should take advantage of the natural energy sources available: wind, sun, and seasonal fluctuations in temperature can all be used to harness and conserve energy. With careful planning, a new home can be designed to maximize the advantages of even an apparently unlikely site, minimize the negative effects of temperature and weather, and cost surprisingly little to maintain at a comfortable temperature year-round.

Here we have used paraphrase to incorporate information from a published source into a paragraph whose topic and structure are our own. This is how paraphrase can be used both responsibly and effectively. If you want to take ideas more directly from a source, retaining the original arrangement and some of the wording, you should use quotations.

Quoting

Of the three ways to introduce ideas from a source into your research paper, direct quotation is the one you should use least. (The exception is the literary essay, in which quotations from the original work are the evidence in your argument; see, for example, Jess Friedland's essay on pages 320–24.) If you use too many quotations, your paper will be a patchwork of the ideas of others, in their words, and very little of your own thinking will be communicated to the reader. Remember that the main reason teachers assign research papers is to test your ability to find, digest, and make sense of specific information about a topic. If what you hand in consists of a string of quotations, your paper will demonstrate only one of these three capabilities.

In most research papers, the ideas, facts, and statistics are the important things, not the wording of an idea or the explanation of facts or statistics. Occasionally, however, you will find that someone else—an expert in a particular field, a well-known author, or a respected public figure—has said what you want to say eloquently, vividly, more memorably than you could ever hope to say it. In such cases, quotations, *as long as they are short and not used too frequently*, are useful in developing your topic. Carefully woven into your paragraphs, they help convince the reader of the validity of what you have to say. Use quotations in writing the way you use salt in cooking: sparingly.

You can quote from two kinds of sources—

- people you know, or have heard speak, or have interviewed
- print, electronic, or recorded materials (e.g., books, articles, CD-ROMs, websites, films, tapes)

—and your quotation may be long or short.

BLOCK AND SPOT QUOTATIONS

If the material you are quoting is more than 40 words or four typed lines, it is a long—or **block**—quotation. After you have introduced it, you begin the quoted passage on a new line and indent all lines of the quotation 10 spaces or 2.5 cm from the left margin. *Do not put quotation marks around a block quotation.* The ten-space indentation is the reader's visual cue that this portion of the paragraph is someone else's words, not yours. Here's an example:

Committees put a lot of thought into the design of fast foods. As David Bodanis points out with such good humour in *The Secret House*, potato chips are an example of total destruction foods. The wild attack on the plastic wrap, the slashing and tearing you have to go through is exactly what the manufacturers wish. For the thing about crisp foods is that they're louder than non-crisp ones. . . . Destructo-packaging sets a favourable mood. . . . Crisp foods have to be loud in the upper register. They have to produce a high-frequency shattering; foods which generate low-frequency rumblings are crunchy, or slurpy but not crisp. . . .

Companies design potato chips to be too large to fit into the mouth, because in order to hear the high-frequency crackling, you need to keep your mouth open. Chips are 80 percent air, and each time we bite one we break open the air-packed cells of the chip, making that noise we call "crispy." Bodanis asks:

How to get sufficiently rigid cell walls to twang at these squeaking harmonics? Starch them. The starch granules in potatoes are identical to the starch in stiff shirt collars. . . . [In addition to starch,] all chips are soaked in fat. . . . So it's a shrapnel of flying starch and fat that produces the conical air-pressure wave when our determined chip-muncher finally gets to finish her chomp.

Ackerman, Diane. *A Natural History of the Senses.* New York: Random House, 1990. 142–43.

Notice that Ackerman is careful to tell her readers the source of her quotations. To introduce the first one, she gives the author's full name and the title of his book. To introduce the second quotation, which is from the same book, she simply identifies the author by surname. Thus, she doesn't waste words by repeating information, nor does she leave readers wondering where the quotation came from. (The only information missing is the publication data—city, publisher, and date—which is provided in the list of sources. See Chapter 20 for information on how to document your sources.)

A **spot quotation** is a word, a phrase, or a short sentence that is incorporated into one of your own sentences. *Put quotation marks before and after a spot quotation.* The quotation marks are a signal to the reader that these aren't your words; a new voice is speaking. The following paragraph contains several spot quotations.

"You are what you quote," in the words of the American essayist Joseph Epstein, himself a heavy user of quotations and the writer who introduced "quotatious" into my vocabulary. Winston Churchill understood the value of a well-aimed quotation: as a young man he read a few pages of *Bartlett's Familiar Quotations* every day to spruce up his style and compensate for his lack of a university education. [Gradually,] he transformed himself from a quotatious writer into the most quoted politician of the western world. . . . Fowler's *Modern English Usage* warns against quoting simply to demonstrate knowledge: "the discerning reader detects it and is contemptuous," while the undiscerning reader finds it tedious. A few years ago Garry Trudeau made fun of George Will's compulsive quoting by inventing a researcher who served as "quote boy" in Will's office: "'Quote boy! Need something on the banality of contemporary society.' 'Right away, Dr. Will!'" . . . As for me, I say don't judge, because you might get judged, too. That's how the quotation goes, right?

Fulford, Robert. "The Use and Abuse of Quotations." *Globe and Mail* 11 Nov. 1992: C1.

HOW TO MODIFY A QUOTATION

In addition to illustrating how to introduce and format block quotations and how to punctuate spot quotations, the examples above also show how to modify a quotation to fit your space and suit your purpose. Although *you must quote exactly and never misrepresent or distort your source's intention*, you may, for reasons of conciseness or smoothness, omit or add a word or phrase or even a sentence or two.

- To leave out a word or words, indicate the omission by replacing the word(s) you've omitted with three spaced dots called **ellipses** (. . .). If the omission comes at the end of your sentence, add a fourth dot as the period.
- If you need to add or change a word or words to make the quoted passage more readable within your paragraph, use **square brackets** around your own words, as we did when we added "[In addition to starch,]" in Ackerman's second block quotation from Bodanis and "[Gradually,]" to Fulford's paragraph.

    If you have omitted some words from a source, you may need to add a transitional phrase or change the first letter of a word to a capital: [T]hus. Another reason for changing words in a quoted passage is to keep the verb tenses consistent throughout your paragraph. If you are writing in the present tense and the passage you are quoting is in the past tense, you can change the verbs to present tense (so long as the change doesn't distort the meaning) and put square brackets around them so the reader knows you have made these changes.

Modifying short quotations to make them fit smoothly into your own sentences without altering the source's meaning takes practice. Reread the paragraph that we have quoted on pages 281–82. Notice that to make Fulford's original slightly shorter and easier to read, we made a couple of minor alterations to the original. The signals to the reader that something has been added or left out are the same as those used in a block quotation: square brackets and ellipses.

HOW TO INTEGRATE QUOTATIONS INTO YOUR WRITING

When you decide to quote source material, you should introduce it so that it will blend as seamlessly as possible into your writing. Don't simply park someone else's words in the middle of your paragraph; you'll disrupt the flow of thought. If Diane Ackerman were not so skillful a writer, she might have "dumped" quotations into her paragraph instead of integrating them. Contrast the readability of the paragraph below with that of Ackerman's second paragraph (on page 281).

> Companies design potato chips to be too large to fit into the mouth because, in order to hear the high-frequency crackling, you need to keep your mouth open. Chips are 80 percent air, and each time we bite one, we break open the air-packed cells of the chip, making that crispy noise. "The starch granules in potatoes are identical to the starch in stiff shirt collars." Starch is just one of the ingredients that contribute to the crispiness of potato chips. "All chips are soaked in fat." "So it's a shrapnel of flying starch and fat that produces the conical air pressure wave when our determined chip-muncher finally gets to finish her chomp."

Without transitional phrases, the paragraph lacks coherence and doesn't make sense. Not convinced? Try reading the two paragraphs aloud.

Every quotation should be introduced and integrated into an essay in a way that makes clear the relationship between the quotation and your own argument. There are four ways to integrate a spot quotation.

1. You can introduce it with a phrase such as "According to X," or "Y states" (or *observes*, or *comments*, or *writes*), followed by a comma. Different verbs suggest different attitudes toward the quoted material. For example, "Fulford *suggests* that writers should not overuse quotations" is more tentative than "Fulford *warns* that writers should not overuse quotations." Other verbs you can use to introduce quotations are *asserts*, *notes*, *points out*, *maintains*, *shows*, *reports*, and *claims*. Choose your introductory verbs carefully, and be sure to use a variety of phrases. The repetitive "X says," "Y says," and "Z says," is a sure way to put your reader to sleep.

2. If your introductory words form a complete sentence, use a colon (:) to introduce the quotation.

   George Bernard Shaw's poor opinion of teachers is well known: "Those who can, do; those who can't, teach."

Oscar Wilde's opinion of teachers is less famous than Shaw's but even more cynical: "Everybody who is incapable of learning has taken to teaching."

3. If the passage you are quoting is a couple of words, a phrase, or anything less than a complete sentence, do not use any punctuation to introduce it.

Oscar Wilde defined fox hunters as "the unspeakable in full pursuit of the uneatable."

Wilde believed that people "take no interest in a work of art until they are told that the work in question is immoral."

4. If you insert your own words into the middle of a quotation, use commas to separate the source's words from yours.

"It is a truth universally acknowledged," writes Jane Austen at the beginning of *Pride and Prejudice*, "that a single man in possession of a good fortune must be in want of a wife."

In general, periods and commas are placed inside the quotation marks (see the examples above). Unless they are part of the quoted material, colons, semicolons, question marks, exclamation marks, and dashes are placed outside the quotation marks. Use single quotation marks to mark off a quotation within a quotation.

According to John Robert Colombo, "The most widely quoted Canadian aphorism of all time is Marshall McLuhan's 'The medium is the message.'"

Block quotations are normally introduced by a complete sentence followed by a colon (for example, "X writes as follows:"). Then you copy the quotation, beginning on a new line and indenting 10 spaces or 2.5 cm. If your introductory statement is not a complete sentence, use a comma or no punctuation, whichever is appropriate. The passage by Diane Ackerman on pages 280–81 contains examples of both ways to introduce block quotations. Turn to it now. Can you explain why Ackerman has used no punctuation to introduce the first block quotation and a colon to introduce the second one?

For each of the following quotations, make up three different sentences as follows:

a. Introduce the complete quotation with a phrase followed by a comma.
b. Introduce the complete quotation with an independent clause followed by a colon.
c. Introduce a portion of the quotation with a phrase or statement that requires no punctuation between it and the quotation. Use ellipses and square brackets, if necessary, to signal any changes you make in the original wording.

Example: Education is the ability to listen to almost anything without losing your temper or your self-confidence. (Robert Frost)

a. According to Robert Frost, "Education is the ability to listen to almost anything without losing your temper or your self-confidence." (complete quotation introduced by phrase + comma)
b. Robert Frost had a peculiar notion of higher learning: "Education is the ability to listen to almost anything without losing your temper or your self-confidence." (complete quotation introduced by independent clause + colon)
c. Robert Frost defined education as "the ability to listen to . . . anything without losing [one's] temper or [one's] self-confidence." (partial quotation introduced by phrase requiring no punctuation; changes indicated with ellipses and square brackets)

1. I find the three major administrative problems on a campus are sex for the students, athletics for the alumni, and parking for the faculty. (Clark Kerr, former president of the University of California)
2. Education is not a *product*: mark, diploma, job, money—in that order; it is a *process*, a never-ending one. (Bel Kaufman, author of *Up the Down Staircase*)
3. School days, I believe, are the unhappiest in the whole span of human existence. (H. L. Mencken, American humorist)
4. In the first place, God made idiots. This was for practice. Then he made school boards. (Mark Twain)
5. Education makes a people easy to lead, but difficult to drive; easy to govern, but impossible to enslave. (Lord Brougham, founder of the University of London, 1825)

TIPS ON USING QUOTATIONS IN YOUR WRITING

1. **Use quotations sparingly and for a specific purpose**, such as *for emphasis* or *to reinforce an important point.* Avoid the temptation to produce a patchwork paper—one that consists of bits and pieces of other people's writing stuck together to look like an original work. Far from impressing your readers, overuse of quotations will give them the impression you have nothing of your own to say.
2. **Be sure every quotation is an accurate reproduction of the original passage.** If you need to change or omit words, indicate those changes with square brackets or ellipses, as appropriate.
3. **Be sure every quotation is relevant.** No matter how interesting or well worded, a quotation that does not clearly and directly relate to your subject does not belong in your essay. An irrelevant quotation will either confuse readers or annoy them (they'll think it's padding), or both.
4. **Make clear the link between the quotation and your controlling idea.** Don't assume readers will automatically see the connection you see between the quotation and your topic sentence. Comment on the quotation so they will be sure to make the connection you intend. If you have used a block quotation, your explanatory comment can sometimes form the conclusion of your paragraph.
5. **Always identify the source of a quotation.** This can be done by mentioning in your paragraph the name of the author and, if appropriate, the title of the source of the quotation. Include the page number(s) in a parenthetical citation. See Chapter 20 for details, and follow the format your instructor prefers.

Exercise 19.7

Read the passages below and then, with your partner, discuss and answer the questions that follow.

1. Whenever college teachers get together informally, sooner or later the conversation turns to students' excuses. The stories students tell to justify absences or late assignments are a source of endless amusement among faculty. These stories tend to fall into three broad thematic categories.

   Accident, illness, and death are at the top of the list. If the stories were true, such incidents would be tragic, not funny. But how could any instructor be expected to keep a straight face at being told, "I can't take the test on Friday because my mother is having a vasectomy"? Or "I need a week's extension because my friend's aunt died"? Or—my personal favourite—"The reason I didn't show up for the final exam was because I have inverse testosterone"?

Problems with pets rank second in the catalogue of student excuses. Animals take precedence over tests: "I can't be at the exam because my cat is having kittens and I'm her coach"; and they are often responsible for a student's having to hand in an assignment late. The age-old excuse "My dog ate my homework" gets no more marks for humour than it does for originality, but occasionally a student puts a creative spin on this old chestnut. Would you believe "My paper is late because my parrot crapped in my computer"?

In third place on the list of students' tales of extenuating circumstances are social commitments of various sorts. "I was being arraigned in Chicago for arms dealing"; "I had to see my fence to pick out a ring for my fiancée"; and "I can't take the exam on Monday because my Mom is getting married on Sunday and I'll be too drunk to drive back to school" are just three examples collected by one college teacher in a single semester.

An enterprising computer programmer could easily compile an "excuse bank" that would allow students to type in the code number of a standard explanation and zap it to their professors. I suspect, however, that there would be little faculty support for such a project. Electronic excuses would lack the humour potential of live ones. Part of the fun comes from watching the student confront you, face to face, shamelessly telling a tale that would make Paul Bunyan blush.

1. Are all the quotations relevant to the subject of this brief essay? Are they sufficiently limited, or could the essay be improved by leaving any out?
2. Underline the specific connections the writer makes between her quotations and her controlling idea.
3. What purpose does the concluding sentence serve? Would the essay be equally effective without it? Why?

2. U.S. federal drug policy, especially the mandatory minimum sentences for drug offenders enacted by Congress in 1987, has so distressed federal judges that approximately 10 percent of them will not hear drug trials. Judge Jack B. Weinstein of Brooklyn, N.Y., is a case in point. In an April 1993 memo to all the judges in his district, he announced that he would no longer preside over trials of defendants charged with drug crimes:

> One day last week I had to sentence a peasant woman from West Africa [with four dependent children] to forty-six months. . . . On the same day I sentenced a man to thirty years as a second drug offender—a heavy sentence mandated by the Guidelines and statute. These two cases confirm my sense of frustration about much of the cruelty I have been party to in connection with the "war on drugs" that is being fought by the military, police, and courts rather than by our medical and social institutions.

I myself am unsure how this drug problem should be handled, but I need a rest from the oppressive sense of futility that these cases leave. Accordingly, I have taken my name out of the wheel for drug cases. This resolution leaves me uncomfortable since it shifts the "dirty work" to other judges. At the moment, however, I simply cannot sentence another impoverished person whose destruction can have no discernible effect on the drug trade. I wish I were in a position to propose a solution, but I am not. I'm just a tired old judge who has temporarily filled his quota of remorselessness.

The sentencing guidelines that Congress requires judges to follow are so harsh they cause, in Weinstein's words, "overfilling [of] our jails and . . . unneccessary havoc to families, society, and prisons." As a senior judge, Weinstein can choose the cases he hears. But 90 percent of judges are not so fortunate. After they have imposed on a low-level smuggler or a poverty-stricken "mule" a sentence far harsher than those mandated for someone convicted of rape or manslaughter, one wonders how—or if—judges can sleep at night.

"The War on Drugs: A Judge Goes AWOL." *Harper's Magazine* Dec. 1993: 18.

1. This writer uses both block and spot quotations to develop her point. Where does she make clear the connection between the block quotation and her topic?
2. The original passage from which the writer extracted her spot quotation reads as follow: "Most judges today take it for granted, as I do, that the applicable guideline for the defendant before them will represent an excessive sentence. The sentencing guidelines result, in the main, in the cruel imposition of excessive sentences, overfilling our jails and causing unnecessary havoc to families, society, and prisons." Why did the writer modify the quotation the way she did?
3. In tip 4 (see page 286), we advise you not to introduce a quotation and just leave it hanging but to comment on it. Where does this writer comment on the quotations she has used?

Additional Suggestions for Writing

1. Interview someone two generations removed from you (e.g., a grandparent, an elderly neighbour) about his or her life as a young person. What were the sources of entertainment? Leisure activities? Work? Family responsibilities? Major challenge or concerns? Goals? Write an essay in which you tell this person's story, using summary, paraphrase,

2. Interview a friend, classmate, or relative on one of the following topics. Then write an essay using summary, paraphrase, and quotation to help tell your reader how your interviewee answered the question.
   a. If you were to live your life over knowing what you know now, what would you do differently?
   b. Explain what being a Canadian (or a parent, or childless, or unemployed, or successful, or a member of a particular religious group) means to you.
   c. "Once I was _____; now I am _____."
3. Research a topic of particular interest to you and write an essay using summary, paraphrase, and quotation to develop your main points.
4. Select a news article or a group of articles dealing with a current issue in your career field. In a paragraph of approximately 200 to 300 words, summarize the issue for your instructor, who has just returned from spending six months in the wilderness without access to either print or electronic media.

20

Documenting
Your Sources

Documentation is the process of acknowledging source material. When you document a source, you provide information that

1. tells your readers that the ideas they are reading have been borrowed from another writer, and
2. enables your readers to find the source and read the material for themselves.

When acknowledging your sources in a research paper, you need to follow a system of documentation. There are many different systems, but one of the most widely used is that of the Modern Language Association (MLA). The instructions and examples in this chapter are a slightly simplified version of the principles outlined by Joseph Gibaldi in the *MLA Handbook for Writers of Research Papers*, 6th ed. (New York: MLA, 2003. http://www.mla.org). Most instructors in English and the humanities require students to use MLA style.

Instructors in the social sciences (psychology, sociology, political science, and economics) usually expect papers to conform to the principles of APA style, based on the *Publication Manual of the American Psychological Association*, 5th ed. (Washington, DC: APA, 2001. http://www.apa.org). You will find instruction and examples of APA style in Appendix B.

For research papers in the biological sciences, your instructor may require Council of Biology Editors (CBE) style, presented in *Scientific Style and Format: The CBE Manual for Authors, Editors, and Publishers* (http://www .councilscienceeditors.org).

Many academic institutions publish their own style guides, which are available in college and university libraries and bookstores. Be sure to ask your instructor which documentation style he or she prefers.

209

Introduction: The Two-Part Principle of Documentation

Documentation styles vary in their details, but all styles require authors to

- identify in a parenthetical reference any information taken from a source, and
- list all sources for the paper on a separate page at the end.

A **parenthetical reference** (called a **parenthetical reference citation** in APA style) tells the reader that the information preceding the parentheses[1] is borrowed from a source and provides a key to the full identification of that source. For the most part, footnotes are no longer used to document source material; they are used to give additional information that cannot be conveniently worked into the body of your paragraph. (Note the example in this paragraph.)

A **Works Cited** list (called **References** in APA style) is a list of all the sources from which you have borrowed words, ideas, data, or other material in your paper.[2] Preparing and presenting a Works Cited list requires paying close attention to the details of presenting the information required in each entry. The format—including the order of information, capitalization, and punctuation—prescribed by your style guide must be followed *exactly*. This requirement may sound picky, but there is a good reason to abide by it.

Every kind of source you use requires a particular format. If entries are formatted correctly, an experienced reader can tell by glancing at them what kinds of sources you have used: books, journal articles, newspaper articles, Web documents, etc. If you use the wrong style, or leave something out, or scramble the elements in a citation, you will mislead or confuse your reader. Fortunately, technology is available to help you make the task of documenting much less onerous than it once was. Before you begin taking notes, find a reference manager program such as EndNote or ProCite. (See http://www.isiresearchsoft.com for these and other managers.) Some programs offer a 30-day free trial. Different programs have different features, but most will help you keep track of the notes you've taken from various sources, and all will format your Works Cited or References list for you.

---

[1]A punctuation note: *parentheses* means the pair of curvy punctuation marks: ( ). *Brackets* are the pair of square marks that surround altered words or phrases in a quotation: [ ].
[2]Formerly, this list was called a *Bibliography*.

How to Punctuate Titles in MLA Style

Depending on your instructor's preference, you may *italicize* or <u>underline</u> titles and subtitles of any work that is published as a whole—e.g., the names of books, plays, periodicals (newspapers, magazines, and journals), films, radio and television programs, compact discs—or underline them if you are using a pen. Put quotation marks around the titles of works published within larger works—e.g., the names of articles, essays, poems, songs, and individual episodes of television or radio programs. Also put quotation marks around the titles of unpublished works, such as lectures and speeches. Use capital letters for the first, the last, and all main words in a title and subtitle even if your source capitalizes only the first word in a title.

Parenthetical References in MLA Style

Every time you include in your paper a quotation, paraphrase, summary, fact, or idea you have borrowed from another writer, you must identify the source in parentheses immediately following the borrowed material. The parenthetical reference tells your reader that what he or she has just read comes from somewhere else, and it points your reader to the complete information about the source in your Works Cited list. Parenthetical references should be as short and simple as possible while still fulfilling these two purposes.

The standard practice in MLA style is to provide the surname of the author of the source material and the page number where the material was taken from. Once your reader has the author's name and page number, he or she can find complete bibliographic information about the source in your Works Cited list at the end of your paper. Of course, electronic sources present a challenge to this author-based citation method because they often lack an identifiable author, and they rarely include page numbers. More on this later.

You need to include a piece of source information only once; don't repeat information unnecessarily. For example, if you've already mentioned the author's name in your paragraph, you only need to give the page reference in the parentheses.

On page 293 is an excerpt from a research paper. The writer uses summary, paraphrase, and quotation, and gives the necessary source information in parentheses immediately following each borrowing. This excerpt also demonstrates how to omit a word or words from a source, using ellipses, and how to add or change a word or words, using square brackets.

The Works Cited list that follows the excerpt gives the reader full bibliographic information about each source.

The attractive young people who are portrayed in tobacco advertising make it easy for viewers to forget the terrible consequences of tobacco addiction. Cigarette advertisements routinely portray happy, energetic young people engaging in athletic activities under invariably sunny skies. The implication of these ads is that smoking is not a deterrent to an active lifestyle; in fact, it may even be a prerequisite (Cunningham 67). — *Full parenthetical citation*

It is difficult to overstate the impact of tobacco advertising on young people. As Cunningham points out,

> Few teenagers begin smoking for cigarettes' inherent physical qualities. Instead, teens are attracted to smoking for its image attributes, such as the five S's: sophistication, slimness, social acceptability, sexual attractiveness, and status. Marketing gives a cigarette a false "personality." (66) — *Block quotation*

— *Abbreviated parenthetical citation*

Is it any wonder that young people continue to take up the habit?

In an effort to reverse the trend of teenage tobacco addiction, the federal government sponsors awareness campaigns to demonstrate how the tobacco industry dupes and manipulates young people. According to Robert Sheppard, the industry plays on teenagers' "need [for] something to rebel against . . . [which] is exactly how cigarette manufacturers market their wares" (20). To counteract the image of smoking as a symbol of rebellion, government anti-tobacco campaigns present smoking as a symbol of conformity. — *Short quotation with • word changed • words left out • parenthetical citation*

Yielding to pressure from the government and the community, the tobacco industry has begun to sponsor programs aimed at restricting youth access to tobacco products. In a comprehensive review, however, the Ontario Medical Association (OMA) concludes that these programs are ineffective and makes several recommendations to strengthen youth reduction initiatives (OMA). — *Parenthetical citation of paraphrase*

The OMA recommends that all parties interested in reducing tobacco use endorse a comprehensive tobacco control program. The Association offers to work with the Canadian Medical Association and other interested parties to ensure that its position statement is published as widely as possible. And finally, the OMA recommends that all tobacco industry-sponsored programs be carefully monitored in the future (OMA). — *Parenthetical citation of summary*

Works Cited

Cunningham, Rob. *Smoke and Mirrors: The Canadian Tobacco War*. Ottawa: IDRC, 1996.

Ontario Medical Association. "More Smoke and Mirrors: Tobacco Industry-Sponsored Youth Prevention Programs in the Context of Comprehensive Tobacco Control Programs in Canada." A Position Statement. Feb. 2002. 3 Feb. 2005 <http://www.oma.org/phealth/ smokeandmirrors.htm>.

Sheppard, Robert. "Ottawa Butts Up against Big Tobacco." *Maclean's* 6 Dec. 1999: 20–24.

The Wadsworth Essential Reference Card to the
MLA Handbook for Writers of Research Papers,
Seventh Edition (2009)

Using MLA Style

The summary below outlines the essential changes to the Modern Language Association's documentation style as described in the recently published *MLA Handbook for Writers of Research Papers*, Seventh Edition.

(1) PARENTHETICAL REFERENCES

MLA documentation uses parenthetical references in the body of the paper that are keyed to a works-cited list at the end of the paper. A typical parenthetical reference consists of the author's last name and page number.

The colony appealed to many idealists in Europe (Kelley 132).

If you state the author's name or the title of the work in your discussion, do not include it in the parenthetical reference.

> **Penn's political motivation is discussed by Joseph J. Kelley in *Pennsylvania, The Colonial years, 1681-1776*(44).**

To distinguish between two or more sources by the same author, include a shortened title after the author's name. When you shorten a title, begin with the word by which the work is alphabetized in the list of works cited.

Penn emphasized his religious motivation (Kelley, *Pennyslvania* 116).

When a reference to an electronic source includes paragraph numbers rather than page numbers, use the abbreviation **par.** or **pars**. followed by the paragraph number or numbers.

> **The earliest type of movie censorship came in the form of licensing fees, and in Deer River, Minnesota, "a licensing fee of $200 was deemed not excessive for a town of 1000" (Ernst, par.20).**

When the electronic source has no page or paragraph numbers, try to cite the work in your discussion rather than in a parenthetical reference. By consulting your works-cited list, readers will be able to determine that the source is electronic and may therefore not have page numbers.

In her article "Limited Horizons", Lynne Cheney observes that schools do best when students read literature not for practical information but for its insights into the human condition.

(2) WORKS CITED LIST

The works-cited list, which appears at the end of your paper, is an alphabetical listing of all the research materials you cite.

Print Sources: Entries for Articles

Article citations include the author's name, the title of the article (in quotation marks); the title of the periodical (italicized); the year or date of publication; the pages on which the full article appears, without the abbreviations **p.** or **pp.**; and the publication medium.

1. **An Article in a Scholarly Journal**

   For an article in a journal with continuous pagination through an annual volume or separate pagination in each issue, include the volume number, a period, and the issue number.

   Hayes, B. Grant. "Group Counseling in Schools: Effective or Not?" *International Journal of Sociology and Social Policy* 21.3 (2001):12-21. Print.

2. **An Article in a Weekly magazine (Signed/Unsigned)**

   For signed articles, start with the author, last name first. In dates, the day precedes the month (abbreviated except for May, June, and July).

   Corliss, Richard. "His Days in Hollywood." *Time* 14 June 2004: 56-62. Print.

For unsigned articles, start with the title of the article.

"Ronald Reagan." *National Review* 28 June 2004:14-17.
    Print.

3. **An Article in a Monthly Magazine**

Thomas, Evan. "John Paul Jones." *American History* Aug.
    2003: 22-25. Print.

4. **An Article that Does Not Appear on Consecutive Pages**

When, for example, an article begins on page 120 and then skips
to page 186, include only the first page number, followed by a
plus sign.

Di Giovanni, Janine. "The Shiites of Iraq." *National*
    Geographic June 2004:2+. Print.

5. **An Article in a Newspaper (Signed/Unsigned)**

Krantz, Matt. "Stock Success Not Exactly Unparalleled."
    Wall Street Journal 11 June 2004: B1+. Print.

"A Steadfast Friend on 9/11 is Buried." *New York Times* 6
    Aug. 2002, late ed.: B8. Print.

NOTE: Omit an initial *The* from the title of a newspaper even if
the newspaper's actual title begins with the article.

6. **An Editorial in a Newspaper**

Brooks, David. "Living in the Age of Political Segregation."
    Editorial. *Dayton Daily News* 1 July 2004, final ed.: A12.
    Print.

7. **A Letter to the Editor of Newspaper**

Chang, Paula. Letter. *Philadelphia Inquirer* 10 Dec. 2006,
    suburban ed.: A17. Print.

8. **A Book Review in a Newspaper**

Straw, Deborah. "Thinking about Tomorrow." Rev. of
    Planning for the 21st Century: A Guide for Community

Colleges, by William A. Wojciechowski and Dedra
Manes. *Community College Week* 7 June 2004: 15. Print.

Print Sources: Entries for Books

Book citations include the author's name, the book's title
(italicized), and publication information (place, publisher, date,
publication medium). Capitalize all major words of the book's
title except articles, coordinating conjunctions, prepositions, and
the *to* of an infinitive (unless such a word is the first or last word
of the title or subtitle).

9. **A Book by One Author**

   **Bettelheim, Bruno. The Uses of Enchantment: The Meaning
   and Importance of Fairy Tales. New York: Knopf, 1976.
   Print.**

10. **A Book by Two or Three Authors**

    List the first author with last name first. List subsequent authors
    with first name first in the order in which they appear on the title
    page.

    Peters, Michael A., and Nicholas C. Burbules.
    ***Poststructuralism and Educational Research.* Lanham:
    Rowman, 2004. Print.**

11. **A Book by a Corporate Author**

    A book is cited by its corporate author when individual members
    of the association, commission, or committee that produced it are
    not identified on the title page.

    **American Automobile Association. *Western Canada and
    Alaska.* Heathrow: AAA, 2004, Print.**

12. **An Edited Book**

    An edited book is a work prepared for publication by a person
    other than the author. If your focus is on the *author's* work,
    begin your citation with the author's name. After the title and

original publication date (if applicable), include the abbreviation **Ed**. ("Edited by") followed by the editor or editors.

Twain, Mark. *Adventures of Huckleberry Finn.* 1884. Ed. Michael Patrick Hearn. New York: Norton, 2001. Print.

If your focus is on the editor's work, begin your citation with the editor's name followed by the abbreviations **ed.** ("editor") if there is one editor or **eds.** (editors") if there are more than one. After the title, give the author's name, preceded by the word **By.**

Hearn, Michael Patrick, ed. *Adventures of Huckleberry Finn.* By Mark Twain. 1884. New York: Norton, 2001. Print.

13. A Subsequent Edition of a Book

When citing an edition other than the first, include the edition number that appears on the work's title page.

Wilson, Charles Banks. *Search for the Native American Purebloods.* 3rd ed. Norman: U of Oklahoma P, 2000. Print.

14. A Multivolume Work

When all volumes of a multivolume work have the same title, include the number of the volume you are using.

Fisch, Max H., ed. *Writings of Charles S. Peirce: A Chronological Edition.* Vol. 4. Bloomington: Indiana UP, 2000. Print.

If you use two or more volumes that have the same title, cite the entire work.

Fisch, Max H. ed. *Writings of Charles S. Peirce: A Chronological Edition.* 6 vols. Bloomington: Indiana UP, 2000. Print.

When the volume you are using has an individual title, you may cite the title without mentioning any other volumes.

Mareš , Milan. **Fuzzy Cooperative Games: Cooperation with Vague Expectations. New York: Physica-Verlag, 2001. Print.**

If you wish, you may include supplemental information such as the number of the volume, the title of the entire work, the total number of volumes, or the inclusive publication dates.

15. An Illustrated Book or a Graphic Narrative

An illustrated book is a work in which illustrations accompany text written by a person other than the illustrator. If your focus is on the *author's* work, begin your citation with the author's name. After the title, include the abbreviation **Illus**. ("Illustrated by") followed by the publication information.

> Frost, Robert. *Stopping by Woods on a Snowy Evening*. Illus. Susan Jeffers. New York: Dutton-Penguin, 2001. Print.

If your focus is on the *illustrator's* work, begin your citation with the illustrator's name followed by the abbreviation **illus**. ("illustrator"). After the title, give the author's name, preceded by the word **By**.

> Jeffers, Susan, illus. *Stopping by Woods on a Snowy Evening*. By Robert Frost. New York: Dutton – Penguin, 2001. Print.

A graphic narrative is a work that contains text and illustrations created by one or more authors. Cite a graphic narrative the same way you would cite a book.

> Bechdel, Alison. *Fun Home: A Family Tragicomic*. Boston: Houghton, 2006. Print.

16. The Foreword, Preface, or Afterword of a Book

> Campbell, Richard. Preface. *Media and Culture: An Introduction to Mass Communication*. By Bettina Fabos. Boston: Bedford, 2005. vi-xi. Print.

17. A Translation

> Garcia Marquez, Gabriel. *One Hundred Years of Solitude*. Trans. Gregory Rabassa. New York: Avon, 1991. Print

18. The Bible

Italicize the title, and give full publication information.

The New English Bible with the Apocrypha. Oxford Study ed. New York: Oxford UP, 1976. Print.

19. The Qur'an

Holy Qur'an. Trans. M. H. Shakir. Elmhurst: Tahrike Tarsile Qur'an, 1999. Print

20. A Short Story, Play or Poem in an Anthology

Chopin, Kate. "The Storm." *Literature: Reading, Reacting, Writing*. Ed. Laurie G. Kirszer and Stephen R. Mandell. 7th ed. Boston: Wadsworth, 2010. 313-17. Print.

21. An Essay in an Anthology

Even if you cite only one page of an essay in your paper, supply inclusive page numbers for the entire essay.

Crevel, Rene. "From *Babylon." Surrealist Painters and Poets: An Anthology*. Ed. May Ann Caws. Cambridge: MIT P, 2001. 175-77. Print.

22. More Than One Work from the Same Anthology

List each work from the same anthology separately, followed by a cross-reference to the entire anthology. Also list complete publication information for the anthology itself.

Agar, Eileen. "Am I a Surrealist?" Caws 3-7

Caws, Mary Ann, ed. *Surrealist Painters and Poets: An Anthology*. Cambridge: MIT P, 2001. Print.

Crevel, Rene. "From Babylon." Caws 175-77.

23. An Article in a Reference Book (Signed/Unsigned)

For a signed article, begin with the author's name. For unfamiliar reference books, do not include full publication information.

Drabble, Margaret. "Expressionism." *The Oxford Companion to English Literature.* 6th ed. New York: Oxford UP, 2000. Print.

If the article is unsigned, begin with the title. For familiar reference books, do not include full publication information.

"Cubism." The Encyclopedia Americana. 2004 ed. Print.

NOTE: Omit page numbers when the reference book lists entries alphabetically. If you are listing one definition among several from a dictionary include the abbreviation **Def.** ("Definition") along with the letter and/or number that corresponds to the definition.

"Justice." Def. 2b. *The Concise Oxford Dictionary.* 10th ed. 1999. Print.

24. A Government Publication

If the publication has no listed author, begin with the name of the government, followed buy the name of the agency. You may use an abbreviation if its meaning is clear: **United States. Cong. Senate.**

United States. Office of Consumer Affairs. *2003 Consumer's Resource Handbook.* Washington: GPO, 2003. Print.

When citing two or more publications by the same government, use three unspaced hyphens (followed by a period) in place of the name for the second and subsequent entries. When you cite more than one work from the same agency of that government, use an additional set of unspaced hyphens in place of the agency name.

United States. FAA. *Passenger Airline Safety in the Twenty-First Century.* Washington: GPO, 2003. Print.

---,---,*Recycled Air in Passenger Airline Cabins.* Washington: GPO, 2002. Print.

Electronic Sources:
Entries for Sources from Internet Sites

MLA style recognizes that full source information for Internet sources is not always available. Include in your citation whatever information you can reasonably obtain: the author or editor of the site (if available); the name of the site (italicized); the version number of the source (if applicable); the name of any institution or sponder (if unavailable, include abbreviation **N.p.** for "no publisher given"); the date of electronic publication or update (if unavailable, include the abbreviation **n.d.** for "no date of publication"); the publication medium; and the date you accessed the source. MLA style recommends omitting the URL from the citation unless it is necessary in finding the source.

25. An Entire Web Site

Nelson, Cary, ed. *Modern American Poetry*. Dept. of English, U of Illinois, Urbana-Champaign, 2002. Web. 26 Mar. 2009

26. A Document within a Web Site

"June 3, 1800: President John Adams Moves into a Tavern in Washington D.C." *History.com*. History Channel, 2007. Web. 23 Mar. 2009.

27. A Home Page

Walker, Janice R. Home page. *Georgia Southern University*. Dept. of Writing and Linguistics, Georgia Southern U, 5 June 2008. Web. 30 Mar. 2009.

28. A Radio Program Accessed from an Internet Archive

"Teenage Skeptic Takes on Climate Scientists." Narr, David Kestenbaum. *Morning Edition*. Natl. Public Radio. WNYC, New York, 15 Apr. 2008. Transcript. *NPR*. Web. 30. Mar 2009.

29. An E-mail

Mauk, Karen R. Message to the author. 28 Mar. 2009. E-mail.

30. An Online Posting

Sethi, Beth. Online posting, *EnviroMom.* EnviroMom, 2 June 2008. Web. 25 Mar. 2009.

31. A Book

Douglass, Frederick. *My Bondage and My Freedom.* Boston, 1855. *Google Book Search.* Web.28 Mar. 2009.

32. An Article in a Scholarly Journal

When you cite information from an electronic source that has a print version, include the publication information for the print source, the inclusive page numbers if available (if unavailable, include the abbreviation **n. pag.** For "no pagnition given"), the publication medium, and the date you accessed it.

DeKoven, Marianne. "Utopiad Limited: Post-Sixties and Postmodern American fiction." *MFS: Modern Fiction Studies* 41.1 (1995): 75-97. Web. 21 Mar. 2009

33. An Article in a Magazine

McFarland, Keith. "myth of the Fearless Entrepeneur." *Time*. Time, 2 June 2008. Web. 23 Mar. 2009.

34. An Article in a Newspaper

Wyatt, Edward. "Electronic Device Stirs Unease at Book fair." *New York Times*. New York Times, 2 June 2008. Web. 22 Mar. 2009.

35. An Article in a Newsletter

Sullivan, Jennifer S., comp. "Documentation Preserved, New Collections." *AIP Center for History of Physics*39.2 (2007): n.pag. Web. 26 Mar. 2009.

36. A Review

Burr, Ty. Rev. of *Indiana Jones and the Kingdom of the Crystal Skull*, dir. Steven Spielberg. *Boston.com.* New York times, 18 May 2008. Web. 25 Mar. 2009

37. A Letter to the Editor

Chen-Cheng, Henry H. Letter. *New York Times.* New York Times, 19 July 1999. Web. 24 Mar. 2009.

38. An Article in an Encyclopedia

Include the article's title, the title of the database (italicized), the version number (if available), the sponsor, the date of electronic publication, the publication medium, and the date of access.

"Hawthorne, Nathaniel." *Encyclopedia Britannica Online.* Encyclopedia Britannica, 2009. Web. 26 Mar. 2009.

39. A Government Publication

Cite an online government publication as you would cite a print version; end with the information required for an electronic source.

United States. Dept. of Justice. Office of Justice Programs. *Violence against Women: Estimates from the Redesigned National Crime Victimization Survey.* By Ronet Bachman and Linda E. Saltzman. Aug. 1995. Bureau of Justice Statistics. Web. 25 Mar. 2009.

Electronic Sources:
Entries for Sources from Online Databases

Cite a source from an online database as you would cite a print version; end with the title of the database (italicized), the publication medium, and the date of access. If inclusive page numbers are unavailable, use **n. pag.**

40. An Article in a Scholarly Journal

> Schaefer, Richard J. "Editing Strategies in Television News Documentaries." *Journal of Communication* 47.4 (1997): 69-89. *InfoTrac OneFile Plus.* Web. 27 Mar. 2009.

41. A Monthly Magazine Article

> Livermore, Beth. "Meteorites on Ice." *Astronomy* July 1993: 54-48. *Expanded Academic ASAP Plus.* Web. 22. Mar.2009.

42. A News Service

> Ryan, Desmond. "Some Background on the Battle of Gettysburg." *Knight Ridder/Tribune News Service* 7 Oct. 1993: n. pag. *InfoTrac OneFile Plus.* Web. 26 Mar. 2009.

43. A Newspaper Article

> Meyer, Greg. "Answering Questions about the West Nile Virus." *Dayton Daily News* 11 July 2002: Z3-7. *LexisNexis.* Web. 27 Mar. 2009.

Additional Common Sources

44. A Painting or Photograph

Hopper, Edward. *Railroad Sunset.* 1929. Oil on canvas. Whitney Museum of American Art, New York.

NOTE: Cite an online painting or photograph as you cite a print version; end with the title of the Web site or database (italicized), the publication medium, and the date of access.

45. A Nonperiodical Publication on DVD-ROM or CD-ROM

Cite a nonperiodical publication on DVD-ROM or CD-ROM the same way you would cite a book, but include the appropriate publication medium.

"Windhover." *The Oxford English Dictionary.* 2nd ed. Oxford: Oxford UP, 2001. DVD-ROM.

46. A Periodical Publication on DVD-ROM or CD-ROM

Zurbach, Kate. "The Linguistic Roots of Three Terms." *Linguist Quarterly* 37 (1994): 12-47. CD-ROM. *InfoTrac: Magazine Index Plus.* Information Access. Jan. 2001.

47. A Digital File

Russell, Brad. "Work Trip Notes." File last modified on 22 Mar. 2009. *Microsoft Word* file.

Content based on Chapter 18, "MLA Documentation Style," in *The Wadsworth Handbook* by Laurie Kirszner and Stephen Mandell.

For each of the following quotations, write a short paragraph in which you use all or a portion of the quotation and credit it in a parenthetical citation. Be sure to punctuate titles correctly.

1. From a book entitled Getting it done: the transforming power of self-discipline by Andrew J. Dubrin, published by Pacesetter Books in Princeton in 1995. This sentence appears on page 182: "Stress usually stems from your interpretation and perception of an event, not from the event itself."

2. From a journal article by Linda A. White that appeared on pages 385 to 405 of Canadian Public Policy, a journal with continuous paging: "If a clear connection exists between the presence of child care and high levels of women's labour market participation, that would provide good reasons for governments and employers to regard child care as part of an active labour market policy." White's article is entitled Child Care, Women's Labour Market Participation and Labour Market Policy Effectiveness in Canada. The quotation appears on page 389 of the fourth issue of the 27th volume, published in 2001.

3. From the American Institute of Stress website, found on May 2, 2005, at http://www.stress.org: "Increased stress results in increased productivity—up to a point."

4. From a newspaper article that appeared on page A2 in the March 30, 2005 issue of The Vancouver Sun by Nancy Cleeland and found on the elibrary Canada database at your college library. The article is entitled As jobs heat up, workers' hearts take a beating. "For years, occupational health researchers have struggled to come up with formulas for measuring job stress and determining its effect on health."

5. From an interview with Hans Selye, conducted on Jan 1, 1982, shortly before his death, on the topic of his pioneering work on stress and illness: "Stress is the non-specific response of a human body to any demand made upon it."

6. From an e-mail message on the subject of time management from your friend, Janet Ford, on March 5, 2005: "Using a daily planner and checking e-mail only once a day are two ways I've found to manage my stress during the school year."

Prepare a Works Cited list in MLA style for the sources in Exercise 20.1 above.

21

Formatting a Research Paper

The appearance of your paper makes an impression on your reader. A correctly formatted paper reflects the care and attention to detail that instructors value in students' work.

Ask your instructor if he or she has any special requirements for the format of your research assignment. If so, follow them carefully. Otherwise, follow the guidelines in this chapter to prepare your paper for submission. These guidelines are based on MLA style. (You will find instruction on formatting in APA style on our website at http://www.essayessentials4e.nelson.com.) After the guidelines, you will find two model research papers, both formatted according to the MLA principles of documentation. The first, "Uncertain Future: Potential Dangers of Genetically Modified Crops," is an essay on a topic of general interest. The second, "The Evolution of Moral Balance in Charlotte Brontë's *Jane Eyre*," is an essay on a literary topic. Together, they provide examples of most of the possibilities you are likely to encounter when writing and formatting your own research paper.

Paper

Compose your final draft on 22 × 28 cm (8.5 × 11 inch) white bond paper. Be sure to use a fresh cartridge in your printer. If your instructor will accept a handwritten document, make sure it adheres to all of the guidelines that follow, including those regarding ink colour, margins, spacing, etc. Print out or write your research paper on *one side* of the paper only.

Fasten your paper together with a paper clip or a single staple in the upper left-hand corner. Unless your instructor specifically requests, don't bother with plastic or paper covers; most teachers find it annoying to disentangle your essay for marking.

Printing/Typing

Choose a standard, easily readable typeface, such as Times New Roman, in a 12-point font. Use black ink (or dark blue, if you are writing by hand).

Spacing and Margins

Unless you are instructed otherwise, double-space throughout your essay, including quotations and the Works Cited list. In a handwritten paper, write on every other line of a ruled sheet of white paper.

Adequate white space on your pages makes your paper more attractive and easier to read. It also allows room for instructors' comments. Leave margins of 2.5 cm at the top, bottom, and both sides of your paper. If you are using a word processor, click on the "justify left" formatting command.

Indent the first line of every paragraph five spaces or 1.25 cm; use the tab default setting in your word-processing program. Indent all lines of a block quotation ten spaces or 2.5 cm from the left margin.

Title Page

Do not prepare a separate title page unless your instructor requires it. Instead, at the top of the left margin of the first page of your essay, on separate lines, type your name, your instructor's name, the course number, and the date. Leave a double space and centre the title of your essay. Capitalize main words (see Chapter 40, page 478), but do not underline, italicize, or put quotation marks around your title (unless it contains the title of another author's work, which you should punctuate in the usual way).

Header and Page Numbers

Number your pages consecutively throughout the paper, including the Works Cited list, in the upper right-hand corner, 1.25 cm from the top and 2.5 cm from the right edge of the page. Type your last name before the page number. Use a word processor to create a running head consisting of your last name, a single space, and the page number—no punctuation or *p*. See the student papers at the end of this chapter for examples.

Copy

Projecting an Image

As well as presenting your understanding of the topic, a research paper demonstrates your writing skills and your ability to follow specific requirements of documentation and format. Meeting your instructor's submission requirements is as important as any other aspect of the preparation of your paper. This may be the last stage of your writing task, but it is the first impression your reader will have of your work.

The paper that follows is an example of a properly formatted, documented essay. Before writing her paper, Soraya prepared an outline. Notice that she included in her outline the sources she wanted to refer to in each section. This technique saves hours of paper shuffling when you sit down to write.

Uncertain Future: Potential Dangers
of Genetically Modified Crops

Attention-Getter: Most people eat genetically modified foods every day, but few of stop to consider their potential dangers.

Thesis Statement: Genetically modified crops may have disastrous health, environmental, and sociopolitical effects.

I.   GM foods pose incalculable risks to human health.
   A. GM foods may contain toxic proteins. (Commoner; Mellon)
   B. Despite the testing that goes on during the genetic engineering process, allergic reactions to GM foods are likely. (Hopkin; Humphrys)
   C. The spread of antibiotic resistant bacteria is also a possibility. (Hopkin)

II.   GM crops may have a catastrophic and unpredictable impact on the environment.
   A. Built-in pesticides have benefits, but they kill creatures other than agricultural pests, destroying the balance of ecosystems. (Brown; Suzuki)
   B. Pests develop tolerance to built-in pesticides. (Brown)

C. The transfer of pollen from genetically modified plants to weeds creates superweeds. (Randerson)

III. The social, economic, and political effects of GM crops may be harmful or even disastrous.

    A. Biotechnology corporations use patents and "terminator technology" to control GM seeds; people become dependent on these companies. (Kneen)

    B. GM crops won't feed the world. (Suzuki; Mellon)

Summary: The health, environmental, and sociopolitical effects of GM crops may be dreadful.

Memorable Statement: More research needs to be done before we can evaluate the impact of GM technology. Right now, the risks are largely unknown and unpredictable.

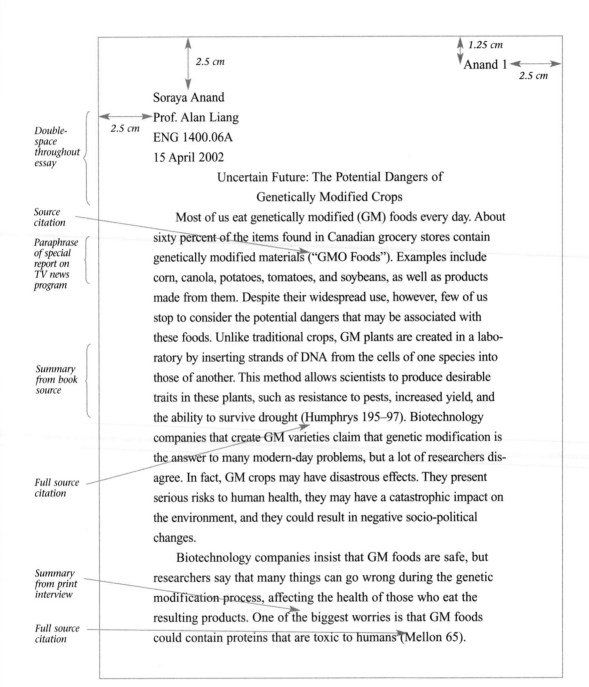

Soraya Anand

Prof. Alan Liang

ENG 1400.06A

15 April 2002

Uncertain Future: The Potential Dangers of

Genetically Modified Crops

Most of us eat genetically modified (GM) foods every day. About sixty percent of the items found in Canadian grocery stores contain genetically modified materials ("GMO Foods"). Examples include corn, canola, potatoes, tomatoes, and soybeans, as well as products made from them. Despite their widespread use, however, few of us stop to consider the potential dangers that may be associated with these foods. Unlike traditional crops, GM plants are created in a laboratory by inserting strands of DNA from the cells of one species into those of another. This method allows scientists to produce desirable traits in these plants, such as resistance to pests, increased yield, and the ability to survive drought (Humphrys 195–97). Biotechnology companies that create GM varieties claim that genetic modification is the answer to many modern-day problems, but a lot of researchers disagree. In fact, GM crops may have disastrous effects. They present serious risks to human health, they may have a catastrophic impact on the environment, and they could result in negative socio-political changes.

Biotechnology companies insist that GM foods are safe, but researchers say that many things can go wrong during the genetic modification process, affecting the health of those who eat the resulting products. One of the biggest worries is that GM foods could contain proteins that are toxic to humans (Mellon 65).

Marginal annotations:

Double-space throughout essay

Source citation

Paraphrase of special report on TV news program

Summary from book source

Full source citation

Summary from print interview

Full source citation

Measurements: 2.5 cm, 1.25 cm, 2.5 cm, Anand 1, 2.5 cm, 2.5 cm

Barry Commoner, a senior scientist at City University of New York, points out that recent discoveries prove that the results of DNA transfer are unpredictable. Transferring genes from one organism to another, he says, "might give rise to multiple variants of the intended protein--or even to proteins bearing little structural relationship to the original one" (45). Margaret Mellon notes that "as scientists manipulate systems that they don't completely understand, one of the unexpected effects could be turning on genes for toxins" (65).

Quotation from magazine article

Abbreviated citation

Summary from article, with full citation

Allergic reactions are also a concern (Hopkin 60). In the mid-1990s, scientists tried to genetically improve soybeans with a gene from brazil nuts. The beans caused allergic reactions in people allergic to brazil nuts, so development was stopped (Humphrys 219–20). Supporters of GM technology cite this case as an example of the effectiveness of the testing process, but John Humphrys, the author of *The Great Food Gamble,* says that we may not be so lucky in the future:

Author and title of book source

> The brazil nut allergen was well known and could be specifically tested for . . . . In other cases, of course, the allergen might not be known. It is entirely possible that its effects might appear only over a period of time. It might produce a form of allergy of which we have no experience. It might simply not be identified. Far from exonerating the industry, what this little tale tells is that the risks exist. (220–21)

10 sp

Block quotation from book

The spread of antibiotic resistant bacteria--bacteria that cannot be killed by known antibiotics--is another potential problem. Food engineers often use antibiotic resistant genes when designing GM crops (Greenpeace). The possibility that "resistance genes might

Paraphrase from website

Abbreviated book citation

Full citation for website

somehow jump from GM foods to bacteria in a consumer's gut" is small, but it cannot be ignored (Hopkin 61). If such a jump occurs, antibiotic resistant bacteria could quickly spread, adding to the already serious medical problem of antibiotic resistance.

Genetically modified crops may also harm the environment. Most GM plant varieties are engineered to be resistant to pests such as insects. Supporters of GM crops point out that the farmers who plant them do not have to spray chemical pesticides on their fields, which is good for the environment (Brown 52). Yet there are other consequences as well. Studies indicate that insect-resistant GM crops may kill not only agricultural pests but also other creatures that happen to be exposed to them, such as monarch butterflies and green lacewing caterpillars (Brown 53–54). Long-term effects could be unpredictable but significant enough to affect whole ecosystems. David Suzuki warns readers:

> If we grow fields of crops that are toxic to all organisms except humans, what will that do to beneficial insects, or to the important microorganisms that live in our soils?
>
> This could have serious repercussions because depletion of insect numbers, for example, would lead to fewer birds and small mammals, and could have other implications up and down the food chain.

In addition, even the defenders of GM crops are realizing that insect pests will develop a tolerance to built-in insecticides (Brown 54; McHughen 108). When this occurs, entire crops may suddenly fail, causing enormous losses. To prevent this disaster, farmers in the United States and elsewhere are now required to set aside a part of their farmland for crops that have not been genetically modified. In

Paragraph topic developed by paraphrase and block quotation

Block quotation from article on website (no page, paragraph, or section numbers given)

Paraphrase of idea found in two sources

these areas, "insects that have acquired some resistance . . . breed with those that have not, diluting the resistance trait" (Brown 57). Many environmentalists question the effectiveness of this strategy. They claim that the areas set aside "are either too small or too poorly designed to keep insect resistance at bay for long" (57). As resistance develops, another form of chemical control will have to be used or food engineers will have to develop new GM crop varieties, causing more environmental devastation.

Short quotation integrated into sentence

The transfer of pollen from a genetically modified species to other plants nearby can also lead to environmental damage. The main reason is that many GM crops are designed to be resistant to herbicides--chemical substances that kill plants. As a result, farmers can spray their fields with herbicides to eliminate weeds without damaging their own crops ("Herbicide"). The problem starts when pollen from one of these GM plants is carried to another plant species, such as a weed. The weed obtains the herbicide-resistant gene and can then grow unchecked, since it can no longer be killed by herbicides. It becomes a so-called superweed (Brown 55). According to a study commissioned by English Nature, the advisory body on conservation for the government of the United Kingdom, many superweeds already exist in Canada. Consequently, farmers are often forced to use older, stronger herbicides to kill them (Randerson).

Summary of encyclopedia article

Summary of online magazine article

The social, economic, and political implications of GM crops are also worrying. One problem often cited by critics is that a few large corporations control the industry. Because GM seeds can be patented, these companies not only dictate the price of seeds but also hold "intellectual property" rights for their products

(Humphrys 197–98). Brewster Kneen, the author of *Farmageddon: Food and the Culture of Biotechnology*, explains the results:

Words left out

> To say the seed is sold . . . is misleading, because in a sense the owners of the technology, the seed companies, do not sell it at all; they rent it out to the farmer for a season. The farmer is not allowed to keep any of the crop for replanting or to share it with a neighbor because the technology [is] owned and patented by one or another major transnational corporation. (107)

Word changed

To protect its interests, one company uses what has been called "terminator technology," which makes plants sterile (Robbins). As a result, farmers cannot save seeds from their plants to produce another harvest; they must buy new seeds instead. Kneen argues that as GM crops become more popular, control of the global food supply shifts dangerously. Eventually, he says, corporate ownership of seeds "will end the ability of the majority of the world's people to feed themselves and will make them dependent on corporate seed suppliers" (61).

Paragraph topic developed by quotations and paraphrase

In light of such practices, many people question what Bill Lambrecht, the author of *Dinner at the New Gene Café*, calls "the grand promise by some of the companies . . . that they will be able to more capably feed the world" with GM crops. Increased productivity will not solve the problem of starvation in developing countries because, as David Suzuki says, "most food shortages are caused by political and social issues, not an overall lack of food production capacity." There is more than enough food in the world, but it doesn't get to those in need (Mellon 64). Drought-tolerant GM crops could potentially benefit people in many countries, but

chances are that these people will not be able to afford them
(Mellon 64).

The jury is out on GM foods. Scientists, corporations, governments, and the public continue to debate their pros and cons. In the
meantime, most of us unknowingly eat products containing genetically modified ingredients every day. As we reach for the corn chips,
we should realize that GM crops may have dreadful and unexpected
health, environmental, and socio-political consequences. More
research and testing need to be done before we can evaluate this
technology and its impact on our lives and on the world. Right now,
the risks are still largely unknown and unpredictable.

Works Cited

Brown, Kathryn. "Seeds of Concern." *Scientific American*
    Apr. 2001: 52–57.

Commoner, Barry. "Unravelling the DNA Myth: The Spurious
    Foundation of Genetic Engineering." *Harper's* Feb. 2002:
    39–47.

"GMO Foods." *The National*. CBC-TV. Toronto. 23 Aug. 2001.
    Transcript.

Greenpeace. "The Secret Ingredient." 10 Apr. 2002
    <http://www.greenpeace.ca/e/resource/publications/gmo/
    secret_ingredient.pdf>.

"Herbicide." *The Columbia Encyclopedia*. 2001 ed. 10 Apr. 2002
    <http:// www.bartleby.com/65/he/herbicid.html>.

Hopkin, Karen. "The Risks on the Table." *Scientific American*
    Apr. 2001: 60–61.

Humphrys, John. *The Great Food Gamble*. London: Hodder and
    Stoughton, 2001.

Kneen, Brewster. *Farmageddon: Food and the Culture of
    Biotechnology*. Gabriola Island: New Society Publishers, 1999.

Lambrecht, Bill. Interview. Canada AM. CTV. 1 Oct. 2001.
    Transcript.

McHughen, Alan. *Pandora's Picnic Basket: The Potential and
    Hazards of Genetically Modified Foods*. New York: Oxford
    UP, 2000.

Mellon, Margaret. Interview. *Scientific American* Apr. 2001: 64–65.

Randerson, James. "Genetically-modified Superweeds 'Not
    Uncommon.'" *New Scientist* 5 Feb. 2002. 10 Apr. 2002
    <http://www.newscientist.com/news/news.jsp?id=ns99991882>.

Robbins, John. Interview. *Times-Herald 13* Jan. 2002: 3.

Suzuki, David. "Genetically Modifying Our Food." Science Matters series. 3
    Nov. 1999; 10 Nov. 1999. 10 Apr. 2002 <http://www
    .davidsuzuki.org/Dr_David_Suzuki/Article_Archives/>.

The following essay won the Sydney Singh Memorial Award at Grant MacEwan College in 2000. This award is given annually to the student who has written the best essay analyzing a work of literature in an English 101 class.

The Evolution of Moral Balance
in Charlotte Brontë's *Jane Eyre*

Introduction: Brontë's use of balancing elements contributes to the impact of *Jane Eyre*.

Thesis statement: Jane is pulled in opposing directions: between the values of Helen Burns and those of Bertha Mason; between the spirituality of St John Rivers and the sensuality of Rochester. Through her struggles with these opposing elements, Jane eventually finds a position on the moral continuum that satisfies her.

I.   Helen Burns and Bertha Mason represent the externalization of "the division of the Victorian female psyche into its extreme components of mind and body." (Showalter 68)

  A. Helen is an asexual child, focused on her spirituality to the point of physical self-denial.

  B. Bertha is a highly sexual woman, whose excessive indulgence has caused her to lose her reason.

  C. Brontë destroys the two "polar personalities" to make way for the integration of Jane's physical and spiritual beings. (Showalter 68)

  D. The values represented by Helen and Bertha influence Jane's moral development.

  E. The lessons she has learned are most clearly evident when she rejects Rochester's proposition.

II.   One of Rochester's arguments for an affair is that nobody will be harmed by it because Jane has no family to offend.

  A. Jane initially seems to accept his reasoning. (356)

  B. Helen's indoctrination about the value of one's good conscience (81) prevents her from acquiescing.

  C. She cannot live without self-respect. (356)

  D. Bertha's story shows her that if she were to become Rochester's mistress, she would share that fate: madness and estrangement from Rochester.

  E. Jane's moral position between the two extremes offered by Bertha and Helen is tested both by Rochester's proposition and by St John's proposal.

III. St John Rivers and Rochester are two characters who balance each other on many levels, from looks to lifestyle. The extremes they represent push her toward middle ground.
   A. Description of Rochester: 129–30.
   B. Description of St John: 386.
   C. Rochester's past: 355.
   D. St John's past: 393.
   E. Jane is offered contrasting choices: a passionate, illicit affair vs. a pious marriage of convenience.
   F. On the surface, the proposals are in contrast, but both would force her to suppress a part of her nature.
   G. Both proposals threaten the fulfillment Brontë has in mind for Jane. (Eagleton 33)
   H. Jane resists temptation; Brontë saves her for a transformed Rochester.
IV. *Jane Eyre* ends with Jane no longer having to compromise herself in order to be with Rochester.
   A. The humbled Rochester is no longer asking Jane to abandon her conscience to live in sin.
   B. Rochester and Jane are now a perfect match because he has moved away from his earlier extremes.
   C. Rochester's physical mutilation is a "symbolic castration" (Chase, qtd. in Gilbert and Gubar 368), but more than his masculinity, his spirit has been transformed.
   D. Humility has taught him wisdom. (495)
   E. Their "perfect concord" (500) is made possible by Rochester's movement away from his earlier extreme to become Jane's ideal mate.
   F. Their blissful marriage is contrasted with the life and death of St John in India.
   G. Brontë pays tribute to St John (417), while still validating Jane's choice.
   H. Jane has achieved an ideal moral balance; she can live a full life on earth and still earn the reward of heaven.
Summary: Jane's refusal to reject the demands of either her mind or her body is the essence of the novel. She is alternately taught and tested by Helen Burns and Bertha Mason, by St John Rivers and Rochester, and ultimately comes to reconcile the two extremes.
Memorable statement: Jane's journey to her own satisfying moral code and a life that celebrates it are intensified by Brontë's use of balancing elements.

Jess Friedland

Professor MacDonald

EN101-354X

1 December 2000

The Evolution of Moral Balance in

Charlotte Brontë's *Jane Eyre*

A profusion of balancing elements contribute to the impact of Charlotte Brontë's novel, *Jane Eyre*. Brontë uses these balances to convey the maturation of Jane's value system. The diametrically opposed characters of Helen Burns and Bertha Mason represent the duality of Jane's nature, and ultimately influence her moral choices. The proposals of Rochester and St John Rivers seem antithetical, but display an underlying similarity. Jane is pulled in opposite directions throughout the novel, but her final address to the reader shows that she has found a position on the moral continuum that satisfies her. The balances utilized to demonstrate her journey enhance both our view of Jane's internal struggle and our understanding of her choices.

According to Elaine Showalter, Helen Burns and Bertha Mason represent the externalization of "the division of the Victorian female psyche into its extreme components of mind and body" (68). Brontë's characterizations support this observation. Helen is an unequivocally asexual child, focused solely on her spirituality to the point of physical self-denial. Bertha is an unequivocally sexual woman, who has seemingly lost her mind through excessive indulgence in bodily pleasure. Showalter goes on to say:

> Brontë gives us not one but three faces of Jane, and she
> resolves her heroine's psychic dilemma by literally and
> metaphorically destroying the two polar personalities to make

way for the full strength and development of the central consciousness, for the integration of the spirit and the body. (68)

Jane's rejection of either extreme validates this statement on a
metaphorical level. In the literal sense, however, both Bertha and
Helen influence Jane's morality in more relevant ways than merely
dying. Jane is neither an angel nor a demon, but she certainly ends
up closer to Helen's end of the spectrum than to Bertha's. Their lessons are most apparent during Jane's rejection of Rochester's
proposition.

One of Rochester's main arguments for an affair is that nobody
will be harmed by it as Jane has no family to offend. Jane pleads
with herself to "tell him you love him and will be his. Who in the
world cares for you? or who will be injured by what you do?"
(Brontë 356; ch. 27). Helen's indoctrination of the intrinsic value of
one's own good conscience prevents her from acquiescing. "If all the
world hated you, and believed you wicked, while your own conscience approved you, and absolved you from guilt, you would not
be without friends" (Brontë 81; ch. 8). The opposite must also hold
true: if Jane's conscience does not approve her, Rochester's love will
not matter. Jane will be without her own self-respect. Therefore, she
cannot stifle the "indomitable [. . .] reply--'I care for myself'"
(Brontë 356; ch. 27). Bertha's lesson is more subtle, but equally
effective. Her sexual nature has led her to madness and estrangement
from Rochester. Once her story is told to Jane, the implications are
clear. She must reject a life as Rochester's mistress or potentially
face similar consequences. Jane's moral position between the two
extremes offered by Bertha and Helen is more a function of their
lives than of their deaths. This moral position is tested most notably
by the aforementioned proposition and by the proposal of her cousin.

St John Rivers and Rochester balance each other on many levels, from looks to lifestyle. Again, these extreme options, which are more literally presented to Jane, push her toward middle ground. Jane's first description of Rochester is of "a dark face, with stern features and a heavy brow"; she implies that he is far from being "a handsome, heroic-looking young gentleman" (Brontë 129–30; ch. 12). St John, on the other hand, is "young [. . .] tall, slender," with "a Greek face, very pure in outline: quite a straight, classic nose; quite an Athenian mouth and chin" (Brontë 386; ch. 29). Rochester's past is riddled with "lust for a passion--vice for an occupation" (Brontë 355; ch. 27), whereas St John is called "blameless in his life and habits [. . .] pure-lived, conscientious" (Brontë 393–94; ch. 30). Jane is offered a passionate, illicit affair by one, and a pious marriage of convenience by the other. These proposals are superficially contrary, but if Jane accepted either one, she would be forced to suppress part of her nature.

As Terry Eagleton states in his study of the novel, "Jane [. . .] must refuse Rivers as she has refused Rochester: loveless conventionalism and illicit passion both threaten the kind of fulfilment the novel seeks for her" (33). Fulfillment involves being accepted and loved without moral modification. Jane is sorely tempted, first to turn her back on her conscience for Rochester, and later to turn her back on her heart for St John. Brontë does not allow her to give in to either man at these crucial points, saving her instead for a revised Rochester.

The conclusion of *Jane Eyre* has Jane and Rochester married at last. Jane no longer needs to compromise herself in order to be with him, and his first wife is not the only obstacle that has been removed. The man who insisted that she abandon her conscience to live in sin has changed significantly. Rochester now complements

Jane as never before. His mutilation has been referred to as a "symbolic castration" by Richard Chase (qtd. in Gilbert and Gubar 368), but it is his spirit rather than his masculinity that seems to have been honed. Rochester has been humbled, and the taste of humility has taught him wisdom. He is able to admit to Jane, "I did wrong: I would have sullied my innocent flower--breathed guilt on its purity" (Brontë 495; ch. 37). During their first engagement, Jane was unsure and often uncomfortable about her place in Rochester's life. In her description of their marriage however, she says that "we are precisely suited in character--perfect concord is the result" (Brontë 500; ch. 38). Such a perfect fit is only made possible by Rochester's movement away from his earlier extreme. He has become a close match for Jane on every level, and therefore becomes her ideal mate.

The final three paragraphs of the novel throw this blissful marriage into sharp contrast with the life and imminent death of St John in India. He is greeting his death at the end of ten years of martyrdom with eagerness, while Jane and Rochester are living life to its fullest. Brontë is giving respectful tribute to St John, but there remains a sense of validation for Jane's choices. St John's reason for clinging solely to his spirituality and rejecting his body is that he will not relinquish his "foundation laid on earth for a mansion in heaven" (Brontë 417; ch. 32). There can be no doubt, however, that Jane will be worthy of heaven upon her death. Jane's moral balance is thus portrayed as ideal; she can live a happy, full life on earth and yet not fear eternal damnation.

Jane's refusal to discount entirely either her mind or her body is the essence of the story. The course by which she comes to reconcile the two is compellingly wrought. She is alternately taught and tested by Helen Burns and Bertha Mason, by St John Rivers and Rochester. Jane's journey to her own satisfying moral code, and a life that celebrates it, are intensified by Brontë's use of balancing elements.

Works Cited

Brontë, Charlotte. *Jane Eyre*. Harmondsworth, England: Penguin,
1996.

Eagleton, Terry. "*Jane Eyre*: A Marxist Study." *Charlotte Brontë's*
Jane Eyre: *Modern Critical Interpretations*. Ed. Harold
Bloom. New York: Chelsea House Publishers, 1987. 29–45.

Gilbert, Sandra M., and Susan Gubar. *The Madwoman in the Attic*.
New Haven: Yale UP, 1984.

Showalter, Elaine. "Charlotte Brontë: Feminine Heroine." Jane
Eyre: *Contemporary Critical Essays*. New Casebooks. Ed.
Heather Glen. New York: St. Martin's Press, 1997. 68–77.

PART 6

22

Cracking the Sentence Code

There is nothing really mysterious or difficult about sentences; you've been speaking them since you were two. The difficulty arises when you try to write—not sentences, oddly enough, but paragraphs. Most college students, if asked to write 10 sentences on 10 different topics, could do so without error. However, when those same students write paragraphs, then fragments, run-ons, and other sentence faults appear.

The solution to sentence-structure problems has two parts.

Be sure every sentence you write
1. has both a subject and a verb
2. expresses a complete thought

If English is your first language, your ear may be the best instrument with which to test your sentences. If you read a sentence aloud, you may be able to tell by the sound whether it is complete and clear. Sometimes, however, your ear may mislead you, so this chapter will show you, step by step, how to decode your sentences to find their subjects and verbs. When you know how to decode sentences, you can make sure that every sentence you write is complete.

Read these sentences aloud.

Snowboarding is one of the world's newest sports.
Although snowboarding is still a young sport.

The second "sentence" doesn't sound right, does it? It does not make sense on its own and is in fact a sentence fragment.

Testing your sentences by reading them aloud won't work if you read your paragraphs straight through from beginning to end. The trick is to read from the end to the beginning. That is, read your last sentence aloud and *listen* to it. If it sounds all right, then read aloud the next-to-last sentence, and so on, until you have worked your way back to the first sentence you wrote.

Now, what do you do with the ones that don't sound correct? Before you can fix them, you need to decode each sentence to find out if it has both a subject and a verb. The subject and the verb are the bare essentials of a sentence. Every sentence you write must contain both. There is one exception:

In a **command**, the subject is suggested rather than stated.

Consider these examples.

Sign here. = [You] sign here. (The subject you is implied or understood.)
Charge it. = [You] charge it.
Play ball! = [You] play ball!

Finding Subjects and Verbs[1]

A sentence is about *someone* or *something*. That someone or something is the **subject**. The word (or words) that tells what the subject *is* or *does* is the **verb**. In the following sentences, the subject is underlined once and the verb twice.

Snow falls.
Kim dislikes winter.
We love snowboarding.
Mt. Whistler offers excellent opportunities for winter sports.
In Canada, winter is six months long.
Some people feel the cold severely.

The subject of a sentence is always a **noun** (the name of a person, place, thing, or concept) or a **pronoun** (a word such as *I, you, he, she, it, we,* or *they* used in place of a noun). In the examples above, the subjects include persons (*Kim, we, people*); a place (*Mt. Whistler*); a thing (*snow*); and a concept (*winter*). In one sentence, a pronoun (*we*) is the subject.

Find the verb first.

[1]If you have forgotten (or have never learned) the parts of speech and the basic sentence patterns, you will find this information on the student page of the *Essay Essentials* website, http://www.essayessentials4e.nelson.com

One way to find the **verb** in a sentence is to ask what the sentence says about the subject. There are two kinds of verbs.

- **Action verbs** tell you what the subject is doing. In the examples above, *falls*, *dislikes*, *love*, and *offers* are action verbs.
- **Linking verbs** link or connect a subject to a noun or adjective describing that subject. In the examples above, *is* and *feel* are linking verbs.

  Linking verbs tell you the subject's condition or state of being. (For example, "Tadpoles *become* frogs," "Frogs *feel* slimy.") The most common linking verbs are forms of *to be* (*am, is, are, was, were, have been*, etc.) and verbs such as *look, taste, feel, sound, appear, remain, seem*, and *become*.

Another way to find the verb in a sentence is to put a pronoun (*I, you, he, she, it*, or *they*) in front of the word you think is the verb. If the result makes sense, it is a verb. For example, you could put *it* in front of *falls* in the first sentence listed above: "it falls" makes sense, so you know *falls* is the verb in this sentence. Try this test with the other five example sentences.

Keep this guideline in mind as you work through the exercises below.

To find the subject, ask <u>who</u> or <u>what</u> the sentence is about.
To find the verb, ask what the subject <u>is</u> or <u>is doing</u>.

Exercise 22.1*

In each of the following sentences, underline the <u>subject</u> with one line and the <u>verb</u> with two. Answers for exercises in this chapter begin on page 523. If you make even one mistake, go to the website and do the exercise listed beside the Web icon that follows this exercise. Be sure you understand this material thoroughly before you go on.

1. I bought a used car.

2. The used car was cheap.

3. It needed some repairs.

4. Unfortunately, the repairs were expensive.

5. Insurance for the car was expensive, too.

6. Buying a car is costly.

7. According to the salesman, the car was not overpriced.

8. Always get a second opinion.

9. After 10 years, cars sometimes develop serious problems.

10. Paying for repairs compensates for the cheap price.

GO TO WEB

EXERCISE **22.1**

Usually, but not always, the subject comes before the verb in a sentence.

Occasionally, we find the subject after the verb:

- In sentences beginning with *Here* + a form of *to be* or with *There* + a form of *to be*

Here and *there* are never the subject of a sentence.

Here <u>are</u> the test <u>results</u>. (Who or what <u>are</u>? <u>Results</u>.)
There <u>is</u> a <u>fly</u> in my soup. (Who or what <u>is</u>? A <u>fly</u>.)

- In sentences that are deliberately inverted for emphasis

Finally, at the end of the long, boring joke <u>came</u> the pathetic <u>punch line</u>.
Out of the stadium and into the pouring rain <u>marched</u> the <u>parade</u>.

- In questions

<u>Are</u> <u>we</u> there yet?
<u>Is</u> <u>she</u> the one?

But notice that in questions beginning with *who, whose, what, where,* or *which,* the subject and verb are in "normal" order: subject followed by verb.

<u>Who</u> <u>ate</u> my sandwich?   Whose <u>horse</u> <u>came</u> first?
<u>What</u> <u>caused</u> the accident?   Which <u>car</u> <u>runs</u> best?

Exercise 22.2*

Underline the subject with one line and the verb with two. Watch out for inverted sentences. If you make an error, do the Web exercises that follow.

1. Here is an idea to consider.

2. William Lyon Mackenzie led a rebellion against the Government of Canada.

3. He later became the mayor of Toronto.

4. Who wants the last piece?

5. Eat slowly.

6. There, beyond the swimming pool, is the gym.

7. A moving chicken is poultry in motion.

8. Far behind the leaders trailed the main group of cyclists.

9. Here are the results of your examination.

10. Irish coffee contains ingredients from all four of the essential food groups: caffeine, fat, sugar, and alcohol.

GO TO WEB

EXERCISES 22.2, 22.3, 22.4

More about Verbs

The verb in a sentence may be a single word, as in the exercises you've just done, or it may be a group of words. When you are considering whether or not a word group is a verb, there are two points you should remember.

1. No verb preceded by *to* is ever the verb of a sentence.[2]
2. **Helping verbs**[3] are often added to main verbs.

---

[2] The form *to* + verb—e.g., *to speak, to write, to help*—is an infinitive. Infinitives can act as subjects or objects, but they are never verbs.

[3] If you are familiar with technical grammatical terms, you will know these verbs as **auxiliary verbs**.

The list below contains the most common helping verbs.

be (all forms of *to be* can act as helping verbs: e.g., *am, are, is, was, were, will be, have/had been*, etc.)	can could/could have do/did have/had may/may have might/might have	must/must have ought shall/shall have should/should have will/will have would/would have

The complete verb in a sentence consists of the main verb together with any helping verbs.

Here are a few of the forms of the verb *write*. Notice that in questions the subject may come between the helping verb and the main verb.

You <u>may write</u> now.
He certainly <u>can write</u>!
We <u>should write</u> home more often.
I <u>shall write</u> tomorrow.
He <u>could have written</u> yesterday.
She <u>is writing</u> her memoirs.
<u>Did</u> he <u>write</u> to you?

You <u>ought to write</u> to him.
We <u>will have written</u> by then.
He <u>had written</u> his apology.
I <u>will write</u> to the editor.
The proposal <u>has been written</u>.
Orders <u>should have been written</u>.
<u>Could</u> you <u>have written</u> it in French?

One verb form *always* takes a helping verb. Here is the rule.

A verb ending in *-ing* MUST have a helping verb (or verbs) before it.

Here are a few of the forms an *-ing* verb can take:

I <u>am writing</u> the report.
<u>Is</u> she <u>writing</u> the paper for him?
You <u>are writing</u> illegibly.
I <u>was writing</u> neatly.
You <u>will be writing</u> a report.
They <u>must have been writing</u> all night.
<u>Have</u> you <u>been writing</u> on the wall?

Beware of certain words that are often confused with helping verbs.

Words such as *not, only, always, often, sometimes, never, ever,* and *just* are NOT part of the verb.

These words sometimes appear in the middle of a complete verb, but they are modifiers, not verbs. Do not underline them.

I <u>have</u> just <u>won</u> a one-way ticket to Moose Factory.
She <u>is</u> always <u>chosen</u> first.
Most people <u>do</u> not <u>welcome</u> unasked-for advice.

Exercise 22.3*

Underline the subject once and the complete verb twice. Check your answers, and if you made even one mistake, try the Web exercises that follow.

1. He has talked nonstop for three hours.

2. I am not going to drive.

3. Could they return the goods tomorrow?

4. You cannot eat your birthday cake before dinner.

5. Carla should have been filing the letters and memos.

6. I will be the first member of my family to graduate from college.

7. Paula's lawsuit should never have been allowed to proceed this far.

8. Have you ever been to the Zanzibar tavern?

9. There has never been a better time to travel to Greece.

10. How are the club members identified?

GO TO WEB

EXERCISES 22.5, 22.6, 22.7, 22.8

More about Subjects

Often groups of words called **prepositional phrases** come before the subject in a sentence or between the subject and the verb. When you're looking for the subject in a sentence, prepositional phrases can trip you up unless you know the following rule.

> The subject of a sentence is never in a prepositional phrase.

You must be able to identify prepositional phrases so that you will know where *not* to look for the subject.

> A prepositional phrase is a group of words that begins with a preposition and ends with a noun or a pronoun that answers the question *what* or *when*.

The noun or pronoun is called the object of the preposition. It is this word that, if you're not careful, you might think is the subject of the sentence.

Below is a list of prepositional phrases. The italicized words are prepositions; the words in regular type are objects of the prepositions.

about the book	*between* the desks	*near* the wall
above the desk	*by* the book	*of* the typist
according to the book	*concerning* the memo	*on* the desk
after the meeting	*despite* the policy	*onto* the floor
against the wall	*down* the hall	*over* a door
along the hall	*except* the staff	*to* the staff
among the books	*for* the manager	*through* the window
among them	*from* the office	*under* the book
around the office	*in* an hour	*until* the meeting
before lunch	*in* front *of* the desk	*up* the hall
behind the desk	*inside* the office	*with* a book
below the window	*into* the elevator	*without* the book
beside the book	*like* the book	*without* them

Before you look for the subject in a sentence, cross out all prepositional phrases.

The keyboard ~~of your computer~~ should be cleaned occasionally.

What <u>should be cleaned</u>? The <u>keyboard</u> (not the computer).

Regardless ~~of the expense~~, one ~~of us~~ should go ~~to the IT conference in Las Vegas~~.

Who <u>should go</u>? <u>One</u> (not the group).

Exercise 22.4*

In the following sentences, first cross out the prepositional phrase(s), then underline the subject once and the verb twice. Check your answers before going on to the Web exercises that follow.

1. Among English teachers, Santa's helpers are known as subordinate clauses.

2. After his death, Terry Fox became a national symbol of heroic courage.

3. In the state of Florida, it is illegal for single, divorced, or widowed women to parachute on Sunday afternoons.

4. In Kentucky, no woman may appear in a bathing suit on any highway in the state unless escorted by two officers or armed with a club.

5. In my wildest imaginings, I cannot understand the reason for these laws.

6. During a break in the conversation, Darryl's embarrassing comment could be heard in every corner of the room.

7. In my lawyer's dictionary, a will is defined as a dead giveaway.

8. To the staff and managers of the project, I extend my congratulations for an excellent job.

9. Against all odds, and despite their shortcomings, the St. John Miners made it into the playoffs of the Southern New Brunswick Little League.

10. Walk a mile in my shoes at high noon with your head held high in order to avoid clichés like the plague.

GO TO WEB

EXERCISES **22.9, 22.10**

Multiple Subjects and Verbs

So far, you have been decoding sentences containing a single subject and a single verb, even though the verb may have consisted of more than one word. Sentences can, however, have more than one subject and one verb.

Multiple subjects are called **compound subjects**; multiple verbs are **compound verbs**.

Here is a sentence with a compound subject:

Esquimalt and Oak Bay border the city of Victoria.

This sentence has a compound verb:

She groped and stumbled her way down the dark aisle of the movie theatre.

And this sentence has a compound subject and a compound verb:

The detective and the police sergeant leaped from their car and seized the suspect.

The parts of a compound subject or verb are usually joined by *and* (sometimes by *or*). Compound subjects and verbs may contain more than two elements, as in the following sentences:

Careful planning, organization, and conscientious revision are the keys to good essay writing.

I finished my paper, put the cat outside, took the phone off the hook, and crawled into bed.

Exercise 22.5*

In the following sentences, cross out any prepositional phrases, then underline the subjects once and the verbs twice. Be sure to underline all the elements in a compound subject or verb. Check your answers before continuing.

1. Management and union met for a two-hour bargaining session.

2. They debated and drafted a tentative agreement for a new contract.

3. The anesthetist and the surgeon scrubbed for surgery and hurried to the operating room.

4. Frederick Banting and Norman Bethune are known around the world as medical heroes.

5. Kevin and Sandra hiked and cycled across most of Newfoundland.

6. My son or my daughter will meet me and drive me home.

7. Knock three times and ask for Stan.

8. In the 17th and 18th centuries, the French and the English fought for control of Canada.

9. Buy the base model and don't waste your money on luxury options.

10. Ragweed, golden rod, and twitch grass formed the essential elements in the bouquet for his English teacher.

GO TO WEB

EXERCISES **22.11, 22.12, 22.13, 22.14**

Here's a summary of what you've learned in this chapter. Keep it in front of you as you write the mastery test.

Summary

- The subject is *who* or *what* the sentence is about.
- The verb tells what the subject *is* or *does*.
- The subject normally comes before the verb (exceptions are questions and sentences beginning with *there* or *here*).
- The complete verb = a main verb + any helping verbs.
- By itself, a word ending in *-ing* is not a verb.
- An infinitive (a phrase consisting of *to* + a verb) is never the verb of a sentence.
- The subject of a sentence is never in a prepositional phrase.
- A sentence can have more than one subject and/or verb.

Exercise 22.6

This challenging exercise will test your ability to find the main subjects and verbs in sentences. In each sentence below, first cross out any prepositional phrases, and then underline each subject with one line and each verb with two lines. Be sure to underline all elements in a multiple subject or verb.

1. The politicians of all parties try in vain to change the world, but they seldom try to change themselves.

2. In the past, men and women had clearly defined roles and seldom broke away from them.

3. Police, firefighters, and paramedics comforted, rescued, and treated my aunt and uncle after their car accident.

4. Among the many kinds of cheese made in Canada are Camembert, Fontina, and Quark.

5. French fries, gravy, and cheese curds are the ingredients in traditional Quebec poutine.

6. Increasingly, in high-end restaurants, chefs are experimenting with Canadian foods like elk meat, fiddlehead greens, and Saskatoon berries.

7. On the Lovers' Tour of Lake Louise were two elderly women with walkers, a couple of elderly gentlemen with very young wives, half a dozen middle-aged divorcées, and me.

8. Negotiate in English, swear in German, argue in Spanish, and make love in French.

9. After the rain, the sun came out, the birds sang, and the tourists returned to their chairs by the pool.

10. According to its campaign literature, the incoming government will provide jobs for all Canadians, eliminate the national debt, find a cure for cancer, land a Canadian on Mars, and reduce income tax by 50 percent, all in its first year in office!

23

Solving Sentence-Fragment Problems

Every complete sentence has two characteristics. It contains a subject and a verb, and it expresses a complete thought. Any group of words that is punctuated as a sentence but lacks one of these characteristics is a **sentence fragment**. Fragments are appropriate in conversation and in some kinds of writing, but normally they are unacceptable in college, technical, and business writing.

There are two kinds of fragments you should watch out for: the "missing piece" fragment and the dependent clause fragments.

"Missing Piece" Fragments

Sometimes a group of words is punctuated as a sentence but is missing one or more of the essential parts of a sentence: a subject and a verb. Consider these examples.

1. Found it under the pile of clothes on your floor.

   Who or what <u>found</u> it? The sentence doesn't tell you. The subject is missing.

2. Their arguments about housework.

   The sentence doesn't tell you what the arguments <u>were</u> or <u>did</u>. The verb is missing.

3. During my favourite TV show.

<u>Who</u> or <u>what</u> <u>was</u> or <u>did</u> something? Both subject and verb are missing.

4. The programmers working around the clock to trace the hacker.

Part of the verb is missing. Remember that a verb ending in *-ing* needs a helping verb to be complete.

Finding fragments like these in your work when you are revising is the hard part. Fixing them is easy. There are two ways to correct sentence fragments. Here's the first one.

> To change a "missing piece" fragment into a complete sentence, add whatever is missing: a subject, a verb, or both.

1. You may need to add a subject:

Your <u>sister</u> found it under the pile of clothes on your floor.

2. You may need to add a verb:

Their arguments <u>were</u> about housework. (linking verb)
Their arguments about housework eventually <u>destroyed</u> their relationship. (action verb)

3. You may need to add both a subject and a verb:

My <u>mother</u> always <u>calls</u> during my favourite TV show.

4. Or you may need to add a helping verb:

The programmers <u>have been</u> working around the clock to trace the hacker.

Don't let the length of a fragment fool you. Students sometimes think that if a string of words is long, it must be a sentence. Not so. No matter how long the string of words, if it doesn't contain both a subject and a verb, it is not a sentence. For example, here's a description of children going from door to door for treats on Halloween:

In twos and threes, dressed in the fashionable Disney costumes of the year, as their parents tarried behind, grownups following after, grownups bantering about the schools, or about movies, about local sports, about their marriages, about the difficulties of long marriages, kids sprinting up the next driveway, kids decked out as demons or superheroes or dinosaurs . . . beating back the restless souls of the dead, in search of sweets.

Moody, Rick. *Demonology.* New York: Little, Brown, 2001. 291.

At 68 words, this "sentence" is long, but it is a fragment. It lacks both a subject and a verb. If you add "The <u>children</u> <u>came</u>" at the beginning of the fragment, you would have a complete sentence.

In the following exercises, decide whether each group of words is a complete sentence or a "missing piece" fragment. Put *S* before each complete sentence and *F* before each fragment. Make each fragment into a complete sentence by adding whatever is missing: the subject, the verb, or both. Then compare your answers with our suggestions. Answers for exercises in this chapter begin on page 524.

Exercise 23.1*

1. _____ About historical events.

2. _____ To decide on the basis of rumour, not facts.

3. _____ Trying to be helpful, I offered to check the files.

4. _____ Cooking my famous tuna casserole.

5. _____ The party members gathering in the campaign office.

6. _____ We won.

7. _____ Hands over your head.

8. _____ To go anywhere without my iPod.

9. _____ Having worked hard all her life.

10. _____ Wanting to please them, she had coffee ready on their arrival.

GO TO WEB

EXERCISES **23.1, 23.2, 23.3, 23.4**

Exercise 23.2*

_____ Professional athletes making millions of dollars a year. _____ At the same time, owners of sports franchises growing fantastically rich from the efforts of their employees, the players. _____ The fans being the forgotten people in the struggle for control over major league sports. _____ The people who pay the money that makes both owners and players rich. _____ I have an idea that would protect everyone's interests. _____ Cap the owners' profits. _____ Cap the players' salaries. _____ And, most important, the ticket prices. _____ A fair deal for everyone. _____ Fans should be able to see their teams play for the price of a movie ticket, not the price of a television set.

Dependent Clause Fragments

Any group of words containing a subject and a verb is a **clause**. There are two kinds of clauses. An **independent clause** is one that makes complete sense on its own. It can stand alone, as a sentence. A **dependent clause**, as its name suggests, cannot stand alone as a sentence; it depends on another clause to make complete sense.

Dependent (also known as **subordinate clauses**) begin with **dependent-clause cues** (subordinating conjunctions).

Dependent-Clause Cues

after	if	until
although	in order that	what, whatever
as, as if	provided that	when, whenever
as long as	since	where, wherever, whereas
as soon as	so that	whether
because	that	which, whichever
before	though	while
even if, even though	unless	who, whom, whose

Whenever a clause begins with one of these words or phrases, it is dependent.

A dependent clause must be attached to an independent clause. If it stands alone, it is a sentence fragment.

Here is an independent clause:

I am a poor speller.

If we put one of the dependent-clause cues in front of it, it can no longer stand alone:

Because I am a poor speller.

We can correct this kind of fragment by attaching it to an independent clause:

Because I am a poor speller, I have a spell checker in my PDA.

Exercise 23.3*

Put an *S* before each clause that is independent and therefore a sentence. Put an *F* before each clause that is dependent and therefore a sentence fragment. Circle the dependent-clause cue in each sentence fragment.

1. _____ Although she practised it constantly.

2. _____ Since the horse stepped on her.

3. _____ As soon as the troops arrived, the fighting stopped.

4. _____ Whichever route the bikers choose.

5. _____ Before Biff bought his bike.

GO TO WEB

EXERCISES **23.5, 23.6, 23.7, 23.8**

Exercise 23.4*

Identify the sentence fragments in the paragraph below by highlighting the dependent-clause cue in each fragment you find.

Although many companies are experiencing growth, thanks to a healthy economy. Middle managers are not breathing easy. As long as there is a surplus of junior executives. Middle managers will continue to look over their shoulders, never sure when the axe will fall. Whether through early retirement, buyout, or termination. Their positions are being eliminated by cost-conscious firms whose eyes are focused on the bottom line. Because the executive branch of many businesses expanded rapidly during the years of high growth. Now there is a large block of managers who have no prospects of advancement. As one analyst observed, when he examined this block of largely superfluous executives and their chances of rising in the company hierarchy, "You cannot push a rectangle up a triangle."

Most sentence fragments are dependent clauses punctuated as sentences. Fortunately, this is the easiest kind of fragment to recognize and fix. All you need to do is join the dependent clause either to the sentence that comes before it or to the one that comes after it—whichever linkage makes better sense.

Read the following example to yourself; then read it aloud (remember, last sentence first).

> Montreal is a sequence of ghettos. Although I was born and brought up there. My experience of French was a pathetically limited and distorted one.

The second "sentence" sounds incomplete, and the dependent-clause cue at the beginning of it is the clue you need to identify it as a sentence fragment. You could join the fragment to the sentence before it, but then you would get "Montreal is a sequence of ghettos, although I was born and brought up there," which doesn't make sense. The fragment should be linked to the sentence that follows it, like this:

> Montreal is a sequence of ghettos. Although I was born and brought up there, my experience of French was a pathetically limited and distorted one. (Mordecai Richler)

If, as in the example above, your revised sentence *begins* with the dependent clause, you need to put a comma after it. If, however, your revised sentence *ends* with the dependent clause, you don't need a comma between it and the independent clause that precedes it.

> My experience of French was pathetically limited although I was born and brought up [in Montreal].

See Chapter 31, Rule 3 (page 419).

Exercise 23.5*

Turn back to Exercise 23.4 and revise it by joining each dependent clause fragment to an independent clause that precedes or follows it, whichever makes better sense.

GO TO WEB

EXERCISE **23.9**

Exercise 23.6*

The following paragraph contains both independent and dependent clauses (fragments), all punctuated as if they were complete sentences. Letting meaning be your guide, join each dependent clause fragment to the independent clause that comes before or after it—whichever makes better sense. Be careful to punctuate correctly between clauses.

In spite of what everyone says about the weak economy and the scarcity of jobs, especially for young people. I have financed my college career with a variety of part-time and seasonal jobs. Right now, for instance, while completing my third year at college. I have not one, or two, but three part-time jobs. I am a short-order cook three nights a week for a local bar and diner. And a telemarketer for a cable company after school. Or whenever I have free time. I'm also a server at a specialty coffee store on weekends. To maintain any kind of social life. While juggling three jobs and the requirements of my third-year program is not exactly easy, but I find it hard to turn down the opportunity for experience. Not to mention cash. I'm willing to put my social life on hold. For a while.

Exercise 23.7

As a final test of your skill in finding and correcting sentence fragments, try this exercise. Make each fragment into a complete sentence.

1. I had never eaten curry. But the first time I tasted it. I decided I liked it.
2. In France, they say that an explosion in the kitchen could have disastrous results. Such as linoleum blown apart.
3. Our family thinks my sister is too young to get married. Since she and her boyfriend want to be registered at Toys "R" Us.
4. It may surprise you to know that Canadians have made significant contributions to world cuisine. Two of the best known being baby pabulum and frozen peas.
5. Bathing the family cat. It's an activity that carries the same risks as tap dancing in a minefield. Or juggling with razor blades.
6. After working for three nights in a row trying to make my essay perfect so that I would get a high grade in my course. I lost my entire project when my brother crashed the computer while playing Grand Theft Auto.
7. I decided to take swimming lessons for two reasons. The first is fitness. Second, water safety.
8. There is good news. The man who was caught in an upholstery machine has fully recovered.
9. All of us are more aware of the effects of pollution now than we were 10 years ago. Because we are continually bombarded with information about the environment and our impact on it. In school, on television, and in newspapers.
10. My second favourite household chore is ironing. The first being hitting my head on the top bunk bed until I faint. (Erma Bombeck)

24

Solving Run-On Problems

Some sentences lack certain elements and thus are fragments. Other sentences contain two or more independent clauses that are incorrectly linked together. A sentence with inadequate punctuation between clauses is a **run-on**. Run-ons tend to occur when you write in a hurry, without first organizing your thoughts. If you think about what you want to say and punctuate carefully, you shouldn't have any problems with them.

There are two kinds of run-on sentences to watch out for: comma splices and fused sentences.

Comma Splices and Fused Sentences

As its name suggests, the **comma splice** occurs when two complete sentences (independent clauses) are joined together with only a comma between them. Here's an example:

I stayed up all night, I am exhausted.

Tea may be good for you, coffee is not.

A **fused sentence** occurs when two complete sentences are joined together with no punctuation at all:

I stayed up all night I am exhausted.

Tea may be good for you coffee is not.

There are four ways to fix run-on sentences.

1. Make the independent clauses into separate sentences.

I stayed up all night. I am exhausted.
Tea may be good for you. Coffee is not.

> 2. Separate the independent clauses with a comma followed by one of these words: *and, but, or, nor, for, so,* or *yet.*[1]

I stayed up all night, and I am exhausted.

You can insert one of the dependent-clause cues listed in Chapter 23, on page 342.

> Because I stayed up all night, I am exhausted.

> 3. Make one clause dependent on the other by adding one of the dependent-clause cues listed on page 342.

Because I stayed up all night, I am exhausted.
I am exhausted because I stayed up all night.
Tea may be good for you although coffee is not.

> 4. Use a semicolon, either by itself or with a transitional word or phrase, to separate the independent clauses. (See Chapter 32.)

I stayed up all night; I am exhausted.
Tea may be good for you; on the other hand, coffee is not.

Note: All four solutions to comma splices and fused sentences require you to use a word or punctuation mark strong enough to come between two independent clauses. A comma by itself is too weak, and so is a dash.

The sentences in the following exercises will give you practice in fixing comma splices and fused sentences. Correct the sentences where necessary and then check your answers, beginning on page 525. Since there are four ways to fix

---

[1]These words are called **coordinating conjunctions** because they are used to join equal (or coordinating) clauses. If you are not sure how to punctuate sentences with coordinating conjunctions, see Chapter 31, Rule 2 (page 418).

each sentence, your answers may differ from our suggestions. If you find that you're confused about when to use a semicolon and when to use a period, be sure to read pages 427–31 before going on.

Exercise 24.1*

1. This is strong coffee, it has dissolved my spoon!
2. Just let me do the talking, we're sure to get a ticket if you open your mouth.
3. I keep buying lottery tickets, but I have won only free tickets.
4. If you have never tried it, hitting a golf ball may look easy, it's not.
5. As long as you smile when you speak, you can get away with saying almost anything.
6. Montreal used to be known as Ville St. Marie, before that it was known as Hochelaga.
7. Students today really need summer jobs and part-time employment, their tuition and living costs are too high for most families to subsidize.
8. Because I'm not very good at calculating odds, I'm afraid to play poker with you.
9. It's very windy, a ball hit deep to centre field will likely go into the stands.
10. "I was married by a judge, I should have asked for a jury." (Groucho Marx)

GO TO WEB

EXERCISES 24.1, 24.2

Exercise 24.2*

1. I use a keyboard all the time and my handwriting has become illegible.
2. Despite my parents' objections, I enjoy having long hair, it makes me feel attractive.
3. Casual meetings are fine for small groups, more formal settings are appropriate for larger groups.
4. I'd be happy to help you, just call when you need me, I'll be here all day.
5. In Canada, winter is more than a season it's a bad joke.
6. Perfection is probably impossible to achieve, but that doesn't mean you should stop trying your best.
7. For students in most technology programs, the future looks bright, however a diploma does not guarantee job security.

8. A Canadian who speaks three languages is called multilingual, one who speaks two languages is called bilingual, one who speaks only one language is called an English Canadian.

9. Skilled people are needed in specialized fields, currently, the top three are geriatrics, hospitality, and environmental technology.

10. I believe in a unified Canada, I believe that in 1867 the Fathers of Confederation were right, a federation of provinces can make a strong nation.

Exercise 24.3

As a final test of your ability to identify and correct run-on sentences, find and correct the 10 errors in the following paragraphs.

According to a news report, a private girls' school in Victoria was recently faced with an unusual problem, they solved it in a way that can only be described as creative, it is also a good example of effective teaching. Some of the grade 10 girls, forbidden by their parents to wear lipstick at home, began to apply it at school, in the second-floor washroom. That was the first problem, the second was that after applying the lipstick, they would press their lips to the mirror, leaving dozens of perfect lip prints. Every night, the maintenance crew would remove the prints, the next day the girls would reapply them and finally the principal decided that something had to be done.

She called the girls into the washroom where she met them with one of the maintenance men and he stood by while the principal addressed the girls. She explained that the lip prints on the mirrors were causing a problem for the maintenance crew, they had to clean the mirrors every night instead of doing other work. To demonstrate how difficult the cleaning job was and how much time was wasted on this needless chore, the principal asked the maintenance man to clean one of the mirrors, the girls watched with interest he took out a long-handled squeegee and began scrubbing at the lipstick prints. When he had scrubbed for a while, he turned, dipped his squeegee into one of the toilets, and continued to work on the mirrors and since then, there has not been another set of lip prints on the washroom mirror.

Sentence Structure

25

Solving Modifier Problems

Felix was complimented on a great game and a fine job of goaltending *by his mother.*

Snarling furiously and baring his teeth, Maurice crawled through a basement window only to confront an angry watchdog.

When she was a first-year student, the English professor told Mara she would *almost* write all her assignments in class.

These sentences show what can happen to your writing if you aren't sure how to use modifiers. A **modifier** is a word or phrase that adds information about another word in a sentence. In the examples above, the italicized words are modifiers. Used correctly, modifiers describe, explain, or limit another word, making its meaning more precise. Used carelessly, however, modifiers can cause confusion or, even worse, amusement.

You need to be able to recognize and solve two kinds of modifier problems: **misplaced modifiers** and **dangling modifiers**.

Misplaced Modifiers

Modifiers must be as close as possible to the words they apply to. Usually, readers will assume that a modifier modifies whatever it's next to. It's important to remember this, because, as the following examples show, changing the position of a modifier can change the meaning of your sentence.

Sentence Structure

Jason walked (only) as far as the corner store. (He didn't walk any farther.)

Jason (only) walked as far as the corner store. (He didn't jog or run.)

(Only) Jason walked as far as the corner store. (No one else went.)

Jason walked as far as the (only) corner store. (There were no other corner stores.)

To make sure a modifier is in the right place, ask yourself "What does it apply to?" and put it beside that word or word group.

When a modifier is not close enough to the word it refers to, it is said to be misplaced. A misplaced modifier can be a single word in the wrong place.

The supervisor told me they needed someone who could use both Word and WordPerfect (badly.)

Is some company really hiring people to do poor work? Or does the company urgently need someone familiar with word processing programs? Obviously, the modifier *badly* belongs next to *needed*.

The supervisor told me they (badly) needed someone who could use both Word and WordPerfect.

Be especially careful with these words: *almost, nearly, just, only, even, hardly, merely, scarcely.* Put them right before the words they modify.

Misplaced: She (nearly) answered every question.

Correctly placed: She answered (nearly) every question.

Misplaced: After driving all night, we (almost) arrived at 7:00 a.m.

Correctly placed: After driving all night, we arrived at (almost) 7:00 a.m.

A misplaced modifier can also be a group of words in the wrong place.

Bundled up in down clothing to keep warm, the dog team waited for the driver.

The modifier, *bundled up in down clothing to keep warm*, is too far away from the word it is supposed to modify, *driver*. In fact, it seems to modify *dog team*, making the sentence ridiculous. We need to rewrite the sentence.

The dog team waited for the driver, bundled up in down clothing to keep warm.

Look at this one:

I drove my mother to Saskatoon, where my aunt lives in a rental car.

In a rental car applies to *drove* and should be closer to it.

I drove my mother in a rental car to Saskatoon, where my aunt lives.

Notice that a modifier need not always go right next to what it modifies; it should, however, be as close as possible to it.

Occasionally, as in the examples above, the modifier is obviously out of place. The writer's intention is clear, and the sentences are easy to correct. But sometimes modifiers are misplaced in such a way that the meaning is not clear, as in the following example:

Raj said after the game he wanted to talk to the press.

Did Raj *say* it after the game? Or does he want to *talk to the press* after the game? To avoid confusion, we must move the modifier and, depending on which meaning we want, write either

After the game, Raj said he wanted to talk to the press.

or

Raj said he wanted to talk to the press after the game.

In Exercises 25.1 and 25.2, rewrite the sentences that contain misplaced modifiers, positioning them closely as possible to the words they modify. Check your answers to the first set before continuing. Answers for this chapter begin on page 526.

Exercise 25.1*

1. Trevor left the can of Pet Grrmet out for the dog that he had opened.

2. Our supervisor told us on the first day that no one takes coffee breaks.

3. I enthusiastically recommend this candidate with no experience whatever.

4. Professor Green told us in September he thought our class was a hopeless case.

5. We almost enjoyed the whole movie; only the ending was a disappointment.

6. Leo and Annie found an apartment in a highrise within walking distance of the campus with two bedrooms and a sunken living room.

7. There just are enough pieces to go around.

8. It almost seems there is a game every day during baseball season.

9. A charming, intelligent companion is sought by a vertically challenged but wealthy gentleman who looks good in evening gowns and diamonds.

10. One of us could only go because there was enough money just to buy one ticket.

Exercise 25.2*

1. One finds the best Chinese food in those restaurants where the Chinese eat usually.

2. He caught sight of a canary and several finches using his new binoculars.

3. Using my new camera, I can take professional-quality pictures with automatic functions.

4. The football practices have been organized for players who are not with a team in the summertime as a keep-fit measure.

5. Vancouver is a wonderful city for anyone who likes rain and fog to live in.

6. Some games are less demanding in terms of time and equipment, such as tiddlywinks.

7. The Human Rights Code prohibits discrimination against anyone who is applying for a job on the basis of race, religion, sex, or age.

8. We looked for a birthday present for our boss in a golf store.

9. Each year, 500,000 Canadian men almost have a vasectomy.

10. We hope to improve our students' performance using cash as a motivator.

Dangling Modifiers

A dangling modifier occurs when there is no appropriate word in the sentence for the modifier to apply to. That is, the sentence does not contain a specific word or idea to which the modifier could sensibly refer. With no appropriate word to modify, the modifier seems to apply to whatever it's next to, often with ridiculous results.

(After a good night's sleep,) my teachers were impressed with my unusual alertness.

This sentence seems to say that the teachers had a good night's sleep.

(Trying desperately to finish an essay,) my roommate's stereo made it impossible to concentrate.

The *stereo* was writing an essay?

Dangling modifiers are harder to correct than misplaced ones; you can't simply move danglers to another spot in the sentence. There are, however, two ways in which you can fix them. One way requires that you remember the following rule.

When a modifier comes at the beginning of a sentence, it modifies the subject of the sentence.[1]

This rule means that you can avoid dangling modifiers by choosing the subjects of your sentences carefully.

---

[1]The rule has exceptions, called adverbial modifiers, but they won't give you any trouble. Example: (Quickly) she did as she was told.

1. Ensure the subject is an appropriate one for the modifier to apply to.

Using this method, we can rewrite our two examples by changing the subjects.

(After a good night's sleep,) I impressed my teachers with my unusual alertness.

(Trying desperately to finish an essay,) I found it impossible to concentrate because of my roommate's stereo.

2. Another way to correct a dangling modifier is by changing it into a dependent clause.

After I had had a good night's sleep, my teachers were impressed with my unusual alertness.

When I was trying desperately to finish an essay, my roommate's stereo made it impossible to concentrate.

Sometimes a dangling modifier comes at the end of a sentence:

A Smart is the car to buy when looking for efficiency and affordability.

Can you correct this sentence? Try it; then look at the suggestions at the foot of the page.

Here is a summary of the steps to follow in solving modifier problems.

Summary

1. Ask "What does the modifier apply to?"
2. Be sure there is a word or group of words *in the sentence* for the modifier to apply to.
3. Put the modifier as close as possible to the word or word group it applies to.

Here are two suggestions.
1. Add a subject: Looking for efficiency and affordability, I decided a Smart was the car to buy.
2. Change the dangler to a dependent clause: A Smart is the car to buy since I am looking for efficiency and affordability.

Exercise 25.3*

Most of the following sentences contain dangling modifiers. Correct each sentence by using whichever solution given on page 357 best suits your purpose. There is no one right way to correct these sentences; our answers are only suggestions.

1. Driving recklessly and without lights, the police stopped Gina at a road block.

2. My supervisor gave me a lecture about punctuality after being late twice in one week.

3. After criticizing both my work and my attitude, I was fired.

4. With enough memory to store her favourite movies and more than 10,000 songs, Hannah knew that the iBook was the computer she needed.

5. After spending two weeks quarrelling over money, their relationship was over.

6. As a dedicated fan of Alice Munro, her last book is her best.

7. In less than a minute after applying the ointment, the pain began to ease.

8. Making her first formal presentation to her colleagues and her supervisor, Jake was probably more nervous than Allison was.

9. When handling hazardous waste, the safety manual clearly outlines the procedures to follow.

10. After spending the day in the kitchen preparing a gourmet meal, the guests drank too much wine to appreciate Kendra's effort.

Exercise 25.4*

In the following sentences, correct the misplaced and dangling modifiers in any way you choose. Our answers are only suggestions.

1. Only she was the baker's daughter, but she could loaf all day.

2. Being horribly hung over, the only problem with a free bar is knowing when to quit.

Sentence Structure

3. Rearing and kicking, Sam finally got the terrified horse under control.

4. In a hurry to get to the interview on time, my résumé was left lying on my desk at home.

5. As a college student constantly faced with new assignments, the pressure is sometimes intolerable.

6. Listening to the rumours, the newlyweds are already on the road to separation.

7. As a nondrinker, the display of liquor in the duty-free outlet held no interest.

8. Quartetto Gelato receives enthusiastic acclaim for its original arrangements and witty presentations from Vancouver to St. John's.

9. Rolling on her back, eager to have her tummy scratched, Queen Elizabeth couldn't resist the little Corgi puppy.

10. Wearing a small Canadian flag on a backpack or lapel, your reception abroad will be warm and enthusiastic.

GO TO WEB

EXERCISES 25.1, 25.2, 25.3, 25.4

Exercise 25.5

As a final test of your ability to use modifiers, correct the misplaced and dangling modifiers in the sentences below, using any solution you choose.

1. Obviously having drunk too much, I drove poor Tanya to her apartment, made her a pot of coffee, and called her mother.

2. When trying for your Red Cross bronze medal, your examiner will evaluate your speed, endurance, and resuscitation techniques.

3. The Riel Rebellion this month will be featured in *Canadian History* magazine.

4. Sinking like a ball of fire below the horizon, our sailboat was the perfect vantage point from which to watch the setting sun.

5. Not being reliable about arriving on time, I can't hire her to supervise others who are expected to be punctual.

6. While they were in my pocket, my children managed to break my glasses by leaping on me from behind.

7. Combining comfortable accommodation and economical travel, my wife and I find a camper van ideal for travelling both here and abroad.

8. The only used motorcycles we could find had been ridden by bikers that were in pretty bad shape.

9. After submitting the lowest bid that met all the developer's criteria, not being awarded the contract was bitterly disappointing.

10. "This bus has a seating capacity of 56 passengers with a maximum height of four metres." (Sign on a double-decker bus in Charlotte-town)

26

The Parallelism Principle

Brevity, clarity, and force: these are three characteristics of good writing style. **Parallelism** will reinforce these characteristics in everything you write.

When your sentence contains a series of two or more items, they must be grammatically parallel. That is, they must be written in the same grammatical form. Consider this example:

Sophie likes *swimming, surfing,* and *to sail.*

The three items in this series are not parallel. Two are nouns ending in *-ing*, but the third, *to sail*, is the infinitive form of the verb. To correct the sentence, you must put all the items in the same grammatical form. You have two choices. You can write

Sophie likes *swimming, surfing,* and *sailing.* (all nouns)

Or you can write

Sophie likes *to swim, to surf,* and *to sail.* (all infinitives)

Now look at this example with two nonparallel elements:

Most people seek happiness in *long-term relationships* and *work that provides them with satisfaction.*

Again, you could correct this sentence in two ways. You could write "Most people seek happiness *in relationships that are long-term* and *in work that provides them with satisfaction,*" but that solution produces a long and clumsy sentence. The shorter version works better: "Most people seek happiness in *long-term relationships* and *satisfying work*." This version is concise, clear, and forceful.

> Correct faulty parallelism by writing all items in a series in the same grammatical form; that is, all words, or all phrases, or all clauses.

One way to tell whether the items in a series are parallel is to write them out in list form, one below the other. That way, you can see at a glance if all the elements are in the same grammatical form.

Not Parallel	**Parallel**
My brother is *messy, rude,* and *an obnoxious person.*	My brother is *messy, rude,* and *obnoxious.*
(This list has two adjectives and a noun phrase.)	(This list has three adjectives.)
I support myself by *delivering pizza, poker,* and *shooting pool.*	I support myself by *delivering pizza, playing poker,* and *shooting pool.*
(This list has two phrases and one single word as objects of the preposition *by*.)	(This list has three phrases as objects of the preposition *by*.)
Jules wants a job that *will interest him, will challenge him,* and *pays well.*	Jules wants a job that *will interest him, (will) challenge him,* and *(will) pay him well.*
(This series of clauses contains two future tense verbs and one present tense verb.)	(All three subordinate clauses contain future tense verbs.)

As you can see, achieving parallelism is partly a matter of developing an ear for the sound of a correct list. A parallel sentence has a smooth, unbroken rhythm. Practice and the exercises in this chapter will help. Once you have mastered parallelism in your sentences, you will be ready to develop ideas in parallel sequence—in thesis statements, for example—and thus to write clear, well-organized prose. Far from being a frill, parallelism is a fundamental characteristic of good writing.

Correct the sentences where necessary in the following exercises. As you work through these sentences, try to spot parallelism errors from the change in rhythm that the faulty element produces. Then revise the sentence to bring the faulty element into line with the other elements in the series. Check your answers to each set of 10 before going on. Answers for this chapter begin on page 528.

Exercise 26.1*

1. This program is easy to understand and using it is not difficult, either.

2. We were told that we would have to leave and to take nothing with us.

3. We organized our findings, wrote the report, and finally our PowerPoint presentation was prepared.

4. Both applicants were unskilled, unprepared, and lacked motivation.

5. Elmer's doctor advised that he should be careful with his back and not to strain his mind.

6. The company is looking for an employee who has a car and knowledge of the city would be a help.

7. If consumers really cared, they could influence the fast-food industry to produce healthy, delicious food that didn't cost very much.

8. When I want to get away from it all, there are three solitary pleasures I enjoy: a walk in the country, reading a good book, and fine music.

9. A recent survey of female executives claims that family responsibilities, being excluded from informal networks, and lacking management experience are the major factors keeping them from advancement.

10. If it is to be useful, your report must be organized clearly, written well, and your research should be thorough.

GO TO WEB

EXERCISES 26.1, 26.2

Exercise 26.2*

1. For my birthday, I requested either a Roots jacket or a scarf from Dior.

2. In my community, two related crimes are rapidly increasing: drug abuse and stealing things.

3. Bodybuilding has made me what I am today: physically perfect, very prosperous financially, and practically friendless.

4. After reading all the explanations and all the exercises have been completed, you'll be a better writer.

5. Bruce claimed that, through repetition and giving rewards, he had trained his centipede to be loyal and demonstrate obedience.

6. During their vacation in New Brunswick, Tracy and Jane visited many beautiful locations and wonderful seafood was eaten.

7. I'm an average tennis player; I have a good forehand, my backhand is average, but a weak serve.

8. The problem with being immortalized as a statue is that you will be a target for pigeon droppings and artists who write graffiti.

9. Never disturb a sleeping dog, a baby that is happy, or a silent politician.

10. I'd like to help, but I'm too tired, and my time is already taken up with other things.

GO TO WEB

EXERCISES 26.3, 26.4, 26.5, 26.6

Exercise 26.3*

Make the following lists parallel. In each case, you can make your items parallel with any item in the list, so your answers may differ from ours.

Example:	Wrong:	report writing	program a computer
	Right:	report writing	computer programming
	Also right:	write a report	program a computer

1. Wrong: wine   women   singing
   Right:
2. Wrong: doing your best   don't give up
   Right:
3. Wrong: lying about all   to do whatever I
            morning   please
   Right:
4. Wrong: information   education   entertaining
   Right:
5. Wrong: individually   as a group
   Right:
6. Wrong: privately   in public
   Right:
7. Wrong: happiness   healthy   wisdom
   Right:
8. Wrong: employers   people working   workers on
                               full-time for an employer contract
   Right:
9. Wrong: insufficient time too little money   not enough
                                                  staff
   Right:
10. Wrong: French is the   English is used   profanity
            language of love   in business   sounds best
                                                  in German
    Right:

(Exercise 26.4*)

Correct the faulty parallelism in these sentences.

1. Not being able to speak the language causes confusion, is frustrating, and it's embarrassing.

2. Trying your best and success are not always the same thing.

3. The first candidate we interviewed seemed frightened and to be shy, but the second was a composed person and showed confidence.

4. To lick one's fingers and picking one's teeth in a restaurant are one way to get attention.

5. Our CEO claims his most valuable business assets are hitting a good backhand and membership at an exclusive golf club.

6. In order to succeed in this economy, small businesses must be creative and show innovation and flexibility.

7. Lowering our profit margin, raising prices, and two management lay-offs will enable us to meet our budget.

8. After an enjoyable dinner, I like to drink a cappuccino, a dark chocolate mint, and, occasionally, a good cigar.

9. Lying in the sun, consumption of high-fat foods, and cigarette smoking are three dangerous activities that were once thought to be healthy.

10. Business travellers complain of long delays at airports, they are paying higher costs for services, and tighter restrictions on their freedom of movement.

Exercise 26.5

As a test of your mastery of parallel structure, correct the six errors in the following paragraph.

The dictionary can be both a useful resource and an educational entertainment. Everyone knows that its three chief functions are to check spelling, for finding out the meanings of words, and what the correct pronunciation is. Few people, however, use the dictionary for discovery as well as learning. There are several methods of using the dictionary as an aid to discovery. One is randomly looking at words, another is to read a page or two thoroughly, and still another is by skimming through words until you find an unfamiliar one. It is by this last method that I discovered the word *steatopygous*, a term I now try to use at least once a day. You can increase your vocabulary significantly by using the dictionary, and of course a large and varied vocabulary can be used to baffle your colleagues, employers will be impressed, and your English teacher will be surprised.

27

Refining by Combining

To reinforce what you've learned about sentence structure, try your hand at **sentence combining**, a technique that enables you to avoid a choppy, monotonous, or repetitious style while at the same time producing correct sentences. Sentence combining accomplishes three things: it reinforces your understanding of sentence structure; it helps you to refine and polish your writing; and it results in a style that will keep your reader alert and interested in what you have to say.

Let's look at two short, technically correct sentences that could be combined:

I prefer champagne.

My budget allows only beer.

There are several ways of combining these two statements into a single sentence.

1. You can connect them with an appropriate linking word, such as *and, but, or, nor,* or *for* (the FANBOYS words).

I prefer champagne, *but* my budget allows only beer.

2. You can change one of the sentences into a subordinate clause.

Although I prefer champagne, my budget allows only beer.

My budget allows only beer *even though I prefer champagne.*

3. You can change one of the sentences into a modifying phrase.

(Living on a beer budget,) I still prefer champagne.

4. Sometimes it is possible to reduce your sentences to single-word modifiers.

I have (champagne) tastes and a (beer) budget.

In sentence combining, you are free to move parts of the sentence around, change words, add or delete words, or make whatever other changes you find necessary. Anything goes, so long as you don't drastically alter the meaning of the base sentences. Remember that your aim in combining sentences is to create effective sentences, not long ones. Clarity is essential, and brevity has force.

In the following exercises, try your solutions aloud before you write them. You may also want to refer to Chapters 31 and 32 for advice on using the comma and the semicolon, respectively.

Exercise 27.1*

Combine each pair of sentences using a FANBOYS connecting word *and, but, or, nor, for, so,* or *yet.* Suggested answers for the exercises in this chapter begin on page 529.

1. We cannot sell our cottage.
   We will live there instead.

2. There are three solutions given for this problem.
   All of them are correct.

3. The people in our firm work very hard.
   They wouldn't want it any other way.

4. We could spend our day off shopping at the mall.
   We could spend the day fishing.

5. Great leaders do not bully their people.
   They do not deceive them.

6. I will not be able to finish my report by the deadline.
   There are only two hours before the deadline.

7. Jennifer knows that she will probably not get the vice-president's job.
   She wants the experience of applying for it.

8. Finish the estimate.
   Do not begin work until the estimate has been approved.

9. Today has been the worst day of my life.
   My horoscope was right today.

10. The government did not offer me a job.
    It did not even reply to my letter.

Exercise 27.2*

Using dependent-clause cues (see Chapter 23, page 342), combine the following sentences into longer, more interesting units.

Hint: Read each set of statements through to the end before you begin to combine them, and try out several variations aloud or in your head before writing down your preferred solution.

1. Leonardo da Vinci was a great artist and inventor.
   He invented scissors, among other things.

2. Cats can produce over 100 vocal sounds.
   Dogs can make only 10 vocal sounds.

3. It is said that men don't cry.
   They do cry while assembling furniture.

4. The name Wendy was made up for a book.
   The book was called *Peter Pan*.

5. Ten percent of Canadians are heavy drinkers.
   Thirty-five percent of Canadians abstain from alcohol.

6. Travel broadens the mind.
   Travel flattens the bank account.

7. We are seeking an experienced and innovative director.
   The candidate should be fluent in French.

8. One hundred thousand Vietnam veterans have taken their own lives.
   This is twice the number who were killed in action.

9. My cooking class went on a field trip to gather greens for a salad.
   We discovered that what we thought was watercress was not watercress.
   It was poison ivy.

10. The classmates ate the salad.
    Eight were hospitalized.
    No one was seriously affected.

Exercise 27.3

Combine the following sentences, using the connecting words listed in Exercise 27.1 and the dependent-clause cues listed on page 342.

1. Mario loses a girlfriend.
   He goes shopping for new clothes.

2. Failure breeds fatigue, according to Mortimer Adler.
   There is nothing more energizing than success.

3. We won't have enough stock to fill our orders.
   A shipment arrives today.

4. Friends may come, and friends may go.
   Enemies accumulate.

5. Marriage is for serious people.
   I have not considered it an option.

6. Divorce is an acknowledgement.
   There was not a true commitment in the first place.
   Some people still believe this.

7. In his essay "A Modest Proposal for a Divorce Ceremony," Pierre Berton
   proposed that Canada institute a formal divorce ceremony.
   The divorce ceremony would be like a formal wedding ceremony.
   All the symbolism would be reversed.

8. The bride, for example, would wear black.
   Immediately after the ceremony, the newly divorced couple would go
   into the vestry.
   They would scratch their names off the marriage register.

9. Twenty percent of adults in Canada are illiterate.
   Fifty percent of the adults who can read say they never read books.
   This is an astonishing fact.

10. Canada is a relatively rich country.
    Most of us brush up against hunger and homelessness almost daily.
    We encounter men, and less often, women begging.
    They are on downtown street corners.

After you have combined a number of sentences, you can evaluate your work. Read your sentences out loud. How they *sound* is important. Test your work against these six characteristics of successful sentences:

Summary

1. **Meaning:** Have you said what you mean?
2. **Clarity:** Is your sentence clear? Can it be understood on the first reading?
3. **Coherence:** Do the parts of your sentence fit together logically and smoothly?
4. **Emphasis:** Are the most important ideas either at the end or at the beginning of the sentence?
5. **Conciseness:** Is the sentence direct and to the point? Have you cut out all redundant or repetitious words?
6. **Rhythm:** Does the sentence flow smoothly? Are there any interruptions in the development of the key idea(s)? Do the interruptions help to emphasize important points, or do they distract the reader?

If your sentences pass all six tests of successful sentence style, you may be confident that they are both technically correct and pleasing to the ear. No reader could ask for more.

28

Mastering Subject–Verb Agreement

Singular and Plural

One of the most common writing errors is lack of agreement between subject and verb. Both must be singular, or both must be plural. If one is singular and the other plural, you have an agreement problem. You have another kind of agreement problem if your subject and verb are not both in the same "person" (see Chapter 30, pages 396–415).

Let's clarify some terms. First, it's important to distinguish between **singular** and **plural**.

- "Singular" means one person or thing.
- "Plural" means more than one person or thing.

Second, it's important to know what we mean when we refer to the concept of **person**:

- "First person" is the person(s) speaking or writing: *I, me; we, us*
- "Second person" is the person(s) being addressed: *you*
- "Third person" is the person(s) being spoken or written about: *he, she, it; they, them*

Here's an example of the singular and plural forms of a regular verb in the present tense.

	Singular	Plural
first person	I win	we win
second person	you win	you win
third person	she wins (*or* he, it, the horse wins)	they win (*or* the horses win)

The form that most often causes trouble is the third person because the verb endings do not match the subject endings. Third-person singular present-tense verbs end in -s, but their singular subjects do not. Third-person plural verbs never end in -s, while their subjects normally do. Look at these examples.

A <u>fire</u> <u>burns</u>.
The <u>car</u> <u>skids</u>.
The <u>father</u> <u>cares</u> for the children.

The three singular verbs, all of which end in -s (*burns, skids, cares*), agree with their singular subjects (*fire, car, woman*), none of which ends in -s. When the subjects become plural, the verbs change form, too.

Four <u>fires</u> <u>burn</u>.
The <u>cars</u> <u>skid</u>.
The <u>fathers</u> <u>care</u> for the children.

Now all of the subjects end in -s, and none of the verbs does.

To ensure **subject–verb agreement**, follow this basic rule:

Subjects and verbs must both be either singular or plural.

This rule causes difficulty only when the writer doesn't know which word in the sentence is the subject and so makes the verb agree with the wrong word. As long as you decode the sentence correctly (see Chapter 22), you'll have no problem making every subject agree with its verb.

If you have not already done so, now is the time to memorize this next rule:

The subject of a sentence is NEVER in a prepositional phrase.

Here's an example of how errors occur.

Only one of the 2,000 ticket buyers are going to win.

What is the subject of this sentence? It's not *buyers*, but *one*. The verb must agree with *one*, which is clearly singular. The verb *are* does not agree with *one*, so the sentence is incorrect. It should read

Grammar

Only <u>one</u> ~~of the 2,000 ticket buyers~~ <u>is</u> going to win.

Pay special attention to words that end in *-one, -thing,* or *-body.* They cause problems for nearly every writer.

Words ending in *-one*, *-thing*, or *-body* are always singular.

When used as subjects, these pronouns require singular verbs.

anyone	anything	anybody
everyone	everything	everybody
no one	nothing	nobody
someone	something	somebody

The last part of the pronoun subject is the tip-off here: every*one,* any*thing,* no*body.* If you focus on this last part, you'll remember to use a singular verb with these subjects. Usually, these words cause trouble only when modifiers crop up between them and their verbs. For example, you would never write "Everyone are here." The trouble starts when you insert a group of words in between the subject and the verb. You might, if you weren't careful, write this: "Everyone involved in implementing the company's new policies and procedures are here." The meaning is plural: several people are present. But the subject (*everyone*) is singular, so the verb must be *is.*

More subject–verb agreement errors are caused by violations of this rule than any other. Be sure you understand it. Memorize it, and then test your understanding by doing the following exercise before you go any further.

Exercise 28.1*

Rewrite each of the following sentences, using the alternative beginning shown. Answers for this chapter begin on page 530.

Example: <u>She</u> <u>wants</u> to make a short documentary.
<u>They</u> <u>want</u> to make a short documentary.

1. He sells used essays to other students.
   They

2. That new guideline affects all the office procedures.
   Those

3. Everyone who shops at Pimrock's receives a free can of tuna.
   All those

4. The woman maintains that her boss has been harassing her.
The women

5. That girl's father is looking for a rich husband for her.
Those

So far, so good. You can match up singular subjects with singular verbs and plural subjects with plural verbs. Now let's take a look at a few of the complications that make subject–verb agreement such a disagreeable problem.

Five Special Cases

Some subjects are tricky. They look singular but are actually plural, or they look plural when they're really singular. There are six kinds of these slippery subjects, all of them common, and all of them likely to trip up the unwary writer.

1. Compound subjects joined by *or; either . . . or; neither . . . nor;* or *not . . . but*

Most of the compound subjects we've dealt with so far have been joined by *and* and have required plural verbs, so agreement hasn't been a problem. But watch out when the two or more elements of a compound subject are joined by *or; either . . . or; neither . . . nor;* or *not . . . but.* In these cases, the verb agrees in number with the nearest subject. That is, if the subject closest to the verb is singular, the verb will be singular; if the subject closest to the verb is plural, the verb must be plural too.

Neither <u>the coach</u> nor <u>the players are</u> ready to give up.

Neither <u>the players</u> nor <u>the coach is</u> ready to give up.

Exercise 28.2*

Circle the correct verb in each of the following sentences.

1. Not your physical charms but your honesty (is are) what I find attractive.

2. Either your job performance or your school assignments (is are) going to suffer if you continue your frantic lifestyle.

3. The college has decided that neither final marks nor a diploma (is are) to be issued to students who owe library fines.

4. Not unemployment but the rising cost of medical care (is are) Canadians' chief concern.

5. Neither the compensation nor the benefits (tempt tempts) me to accept your offer.

2. Subjects that look like compound subjects but really aren't

Don't be fooled by phrases beginning with words such as *with, like, together with, in addition to,* or *including.* These prepositional phrases are NOT part of the subject of the sentence. Since they do not affect the verb, you can mentally cross them out.

> Mario's <u>brother</u>, ~~together with three of his buddies~~, <u>is going</u> to the Yukon to look for work.

Obviously four people are looking for work. Nevertheless, the subject (<u>brother</u>) is singular, and so the verb must be singular (<u>is going</u>).

> All my <u>courses</u>, ~~except economics~~, <u>are</u> easier this term.

If you mentally cross out the phrase *except economics,* you can easily see that the verb (<u>are</u>) must be plural to agree with the plural subject (<u>courses</u>).

Exercise 28.3*

Circle the correct verb in each of the following sentences.

1. Some meals, like tagine, (is are) best enjoyed in a large group.

2. Our city, along with many other North American urban centres, (register registers) a dangerous level of carbon monoxide pollution in the summer months.

3. The Tour de France, like the Olympic Games, (is are) a world-class athletic competition.

4. Lori's mother, along with her current boyfriends, (wonder wonders) when she'll decide to settle down.

5. My English instructor, in addition to my math, biology, and even my learning skills instructor, (put, puts) a lot of pressure on me.

3. *Each (of), either (of), neither (of)*

Used as subjects, these words (or phrases) take singular verbs.

<u>Either</u> <u><u>is</u></u> acceptable to me.

<u>Each</u> <u>wants</u> desperately to win.

<u>Neither</u> of the stores <u><u>is</u></u> open after six o'clock. (Remember, the subject is never in a prepositional phrase.)

Exercise 28.4*

Circle the correct verb in each of the following sentences.

1. Unless we hear from the coach, neither of us (is are) playing this evening.
2. Each of these courses (involve involves) field placement.
3. When my girlfriend asks if she has lost weight, I know that either of my answers (is are) bound to be wrong.
4. Each of the women (want wants) desperately to win the Ms. Nanaimo bodybuilding competition.
5. Strict discipline is what each of our teachers (believe believes) in.

4. Collective nouns

A **collective noun** is a word that names a group. Some examples are *company, class, committee, team, crowd, band, family, audience, public,* and *jury.* When you are referring to the group acting as a *unit,* use a *singular* verb. When you are referring to the *members* of the group acting *individually,* use a *plural* verb.

The <u>team</u> <u><u>is</u></u> sure to win tomorrow's game. (Here *team* refers to the group acting as a whole.)

The <u>team</u> <u>are</u> getting into their uniforms now. (The members of the team are acting individually.)

Exercise 28.5*

Circle the correct verb in each of the following sentences.

1. The whole gang (plan plans) to attend the bikers' rally.

Grammar

2. The wolf pack (has have) been almost wiped out by local ranchers.
3. By noon on Friday, the whole dorm (has have) left their rooms and headed for the local pubs and coffeehouses.
4. After only two hours' discussion, the committee (was were) able to reach consensus.
5. The majority of Canadians, according to a recent survey, (is are) not so conservative about sex and morality as we had assumed.

5. Units of money, time, mass, length, and distance

When used as subjects, they all require singular verbs.

Four kilometres is too far to walk in this weather.

Remember that 2.2 pounds equals a kilogram.

Three weeks is a long time to wait to get your paper back.

Exercise 28.6*

Circle the correct verb in each of the following sentences.

1. No wonder you are suspicious if $70 (was were) what you paid for last night's pizza.
2. Tim told his girlfriend that nine years (seem seems) like a long time to wait.
3. Forty hours of classes (is are) too much in one week.
4. When you are anxiously looking for a gas station, 30 km (is are) a long distance.
5. Ninety cents (seems seem) very little to tip, even for poor service.

In Exercises 28.7 and 28.8, correct the errors in subject–verb agreement. (Some rephrasing may be required.) Check your answers to each exercise before going on.

Exercise 28.7*

1. Neither of the following two sentences are correct.

2. The teachers, with the full support of the college administration, treats plagiarism as a serious offence.

3. Either good looks or intelligence run in our family, but never at the same time.

4. None of these computer programs are able to streamline our billing procedures.

5. The enjoyment of puns and jokes involving plays on words are the result of having too little else on your mind.

6. Anyone who jumps from one of Paris's many bridges are in Seine.

7. It is amazing how much better the orchestra play now that the conductor is sober.

8. The number of layoffs reported in the headlines seem to be rising again.

9. Her supervisors all agree that Emily need further training to be effective.

10. Canada's First Nations population are thought to have come to this continent from Asia thousands of years before the Europeans arrived in North America.

Grammar

Exercise 28.8*

   Quebec City, along with Montreal, Toronto, and Vancouver, are among Canada's great gourmet centres. Whereas Toronto is a relative latecomer to this list, neither Quebec City nor Montreal are strangers to those who seeks fine dining. Indeed, travel and food magazines have long affirmed that the inclusion of these two cities in a Quebec vacation are a "must." Montreal is perhaps more international in its offerings, but Quebec City provides exquisite proof that French-Canadian cuisine and hospitality is second to none in the world. Amid the Old World charm of the lower city is to be found some of the quaintest and most enjoyable traditional restaurants; the newer sections of town boasts equally fine dining in more contemporary surroundings. The combination of the wonderful food and the city's fascinating charms are sure to make any visitor return frequently. Either the summer, when the city blooms and outdoor cafés abound, or the winter, when Carnaval turns the streets into hundreds of connecting parties, are wonderful times to visit one of Canada's oldest and most interesting cities.

GO TO WEB

EXERCISES **28.1, 28.2, 28.3, 28.4**

Summary

- Subjects and verbs must agree: both must be singular, or both must be plural.
- The subject of a sentence is never in a prepositional phrase.
- Pronouns ending in *-one, -thing,* or *-body* are singular and require singular verbs.
- Subjects joined by *and* are always plural.
- When subjects are joined by *or; either . . . or; neither . . . nor;* or *not . . . but,* the verb agrees with the subject that is closest to it.
- When looking for the subject in a sentence, ignore phrases beginning with *as well as, including, in addition to, like, together with,* etc. They are prepositional phrases.
- When *each, either,* and *neither* are used as subjects, they require singular verbs.
- Collective nouns are usually singular.
- Units of money, time, mass, length, and distance are always singular.

Exercise 28.9

As a final check of your mastery of subject–verb agreement, correct the following sentences as necessary.

1. Each of the options you outlined in your concluding remarks are worth examining further.

2. My opinion of the college's accounting programs are that neither of them are what I need.

3. Every one of the dozen people we interviewed qualify for the position.

4. My whole family, with the exception of the cat, dislike anchovies on pizza.

5. The applause from a thousand enthusiastic fans were like music to the skaters' ears.

6. Neither of your decisions are likely to improve sales, let alone morale.

7. Three thousand dollars per term, the students agree, are too much to pay for their education.

8. Neither age nor illness prevents Uncle Alf from leering at the nurses.

9. The birth of triplets, after six other children in eight years, were too much for the parents to cope with.

10. Everything you have accomplished in the last three years are wasted if you fail this assignment.

29

Using Verbs Effectively

Good writers pay especially careful attention to verbs. A verb is to a sentence what an engine is to a car: it's the source of power—but it can also be a source of trouble. Now that you've conquered subject–verb agreement, it's time to turn to the three remaining essentials of correct verb use: **form**, **consistency**, and **voice**.

Choosing the Correct Verb Form

Every verb has four forms, called its **principal parts**:

1. The **infinitive** form: used with *to* and with *can, may, might, shall, will, could, should, would, must*
2. The **simple past** (also called the **past tense**)
3. The **present participle** (the **-ing**) form
4. The **past participle** form: used with *has* or *have*

Here are some examples:

Infinitive	Simple Past	Present Participle	Past Participle
dance	danced	dancing	danced
learn	learned	learning	learned
play	played	playing	played
seem	seemed	seeming	seemed

To use verbs correctly, you must be familiar with their principal parts. Knowing three facts will help you.

- The present participle, the *-ing* form, is always made up of the base form of the verb + *ing*.
- Your dictionary gives you the principal parts of all **irregular** verbs. Look up the base form, and you'll find the simple past and the present and past participles given beside it, usually in parentheses. For example, if you look up *sing* in your dictionary, you will find *sang* (simple past), *sung* (past participle), and *singing* (present participle) listed immediately after the verb itself. If the past tense and past participle are not given, the verb is **regular**.
- To form the simple past and the past participle of regular verbs: add *-ed* to the base form. The examples listed above — *dance, learn, play, seem* — are all regular verbs.

Unfortunately, many of the most common English verbs are irregular. Their past tenses and past participles are formed in unpredictable ways. The verbs in the list that follows are used so often that it is worth your time to memorize their principal parts. (We have not included the *-ing* form because, as we have noted above, it never causes any difficulty.)

The Principal Parts of Irregular Verbs

Infinitive	Simple Past	Past Participle
(Use with *to* and with helping/ auxiliary verbs)		(Use with *have, has, had*)
awake	awoke/awaked	awaked/awoken
be (am, is)	was/were	been
bear	bore	borne
beat	beat	beaten
become	became	become
begin	began	begun
bid (offer to pay)	bid	bid
bid (say, command)	bid/bade	bid/bidden
bite	bit	bitten
bleed	bled	bled
blow	blew	blown
break	broke	broken
bring	brought (*not* brang)	brought (*not* brung)

Grammar

Infinitive	Simple Past	Past Participle
(Use with *to* and with helping/ auxiliary verbs)		(Use with *have, has, had*)
broadcast	broadcast	broadcast
build	built	built
burst	burst	burst
buy	bought	bought
catch	caught	caught
choose	chose	chosen
come	came	come
cost	cost	cost
cut	cut	cut
deal	dealt	dealt
dig	dug	dug
dive	dived/dove	dived
do	did (*not* done)	done
draw	drew	drawn
dream	dreamed/dreamt	dreamed/dreamt
drink	drank (*not* drunk)	drunk
eat	ate	eaten
fall	fell	fallen
feed	fed	fed
feel	felt	felt
fight	fought	fought
find	found	found
fling	flung	flung
fly	flew	flown
forget	forgot	forgotten/forgot
forgive	forgave	forgiven
freeze	froze	frozen
get	got	got/gotten
give	gave	given
go	went	gone (*not* went)
grow	grew	grown
hang (suspend)	hung	hung
hang (put to death)	hanged	hanged
have	had	had
hear	heard	heard
hide	hid	hidden

NEL

Infinitive	Simple Past	Past Participle
(Use with *to* and with helping/ auxiliary verbs)		(Use with *have, has, had*)
hit	hit	hit
hold	held	held
hurt	hurt	hurt
keep	kept	kept
know	knew	known
lay (put or place)	laid	laid
lead	led	led
leave	left	left
lend	lent (*not* loaned)	lent (*not* loaned)
lie (recline)	lay	lain (*not* layed)
light	lit/lighted	lit/lighted
lose	lost	lost
mean	meant	meant
meet	met	met
pay	paid	paid
raise (lift up, increase, bring up)	raised	raised
ride	rode	ridden
ring	rang	rung
rise	rose	risen
run	ran	run
say	said	said
see	saw (*not* seen)	seen
sell	sold	sold
set (put or place)	set	set
shake	shook	shaken (*not* shook)
shine	shone	shone
sing	sang	sung
sink	sank	sunk
sit	sat	sat
sleep	slept	slept
slide	slid	slid
speak	spoke	spoken
speed	sped	sped
steal	stole	stolen
stick	stuck	stuck
strike (hit)	struck	struck

Infinitive	Simple Past	Past Participle
(Use with *to* and with helping/ auxiliary verbs)		(Use with *have, has, had*)
strike (affect)	struck	stricken
swear	swore	sworn
swim	swam	swum
swing	swung (*not* swang)	swung
take	took	taken
teach	taught	taught
tear	tore	torn
tell	told	told
think	thought	thought
throw	threw	thrown
wake	woke/waked	waked/woken
wear	wore	worn
weave	wove	woven
win	won	won
wind	wound	wound
wring	wrung	wrung
write	wrote	written

Exercise 29.1*

Find and correct the verbs in the following sentences. When you have finished, check your answers on page 532.

1. Once I laid down, I found it very hard to get up again.

2. The staff have ate all the sandwiches that were ordered for the board's lunch.

3. Have you ever rode in a Porsche?

4. Having finished his presentation, Greg set down to answer questions.

5. After spending all day in class, I need to lay down for an hour or two.

6. The contractor who was eventually chose was the one who submitted the lowest bid.

7. My computer has print the document in a font so small I can't read it.

8. When will I get back the money I loaned you last month?

9. After three years of constant use, our copier is practically wore out.

10. I should have knew that all generalizations are false.

GO TO WEB

EXERCISES **29.1, 29.2, 29.3, 29.4**

Exercise 29.2

As a final test of your mastery of verb forms, correct the errors in the following sentences.

1. We swum in the pool until my toes were almost froze.

2. The stars shined like diamonds the night I told Emmy-Lou how I feeled about her and gave her the ring that costed me a week's pay.

3. Dan had drove very slowly on the gravel road, but once he reached the highway he speeded away into the night.

4. She had forgot how much I dislike the green dress and weared it at the wedding rehearsal.

5. If only we had knew then what we know now, we wouldn't have spoke so quickly.

6. We have never forgave her for the time when her cell rung during the scariest part of the movie.

7. It finally sunk in that he had stole my heart.

8. After the band had sang "The Lion Sleeps Tonight" seven times, we realized that they had been payed too much because they only knowed four tunes.

9. The priest has spoke with the condemned man who will be hung in the morning unless the governor gives him a stay of execution.

10. I played the guitar they loaned me and sung an old tune that I had wrote when I was much younger.

Keeping Your Tenses Consistent

Verbs are time markers. Changes in tense express changes in time: past, present, or future.

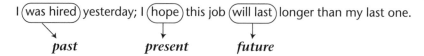

I (was hired) yesterday; I (hope) this job (will last) longer than my last one.

past   *present*   *future*

Sometimes, as in the example above, it is necessary to use several different tenses in a single sentence to get the meaning across. But most of the time, whether you're writing a sentence or a paragraph, you use one tense throughout. Normally, you choose either the past or the present tense, depending on the nature of your topic. (Few paragraphs are written completely in the future tense.) Here is the rule to follow.

> Don't change tense unless meaning requires it.

Readers like and expect consistency. If you begin a sentence with "I worried and fretted and delayed," your readers will tune in to the past-tense verbs and expect any other verbs in the sentence to be in the past tense too. Therefore, if you finish the sentence with ". . . and then I decide to give it a try," your readers will be jolted abruptly out of one time frame and into another. This sort of jolting is uncomfortable, and readers don't like it.

Shifting tenses is like shifting gears: it should be done smoothly and only when necessary. Avoid causing verbal whiplash: keep your tenses consistent.

Wrong: Monika starts the car and revved the engine.
Right: Monika started the car and revved the engine.
Also right: Monika starts the car and revs the engine.

Wrong: Carrie flounces into the room and sat down. Everyone stares.
Right: Carrie flounced into the room and sat down. Everyone stared.
Also right: Carrie flounces into the room and sits down. Everyone stares.

Exercise 29.3*

In this exercise, most of the sentences contain unnecessary tense shifts. Use the first verb in each sentence as your time marker and change the tense(s) of the other verb(s) in the sentence to agree with it. Answers are on page 532.

1. After he accused me, I call him a liar.

2. Hank Aaron broke Babe Ruth's record of 714 home runs in a lifetime when he hits number 715 in 1974.

3. Children are quite perceptive and will know when you are lying to them.

4. She went up to the counter and asks for a refund.

5. When Brad Pitt walked into the room, the girls go crazy.

6. You should not go into that building until the police arrive.

7. Tim walked into the room, took one look at Leroy, and smashes him right through the wall.

8. First you will greet the guests; then you show them to their rooms.

9. The largest cheese ever produced took 43 hours to make and weighs a whopping 15,723 kg.

10. He watches television until he finally went to sleep.

Grammar

Exercise 29.4*

Correct the 15 faulty tense shifts in this passage.

For some reason, when mistakes or accidents happen in radio or television, they were often hilariously funny. If, in the course of a conversation, someone said, "Here come the Duck and Doochess of Kent," listeners would probably be mildly amused. But many years ago, when an announcer makes that slip on a live radio broadcast, it becomes one of the most famous blunders in radio history. Tapes of the slip will be filed in "bloopers" libraries all over the world. This heightened sense of hilarity is the reason that so many people who work in radio dedicated their creativity to making the on-air announcer laugh while reading the news. To take one example, Lorne Greene's is the deeply serious voice that is heard on the CBC news during World War II. He is the victim of all kinds of pranks aimed at getting him to break up while reading the dark, often tragic, news of the combat overseas.

The pages of his news script are set on fire while he reads. He is even stripped naked as he reads, calmly, and apparently without strain. Lorne Greene will be a true professional. Many other newscasters, however, will have been highly susceptible to falling apart on air at the slightest provocation. And there were always people around a radio station who cannot resist giving them that little push.

GO TO WEB

EXERCISE 29.5

Exercise 29.5

To test and reinforce your mastery of correct verb forms and tense consistency, correct the 10 errors in the following paragraph. Use the italicized verb as your time marker.

The art of writing *is* not dead. Thanks to the use of computers in homes and businesses, it will now be more important than ever to be able to write competently. Not everyone agrees with this statement. Many people will continue to think that electronic technology has eliminated the need to learn how to write, but it will be clear that reports of the death of the written word were premature. Computer networking, bulletin boards, e-mail, and electronic forums made it more important than ever to write well. In the past, when letters were written on paper, writers could have checked their messages over before mailing them to ensure that there were no errors or embarrassing miscommunications. Now, however, communication is instantaneous, and any writing faults will be immediately apparent. The exposure of writing flaws, however, is not the only reason electronic communication links require the ability to write clear, unambiguous prose. Paper letters were normally mailed to a few people, at most.

Electronic mail, on the other hand, will often be sent to dozens, even hundreds, of receivers; therefore, the message will need to be carefully composed if all recipients are to understand what the writer intended. In today's world of electronic communication, good writing skills will be more important than ever before.

Choosing between Active and Passive Verbs

Verbs have another quality besides tense (or time). Verbs also have what is called "voice," which means the quality of being either active or passive. In sentences with **active voice** verbs, the "doer" of the action is the grammatical subject of the sentence.

Active voice: Good parents <u>support</u> their children.
A car <u>crushed</u> the cat.
Someone <u>will show</u> a movie in class.

In sentences with **passive voice** verbs, the grammatical subject of the sentence is the "receiver" of the action (that is, the subject is passively acted upon), and the "doer" becomes an object of the preposition *by* or is absent from the sentence entirely, as in the third example below.

Passive voice: Children <u>are supported</u> by good parents.
The cat <u>was crushed</u> by a car.
A movie <u>will be shown</u> in class.

You probably use the passive voice more often than you think you do. To be a better writer, you need to know the distinction between active and passive, to understand their different effects on the reader, and to use the passive voice only when it is appropriate to your meaning.

Grammar

There are three good reasons for choosing a passive verb rather than an active one.

> 1. The person or agent that performed the action is unknown (or the writer does not wish to disclose the identity).

My books <u>were stolen</u> from my locker this morning.

Giovanna's father <u>was killed</u> in Bosnia.

Unlike the streets of a typical prairie city, which <u>are laid out</u> on a grid, Vancouver's streets <u>are laid out</u> to follow the curves and bends of the harbour and the Fraser River.

> 2. You want to place the emphasis on the person, place, or object that was acted upon rather than on the subject that performed the action.

Early this morning, the Bank of Montreal at 16th and Granville <u>was robbed</u> by four men wearing nylon stockings over their heads and carrying shotguns.

This sentence focuses the reader's attention on the bank rather than on the robbers. A quite different effect is produced when the sentence is reconstructed in the active voice:

Four men wearing nylon stockings over their heads and carrying shotguns <u>robbed</u> the Bank of Montreal at 16th and Granville early this morning.

> 3. You are writing a technical or scientific report or a legal document.

Passive verbs are the appropriate choice when the focus is on the facts, methods, or procedures involved rather than on who discovered or performed them. Passive verbs also tend to establish an impersonal tone that is appropriate in these kinds of writing. Contrast the emphasis and tone of the following sentence pairs:

Passive: The heat <u>was increased</u> to 200°C and <u>was maintained</u> at that temperature.

Active: My lab partners and I <u>increased</u> the heat to 200°C and <u>maintained</u> it at that temperature.

Passive: Having been found guilty, the accused <u>was sentenced</u> to two years.

Active: The jury <u>found</u> the accused guilty, and the judge <u>sentenced</u> him to two years.

In general, because active verbs are more concise and forceful than passive verbs, they add vigour and impact to your writing. The distinction between active and passive is not something you should worry about during the drafting stage, however. The time to focus on verbs and decide whether active or passive would best serve your purpose is during revision. When you find a passive verb in your draft, think about who is doing what. Ask yourself why the "who" is not the subject of the sentence. If there's a good reason, then use the passive verb. Otherwise, choose an active verb.

Grammar

Exercise 29.6*

Rewrite the sentences below, changing their verbs from passive to active. Note that you may have to add a word or word group to identify the "doer" of the action of the verb.

Example: Matt's two front teeth <u>were knocked out</u> by Clark's shot.

Clark's shot <u>knocked out</u> Matt's two front teeth.

1. A meeting was called by the department head.
2. The espresso will be made by the server in a few minutes.
3. When it gets cold, the block heater is plugged in overnight.
4. For many years, steroids have been used by professional athletes to improve speed and endurance.
5. The dough must not be kneaded, or your pastry will be tough.
6. This postcard was written by my parents while they were hiking in Nepal.
7. This movie was made for less than $900,000 by a crew of students.
8. While our neighbours were vacationing in the Caribbean, their house was broken into by thieves.
9. An error was made in the code you wrote for this program.
10. The Red Sox and the White Sox have been replaced as the stupidest team names in sports by the Mighty Ducks.

Exercise 29.7*

Rewrite each of the sentences below, changing the verbs from active to passive or vice versa, and then decide which sentence is more effective.

1. Sarah McLachlan won another Juno.
2. Carl spiked the ball after scoring the winning points.
3. City council passed a bylaw forbidding smoking in bars and restaurants.
4. Forty-eight hours later, 2 mL of sterile water was added to the culture in the petri dish.
5. By standing in line all night, Courtenay managed to get four tickets for the concert.
6. The 10 p.m. news revealed the truth behind the famous Doobie Brothers scandal.
7. The judgment was finally announced today, almost a year after the environmental hearings were concluded.
8. After a long debate, the committee finally agreed to endorse Yasmin's fundraising proposal.
9. A computer program that analyzes speech patterns has been developed by psychologist Dr. Hans Steiner of Stanford University.
10. After years of research among college students, it has been concluded by Dr. Steiner that people who frequently use passive-voice constructions tend to be maladjusted.

Exercise 29.8

Rewrite the following paragraphs, changing the 15 misused passive verbs to active verbs. (Remember, passive voice verbs are sometimes appropriate.)

The last time Glenn had his hair cut by the barber at the local mall was the day of the big high-school graduation dance. One of the prettiest girls in the school had been invited to the prom by Glenn, and to make a good impression was what was wanted. The barber was thought to be talented, if a little unconventional: he had long hair and a vaguely dreamy smile. It was well known by everybody that he had been a hippie back in the 1970s; it was thought by some that his youthful excesses might be responsible for his soft voice and mumbling speech.

Glenn settled into the chair, and a few inaudible words were muttered by the barber. Glenn made a guess at what had been said and replied that the weather was fine. Another mumble from the barber. This time, Glenn thought he'd been asked which college he planned to attend in the fall, and he answered politely. At this point, the conversation was stopped, and the barber got on with his work.

Half an hour later, the sheet was swept away, and the chair was spun so that Glenn could see his image in the mirror. To his horror, it was discovered that he was practically bald, except for an 8 cm high strip of hair running from his forehead to the nape of his neck. Glenn's scream was heard through the entire mall. After the excitement died down, it was learned by the crowds of curious shoppers that when Glenn had been asked what kind of haircut he wanted, Glenn had replied, "Mohawk."

So the prom was attended by Glenn in a tux, a startling haircut, and with a very unsympathetic date. The following week, Glenn left for Hamilton and Mohawk College. His high-school sweetheart was never seen by him again.

Grammar

30

Solving
Pronoun Problems

Look at the following sentences. Can you tell what's wrong with them?

"Dev must choose between you and I," Miranda said.

When you are on a diet, it is a good idea for one to avoid Bagel World.

We had invited everybody to come with their partner, so we were a little surprised when Marcel showed up with his Doberman.

Everyone is expected to do their duty.

Mohammed's nose was badly sunburned, but it has now completely disappeared.

Most of the students that were protesting tuition increases were ones which had been elected to council.

These sentences all contain pronoun errors. After verbs, pronouns are the class of words most likely to cause problems for writers. In this chapter, we will look at the three aspects of pronoun usage that can trip you up if you're not careful: pronoun form, agreement, and consistency. We'll also look at the special problems of usage that can lead to sexist language.

Choosing the Correct Pronoun Form

First you need to be sure you are using the "right" pronouns—that is, the correct pronoun forms—in your sentences. Here are some examples of incorrect pronoun usage:

Her and me can't agree on anything.

The reason for the quarrel is a personal matter between he and I.

How do you know which form of a pronoun to use? The answer depends on the pronoun's place and function in your sentence.

SUBJECT AND OBJECT PRONOUNS

There are two forms of personal pronouns: one is used for subjects, and the other is used for objects. Pronoun errors occur when you confuse the two. In Chapter 22, you learned to identify the subject of a sentence. Keep that information in mind as you learn the following basic rule.

When a subject or a complement is a pronoun, the pronoun must be in **subject form**. Otherwise, use the **object form**.

Subject Pronouns

Singular	Plural
I	we
you	you
he, she, it, one	they

She and *I* tied for first place. (The pronouns are the subject of the sentence.)

The lucky winners of the all-expenses-paid weekend in Paris are *they*. (The pronoun is the complement and refers to the subject of the sentence, *winners*.)

The student who regularly asks for extra help is *he*. (The pronoun is the complement and refers to the subject of the sentence, *student*.)

Object Pronouns

Singular	Plural
me	us
you	you
him, her, it, one	them

Between you and *me*, I think he's cute. (*Me* is not the subject of the sentence; it is one of the objects of the preposition *between*.)

Omar asked *him* and *me* for help. (*Him* and *me* are not the subject of the verb *asked*; *Omar* is, so the pronouns need to be in the object form.)

Be especially careful when using pronouns in compound subjects or after prepositions. If you can remember the following two rules, you'll be able to eliminate most potential errors.

1. A pronoun that is part of a compound subject is *always* in subject form.
2. A pronoun that follows a preposition is *always* in object form.

Examples:

She and *I* had tickets to U2. (The pronouns are used as a compound subject.)

It is up to *you* and *her* to pay for the damage. (The pronouns follow the preposition *to*.)

When you're dealing with a pair of pronouns and can't decide which form to use, try this test.[1] Mentally cross out one pronoun at a time, then read aloud the sentence you've created. Applying this technique to the first example above, you get "*She* has tickets" and "*I* have tickets." Both sound right and are correct. In the second sentence, if you try the pronouns separately, you get "It is up to *you*" and "It is up to *her*." Again, you know by the sound that these are the correct forms. (You would never say "*Her* had tickets," or "*Me* had tickets," or "It is up to *she*.") If you deal with paired pronouns one at a time, you are unlikely to choose the wrong form.

Note, too, that when a pair of pronouns includes "I" or "me," that pronoun comes last. For example, we write "between *you* and *me*" (not

---

[1] This test is reliable only for those who are fluent in English. ESL students must rely on memorizing the rules.

"between *me* and *you*"); we write *"she* and *I"* (not *"I* and *she"*). There is no grammatical reason for this rule. It's based on courtesy. Good manners require that you speak of others first and yourself last.

Exercise 30.1*

Correct the pronouns in these sentences as necessary. Answers for the exercises in this chapter begin on page 534.

1. No one except you and I would go camping in this weather.
2. Him and I can't figure out this problem set any better than you and her could.
3. George and him fell asleep in class, as usual.
4. Do you want to work with Emma and she?
5. We can use the film passes all week, and you and her can use them on the weekend, when Biff and me are going skiing.
6. Thanks to the recommendations provided by your math instructor and I, you and her got the tutorial jobs.
7. As we were going to class, Karl and me heard that there had been an explosion in the lab.
8. If it hadn't been for Hassan and he, the only ones to show up would have been you and I.
9. Quentin and him agreed to split the price of a case with Stan and I.
10. Only two students passed the midterm: Nadia and me.

GO TO WEB

EXERCISES 30.1, 30.2

Using Pronouns in Contrast Constructions

Choosing the correct pronoun form is more than just a matter of not wanting to appear ignorant or careless. Sometimes the form you use determines the meaning of your sentence. Consider these two sentences:

Stefan is more interested in his new car than *I.*

Stefan is more interested in his new car than *me.*

There's a world of difference between the meaning of the subject form ("Stefan is more interested in his new car than *I* [am]") and the object form ("Stefan is more interested in his new car than [in] *me*").

When using a pronoun after *than*, *as well as*, or *as*, decide whether you mean to contrast the pronoun with the subject of the sentence. If you do, use the subject form of the pronoun. If not, use the object form.

Jay would rather watch television than I. (*I* is contrasted with the subject, *Jay*.)

Jay would rather watch television than me. (*Me* is contrasted with the object, *television*.)

To test your sentence, try putting a verb after the pronoun. If the sentence makes sense, then the subject form is the form you want.

Jay would rather watch television than I [would].

Some writers prefer to leave the added verb in place, a practice that eliminates any possibility of confusion.

Exercise 30.2*

Correct the following sentences where necessary.

1. At 14, my younger brother is already taller than me.

2. No one likes partying more than him and Anne.

3. Would you like to join Daniel and I for dinner and a movie?

4. Only one person in this firm could manage the department as well as him.

5. At last I have met someone who enjoys grilled liver as much as me!

6. We can skate as well as them, but they are much better at shooting and defending than us.

7. More than me, Serge uses the computer to draft and revise his papers.

Exercise 30.3*

Revise the following paragraph to correct the errors in pronoun form.

(1) My boyfriend and me have different opinions when it comes to food. (2) I like fast food better than him. (3) He likes vegetables better than me. (4) In fact, between you and I, he is a vegetarian, though he would deny it. (5) When we go out with friends, it is difficult for they to know where to take him and I because our tastes are so different. (6) The only type of restaurant where us and them can all have what we like is Italian. (7) There, him and his friends can sample pasta primavera and eggplant parmigiana while my friends and I tuck into spaghetti and meatballs and pepperoni pizza. (8) We are probably not as healthy as they, but they don't seem to enjoy their food as much as us.

Now that you know how to choose the correct form of pronouns within a sentence, let's turn to the problems of using pronouns consistently throughout a sentence and a paragraph.

Pronoun–Antecedent Agreement

The name of this pronoun problem may sound difficult, but the idea is simple. Pronouns are words that substitute for or refer to the name of a person, place, or thing mentioned elsewhere in your sentence or your paragraph. The word(s) that a pronoun substitutes for or refers to is called the **antecedent**.

(Hannibal) had (his) own way of doing things. (The pronoun *his* refers to the antecedent *Hannibal*.)

Grammar

Chantal respects her boss. (The pronoun *her* refers to the antecedent *Chantal*.)

The computer is processing as fast as it can. (The pronoun *It* substitutes for the antecedent *computer*.)

Usually, as in these three examples, the antecedent comes before the pronoun that refers to it. Here is the rule to remember.

A pronoun must agree with its antecedent in
- number (singular or plural)
- person (first, second, or third)
- gender (masculine, feminine, or neuter)

Most of the time, you follow this rule without even realizing that you know it. For example, you would never write

Hannibal had *your* own way of doing things.

Chantal respects *its* boss.

The computer is processing as fast as *she* can.

You know these sentences are incorrect even if you may not know precisely why they are wrong.

There are three kinds of pronoun–antecedent agreement that you do need to learn about. They lead to errors that, unlike the examples above, are not obvious, and you need to know them so you can watch out for them. The rules you need to learn involve **indefinite pronouns ending in -one, -body, or -thing; vague references; and relative pronouns.**

1. INDEFINITE PRONOUNS: PRONOUNS ENDING IN *-ONE, -BODY*, OR *-THING*

The most common pronoun–antecedent agreement problem involves **indefinite pronouns:**

anyone	anybody	anything
everyone	everybody	everything

no one	nobody	nothing
someone	somebody	something
each (one)		

In Chapter 28, you learned that when these words are used as subjects they are singular and take singular verbs. So it makes sense that the pronouns that stand for or refer to them must also be singular.

> Antecedents ending in *-one*, *-body*, or *-thing* are singular and must be referred to by singular pronouns: *he, she, it; his, her, its.*

Please put everything back in *its* place.

Anybody can retire comfortably if *he* or *she* begins planning now.

Everyone is expected to do *his* share.

No one in *his* right mind would claim *he* enjoys living in this climate.

Now take another look at the last two sentences. Until about 30 years ago, the pronouns *he, him,* and *his* were used with singular antecedents to refer to both men and women. In order to appeal to the broadest possible audience, most writers today are careful to avoid this usage and other examples of what may be seen as sexist language.

In informal speech, it has become acceptable to use plural pronouns with *-one, -body,* or *-thing* antecedents. Although these antecedents are grammatically singular and take singular verbs, they are often plural in meaning, and in conversation we find ourselves saying

Everyone is expected to do *their* share.

No one has to stay if *they* don't want to.

This usage is acceptable in speech, but it is not acceptable in academic or professional writing.

Writers sometimes make errors in pronoun–antecedent agreement because they are trying to write without indicating whether the person referred to is male or female. A sentence such as "Everyone is required to do *their* oral presentation" is incorrect, as we have seen, but it does avoid making "everyone" male. It also avoids the awkwardness of "Everyone is required to do *his* or *her* oral presentation." There are two better ways to solve this problem.

Grammar

1. Revise the sentence to leave the pronoun out.

Everyone is required to deliver an oral presentation in the last week of class.

or

An oral presentation is required of everyone in the last week of class.

Such creative avoidance of gender-specific or incorrect constructions can be an interesting challenge. The results often sound a little artificial, however. The second method is easier to accomplish.

2. Revise the sentence to make both the antecedent and the pronoun plural.

You are all required to deliver an oral presentation in the last week of class.

or

All students are required to deliver an oral presentation in the last week of class.

Here are two more examples for you to study.

Problem: Everybody has been given his or her assignment.
Revision 1:   Everybody has been given an assignment.
Revision 2:   All of the students have been given their assignments.

Problem: No one wants his copy edited.
Revision 1:   No one wants copy editing.
Revision 2:   Most writers object to having their copy edited.

Exercise 30.4*

In the following sentences, identify the most appropriate word(s) from the choices given in parentheses. (Note: the options may not be the best choices stylistically; just select the one that is grammatically correct in each case.) Check your answers on page 534 before continuing.

1. Everyone who enjoys a thrilling match will reserve (his their) seat for today's chess club meeting.

2. Despite the inconvenience, everyone climbed to the fourth floor to hand in (her their) course evaluation.
3. Each of her sons has successfully completed (his their) diploma.
4. Someone with a lot of cash left (her their) purse in the women's washroom.
5. Every reporter must decide for (himself themselves) how far (he they) will go in pursuit of a story.

Exercise 30.5*

Rewrite the sentences in Exercise 30.4 to eliminate sexist language.

Exercise 30.6*

Correct the following sentences where necessary, being careful to avoid awkward repetition and sexist language.

1. Virginia claims that every one of her male friends has a room of their own.
2. Almost everyone I know is concerned about finding a job that will be suitable for him or her.
3. Anybody who applies for a job with this institution can expect to spend a lot of their time in selection committee interviews.
4. Taking a picture of someone when they are not looking can produce interesting results.
5. Nearly every man who can cook will tell you that they enjoy preparing food.

2. VAGUE REFERENCE

Avoiding the second potential difficulty with pronoun–antecedent agreement requires common sense and the ability to think like your readers. If you look at your writing from your readers' point of view, it is unlikely that you will break the following rule.

Every pronoun must have a clearly identifiable antecedent.

The mistake that occurs when you fail to follow this rule is called **vague reference.**

Chris told his brother that he was losing his hair.

Who is going bald? Chris or his brother?

Here's another example:

The faculty are demanding higher salaries and fewer teaching hours, but the administration does not support them.

What does the administration not favour: higher salaries, fewer classes, or the faculty themselves?

In sentences like these, you can only guess the meaning because you don't know who or what is being referred to by the pronouns. You can make such sentences less confusing by using either more names or other nouns and by using fewer pronouns. For example:

Chris told his brother Sam that Sam was losing his hair.

The faculty are demanding higher salaries and fewer teaching hours, but the administration does not support their demands.

Another type of vague reference occurs when there is no antecedent at all in the sentence for the pronoun to refer to.

I sold my skis last year and can't even remember how to do it anymore. (Do what?)

Reading is Sophia's passion, but she says she doesn't have a favourite. (A favourite what?)

My roommate smokes constantly, *which* I hate. (There is no noun or pronoun for *which* to refer to.)

I hate homework; this is my downfall. (*This* refers to homework, but homework is not my downfall. My hatred of doing it is.)

How would you revise these sentences? Try it, then see our suggestions in the footnote below.[2]

Be sure that every pronoun has a clear antecedent with which it agrees in number, person, and gender. Once you have mastered this principle, you'll have no further trouble with pronoun–antecedent agreement.

---

[2]I sold my skis last year and can't even remember how to *slalom* anymore.

Reading is Sophie's passion, but she says she doesn't have a favourite *writer*.

My roommate is constantly smoking, *which* I hate.

She hates doing homework; *this* is her downfall.

Exercise 30.7*

Correct the following sentences where necessary. There are several ways to fix these sentences. In some cases, the antecedent is missing, and you need to supply one. In other cases, the antecedent is so vague that the meaning of the sentence can be interpreted in more than one way. You need to rewrite these sentences to make the meaning clear.

1. I know that smoking is bad for me and everyone else, but I can't give them up.

2. If your pet rat won't eat its food, feed it to the kitty.

3. Our cat is a picky eater, which is inconvenient and expensive.

4. Whenever Stefan and Matt played poker, he stacked the deck.

5. The gorilla was mean and hungry because he had finished it all in the morning.

6. Madonna has transformed herself at least four times in her career, which makes her unique.

7. Dani backed her car into a garbage truck and dented it.

8. Rocco was suspicious of handgun control because he thought everyone should have one for late-night subway rides.

9. Get your ears pierced during this week's special and take home an extra pair free.

10. Our car is in the shop, but this won't keep us from going to the party.

Exercise 30.8

To test your understanding of the pronoun problems we have covered so far, try this exercise, which contains all three kinds of pronoun–antecedent agreement errors. Correct the following sentences where necessary.

1. Each of her suitors had their faults, but Denise decided to overlook the shortcomings of the one that had the most money.

2. Embezzling is what he does best, but he hasn't been able to pull one off lately.

3. Everyone may pick up their exams in my office on Tuesday after 9:00 a.m.

4. None of the candidates came with their résumé, so we had to reject them all.

5. Every applicant must submit their portfolio of work, their essay on why they want to enter the program, and a neatly folded $50 bill.

6. When I go fishing, I expect to catch at least a few.

7. Every secretary knows that their boss is someone that could not survive for 15 minutes without competent secretarial assistance.

8. All the women in this beauty pageant are treated like a sister even though the competition is fierce.

9. Everybody that joins the tour will receive their own souvenir hat.

10. Before a Canadian votes, it is their responsibility to make themselves familiar with the candidates and the issues.

---

3. RELATIVE PRONOUNS

The third potential difficulty with pronoun–antecedent agreement is how to use relative pronouns—*who/whoever, whom/whomever, which,* and *that*—correctly. Relative pronouns refer to someone or something already mentioned in the sentence or paragraph. Here is the guideline to follow.

Use *who/whom* and *whoever/whomever* refer to people.
Use *that* and *which* to refer to everything else.

The student *who* won the Governor General's Academic Medal decided to go to Dalhousie.

For *whom* are you voting: the Liberals or the New Democrats?

The moose *that* I met looked hostile.

Her car, *which* is imported, is smaller than cars *that* are built here.

Tips:

1. Whether you need *who* or *whom*, *whoever* or *whomever*, depends on the pronoun's place and function in your sentence. Apply the basic rule of pronoun usage: if the pronoun is acting as, or refers to, the subject or the complement, use *who/whoever*. Otherwise, use *whom/whomever*.

My husband was the idiot *who* entered a contest to win a trip to Moose Factory. (The pronoun refers to the subject of the sentence, *husband*.)

The trip's promoters were willing to settle for *whomever* they could get. (The pronoun does not refer to the sentence's subject, *promoters*; it is the object of the preposition *for*.)

An even simpler solution to this problem is to rewrite the sentence so you don't need either *who* or *whom*.

My husband entered a contest to win a trip to Moose Factory.

The trip's promoters were willing to settle for anyone they could get.

2. *That* is required more often than *which*. You should use *which* only in a clause that is separated from the rest of the sentence by commas. (See Comma Rule 4 on page 420.)

The moose *that* I met looked hostile.

The moose, *which* was standing right in front of my car, looked hostile.

Exercise 30.9*

Correct the following sentences where necessary.

1. The actress that saw her first grey hair thought she'd dye.

2. I am a longtime fan of David Cronenberg, a director that began his career in Canada.

3. I wonder why we are so often attracted to people which are completely opposite to us.

4. I'm one of those people that should stay out of the sun.

5. People that take afternoon naps often suffer from insomnia as a result.

6. The vacuum-cleaner salesperson which came to our door was the sort of person that won't take no for an answer.

Grammar

7. This is the brilliant teacher that helped me achieve the grades which I had thought were beyond me.

8. Marathon runners that wear cheap shoes often suffer the agony of defeat.

9. The math problems which we worked on last night would have baffled anyone that hadn't done all the problem sets.

10. We took the ancient Jeep, that we had bought from a friend that had lost his licence, to a scrapyard who paid us $200 for it.

GO TO WEB

EXERCISES 30.3, 30.4, 30.5, 30.6

Person Agreement

So far, we have focused on using pronouns correctly and clearly within a sentence. Now let's turn to the problem of **person agreement**, which means using pronouns consistently throughout a sentence or a paragraph. There are three categories of person that we use when we write or speak:

	Singular	**Plural**
First person	I; me	we; us
Second person	you	you
Third person	she, he, it, one; her, him *and all pronouns ending in* -one, -thing, -body	they; them

Here is the rule for person agreement.

Do not mix "persons" unless meaning requires it.

In other words, be consistent. If you begin a sentence using a second-person pronoun, you must use second person all the way through. Look at this sentence:

If *you* wish to succeed, *one* must work hard.

This is the most common error—mixing second-person *you* with third-person *one*.

Here's another example:

One can live happily in Vancouver if *you* have a sturdy umbrella.

1. We can correct this error by using the second person throughout:

You can live happily in Vancouver if *you* have a sturdy umbrella.

2. We can also correct it by using the third person throughout:

a. *One* can live happily in Vancouver if *one* has a sturdy umbrella.

or

b. *One* can live happily in Vancouver if *he* or *she* has a sturdy umbrella.

These examples raise two points of style that you should consider.

1. Don't overuse *one*.

All three revised sentences are grammatically correct, but they make different impressions on the reader, and impressions are an important part of communication.

- The first sentence, in the second person, sounds the most informal—like something you would say. It's a bit casual for general writing purposes.
- The second sentence, which uses *one* twice, sounds the most formal—even a little pretentious.
- The third sentence falls between the other two in formality. It is the one you'd be most likely to use in writing for school or business.

Although it is grammatically correct and nonsexist, this third sentence raises another problem. Frequent use of *he or she* in a continuous prose passage, whether that passage is as short as a paragraph or as long as a paper, is guaranteed to irritate your reader.

2. Don't overuse *he or she*.

He or she is inclusive, but it is a wordy construction. If used too frequently, the reader cannot help shifting focus from what you're saying to how

Grammar

you're saying it. The best writing is transparent—that is, it doesn't call attention to itself. If your reader becomes distracted by your style, your meaning gets lost. Consider this sentence:

A student can easily pass this course if he or she applies himself or herself to his or her studies.

Readers deserve better. A paper—or even a single paragraph—filled with this clumsy construction will annoy even the most patient reader. There are two better solutions to the problem of sexist language, and they are already familiar to you because they are the same as those for making pronouns ending in -one, -body, or -thing agree with their antecedents.

- You can change the whole sentence to the plural.

   Students can easily pass this course if they apply themselves to their studies.

- You can rewrite the sentence without using pronouns.

   A student can easily pass this course by applying good study habits.

(Exercise 30.10*)

In each of the following sentences, select the correct word from the choices given in parentheses. Check your answers before continuing.

1. If you want to make good egg rolls, I advise (them her you) to buy the ready-made wrappings.

2. If you win tonight's lottery, will (one he you) tell (one's his your) friends?

3. Anyone who wants to swim should bring (their your his her a) bathing suit and towel.

4. Every person working in this office should know that (they she) helped to finish an important project.

5. When we toured the House of Commons, (you we he one) didn't see a single MP.

Exercise 30.11*

Correct the following sentences where necessary.

1. When a person lives in a glass house, they shouldn't throw stones.

2. Experience is something one acquires just after you need it.

3. Anyone who enjoys snowboarding can have your best holiday ever in western Alberta.

4. When she asked if Peter Tchaikovsky played for the Canucks, you knew she wasn't the woman for me.

5. From time to time, most of us think about the opportunities we've missed even if you are happy with what you have.

6. Managers who are concerned about employee morale should think about ending your policy of threats and intimidation and consider other means to improve your efficiency.

7. If you are afraid of vampires, one should wear garlic around one's neck and carry a silver bullet.

8. Any woman who wears a garlic necklace probably won't have to worry about men harassing them, either.

9. Can you really know another person if you have never been to their home?

10. A sure way to lose one's friends is to eat all the ice cream yourself.

Exercise 30.12*

Revise the following passage to make the nouns and pronouns agree in person (first, second, or third) and number (singular or plural). Use the italicized word in the first sentence of each paragraph as your marker.

When *people* see a dreadful occurrence on television, such as a bombing, an earthquake, or a mass slaughter, it does not always affect one. It is one thing for people to see the ravages of war oneself and another thing to see

Grammar

a three-minute newscast of the same battle, neatly edited by the CBC. Even the horrible effects of natural catastrophes that wipe out whole populations are somehow minimized or trivialized when I see them on TV. And though viewers may be horrified by the gaunt faces of starving children on the screen, you can easily escape into your familiar world of Egg McMuffins, Shake'n Bake, and Labatt Blue that is portrayed in commercial messages.

Thus, the impact of television on *us* is a mixed one. It is true that one is shown terrible, sometimes shocking, events that you could not possibly have seen before television. In this way, one's world is drawn together more closely. However, the risk in creating this immediacy is that one may become desensitized and cease to feel or care about one's fellow human beings.

GO TO WEB

EXERCISES 30.7, 30.8

Exercise 30.13

Revise the following paragraph, which contains 15 errors representing the three different kinds of pronoun–antecedent agreement error. If you change a subject from singular to plural, don't forget to change the verb to agree. Some of your answers may differ from our suggestions and still be correct. Check with your instructor.

Everyone that has been to Newfoundland knows that an outport is a small fishing community along the coast of that vast island province. Ladle Cove, for example, is a tiny outport with fewer than 200 residents that live there all year. Despite its small population, Ladle Cove is a village which enjoyed a nation-wide moment of fame when a man that lives there met the Queen. Fred had left Ladle Cove, as just about every man does when they need to find work, and gone to St. John's. Fred wanted to work, but he had few marketable skills to help him get one. Fortunately, he had relatives in St. John's that helped him find a place to stay and eventually found him a job at Purity Foods, a company famous for their baked goods—and for Newfoundland's favourite treat, Jam Jam cookies.

During Queen Elizabeth's visit to St. John's, the officials that organized her tour decided it would be a good idea for her to visit a local industry which had a national reputation. Purity Foods was the logical choice. While touring the plant, the Queen stopped to talk to a few of the men and women that were on the production line. Near the end of the tour, that was being filmed by the national media, the Queen stopped by one of the workers that were making the famous Jam Jams: Fred. As the television lights glared and each reporter held their pencil poised over their notebook, the Queen leaned toward Fred and asked, "And what are we making here?" With a courteous bow in Her Majesty's direction, Fred replied, "Ten-fifty an hour, Ma'am. Ten-fifty an hour."

31

The Comma

Many writers-in-training tend to sprinkle punctuation like pepper over their pages. Do not use punctuation to spice up your writing. Punctuation marks are functional: they indicate to the reader how the various parts of a sentence relate to one another. By changing the punctuation, you can change the meaning of a sentence. Here are two examples to prove the point.

1. An instructor wrote the following sentence on the board and asked the class to punctuate it: "Woman without her man is nothing."

   The men wrote, "Woman, without her man, is nothing."
   The women wrote, "Woman! Without her, man is nothing."

2. Now it's your turn. Punctuate this sentence: "I think there is only one person to blame myself."
   If you wrote, "I think there is only one person to blame, myself," the reader will understand that you believe only one person—who may or may not be known to you—is to blame.
   If you wrote, "I think there is only one person to blame: myself," the reader will understand that you are personally accepting responsibility for the blame.

The comma is the most frequently used—and misused—punctuation mark in English. One sure sign of a competent writer is the correct use of commas, so it is very important that you master them. This chapter presents five comma rules that cover most instances in which you need to use commas. If you apply these five rules faithfully, your reader will never be confused by missing or misplaced commas in your writing. And if, as occasionally happens, the sentence you are writing is not covered by one of our five rules, remember the first commandment of comma usage: WHEN IN DOUBT, LEAVE IT OUT.

Five Comma Rules

1. Use commas to separate three or more items in a series. The items may be expressed as words, phrases, or clauses.

Words   The required subjects in this program are *math, physics,* and *English.*

Phrases   Punctuation marks are the traffic signals of prose. They tell us *to slow down, notice this, take a detour,* and *stop.* (Lynne Truss)

Clauses   *Karin went to the movies, Jan and Yasmin went to play pool, and I went to bed.*

The comma before the *and* at the end of the list is optional, but we advise you to use it. Occasionally, misunderstandings can occur if it is left out.

Exercise 31.1*

Insert commas where necessary in the following sentences. Answers for exercises in this chapter begin on page 536.

1. Holly held two aces a King a Queen and a Jack in her hand.

2. The food at the Thai Palace is colourful spicy delicious and inexpensive.

3. Life would be complete if I had a Blackberry a Porsche a Sea-Doo and a job.

4. The gear list for the Winter Wilderness course includes woollen underwear snowshoes Arctic boots and a toque.

5. In the summer, a cup of coffee a croissant and a glass of juice are all I want for breakfast.

6. Don't forget to bring the videos maps and souvenirs of your trip to Australia.

7. In Ontario, the four seasons are summer winter winter and winter.

Punctuation

8. My doctor and my nutritionist agree that I should eat better exercise more and take vitamins.

9. Sleeping through my alarm dozing during sociology class napping in the library after lunch and snoozing in front of the TV after supper are symptoms of my overactive nightlife.

10. Welcome home! Once you have finished your homework taken out the garbage and done the dishes, you can feed the cat clean your room and do your laundry.

---

2. Put a comma between independent clauses when they are joined by these connecting words:

for	but	so
and	or	
nor	yet	

(You can remember these words easily if you notice that their first letters spell FANBOYS.)

I hope I do well in the interview, for I really want this job.

I like Norah Jones, but I prefer Diana Krall.

We shape our tools, and our tools shape us. (Marshall McLuhan)

I knew I was going to be late, so I went back to sleep.

Be sure that the sentence you are punctuating contains two independent clauses rather than one clause with a single subject and a multiple verb.

We loved the book but hated the movie.
(We is the subject, and there are two verbs, loved and hated. Do not put a comma between two or more verbs that share a single subject.)

We both loved the book, but Kim hated the movie.
(This sentence contains two independent clauses—We loved and Kim hated—joined by but. The comma is required here.)

Exercise 31.2*

Insert commas where they are needed in the following sentences, then check your answers.

1. Either it is very foggy this morning or I am going blind.

2. We have an approved business plan and budget but we're still looking for qualified and experienced staff.

3. Talk shows haven't said anything new in years nor have they solved a single one of the problems they endlessly discuss.

4. We discovered that we both had an interest in fine art so we made a date to go to an exhibition at the art gallery next week.

5. Canadians are proud of their country but they don't approve of too much flag-waving.

6. Take good notes for I'll need them in order to study for the exam.

7. I'll rent a tux but I will not get a haircut or my shoes shined.

8. I chose a quiet seat on the train and two women with bawling babies boarded at the next station.

9. I have travelled all over the world yet my luggage has visited at least twice the number of countries that I have.

10. Jet lag makes me look haggard and ill but at least I resemble my passport photo.

3. Put a comma after an introductory word, phrase, or dependent clause that comes before an independent clause.

Lucas, you aren't paying attention. (word)

After staying up all night, I staggered into class 15 minutes late. (phrase)

If that's their idea of a large pizza, we'd better order two. (clause)

Until she got her promotion, she was quite friendly. (clause)

Punctuation

> **4.** Use commas to set off any word, phrase, or dependent clause that is NOT ESSENTIAL to the main idea of the sentence.

Following this rule can make the difference between your reader's understanding and misunderstanding what you write. For example, the following two sentences are identical, except for a pair of commas. But notice what a difference those two tiny marks make to meaning:

> The children who were dressed in clown costumes had ice cream. (Only the children wearing clown costumes ate ice cream.)

> The children, who were dressed in clown costumes, had ice cream. (All the children wore costumes and had ice cream.)

To test whether a word, phrase, or clause is essential to the meaning of your sentence, mentally put parentheses around it. If the sentence still makes complete sense (i.e., the main idea is unchanged; the sentence just delivers less information), the material in parentheses is *not essential* and should be set off from the rest of the sentence by a comma or commas.

Nonessential information can appear at the beginning of a sentence,[1] in the middle, or at the end of a sentence. Study the following examples.

> Alice Munro (one of Canada's best-known novelists) spends summer in Clinton and winter in Comox.

Most readers would be puzzled the first time they read this sentence because all the information is presented without punctuation, so the reader assumes it is all equally important. In fact, the material in broken parentheses is extra information, a supplementary detail. It can be deleted without changing the sentence's meaning, and so it should be separated from the rest of the sentence by commas:

> Alice Munro, one of Canada's best-known novelists, spends summer in Clinton and winter in Comox.

Here's another example to consider:

> The Queen (who has twice as many birthdays as anyone else) officially celebrates her birthday on May 24.

---

[1] Comma Rule 3 covers nonessential information at the beginning of a sentence.

Again, the sentence is hard to read. You can't count on your readers to go back and reread every sentence they don't understand at first glance. As a writer, your responsibility is to give readers the clues they need as to what is crucial information and what isn't. In the example above, the information in broken parentheses is not essential to the meaning of the sentence, so it should be set off by commas:

> The Queen, who has twice as many birthdays as anyone else, officially celebrates her birthday on May 24.

In this next sentence, the nonessential information comes at the end.

> Writing a good letter of application isn't difficult ⸨ if you're careful ⸩ .

The phrase "if you're careful" is not essential to the main idea, so it should be separated from the rest of the sentence by a comma:

> Writing a good letter of application isn't difficult, if you're careful.

And finally, consider this sentence:

> Writing a letter of application ⸨ that is clear, complete, and concise ⸩ is a challenge.

If you take out "that is clear, complete, and concise," you change the meaning of the sentence. Not all letters of application are a challenge to write. Writing vague and wordy letters is easy; anyone can do it. The words "that is clear, complete, and concise" are essential to the meaning of the sentence, and so they are not set off by commas.

> Writing a letter of application that is clear, complete, and concise is a challenge.

Punctuation

Exercise 31.3*

Insert commas where they are missing in the following sentences, then check your answers.

1. A good day in my opinion always starts with a few cuts of high-volume heavy metal.
2. This photograph which was taken when I was four embarrasses me whenever my parents display it.
3. Mira's boyfriend who looks like an ape is living proof that love is blind.

4. Isn't it strange that the poor who often are bitterly critical of the rich keep buying lottery tickets?
5. A nagging headache the result of last night's great party made me miserable all morning.
6. Our ancient car made it all the way to Saskatoon without anything falling off or breaking down a piece of good luck that astonished everyone.
7. Professor Repke a popular mathematics teacher won the Distinguished Teaching Award this year.
8. We're going to spend the afternoon at the mall a weekly event that has become a ritual.
9. No one who ever saw Patrick Roy play doubts that he was a superstar.
10. Classical music which I call Prozac for the ears can be very soothing in times of stress.

Exercise 31.4*

Insert commas where they are needed in the following sentences. Check your answers on page 538 before continuing.

1. Unfortunately we'll have to begin all over again.
2. Mr. Dillinger the bank would like a word with you.
3. In college the quality of your work is more important than the effort you put into it.
4. Hopelessly lost my father still refused to stop and ask for directions.
5. Finally understanding what she was trying to say I apologized for being so slow.
6. After an evening of watching television I have accomplished as much as if I had been unconscious.
7. Since the doctor ordered me to walk to work every morning I have seen three accidents involving people walking to work.
8. Having munched our way through a large bag of peanuts while watching the game we weren't interested in supper.
9. Whenever an optimist is pulled over by a police officer the optimist assumes it's to ask for directions.
10. That same year Stephen Leacock bought his summer home in Orillia, Ontario.

---

5. Use commas between coordinate adjectives but not between cumulative adjectives.

Coordinate adjectives are those whose order can be changed, and the word *and* can be inserted between them without changing the meaning of the sentence.

> Our company is looking for energetic, courteous salespeople.

The adjectives *energetic* and *courteous* could appear in reverse order, and you could put *and* between them: "Our company is looking for courteous and energetic salespeople."

In a series of **cumulative adjectives**, however, each adjective modifies the word that follows it. You cannot change their order, nor can you insert *and* between them.

> The bride wore a pale pink silk dress, and the groom wore a navy wool suit.

You cannot say "The bride wore a silk pink pale dress" or "The groom wore a navy and wool suit," so no commas are used with these adjectives.

One final note about commas before you try the review exercises: never place a SINGLE comma between a subject and its verb.

> Wrong: <u>Those</u> who intend to register for hockey, <u>must be</u> at the arena by 8:00 a.m.

> Right: <u>Those</u> who intend to register for hockey <u>must be</u> at the arena by 8:00 a.m.

Two commas, however, between a subject and its verb are correct if the commas set off nonessential material.

> <u>Saied and Mohamed</u>, who intend to register for hockey, <u>have</u> never <u>played</u> before.

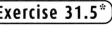

Exercise 31.5*

Insert commas where they are needed in the following sentences. Check your answers before continuing.

1. The desk was made of dark brown carved oak.
2. Do you want your portrait in a glossy finish or a matte finish?
3. Bright yellow fabric that repels stains is ideal for rain gear.
4. Toronto in the summer is hot smoggy and humid.

5. Today's paper has an article about a new car made of lightweight durable aluminum.

6. Dietitians recommend that we eat at least two servings daily of green leafy vegetables.

7. This ergonomic efficient full-function keyboard comes in a variety of pastel shades.

8. We ordered a large nutritious salad for lunch, then indulged ourselves with a redcurrant cheesecake for dessert.

9. Danny bought a cute cuddly purebred puppy.

10. Ten months later that cute puppy turned into a vicious man-eating monster.

The rest of the exercises in this chapter require you to apply all five comma rules. Before you start, write out the five rules and keep them in front of you as you work through the exercises. Refer to the rules frequently as you punctuate the sentences. After you've finished each exercise, check your answers and make sure you understand any mistakes you've made.

Exercise 31.6*

1. Pinot noir which is a type of grape grown in California Oregon British Columbia and Ontario produces a delicious red wine.

2. There are I am told people who don't like garlic but you won't find any of them eating at Freddy's.

3. I use e-mail to communicate with my colleagues a fax machine to keep in touch with clients and Canada Post to send greetings to my relatives.

4. Your dogs Mr. Pavlov seem hungry for some reason.

5. According to G. K. Chesterton "If a thing is worth doing it is worth doing badly."

6. Looking for a competent computer technologist we interviewed tested investigated and rejected 30 applicants.

7. How you choose to phrase your resignation is up to you but I expect to have it on my desk by morning.

8. Your superstitious dread of March 13 Senator Caesar is irrational and silly.

9. The lenses of my new high-fashion sunglasses are impact-resistant yellow UV-reflective optical plastic.

10. Canada a country known internationally for beautiful scenery peaceful intentions and violent hockey always places near the top of the United Nations' list of desirable places to live.

Exercise 31.7*

1. Whereas the Super Bowl tradition goes back about four decades the Grey Cup has a history that stretches back to the 19th century.
2. Otherwise Mrs. Lincoln said she had very much enjoyed the play.
3. Our guard dog a Rottweiler caught an intruder and maimed him for life.
4. Unfortunately my Uncle Ladislaw was the intruder and he intends to sue us for every penny we have.
5. The year 1945 marked the end of World War II and the beginning of assistance to war-torn nations.
6. We bought a lovely old mahogany dining table at auction for $300.
7. If there were more people like Gladys global warming would be the least of our worries.
8. We are pleased with your résumé and are offering you an interview this week.
9. Deciding on the midnight blue velvet pants was easy but paying for them was not.
10. Igor asked "May I show you to your quarters or would you prefer to spend the night in the dungeon?"

GO TO WEB

EXERCISES 31.1, 31.2, 31.3

Exercise 31.8

To test your mastery of commas, provide the necessary punctuation for the following paragraph. There are 15 errors.

When my brother and I were growing up my mother used to summon us home from playing by ringing a solid brass bell that could be heard for miles. All of the other kids to our great embarrassment, knew when our mother was calling us and they would tease us by making ringing noises. We begged her to yell like all the other moms but she knew she had a foolproof system and wouldn't change. One day while we were playing with our friends in the fields behind our homes the bell rang in the middle of

Punctuation

an important game. The other kids began their usual taunts that our mother was calling but this time we bravely ignored the bell. When it rang the second time we ignored it again. By the third ring, however we knew that we were in big trouble so we dashed for home. We agreed on the way that we would tell our mother that we just didn't hear the bell. We arrived hot sweaty and panting from our run. Before Mom could say a word my brother blurted out, "We didn't hear the bell until the third ring!" Fortunately for us our mother couldn't stop laughing and we escaped the punishment we deserved.

Summary

The Five Comma Rules

1. Use commas to separate items in a series of three or more. The items may be expressed as words, phrases, or clauses.
2. Put a comma between independent clauses when they are joined by *for, and, nor, but, or, yet,* or *so.*
3. Put a comma after an introductory word, phrase, or dependent clause that comes before an independent clause.
4. Use commas to set off a word, phrase, or dependent clause that is NOT ESSENTIAL to the main idea of the sentence.
5. Use commas between coordinate adjectives but not between cumulative adjectives.

32

The Semicolon

The semicolon and the colon are often confused and used as if they were interchangeable. They have distinct purposes, however, and their correct use can dramatically improve a reader's understanding of your writing. The semicolon has three functions.

1. A semicolon can replace a period; in other words, it can appear between two independent clauses.

You should use a semicolon when the two clauses (sentences) you are joining are closely connected in meaning, or when there is a cause-and-effect relationship between them.

I'm too tired; I can't stay awake any longer.

Montreal is not the city's original name; it was once called Ville Marie.

A period could have been used instead of a semicolon in either of these sentences, but the close connection between the clauses makes a semicolon more effective in communicating the writer's meaning.

2. Certain transitional words or phrases can be put between independent clauses to show a cause-and-effect relationship or the continuation of an idea.

Words or phrases used in this way are usually preceded by a semicolon and followed by a comma:

; also,	; furthermore,	; nevertheless,
; as a result,	; however,	; on the other hand,
; besides,	; in addition,	; otherwise,
; consequently,	; in fact,	; then,
; finally,	; instead,	; therefore,
; for example,	; moreover,	; thus,

The forecast called for sun; instead, we got snow.

My monitor went blank; nevertheless, I kept on typing.

"I'm not offended by dumb blonde jokes because I know I'm not dumb; besides, I also know I'm not blonde." (Dolly Parton)

In other words, *a semicolon + a transitional word/phrase + a comma* = a link strong enough to come between two related independent clauses.

Note, however, that, when these transitional words and phrases are used as nonessential expressions rather than as connecting words, they are separated from the rest of the sentence by commas (Chapter 31, Rule 4, page 420).

I just can't seem to master particle physics, however hard I try.

The emissions test, moreover, will ensure that your car is running well.

3. To make a COMPLEX LIST easier to read and understand, put semicolons between the items instead of commas.

A complex list is one in which at least one component part already contains commas. Here are two examples:

I grew up in a series of small towns: Cumberland, B.C.; Red Deer, Alberta; and Timmins, Ontario.

When we opened the refrigerator, we found a limp, brown head of lettuce; two small containers of yogurt, whose "best before" dates had long since passed; and a hard, dried-up piece of cheddar cheese.

Exercise 32.1*

Put a check mark next to the sentences that are correctly punctuated. Check your answers before continuing. Answers for this chapter begin on page 539.

1. _____We've eaten all the food, it's time to go home.
2. _____Many doctors claim weather affects our health; in fact, barometric pressure has a direct effect on arthritis.
3. _____ Your instructor would like to see you pass, however, there may be a small fee involved.
4. _____ Molly is going to Chicago, she wants to appear on *Oprah*.
5. _____ Many people dislike hockey; because some of the players act like goons rather than athletes.
6. _____ Orville tried and tried; but he couldn't get the teacher's attention.
7. _____ She presented her report using coloured charts and diagrams; these visual aids woke up even the accountants.
8. _____ Tomorrow is another day, unfortunately it will probably be just like today.
9. _____ Rumours of a merger had begun to circulate by five o'clock; so it's no wonder many employees looked nervous on their way home.
10. _____ We knew the party had been a success when Uncle Morty, drunk as usual, tap-danced across the top of the piano, Aunt Madeline, who must weigh at least 80 kg, did her Cirque du Soleil routine, and Stan punched out two of his cousins.

Exercise 32.2*

Correct the faulty punctuation in Exercise 32.1.

GO TO WEB

EXERCISES 32.1, 32.2

Punctuation

Exercise 32.3*

Insert semicolons where necessary in these sentences. Then check your answers.

1. The rain has to stop soon otherwise, we'll have to start building an ark.
2. Our finances are a mess the only way we can repay our debts would be to stop paying for rent and food.
3. We need you at the meeting, however, since you have another engagement, we will have to reschedule.
4. A day without puns is like a day without sunshine, it leaves gloom for improvement.
5. I work on an assembly line, all of us workers believe that if a job is worth doing; it's worth doing 11,000 times a day.
6. It is not impossible to become wealthy, if you're under 20, all you need to do is put the price of a pack of cigarettes into an RRSP every day, and you'll be a millionaire by the age of 50.
7. If, on the other hand, you continue to spend your money on smokes, the government will make the millions that could have been yours, you'll die early and broke.
8. As a dog lover and the owner of an Afghan, I suffer a great deal of abuse, for example, for my birthday, my wife gave me a book rating the intelligence of Afghans as 79th out of 79 breeds tested.
9. A plateau, according to the *Dictionary of Puns*, is a high form of flattery, this may be low humour, but it's a clever remark.
10. According to a *Gourmet Magazine* poll, four of the top ten restaurants in the world are in Paris, three—those ranking eighth, ninth, and tenth—are in the United States, two are in Tokyo and the other is in Thailand.

GO TO WEB

EXERCISE **32.3**

Exercise 32.4

Test your mastery of semicolons and commas by correcting the punctuation in these sentences.

1. Growing old has never really bothered me in fact I consider aging a huge improvement over the alternative.
2. I visit a chiropractor twice a month, if I miss a treatment I have to crawl into work.

3. Our marketing campaign is based on sound principles, for example if we are sufficiently annoying people will buy our product just to make us go away.

4. The construction was so far behind schedule that we couldn't make up the time, consequently we lost our performance bonus our chance to bid on the next contract and an important client.

5. Among the many products being standardized by the European Community is the condom however a number of nations have officially complained that the standard size is too small.

6. Failing to stop at the light turned out to be the least of his offences the police were much more interested in his expired driving licence.

7. In her fridge we found a pound of butter dating from last August a mouldy piece of cake three containers of unidentifiable fur-bearing substances and an open can of beer.

8. A practice that works well in one country may not work in another for example every man in Switzerland is required to own a rifle. Such a policy might find acceptance in the United States however anyone who proposed it in Canada would be thought insane.

9. While some people find bird watching an exciting hobby and others are drawn to rock climbing or heli-skiing my own preference is for less strenuous pastimes such as those involving food.

10. To use or not to use the semicolon is sometimes a matter of the writer's choice, on the other hand, a few syntactical constructions require a semicolon, no other punctuation mark will do.

Punctuation

33

The Colon

The **colon** functions as an introducer. When a statement is followed by a list, one or more examples, or a quotation, the colon alerts the reader that some sort of explanatory detail is coming up.

When I travel, I am never without three things: sturdy shoes, a money belt, and my journal.

There is only one enemy we cannot defeat: time.

We have two choices: to study or to fail.

Early in his career, Robert Fulford did not think very highly of intellectual life in Canada: "My generation of Canadians grew up believing that, if we were very good or very smart, or both, we would someday *graduate* from Canada."

The statement that precedes the colon must be a complete sentence (independent clause).

A colon should never come immediately after *is* or *are*. Here's an example of what *not* to write.

The only things I am violently allergic to are: cats, ragweed, and country music.

This is incorrect because the statement before the colon is not a complete sentence.

1. Use a colon between an independent clause and a LIST or one or more EXAMPLES that define, explain, or illustrate the independent clause.

The information after the colon often answers the question "what?" or "who?"

I am violently allergic to three things: (what?) cats, ragweed, and country music.

Business and industry face a new challenge: (what?) offshore out-sourcing.

The president has found the ideal candidate for the position: (who?) her brother.

2. Use a colon after a complete sentence introducing a quotation.

Lucille Ball observed that there were three secrets to staying young: "Live honestly, eat slowly, and lie about your age."

3. Finally, use a colon to separate the title of a book, film, or TV show from a subtitle.

Word Play: What Happens When People Talk

Ace Ventura: Pet Detective

Trading Spouses: Meet Your New Mommy

If you remember this summary, you'll have no more trouble with colons: the colon follows an independent clause and introduces an example, a list, or a quotation that amplifies the meaning of that clause.

Punctuation

Exercise 33.1*

Put a check mark next to the sentences that are correctly punctuated. Check your answers before going on. Answers for this chapter begin on page 540.

1. _____ Believe it or not, the country that produces the most films every year is: India.

2. _____ Jordan wants to go home to be comforted by the only person in the world who truly understands him: his mother.

3. _____ In this region, the three grapes most commonly grown for wine are Chardonnay, Merlot, and Riesling.

4. _____ The most annoying sound in the world has to be that produced by: bagpipes.

5. _____ The company's bankruptcy resulted from the CEO's management style. He relied on: crisis management, seat-of-the-pants planning, and excessive profit-taking.

6. _____ One topic has dominated the health concerns of the world since the late 1980s: AIDS.

7. _____ Two of Canada's highest awards in professional sports are the Stanley Cup and the Grey Cup.

8. _____ All most students ask is that their teachers treat them with: courtesy, fairness, and respect.

9. _____ Of course, there are always a few students who demand what no true professional will provide special treatment.

10. _____ Our department's proposal is unique it has the CEO's approval.

Exercise 33.2*

Insert colons in the following sentences where necessary and then check your answers. If you find you've made any mistakes, review the explanations on pages 432–33, study the examples, and be sure you understand why your answers were wrong before going on.

1. I have set myself three goals this year to achieve an 80 percent average, to get a good summer job, and to buy a car.

2. Right after we moved in, we discovered we had a problem termites.

3. After our bankruptcy, our credit card consultant asked us an interesting question "Why don't you cut up your credit cards?"

4. Several Canadian writers are even better known abroad than they are at home Carol Shields, Neil Bissoondath, and Michael Ondaatje are three examples.

5. There are a number of inexpensive activities that will improve physical fitness; swimming, tennis, jogging, even brisk walking.

6. Jocelyn is trying to accomplish two mutually contradictory tasks a significant weight loss and success as a restaurant critic.

7. Several of the animals on the international list of endangered species are native to Canada; the wood bison, the northern kit fox, and the whooping crane.

8. We'll finish the assignment by tomorrow only if we stay up all night and consume vast quantities of pizza and black coffee.

9. The majority of Canada's population is worn out and exhausted at the end of a long, hard winter, but most people are able to console themselves with one comforting thought, spring will arrive sometime in May or June.

10. There are several troublesome implications of biological engineering, but one in particular is frightening to most people the cloning of human beings.

Exercise 33.3*

Correct the incorrectly punctuated sentences in Exercise 33.1.

EXERCISES **33.1, 33.2, 33.3, 33.4**

Exercise 33.4

To test your mastery of colons and semicolons, correct the errors in the following sentences.

1. The person who comes to mind when I am asked to name a female role model is: Adrienne Clarkson.

2. The TV is always asking me challenging questions "It's 11:05. Do you know where your children are?"

3. You have all the qualities of a pit bull: except one, loyalty.

4. Hippocrates, the father of modern medicine, is responsible for the first rule of medical practice "First, do no harm."

5. One of the symptoms of an approaching nervous breakdown is: the belief that one's work is terribly important. (Bertrand Russell)

6. You should use a colon in this sentence: and there's one place to put it here.

7. Contrary to the words of the popular song from the 1950s: breaking up is easy to do.

8. There are many countries on my "must visit" list, including: Brazil, Ukraine, Sweden, and Slovenia.

9. Studies have shown that in most offices the Internet is used primarily for nonwork-related activities: such as personal e-mail, random surfing, and game playing.

10. Having failed to impress Cara with his charm, Sean decided to try gifts; roses, chocolates, and perfume.

34

Quotation Marks

Quotation marks are used to set off direct speech (dialogue), quoted material, and some titles. For information how to punctuate and insert quoted material into your papers, see pages 280–86. To review when to use quotation marks for titles, see page 292.

Direct Quotations

A **direct quotation** is someone's exact words, spoken or written. It is usually introduced by a reporting expression such as *she said, he replied,* or *they shouted.* Put quotation marks before and after the person's exact words.

> Tim asked angrily, "Did you delete my entire address book?"

> "No, a virus attacked the computer and ate your files," I replied.

Do not use quotation marks with **indirect quotations** (reported speech):

> Tim asked angrily if I had deleted his entire address book. (These are not Tim's exact words, so no quotation marks are necessary.)

> I replied that a virus attacked his computer and ate his files. (Note that indirect quotations are often introduced by *that.*)

Use single quotation marks to enclose a quotation within a quotation:

> "I don't understand what you mean by the term 'creative memory,'" said Lauren.

The final thing you need to know about direct quotations is how to punctuate them. Here are the rules to follow.

1. Separate a reporting expression and a quotation with a comma.

Professor Lam announced, "You will write the mid-term test on Tuesday."

"You will write the mid-term test on Tuesday," announced Professor Lam.

2. If there is no reporting verb, use a colon after an independent clause to introduce a quotation.

Too late, I remembered Professor Lam's advice at the beginning of term: "Keep up with your work each week, and the tests will cause you no trouble."

3. Begin each quoted sentence with a capital letter. If a quoted sentence is divided into two parts, begin the second part with a small letter.

"Our national anthem," John informed us, "was written by Calixa Lavillée. First composed in French, it was later translated into English."

4. If the end punctuation is part of the direct quotation, put commas, periods, question marks, and exclamation marks *inside* the second quotation mark of a pair.

"Could you help me?" the woman asked. "I'm trying to find Melrose Avenue." Almost in tears, she went on, "I'm already late for my job interview!"

5. If the end punctuation is *not* part of the direct quotation, put it *outside* the second quotation mark. (It's part of your sentence, not the speaker's.)

Did the woman say, "I'm late for my job interview"?

6. Put colons and semicolons *outside* the second quotation mark (unless they are part of the direct quotation).

Near tears, the woman cried, "Please help me": we could hardly leave her standing there alone.

The woman cried, "Please help me"; she was near tears.

"Please help me; I'm late for my job interview," cried the woman.

Exercise 34.1*

Punctuate the following sentences correctly, using quotation marks and other punctuation marks where they are needed. Answers are provided on page 541.

1. Did you see the look on her face asked Roderick.
2. Frank asked Jenna if she would like to play bridge.
3. I'd love to, she replied, if only I knew how.
4. Pardon me, boys, is this the Transylvania Station asked the man in the black cape.
5. When I pointed out to Wayne that he was wearing one green sock and one brown sock, he replied what's wrong with that? My brother has a pair just like it.
6. When I asked the guide if people jumped from the CN Tower very often, he replied no, just the once.
7. Pierre Trudeau once told Canadians that the state had no business in the nation's bedrooms.
8. Just as well, muttered Terry, because I wouldn't want the state to see what's growing on my bedroom windowsill.
9. I knew that Microsoft had lost its corporate mind when my computer flashed the following blue-screen error message No keyboard detected. Press any key to continue.
10. The psychiatrist said to the woman whose husband thought he was a horse I can cure your husband, but it will take a long time and be very costly. Money is no object, replied the woman. He just won the Queen's Plate.

35

Question and Exclamation Marks

The Question Mark

Everyone knows that a question mark follows an interrogative, or asking, sentence, but we all sometimes forget to include it. Let this chapter serve as a reminder not to forget!

> The **question mark** is the end punctuation for all interrogative sentences.

The question mark gives your readers an important clue to the meaning of your sentence. "There's more?" is vastly different in meaning from "There's more!" and that difference is communicated to readers by the punctuation alone.

The only time you don't end a question with a question mark is when the question is part of a statement.

Is anyone there? (question)
I asked if anyone was there. (statement)
Do you understand? (question)
I wonder whether you understand. (statement)

Exercise 35.1*

Supply the correct end punctuation for the following sentences. Then check your answers. Answers for this chapter are on page 542.

1. Do you ever wonder why we park in a driveway and drive on a parkway

2. I cannot understand how you can listen to that music

3. I cannot believe that you would question my integrity

4. I wonder if my apartment will ever be the same after their visit

5. What's another word for thesaurus

6. If we can't finish the project on time, will we lose the contract

7. I question the results you got on your survey

8. Did you know there are only 18,000 elephants in all of India

9. Human Resources wants to know why we hired an unqualified, inexperienced person for such a sensitive position

10. If corn oil comes from corn, where does baby oil come from

---

GO TO WEB

EXERCISES 35.1, 35.2

The Exclamation Mark

In informal or personal writings, the exclamation mark is a useful piece of punctuation for conveying your tone of voice to your readers. There is a distinct difference in tone between these two sentences:

There's a man behind you.

There's a man behind you!

In the first sentence, information is being supplied, perhaps about the line-up at a grocery-store checkout counter. The second sentence might be a shouted warning about a mugger.

Punctuation

Use an **exclamation mark** as end punctuation in sentences requiring extreme emphasis or dramatic effect.

Exclamation marks have "punch" or drama only if you use them sparingly. If you use an exclamation mark after every third sentence, how will your readers know when you really mean to indicate excitement? Note also that exclamation marks are seldom used in academic or professional writing.

Practically any sentence could end with an exclamation mark, but remember that the punctuation changes the meaning of the sentence. Read each of the following sentences with and without an exclamation mark and picture the situation that would call for each reading.

He's gone   Don't touch that button

The room was empty   There she goes again

Exercise 35.2*

Supply the correct end punctuation for each of the following sentences. In many cases, the punctuation you use will depend on how you want the sentence to be read.

1. You must be kidding

2. Turn left Now

3. I can't believe I actually passed

4. Oh, great We're moving to Backwater, Alberta

5. Run It's right behind you

6. I'm freezing Turn the heat up

7. "Workers of the world, unite" (Karl Marx)

8. Finally Someone is coming to take our order

9. For the last time, leave me alone

10. What a great game I've never seen a better one.

GO TO WEB

EXERCISES **35.3, 35.4, 35.5**

Exercise 35.3

1. We asked whether there is intelligent life in Arkansas

2. Don't shoot I'm on your side

3. What in the world were you thinking when you had "file not found" tattooed on your arm

4. Whenever the power goes out, we wonder if the outage affects everyone or just us

5. Would you believe that the heaviest world-champion boxer, Primo Carnera, weighed 123 kg for a 1933 fight

6. That's one king-size heavyweight

7. Do you really believe that Al found a lamp that held a genie who gave him three wishes

8. That's outrageous

9. I often think about my future. Will I become an architect A fashion designer Or a movie director

10. Hooray This chapter is finished

36

Dashes and Parentheses

When you are talking with someone, you use your voice to punctuate: you pause for a short time (commas) or for a longer time (semicolons and periods); you shout (exclamation marks); or you query (question marks). In writing, punctuation substitutes for these vocal markers: it helps you ensure that your writing will make sense to your readers.

One way you can add variety and flexibility to your sentences is by inserting words or phrases that add to but are not essential to the sentence's meaning. That is, the word or phrase could be omitted, and the sentence would still be complete and would still make sense. It might, however, lack grace or interest.

You can use three punctuation marks to add nonessential material to your sentences: commas, dashes, and parentheses. You are already familiar with the first one. Here is your opportunity to master the last two: the **dash**—which looks like this—and **parentheses** (round brackets). (If you are typing, the dash is two hyphens with no space on either side.)

Dashes

Dashes are used to mark a break in thought or an abrupt shift in emphasis.

1. Use a dash to introduce a word, phrase, or clause that summarizes or restates what has just been said.

I still love dried apricots and pickled beets—foods my mother gave me as treats when I was a child.

Perseverance, spirit, and skill—these three qualities ensure a good game.

Atwood, Ondaatje, Laurence, Davies, Clarke, and Richler—for a country with a relatively small population, Canada has produced an extraordinary number of internationally acclaimed novelists.

2. Use a pair of dashes to enclose a series of items separated by commas.

Four of the managers—Olive, Muhsin, Luis, and Neville—are new to the McDonald's franchise at the zoo.

Because they were afraid of the police, my so-called friends—Roman, Shane, and Mark—all betrayed me.

The apartment he showed me would have been fine, had it not been for the tenants—moths, cockroaches, and silverfish—already making it their home.

3. Use a dash or a pair of dashes to set off from the rest of the sentence a climactic or emphatic moment.

I expect—and so does the college—that students at this level should be self-motivated.

Our neighbour—an animal-rights activist—keeps rabbits in his backyard.

If you really want to go—even though you haven't been invited—I'll take you.

Note that dashes set off material that is not grammatically part of the sentence. If you were to omit the words between the dashes, the sentence would still make sense.

Dashes can be misused if you use them too frequently. Unless you are writing very informally—in a personal letter, for instance—save dashes for the very occasional phrase to which you want to draw emphatic attention.

Punctuation

Exercise 36.1*

Add dashes where they are appropriate. Answers for this chapter begin on page 542.

1. One Aboriginal tribe in England painted themselves blue with dye made from a plant woad.
2. My purpose in moving from Vancouver to Hope like that of hundreds of people before me was to find affordable housing.
3. We shall have to start without her again!
4. Skiing and skating if you like these sports, you'll love Quebec.
5. Tending to his garden, writing his memoirs, and dining with friends these were the pleasures Arnold looked forward to in retirement.
6. What is missing in his life is obvious rest and relaxation!
7. Zoe should do well in fact, I'm sure she will in the engineering program.
8. Alexei was amazed positively thunderstruck when he learned Uncle Vladimir had won a million dollars.
9. Historians, diarists, and chroniclers these are the recorders of our past.
10. Dashes a kind of silent shout allow you to insert an occasional exclamation into your sentences.

Parentheses

Like dashes, parentheses are used to enclose an interruption in a sentence. The difference between them is a matter of tone: dashes SHOUT—they serve to draw the reader's attention to the material they enclose—but parentheses (which should be used sparingly) "whisper." Parentheses are similar to theatrical asides; they are subordinate to the main action but are not to be missed.

> 1. Use parentheses around additional information that you wish to include but not emphasize.

Giselle's teaching schedule (she is in class seven hours a day) gives her little time to meet with students individually.

They brought me to their village and presented me to their chief (a woman) and to the tribal councillors.

Note the difference in tone your choice of punctuation makes. Compare the examples above with the following versions.

Giselle's teaching schedule—she is in class seven hours a day—gives her little time to meet with students individually.

They brought me to their village and presented me to their chief—a woman—and to the tribal councillors.

2. Use parentheses to enclose explanatory material that is not part of the main sentence.

"Lightweight Lit." (an essay in Part 4) was written by an English teacher who would have preferred to remain anonymous.

The Malagasy (people of Madagascar) like to eat a kapoaka of rice (enough to fill a condensed-milk can) three times a day.

3. Use parentheses to enclose reference data in a research paper. (See Chapter 20.)

Exercise 36.2*

Add parentheses where they are appropriate.

1. Five of the students I was asked not to name them have volunteered to be peer tutors.
2. The apostrophe is explained in the unit on spelling pages 463–70.
3. Jason complained that being a manager he became one in March was like being a cop.
4. I have enclosed a cheque for one hundred and fifty dollars $150.
5. More members of the Canadian Armed Forces died in World War I 1914–18 than in any war before or since.
6. Although Mozart lived a relatively short time he died when he was 36, he composed hundreds of musical masterpieces.
7. As news of her miracle cures spread patients began to come to her from all over the province, the doctor had to move her clinic to a more central location.
8. The new contract provided improved working conditions, a raise in salary 3 percent, and a new dental plan.

Punctuation

9. Ontario and British Columbia now produce world-class wines from their small estate wineries Inniskillin, Hillebrand, Quails' Gate that compete and win internationally.

10. "One of the most important tools for making paper speak in your own voice is punctuation; it plays the role of body language; it helps readers hear you the way you want to be heard" Baker, 48–49.

GO TO WEB

EXERCISE 36.1

Exercise 36.3

Insert dashes and parentheses where appropriate in the following sentences.

1. The function of parentheses see the explanation on page 446 is to set apart material that interrupts the main idea of the sentence and that the writer does not want to emphasize.

2. Dashes, on the other hand bold, dramatic dashes are used to set off an emphatic interruption.

3. We should we must find a way to cut expenses by at least 10 percent.

4. On their first and last date, Rupert took Freda bowling.

5. Proof of the need for investment in infrastructure see the appendix to the Building Committee Report is that the building has twice failed fire code inspections.

6. We wanted it to be warm for our week at the ocean, but it was so hot 40 degrees hot that we didn't even want to leave the hotel to go to the beach.

7. This comic book comics may not be great literature, but they are important cultural documents cost me 10 cents and is now worth more than $4,000.

8. There are a few people obnoxious people like Dwight and Daisy who light up the room when they leave.

9. For my birthday, my sister gave me a pair of hand-knit socks I'm allergic to wool, a box of chocolates I'm on a diet, and a coffee mug with the Nortel logo on it.

10. Canadian sports broadcaster, Foster Hewitt, created a sports catch phrase "He shoots! He scores!" during an overtime game between the Rangers and the Leafs on April 4, 1933. The Rangers won.

Exercise 36.4

Correct the following paragraph, which contains 20 errors (each set of dashes and parentheses counts as two errors).

As a final review of punctuation here's a paragraph that should contain all the punctuation marks we have discussed in this section of the book however 20 pieces of punctuation are missing. Your job is to provide the missing punctuation. Let's quickly deal with punctuation marks one by one. The comma probably the hardest-working of them all is used to separate items in a series to set off nonessential material to join with a conjunction to separate independent clauses and to set off material that comes before a main clause. Whew. The semicolon can replace a period it often separates two independent clauses that are closely connected in meaning. The colon has a different function it follows an independent clause and introduces a list a clarification or a quotation. Did you remember that a colon should never follow "is" or "are". A question mark must be used at the end of all interrogative sentences. We all know this but sometimes we forget. Exclamation marks are used at the end of sentences for one purpose only to supply dramatic effect. But remember that they are seldom used in academic writing. Finally dashes and parentheses allow a writer to interrupt a train of thought and insert an "aside" into a sentence. That's it. If you have correctly inserted all the punctuation in this paragraph then you are ready to tackle Hazardous Homonyms.

Punctuation

37

Hazardous Homonyms

This chapter focuses on homonyms—words that sound alike or look alike and are easily confused: *accept* and *except*; *weather* and *whether*; *whose* and *who's*; *affect* and *effect*. A spell checker will not help you find spelling mistakes in these words because the "correct" spelling depends on the sentence in which you use the word. For example, if you write, "Meat me hear inn halve an our," no spell checker will find fault with your sentence—and no reader will understand what you're talking about.

Careful pronunciation can sometimes help you tell the difference between words that are often confused. For example, if you pronounce the words *accept* and *except* differently, you'll be less likely to use the wrong one when you write. You can also make up memory aids to help you remember the difference in meaning between words that sound or look alike.

Below is a list of the most common homonym hazards. Only some of the words on this list will cause you trouble. Make your own list of problem pairs and tape it on the inside cover of your dictionary or post it close to your computer. Get into the habit of checking your document against your list every time you write.

accept
except
Accept means "take" or "receive." It is always a verb. *Except* means "excluding."

> I *accepted* the spelling award, and no one *except* my mother knew I cheated.

advice
advise
The difference in pronunciation makes the difference in meaning clear. *Advise* (rhymes with *wise*) is a verb. *Advice* (rhymes with *nice*) is a noun.

> I *advise* you not to listen to free *advice*.

affect
effect

Affect as a verb means "change." Try substituting *change* for the word you've chosen in your sentence. If it makes sense, then *affect* is the word you want. As a noun, *áffect* means "a strong feeling." *Effect* is a noun meaning "result." If you can substitute *result,* then *effect* is the word you need. Occasionally, *effect* is used as a verb meaning "to bring about."

> Learning about the *effects* (results) of caffeine *affected* (changed) my coffee-drinking habits.
> Depressed people often display inappropriate *affect* (feelings).
> Antidepressant medications can *effect* (bring about) profound changes in mood.

a lot
allot

A lot (often misspelled *alot*) should be avoided in formal writing. Use *many* or *much* instead. *Allot* means "distribute" or "assign."

>   *many*   *much*
> He still has a lot of problems, but he is coping a lot better.
> The teacher will *allot* the marks according to the difficulty of the questions.

aloud
allowed

Aloud means out loud, not a whisper. *Allowed* means permitted.

> We were not *allowed* to speak *aloud* during the performance.

amount
number

Amount is used with uncountable things; *number* is used with countable things.

> You may have a large *number* of jelly beans in a jar but a small *amount* of candy.
> (Jelly beans are countable; candy is not.)

are
our

Are is a verb. *Our* shows ownership.

> Marie-Claire Blais and Margaret Atwood *are* two of Canada's best-known writers.

> Canada is *our* home and native land.

assure
ensure
insure

Assure means "state with confidence; pledge or promise."

> She *assured* him she would keep his letters always.

> The prime minister *assured* the Inuit their concerns would be addressed in the near future.

Spelling

Ensure means "make certain of something."

> The extra $20 will *ensure* that you get a good seat.
>
> No number of promises can *ensure* that love will last.

Insure means "guarantee against financial loss." We *insure* lives and property.

> Kevin *insured* the book before he sent it airmail.
>
> We have *insured* both our home and our car against fire and theft.

choose
chose

Pronunciation gives the clue here. *Choose* rhymes with *booze* and means "select." *Chose* rhymes with *rose* and means "selected."

> Please *choose* a topic.
>
> I *chose* filmmaking.

cite
sight
site

To *cite* is to quote or mention. A lawyer *cites* precedents. Writers *cite* their sources in research papers. You might *cite* a comedian for her wit or a politician for his honesty. A *site* is a place.

> You have included only Internet sources in your Works *Cited* list.
>
> The Plains of Abraham is the *site* of a famous battle.
>
> Tiananmen Square is the *site* of the massacre.
>
> Pape and Mortimer is the *site* of our new industrial design centre.

A *sight* is something you see.

> With his tattooed forehead and three nose rings, he was a *sight* to behold.

coarse
course

Coarse means "rough, unrefined." (Remember: the word **arse** is co**arse**.) For all other meanings, use *course*.

> That sandpaper is too *coarse*.
>
> You'll enjoy the photography *course*.
>
> Of *course* you'll do well.

complement
compliment

A *complement* completes something. A *compliment* is a gift of praise.

A glass of wine would be the perfect *complement* to the meal.

Some people are embarrassed by *compliments*.

conscience
conscious

Your *conscience* is your sense of right and wrong. *Conscious* means "aware" or "awake"—able to feel and think.

After Katy cheated on the test, her *conscience* bothered her.

Katy was *conscious* of having done wrong.

The injured man was *unconscious* for an hour.

consul
council
counsel

A *consul* is a government official stationed in another country. A *council* is an assembly or official group. (Members of a council are *councillors*.) *Counsel* can be used to mean both "advice" and "to advise." (Those who give advice are *counsellors*.)

The Canadian *consul* in Mexico was very helpful.

The Women's Advisory *Council* meets next month.

Maria gave me good *counsel*.

She *counselled* me to hire a lawyer.

continual
continuous

Continual refers to an action that goes on regularly but with interruptions. *Continuous* refers to an action that goes on without interruption.

The student *continually* tried to interrupt the lecturer, who droned on *continuously*.

There is a *continuous* flow of traffic during rush hour.

credible
credulous
creditable

Credible means "believable"; *credulous* describes the person who believes an incredible story.

Nell was fortunate that the police officer found her story *credible*.

My brother is so *credulous* that we call him Gullible Gus.

Creditable means "worthy of reward or praise."

Spelling

After two semesters, Eva has finally begun to produce *creditable* work.

desert
dessert

A *désert* is a dry, barren place. As a verb, *desért* means "leave behind." *Dessért* is the part of the meal you'd probably like a double serving of, so give it a double *s*.

The tundra is Canada's only *desert* region.

My neighbour *deserted* her husband and children.

Dessert is my favourite part of the meal.

dining
dinning

You'll spell *dining* correctly if you remember the phrase "wining and dining." You'll probably never use *dinning*. It means "making a loud noise."

The children are in the *dining* room.

We are *dining* out tonight.

The noise from the bar was *dinning* in our ears.

disburse
disperse

Disburse means "to pay out money," which is what **bursars** do. *Disperse* means "to break up"; crowds are sometimes *dispersed* by the police.

The college's financial-aid officer will *disburse* the students' loans at the end of this week.

The protesters were *dispersed* by the police.

does
dose

Pronunciation provides the clue. *Does* rhymes with *buzz* and is a verb. *Dose* rhymes with *gross* and refers to a quantity of medicine.

John *does* drive quickly, doesn't he?

My grandmother gave me a *dose* of cod liver oil.

farther
further

You'll have no trouble distinguishing between these two if you associate *farther* with *distance* and *further* with *time*.

Dana wanted me to walk a little *farther* so we could discuss our relationship *further*.

faze
phase

Fazed usually has a *not* before it; to be *not fazed* means to be not disturbed, or concerned, or taken aback. *Phase* means "stage of development or process."

Unfortunately, Theo was not the least bit *fazed* by his disastrous grade report.

Since Mei Ling works full-time, she has decided to complete her degree in *phases*.

fewer
less

Fewer is used with countable things, *less* with uncountable things.

In May, there are *fewer* students in the college, so there is *less* work for the faculty to do.

The *fewer* attempts you make, the *less* your chance of success.

With units of money or measurement, however, use *less*:

I have *less* than $20 in my wallet.

Our house is on a lot that is *less* than four metres wide.

forth
fourth

Forth means "**forward**" or "**onward.**" **Fourth** contains the number **four**, which gives it its meaning.

Please stop pacing back and *forth*.

The B.C. Lions lost their *fourth* game in a row.

hear
here

Hear is what you do with your **ears**. *Here* is used for all other meanings.

Now *hear* this!

Ray isn't *here*.

Here is your assignment.

imply
infer

A speaker or writer *implies*; a listener or reader *infers*. To *imply* is to hint or say something indirectly. To *infer* is to draw a conclusion from what is stated or hinted at.

I *inferred* from his sarcastic remarks that he was not very fond of Sheila.

In her introduction of the speaker, Sheila *implied* that she greatly admired him.

it's
its

It's is a shortened form of *it is*. The apostrophe takes the place of the *i* in *is*. If you can substitute *it is*, then *it's* is the form you need. If you can't substitute *it is*, then *its* is the correct word.

Spelling

It's really not difficult. (*It is* really not difficult.)

The book has lost *its* cover. ("The book has lost *it is* cover" makes no sense, so you need *its*.)

It's is also commonly used as the shortened form of *it has*. In this case, the apostrophe replaces the *ha* in *has*.

It's been a good year for us.

later
latter

Later refers to time and has the word **late** in it. *Latter* means "the second of two" and has two *t*s. It is the opposite of *former*.

It is *later* than you think.

You take the former, and I'll take the *latter*.

loose
lose

Pronunciation is the key to these words. *Loose* rhymes with *goose* and means "not tight." *Lose* rhymes with *ooze* and means "misplace" or "be defeated."

A *loose* electrical connection is dangerous.

Some are born to win, some to *lose*.

martial
marshal

Martial refers to warfare or military affairs. *Marshal* has two meanings. As a noun, it refers to a person who has high office, either in the army or (especially in the United States) the police. As a verb, it means to arrange or assemble in order.

She is a *martial* arts enthusiast.

When the troops were *marshalled* on the parade grounds, they were reviewed by the army *marshal*.

miner
minor

A *miner* works in a **mine**. *Minor* means "lesser" or "not important." For example, a *minor* is a person of less than legal age.

Liquor can be served to *miners*, but not if they are *minors*.

For me, spelling is a *minor* problem.

moral
morale

Again, pronunciation provides the clue you need. *Móral* refers to the understanding of what is right and wrong. *Morále* refers to the spirit or mental condition of a person or group.

> People often have to make *moral* decisions.
> The low *morale* of the workers prompted the strike.

peace
piece

Peace is what we want on **Earth**. *Piece* means "a part or portion of something," as in "a **piece** of **pie**."

> Everyone hopes for *peace* in the Middle East.
> A *piece* of the puzzle is missing.

personal
personnel

Personal means "private." *Personnel* refers to the group of people working for a particular employer or to the office responsible for maintaining employees' records.

> The letter was marked "*Personal* and Confidential."
> We are fortunate in having qualified *personnel*.
> Fatima works in the *Personnel* Office.

principal
principle

Principal means "main." A *principle* is a rule.

> A *principal* is the main administrator of a school.
> Oil is Alberta's *principal* industry.
> I make it a *principle* to submit my essays on time.

quiet
quite

If you pronounce these words carefully, you won't confuse them. *Quiet* has two syllables; *quite* has only one.

> The librarian asked us to be *quiet*.
> We had not *quite* finished our homework.

roll
role

Turning over and over like a wheel is to *roll*; a bun is also a *roll*. An actor playing a part is said to have a *role*.

> His *role* called for him to fall to the ground and *roll* into a ditch, all the while munching on a bread *roll*.

Spelling

simple
simplistic

Simple means uncomplicated, easily understood. Something described as *simplistic* is too simple to be acceptable; essential details or complexities have been overlooked.

This problem is far from *simple*. Your solution to it is *simplistic*.

stationary
stationery

Stationary means "fixed in place." *Stationery* is writing paper.

Sarah Ferguson works out on a *stationary* bicycle.
Please order a new supply of *stationery*.

than
then

Than is used in comparisons. Pronounce it to rhyme with *can*. *Then* refers to time and rhymes with *when*.

Rudi is a better speller *than* I.
He made his decision *then*.
Eva withdrew from the competition; *then* she realized the consequences.

their
there
they're

Their indicates ownership. *There* points out something or indicates place. It includes the word *here*, which also indicates place. *They're* is a shortened form of *they are*. (The apostrophe replaces the *a* in *are*.)

It was *their* fault.
There are two weeks left in the term.
You should look over *there*.
They're late, as usual.

too
two
to

The *too* with an extra *o* in it means "more than enough" or "also." *Two* is the number after one. For all other meanings, use *to*.

He thinks he's been working *too* hard. She thinks so *too*.
There are *two* sides *to* every argument.
The *two* women knew *too* much about each other *to* be friends.

weather
whether
wether

Whether means "which of the two" and is used in all cases when you aren't referring to the climatic conditions outside (*weather*). A *wether* is a castrated ram, so that word's uses are limited.

Whether you're ready or not, it's time to go.

No one immigrates to Canada for its *weather.*

were
where
we're

If you pronounce these three carefully, you won't confuse them. *Were* rhymes with *fur* and is a verb. ***Where*** is pronounced "hwear," includes the word ***here***, and indicates place. *We're* is a shortened form of *we are* and is pronounced "weer."

You were joking, *weren't* you?

Where did you want to meet?

We're on our way.

who's
whose

Who's is a shortened form of *who is* or *who has*. If you can substitute *who is* or *who has* for the *who's* in your sentence, then you are using the right spelling. Otherwise, use *whose*.

Who's coming to dinner? (*Who is* coming to dinner?)

Who's been sleeping in my bed? (*Who has* been sleeping in my bed?)

Whose calculator is this? ("*Who is* calculator" makes no sense, so you need *whose*.)

woman
women

Confusing these two is guaranteed to irritate your female readers. *Woman* is the singular form; compare ***man***. *Women* is the plural form; compare ***men***.

A *woman's* place is wherever she chooses to be.

The *women's* movement promotes equality between women and men.

you're
your

You're is a shortened form of *you are*. If you can substitute *you are* for the *you're* in your sentence, then you're using the correct form. If you can't substitute *you are*, use *your*.

You're welcome. (*You are* welcome.)

Unfortunately, *your* hamburger got burned. ("*You are* hamburger" makes no sense, so *your* is the word you want.)

Spelling

In Exercises 37.1 and 37.2, choose the correct word from those in parentheses. If you don't know an answer, go back and reread the explanation. Check your answers after each set. Answers for this chapter begin on page 543.

Exercise 37.1*

1. The limited (coarse course) selection will (affect effect) our academic development and subsequent job opportunities.
2. (Are Our) you going to (accept except) the offer?
3. Eat your vegetables; (than then) you can have your (desert dessert).
4. If (your you're) overweight by 20 kg, (loosing losing) the excess will be a long-term proposition.
5. It's (quiet quite) true that they did not get (hear here) until 2:00 a.m.
6. It is usually the saint, not the sinner, (who's whose) (conscience conscious) is troubled.
7. He (assured ensured insured) me he would keep the (amount number) of changes to a minimum.
8. (Its It's) hard to tell the dog from (its it's) owner.
9. To (choose chose) a (coarse course) of action against your lawyer's (advice advise) would be foolish.
10. (Continual Continuous) (dining dinning) out becomes boring after a while.

Exercise 37.2*

1. It is (simple simplistic) to claim that our society's (morals morales) have declined drastically over the last 20 years; to do so (infers implies) that morality is an absolute value.
2. After the accident, the (moral morale) of the (miners minors) did not recover for many months, but the owners appeared not to be (fazed phased) by the disaster.
3. The chief librarian did not mean to (imply infer) that (farther further) cuts to services are being considered by the board, which, in the circumstances, has done a very (credible credulous creditable) job.
4. The (affect effect) of trying to (disperse disburse) the mob of (less fewer) than 20 people was to cause a riot involving hundreds.
5. (Who's Whose) (principals principles) are so firm that they wouldn't pay (fewer less) tax if they could get away with it?
6. By reading between the lines, we can (infer imply) (wether weather whether) the author intends his (forth fourth) chapter to be taken seriously.

7. It's (your you're) fault that we are (continually continuously) harassed by salespeople because your welcoming smile (assures insures ensures) that they will return again and again.

8. Are you (conscious conscience) of the fact that (choosing chosing) this (site cite sight) for your business will take you (farther further) away from your client base?

9. Gloria could not (accept except) the fact that the (councillors counsellors) rejected her plan to (phase faze) out parking in the downtown core.

10. The (amount number) of people (aloud allowed) to participate depends on (fewer less) (then than) a dozen (woman women) who are entrusted with making the decision.

Exercise 37.3*

Each of the items below is followed by two statements. Identify the one that makes sense as a follow-up to the introductory sentence.

1. All former students will be welcomed back to class.
   a. We will except all former students.
   b. We will accept all former students.

2. The lawn mower next door has been running nonstop for over an hour.
   a. The continual noise is driving me crazy.
   b. The continuous noise is driving me crazy.

3. This author only hints at how the story ends.
   a. She implies that they live happily ever after.
   b. She infers that they live happily ever after.

4. Your proposal is not worth our consideration
   a. It's simple.
   b. It's simplistic.

5. We're looking for a female role model.
   a. The women must lead by example.
   b. The woman must lead by example.

6. How many assistants will be required?
   a. The amount of help we will need is hard to estimate.
   b. The number of helpers we will need is hard to estimate.

7. While their skill sets are very different, together, the two make a good team.
   a. She compliments his weaknesses.
   b. She complements his weaknesses.

8. Are you permitted to talk during the lectures?
   a. It is not allowed.
   b. It is not aloud.

Spelling

9. When did she wake up?
    a. She regained her conscience during the prayers.
    b. She regained her consciousness during the prayers.
10. How many kilometres are left in your journey?
    a. We have only a little farther to go.
    b. We have only a little further to go.

GO TO WEB

EXERCISES **37.1, 37.2, 37.3, 37.4**

Exercise 37.4

Now test your mastery of homonyms by correcting the 10 errors in the following paragraph.

I would advice anyone who's schedule seems to be full to try the solution I came up with less then three months ago. I pulled the plug on my TV. Overwhelmed with assignments and unable to chose among priorities, I realized I was making the problem worse by sitting for three or four hours a night in front of the tube. I decided I should spend more time on my coarses and less on watching television. To avoid temptation, I put the TV set in the closet. The results have been more dramatic then I thought possible. My apartment is now a haven of piece and quiet, and some of my assignments are actually handed in before their due. Occasionally there is a twinge of regret that I no longer know whose doing what to whom in the latest reality contest, but overall, I'm much happier for choosing to loose the tube.

38

The Apostrophe

Most punctuation marks indicate the relationship among parts of a sentence. Apostrophes and hyphens, on the other hand, indicate the relationship between the elements of a word. That's why we've chosen to discuss them in this section, along with other spelling issues.

Misused apostrophes display a writer's ignorance or carelessness. They can also confuse, amuse, and sometimes annoy readers.

- Sometimes you need an apostrophe so that your reader can understand what you mean. For example, there's a world of difference between these two sentences:

The instructor began class by calling the students' names.

The instructor began class by calling the students names.

- In most cases, however, misused apostrophes just amuse or irritate an alert reader:

The movie had it's moments.

He does a days work for every weeks salary.

The Lion's thank you for your contribution.

It isn't difficult to avoid such mistakes. Correctly used, the apostrophe indicates either **contraction** or **possession**. It never makes a singular word plural. Learn the simple rules that govern these uses and you'll have no further trouble with apostrophes.

Spelling

Contraction

Contraction is the combining of two words into one, as in *they're* or *can't*. Contractions are common in conversation and in informal written English. Unless you are quoting someone else's words, however, you should avoid them in the writing you do for college or work.

The rule about where to put an apostrophe in a contraction is one of those rare rules that has no exception. It *always* holds.

> When two words are combined into one, and one or more letters are left out, the apostrophe goes in the place of the missing letter(s).

Here are some examples.

I am	→ I'm	they are	→ they're
we will	→ we'll	it is	→ it's
she is	→ she's	it has	→ it's
do not	→ don't	who has	→ who's

Exercise 38.1*

Correct these sentences by placing apostrophes where needed. Answers for this chapter begin on page 544.

1. Yes, its a long way from Halifax to Vancouver, but weve been in training for three months.
2. Were taking the train to Antigonish, and were biking to Halifax; then well begin the big trip west.
3. There wasnt a dry eye in the theatre when Spielbergs film reached its climax.
4. Whos discovered whats wrong with this sentence?
5. Wasnt it Mark Twain who said, "Its easy to stop smoking; Ive done it dozens of times"?

GO TO WEB

EXERCISES 38.1, 38.2

Exercise 38.2[*]

In some formal kinds of writing—academic, legal, and technical, for example—contractions are not acceptable. A good writer is able not only to contract two words into one, but also to expand any contraction into its original form: a two-word phrase. In the following paragraph, find and expand the contractions into their original form.

I'm writing to apply for the position of webmaster for BrilloVision.com

that you've advertised in the *Daily News*. I've got the talent and background

you're looking for. Currently, I work as a Web designer for an online publi-

cation, Vexed.com, where they're very pleased with my work. If you click on

their website, I think you'll like what you see. There's little in the way of

Web design and application that I haven't been involved in during the past

two years. But it's time for me to move on to a new challenge, and

BrilloVision.com promises the kind of opportunity I'm looking for. I

guarantee you won't be disappointed if I join your team!

Possession

The apostrophe is also used to show ownership or possession. Here's the rule that applies in most cases.

> Add *'s* to the word that indicates the *owner*.
> If the resulting word ends in a double or triple *s*, delete the last *s*, leaving the apostrophe in place.[1]

---

[1]Many writers today prefer to keep the final *s* when it represents a sound that is pronounced, as it is in one-syllable words such as *boss* and *class*, and in some names such as *Harris* and *Brutus*.

Spelling

Here are some examples that illustrate the rule.

singer + 's = singer's voice   women + 's = women's voices
band + 's = band's instruments   student + 's = student's transcript
players + 's = players'$ uniforms   students + 's = students'$ transcripts

To form a possessive correctly, you must first identify the word in the sentence that indicates possession and determine whether it is singular or plural. For example, "the managers duties" can have two meanings, depending on where you put the apostrophe:

the manager's duties (the duties belong to one *manager*)
the managers' duties (the duties belong to two or more *managers*)

To solve an apostrophe problem, follow this two-step process:
1. Find the owner word.
2. Apply the possession rule.

Problem: Carmens hair is a mess.
Solution: 1. The word that indicates possession is *Carmen* (singular).
          2. Add *'s* to *Carmen*.

Carmen's hair is a mess.

Problem: The technicians strike halted the production.
Solution: 1. The word that indicates possession is *technicians* (plural).
          2. Add *'s* to *technicians*, then delete the second *s*, leaving the apostrophe.

The *technicians'* strike halted the production.

Sometimes the meaning of your sentence is determined by where you put the apostrophe.

Problem: I was delighted by the critics response to my book.

Now you have two possibilities to choose from, depending on your meaning.

Solution A: 1. The owner word is *critic* (singular).
            2. Add *'s* to *critic*.

I was delighted by the *critic's* response to my book.

Solution B: 1. The owner word is *critics* (plural).
2. Add *'s* to *critics*, then drop the second *s*, leaving the apostrophe.

I was delighted by the *critics'* response to my book.

Both solutions are correct, depending on whether the book was reviewed by one critic (A) or by more than one critic (B).

Possession does not have to be literal. It can be used to express the notion of "belonging to" or "associated with." That is, the owner word need not refer to a person or group of people. Ideas or concepts (abstract nouns) can be "owners" too.

a month's vacation = a vacation of one month
a year's salary = the salary of one year
"A Hard Day's Night" = the night that follows a hard day

Note that a few words, called **possessive pronouns**, are already possessive in form, so they don't have apostrophes.[2]

yours	ours	whose
hers, his, its	theirs	

His music is not like *yours*.

Whose lyrics do you prefer, *theirs* or *ours*?

The dog lost *its* bone.

Four of these possessive pronouns are often confused with the contractions that sound like them. It's worth taking a moment to learn how to avoid this confusion. When you are trying to decide which spelling to use,

1. Expand the contraction into its original two words.
2. Then substitute those words for the contraction in your sentence.
3. If the sentence still makes sense, use the contraction. If it doesn't, use the possessive spelling.

---

[2]If you add an apostrophe to any of these words, you create an error. There are no such words as *your's*, *her's*, *their's*, or *our's*.

Spelling

Possessive		**Contraction**	
its	= *It* owns something	it's	= it is/it has
their	= *They* own something	they're	= they are
whose	= *Who* owns something	who's	= who is/who has
your	= *You* own something	you're	= you are

Error: They're (they are) going to sing they're (~~they are~~) latest song.
Revision: They're going to sing *their* latest song.

Exercises 38.3 and 38.4 will test and reinforce your understanding of both contraction and possession.

Exercise 38.3*

Correct the following sentences by adding apostrophes where necessary.

1. The cars brakes are worn and its tires are nearly bald.
2. Diplomatic ambassadors wives or husbands are often as important to a missions success as the ambassadors themselves.
3. Near Chicoutimi is one of the countrys most beautiful parks, where the skills of canoeists, fishermen, and wildlife photographers can be put to the test on a summers day.
4. Janis career got its start when she sang seafarers songs in the yacht clubs dining lounge.
5. A countrys history is the main determinant of its national character.

Exercise 38.4*

In each of the sentences below, choose the correct word from those in parentheses. Check your answers before going on.

1. Where (your you're) going, (your you're) biggest problem will be maintaining (your you're) health.
2. (Someones Someone's) got to take responsibility for the large numbers of domestic animals (whose who's) owners have abandoned them.
3. The (ships ship's ships') captain agreed to donate a (weeks week's weeks') salary to the Scott Mission.
4. Contrary to some (people's peoples) opinions, postal (workers worker's workers') contracts are most often settled by both (sides side's sides') willingness to bend long before a strike is necessary.
5. My (turtles turtle's) legs are shorter than your (turtles turtle's), but I bet (its it's) going to run (its it's) laps faster than (yours your's).

EXERCISES **38.3, 38.4**

Plurals

The third apostrophe rule is very simple. Memorize it, apply it, and you will instantly correct many of your apostrophe errors.

> Never use an apostrophe to make a word plural.

The plural of most English words is formed by adding *s* to the root word (not *'s*). The *s* alone tells the reader that the word is plural: e.g., *memos, letters, files, broadcasts, newspapers, journalists.* If you add an apostrophe + *s*, you are telling your reader that the word is either a contraction or a possessive.

> Incorrect: Never use apostrophe's to make word's plural.
> Correct: Never use apostrophes to make words plural.

Exercise 38.5*

Correct the misused and missing apostrophes in the following sentences. There are 10 errors in this exercise.

1. When you feel like a snack, you can choose between apples and Timbit's.

2. Annas career took off when she discovered its easy to sell childrens toys.

3. Golfing requires the use of different club's: woods for long shots, irons for short ones.

4. Poker's an easy game to play if you are dealt ace's more often than your opponent's are.

5. Good writing skill's dont guarantee success in you're career, but they help.

Spelling

Exercise 38.6

Before you try the final exercise in this chapter, carefully review the information in the Summary box below. Then test your mastery of apostrophes by correcting the 15 errors in the passage below.

The following advisory for American's heading to Canada was compiled from information provided by the U.S. State Department and the CIA. It is intended as a guide for American traveller's:

Canada is a large foreign country, even bigger than Texas. It has 10 states (called provinces) and it's only neighbour is America. Canadas contributions to Western civilization include bacon, hockey players, geese, doughnut's, and the Mountie's red uniform's.

Canadians stand in line without complaining, seldom raise they're voices, and cheer politely when the home or visiting teams players do something worthwhile. Canada has two language's: French and American. Other linguistic oddities include "eh," which can turn any statement into a question, and the pronunciation of *ou* as *uoo*, as in *huoose* or *abuoot*.

The bright color's and funny picture's of Canadian currency may make the unwary tourist think of it as play money, but each blue Canadian five-dollar bill is worth about two real dollars. The one- and two-dollar coins, called loonies and toonies, make good souvenir's.

The Canadian government is somewhat left-leaning, providing health care for all and refusing to execute criminal's. Tourists are advised to avoid all political discussion and to remember that politician's in Canada are like politician's anywhere: popular with some people, unpopular with others.

Summary

- When contracting two words into one, put an apostrophe in the place of the missing letters.
- Watch for owner words: they need apostrophes.
- To indicate possession, add *'s* to the owner word. (If the owner word already ends in *s*, just add the apostrophe.)
- Possessive pronouns (e.g., *yours, its, ours*) do not take apostrophes.
- Never use an apostrophe to form the plural of a word.

39

The Hyphen

The **hyphen** (-) has three different functions:

- as part of the correct spelling of a word (e.g., mother-in-law, self-esteem)
- to divide a word at the end of a line
- to separate or join two or more words or parts of words. There are five rules to follow.

1. Use a hyphen to divide a word at the end of a written or typed line.

Your dictionary tells you where words can be divided. Most dictionaries mark the syllables of a word with a dot: syl·lables = syl-lables.

Never divide a word of only one or two syllables. Use a hyphen at the end of a line for words of three or more syllables (e.g., commu-nity). If the word is already hyphenated (e.g., self-reliance, ex-president), break it after the hyphen.

2. Use a hyphen to separate a prefix from the main word when two of the same vowels occur together.

Examples: re-elected, co-operate, anti-imperalism

When the two vowels are different, however, no hyphen is required: semiautomatic, realign, preamble

3. Use a hyphen with compound numbers from twenty-one to ninety-nine, with fractions, and with dimensions.

Spelling

Examples: forty-six, one-eighth, ninety-eight, six-by-eight

4. Use a hyphen to join two or more words that serve as an adjective *before* a noun.

Examples: The (first-born) child is often the best loved.

The (best-loved) child is often the first born.

(Word-of-mouth) advertising is very effective.

A good writer has a (well-thumbed, up-to-date) dictionary.

5. Use a hyphen to avoid ambiguity.

Examples: The contractor re-covered the roof with asphalt shingles. (He repaired the roof.)

The contractor recovered his money. (He got his money back.)

The government's plan provided for nursing-home care. (care in a nursing home)

The government's plan provided for nursing home-care. (care at home by nurses)

The prime minister will address small business owners. (Do you really want to say he will talk only to short people?)

The prime minister will address small-business owners. (These people are owners of small businesses.)

Exercise 39.1*

Most of the following sentences require one or more hyphens. Review the rules in the boxes above, then try your hand at correcting these sentences. Answers for this chapter are on page 545.

1. Jill decided to sublet her fifth floor apartment.

2. Fraser claims he is allergic to classical music but addicted to hip hop music.
3. Just before the critical play, the hard fought game was preempted by the movie *Heidi*!
4. Hand knit sweaters are usually more expensive than factory produced ones.
5. In 1950, at the age of forty seven, George Orwell died of tuberculosis.

GO TO WEB

EXERCISE **39.1**

Exercise 39.2*

In the following sentences, some hyphens are missing, and some are included where they don't belong. Correct the errors in these sentences.

1. For months after Saddam Hussein was over-thrown, the world was shocked by revelations of the repression suffered by the Iraqi people.
2. Would you re-lay this message to Mr. Chan: the masons would like to relay the bricks this evening?
3. Our next door neighbour teaches in a high-school, but she does not like to be introduced as a high school teacher.
4. A face to face meeting with an antiintellectual always gets my adrenalin going.
5. Because Angela was an attorney at law and had once been an all Canadian athlete, her former coach was not surprised when she became Minister-of-Recreation.

Exercise 39.3

This last exercise is a mastery test. Insert hyphens where they are needed and delete them where they are not.

1. At 20 years-of-age, Trudy began to reorganize her life.
2. Because she is the instructor who is the most up to date with trends in the industry, Alysha is the coordinator of our program.
3. Only one third of the team seemed to be reenergized by the 20 minute break.
4. Vernon wore his hand tailored three piece suit to his former-girlfriend's wedding.
5. In spite of its country garden atmosphere, the hotel's up to the minute décor and facilities could not be faulted.

Spelling

6. The space shuttle will reenter the atmosphere in exactly eighty five seconds.
7. Tim began to recover from his career threatening injury after taking an antiinflammatory.
8. Some very successful businesses are coowned by the employees; these cooperative ventures ensure that workers' hard earned dollars are put to work on their-own behalf.
9. Computer generated graphics are ninety nine percent of our over the counter business.
10. Trevor was treated for post traumatic stress after his no hope last minute attempt to pass chemistry.

40

Capital Letters

Capital letters belong in a few specific places and nowhere else. Some writers suffer from "capitalitis." They put capital letters on words without thinking about their position or function in a sentence.

Capitalize the first letter of a word that fits into one of the six categories listed below:

1. The first word of a sentence, a direct quotation, or a sentence from a quoted source.

Are you illiterate? Write to us today for free help.
The supermodel cooed, "I just love the confidence makeup gives me."
Lister Sinclair claims that the only thing Canadians have in common is that "We all hate Toronto."

Exercise 40.1*

Add the seven missing capital letters to the following sentences. Answers for exercises in this chapter begin on page 545.

1. time is nature's way of keeping everything from happening at once.

2. Brad sang, "there's a light in the Frankenstein house."

3. Learning Standard english is, for many people, like learning another Language.

4. Richard Harkness, writing in *The New York Times*, said "a committee is a group of the unwilling, picked from the unfit, to do the unnecessary."

Spelling

5. in conclusion, I want you to consider the words of Wendell Johnson: "*always* and *never* are two words you should always remember never to use."

---

2. The names of specific people, places, and things.

Names of people (and their titles):

> Shania Twain, Governor General Michaëlle Jean, the Rev. Henry Jones, the Hon. Eugene Forsey, Senator Anne Cools

Names of places, regions, and astronomical bodies (but not general geographic directions):

> Stanley Park, Lake Superior, Cape Breton Island; Nunavut, the Prairie Provinces, the Badlands; Saturn, Earth, the Moon, the Asteroid Belt; south, north

Names of buildings, institutions, organizations, companies, departments, products, etc.:

> the Empress Hotel; McGill University, Red Deer College; the Liberal Party, the Kiwanis Club; Petro-Canada, Radio Shack; the Department of English, the Human Resources Department; Kleenex, Volvo, Labatt's

Exercise 40.2*

Add capital letters where necessary in the following sentences. There are 30 errors in this exercise.

1. After a brief stay in the maritimes, captain tallman and his crew sailed west up the st. lawrence.

2. The broadcast department of niagara college has ordered six sony cameras for their studios in welland, ontario.

3. Do you find that visa is more popular than American express when you travel to faraway places such as mexico, france, or jupiter?

4. Our stay at the seaview hotel, overlooking the pacific ocean, certainly beat our last vacation at the bates motel, where we faced west, overlooking the city dump.

5. As the fundraiser for our alumni association, I am targeting companies like disney, canadian tire, the bank of montreal, and the cbc, all of which employ our graduates.

---

3. Names of major historical events, historical periods, religions, holy texts, and holy days.

World War II, the Depression; the Renaissance; Islam, Judaism, Christianity, Buddhism, Hinduism; the Torah, the Koran, the Bible, the Upanishads; Ramadan, Yom Kippur, Easter

---

Exercise 40.3*

Add the 20 capital letters that are missing from the following sentences.

1. The crusades, which were religious wars between muslims and christians, raged through the middle ages.

2. The hindu religion recognizes and honours many gods; islam recognizes one god, allah; buddhism recognizes none.

3. The koran, the bible, and the torah agree on many principles.

4. The jewish festival of hanukkah often occurs near the same time that christians are celebrating christmas.

5. After world war I, many jews began to emigrate to Palestine, where they and the muslim population soon came into conflict.

Spelling

GO TO WEB

EXERCISE **40.1**

4. The days of the week, months of the year, and specific holidays, but not the seasons.

Wednesday; January; Remembrance Day, Canada Day; spring, autumn

Exercise 40.4*

The following sentences contain both missing and unnecessary capitals. Find and correct the 15 errors.

1. My favourite months are january and february because I love all Winter sports.

2. This monday is valentine's day, when messages of love are exchanged.

3. In the summer, big meals seem too much trouble; however, after thanksgiving, we need lots of food to survive the winter cold.

4. A National Holiday named flag day was once proposed, but it was never officially approved.

5. By thursday, I'll have finished my st. patrick's day costume.

5. The main words in titles of published works (books, magazines, films; essays, poems, songs; works of art; etc.). Do not capitalize minor words (articles, prepositions, conjunctions) in titles unless the word is the first word in the title.

The Colony of Unrequited Dreams   *The Thinker*
Of Mice and Men   "An Immigrant's Split Personality"
Maclean's   "In Flanders Fields"
A Room with a View   "If I Had a Million Dollars"

Exercise 40.5*

Add the 30 capital letters that are missing from the following sentences.

1. The review of my book, *the life and times of a chocoholic*, published in *the globe and mail*, was not favourable.

2. Clint eastwood fans will be delighted that the two early movies that made him internationally famous, *a fistful of dollars* and *for a few dollars more,* are now available on DVD.

3. Joseph Conrad's short novel *heart of darkness* became the blockbuster movie *apocalypse now.*

4. My poem, "a bright and silent place," was published in the april issue of *landscapes* magazine.

5. Botticelli's famous painting, "birth of venus," inspired my poem "woman on the half shell."

Pay special attention to this next category. It is one that often causes trouble.

6. The names of specific school courses.

Marketing 101, Psychology 100, Mathematics 220, English 110,

but

a) not the names of general school subjects

e.g., marketing, sociology, mathematics

b) *unless* the subjects are languages or pertain to specific geographical areas whose names are capitalized

e.g., English, Greek, the study of Chinese history, modern Caribbean literature, Latin American poetry

(Names of languages, countries, and geographical regions are always capitalized.)

Spelling

Exercise 40.6*

Add capital letters where necessary in the following sentences. There are ten errors in this exercise.

1. After studying geography for two years, I began taking courses in ancient greek and modern history.

2. We began our study of sociology with the concept of relationships.

3. By taking Professor Subden's noncredit course, introduction to wine, I qualified to register for oenology 120 the next semester.

4. While math is her strong subject, Laurie has trouble with accounting, english, and conversational french.

5. The prerequisite for theology 210 is introduction to world religions, taught by Professor Singh.

GO TO WEB

EXERCISE 40.2

Exercise 40.7

The following exercise is the mastery test and contains 30 errors. Before you begin, it would be a good idea to review the six capitalization rules presented in this chapter.

1. On the first official friday of Spring, we always celebrate by going fishing on lake winnipeg.

2. Failing Sociology is like eating soup with a fork: it's difficult, but you can do it if you really try.

3. July First is Canada day, when we celebrate the anniversary of confederation, which occurred in 1867.

4. Although Ms. Lau is a member of the new democratic party, she is quite Conservative in her thinking on Economic and social issues.

5. She may look like a sheep, but I'll have you know she's a purebred afghan hound.

6. Trying to learn english as quickly as possible, Wong Bao Lin took two Night School classes a week and listened to audiotapes several hours every day.

7. When travelling abroad, canadians can readily identify each other by their mountain equipment co-op backpacks, tilley hats, and roots clothing.

8. If I drop Math and Accounting, I will be able to concentrate on english and Marketing, but it will mean adding a semester to my program.

9. Citroen, Renault, and Peugeot are french cars that sell well in Europe, but have never caught on in north America.

10. Sally and Kendra are packing away the essentials like cigarettes, doritos, and Beer in preparation for the end of the World, which, they are convinced, will occur on December 31, 2010.

Spelling

41

Numbers

Numbers may be expressed as words (*one, four, nine*) or as figures (*1, 4, 9*), depending on the kind of assignment you are writing and what the numbers refer to. In a few circumstances, a combination of words and figures is required. In scientific and technical papers, numbers are normally given in figures; in humanities papers, numbers that can be expressed in one or two words are spelled out. For college papers, ask your instructor which style he or she prefers. For general purposes, including most business writing, follow the guidelines given below.

When to Use Words

1. Use words to express whole numbers one through nine and simple fractions. Use figures for numbers 10 and above.

The novel's three parts chronicle the nine-week journey of the five Acadian teenagers.

China and India together account for more than one-third of the Earth's population.

Approximately 30 years ago, Paul Henderson scored the most famous goal in the history of Canadian hockey.

There are two exceptions to this general rule.

A. Spell out any number that begins a sentence, or rewrite the sentence so that the number does not come first.

Incorrect: 157 students submitted essays to the awards committee.

Correct: One hundred and fifty-seven students submitted essays to the awards committee.

Also correct: The awards committee received essays from 157 students.

B. Use either figures *or* words to express numbers that modify the same or similar items in one sentence. (That is, be consistent within a sentence.)

We are looking for 3 accountants, 15 salespeople, and 2 customer service representatives. (*not* "three, 15, and two")

Only 9 of the 55 applicants had both the qualifications and the experience we required. (*not* "nine of the 55 applicants")

2. Treat ordinal numbers (first, second, etc.) as you would cardinal numbers (one, two, etc.).

Up to its sixth or seventh month, an infant can breathe and swallow at the same time.

In a 1904 speech, Sir Wilfrid Laurier declared that the 20th century would belong to Canada.

Exercise 41.1*

Applying the two highlighted rules in this chapter, correct any errors in the following sentences. Answers begin on page 547.

1. This applicant claims to speak more than 7 languages, but from her résumé, I'd say that English is not 1 of them.

2. This is the 3rd time the Accounting Department has filed its report 2 days late.

Spelling

3. 54 eager people have signed up for the 2nd annual Pool Tournament.

4. Of the 12 cuts on her new DVD release, the 1st two are my favourites.

5. Gavin, who works for the garage where I take my car, was unable to answer twelve of the twenty-three questions on the Mechanic Certification Exam.

6. In the Great Fire of 1666, 1/2 of London burned down, but only 6 people lost their lives.

7. If the diesel mixture contains 3/4 of a litre of regular gasoline, it will make your truck easier to start in those 4 or 5 really cold weeks of winter.

8. When I was twenty-seven and had been unemployed for nearly 3 years, I decided to return to college for 2 years of practical training.

9. In the United States, 1 of the reasons that hemp is illegal is that about eighty years ago, cotton growers lobbied against its cultivation because they saw it as competition.

10. Only eight out of forty-seven trivia players were able to name Jay Silverheels of Brantford, Ontario, as the original Tonto in *The Lone Ranger.*

GO TO WEB

EXERCISE **41.1**

When to Use Figures

As a general rule, you should use figures when you are presenting technical or precise numerical information or when your sentence or paragraph contains several numbers.

3. Use figures to express dates, specific times, addresses, and percentages; with abbreviations or symbols; and with units of currency.

Dates	April 1, 2006, *or* 1 April 2006
Times	8:45 a.m. *or* 08:45, 7:10 p.m. *or* 19:10 (Use words with *o'clock*: e.g., *nine o'clock*)
Addresses	24 Sussex Drive, 2175 West 8th Street
Percentages	19 percent, a 6.5-percent interest rate (Use the % sign only with figures in tables or in series: e.g., "From 2003 to 2005, our sales increased by 8%, 13%, and 19%.")
With abbreviations or symbols	7 mm, 293 km, 60 km/h, 40 g, 54 kg, 18°C, 0.005 cm, 1.5 L, 8½", p. 3
Amounts of money	79 cents *or* $0.79, $2, $100, $30,000, $20 million, $65 billion (Use words if the unit of currency follows whole numbers one through nine: e.g., *two dollars*, *seven euros*, unless the number includes a decimal: e.g., *1.5 trillion dollars*.)

Exercise 41.2*

With rule 3 in mind, correct the errors in the following sentences.

1. Researchers at Cornell University conducted a study that showed that sixty-six percent of all businessmen wear their ties too tight.

2. More than ten percent of those studied wore their ties so tight that blood flow to the brain was diminished.

3. 99 percent of the people who read the report wondered why Cornell had conducted such a study.

4. 1 plan is to retire on December seventeenth, 2055.

5. At precisely eight-ten p.m. on June third, your flight will leave for Whitehorse.

6. You will arrive at approximately 10 o'clock on June fourth if you make all your connections.

7. I won 5 dollars from Ted by proving that February Eighteen Sixty-five was the only month in recorded history not to have a full moon.

Spelling

8. You must be present at one thirty-three West Eighteenth Street by exactly 7:00 o'clock to claim your prize.

9. So far this year, I have spent thirty-eight thousand dollars, or twenty percent more than my anticipated income for the entire year, and it's only May fifteenth!

10. At the Indianapolis Speedway, the race cars burn approximately four L of fuel for each lap, while the ship *Queen Elizabeth II* moves just fifteen cm for every 4 L of fuel it burns.

GO TO WEB

EXERCISE **41.2**

When to Use Both Words and Figures

4. When one number immediately follows another, spell out the one that makes the shorter word.
5. For numbers over a million, express introductory whole numbers 10 and above in figures, and the quantity in words. (If the numbers involve decimals, use figures.)

The Grey Cup is contested by *two 12-man* teams of heavily padded and helmeted warriors.

Our local car dealers sold more than *200 four-wheel* drive vehicles the day after our first big storm.

The human stomach contains more than *35 million* digestive glands.

The Earth's population in 2005 was *6.54 billion*.

The following exercises will test your ability to apply all of the rules and exceptions presented in this chapter.

Exercise 41.3*

Correct any errors in the expression of numbers in the following sentences.

1. The speedboat is powered by 2 80-horsepower outboard motors.

2. 1 8-cylinder SUV emits more pollution than two four-cylinder Volkswagens or 3 Toyota gas-electric hybrids.

3. Because she sold seven $2,000,000 homes last year, she topped the agency's earnings list.

4. Eighty-two percent of people whose net worth is over two million dollars say they got rich by hard work.

5. 200 people were invited to celebrate my parents' twenty-fifth wedding anniversary on August Thirty-first, 2005.

6. A total of 10 fifteen-year-old girls and 4 fifteen-year-old boys applied for the commercial acting position we advertised.

7. Our lawyer told us that thirty-eight % of people who die between the ages of 45 and 54 have not prepared a will.

8. Canada's population of about 30,000,000 puts us in twenty-ninth place on the list of most populous countries.

9. 10 years ago, the average speed on urban freeways was fifty kph, but it has been steadily declining and is expected to be thirty kph within the next 5 years.

10. 7,000 ecstatic fans celebrated their team's unexpected two–one win in the Memorial Cup final, partying in the streets until four-thirty a.m.

GO TO WEB

EXERCISE 41.3

Spelling

Exercise 41.4

Before you tackle this final exercise, review the five highlighted rules given in this chapter. It's a good idea to write them out on a single sheet of paper and keep them before you as you go through this exercise. There are 15 errors in this paragraph.

Here's a news flash: Canadians trust neither politicians nor the media! A poll conducted for the CBC revealed that just under 2/3 of Canadians have little or no confidence in their political leaders. Furthermore, 1/3 of the respondents said they have little or no confidence in the media who report on the politicians; only eleven percent had a great deal of confidence in the media. But Canadians aren't just unhappy with the usual targets; they also have lost confidence in religious leaders (forty % have little or no confidence in them). Business leaders are slightly more trusted than religious leaders, with four % more people showing faith in them. In the poll, which surveyed just one thousand five hundred of Canada's 33,000,000 citizens, there was a little good news: seventy-two % of those polled said they didn't really expect politicians to keep their promises. That's down 2 percentage points from 2004. The CBC is careful to point out that the poll is accurate to within two point six percentage points nineteen times out of twenty, but even within that small margin of error, there is little here to surprise anyone. In their report on the poll, the CBC seemed most perturbed by the finding that so few had faith in the media. If Canadians are anything, it's news-savvy, and they are perfectly aware of the media's tendency to sensationalism, simplistic reporting of complex stories, and editorial bias. This distrust is most evident among young people: ask ten nineteen-year-old Canadians where they get their information about the world, and 8 will tell you, "The Internet."

ESSAY ESSENTIALS

INTRODUCTION TO *SHAKE HANDS WITH THE DEVIL: THE FAILURE OF HUMANITY IN RWANDA*

LT.-GEN. ROMÉO DALLAIRE (WITH BRENT BEARDSLEY)

Born in 1946 and brought up in Montreal, Roméo Dallaire was, in 1993, appointed by the United Nations to command an international peacekeeping force to prevent ethnic cleansing in Rwanda, a small African country. Lieutenant-General Dallaire foresaw and then witnessed the genocide taking place, and though his efforts were genuinely heroic, he had little on-the-spot support to do much more than act as a witness to the slaughter of 800,000 people over the period of a few months. His story and struggle has become well known internationally.

It was an absolutely magnificent day in May 1994. The blue sky was cloudless, and there was a whiff of breeze stirring the trees. It was hard to believe that in the past weeks an unimaginable evil had turned Rwanda's gentle green valleys and mist-capped hills into a stinking nightmare of rotting corpses. A nightmare we all had to negotiate every day. A nightmare that, as commander of the UN peacekeeping force in Rwanda, I could not help but feel deeply responsible for.

In relative terms, that day had been a good one. Under the protection of a limited and fragile ceasefire, my troops had successfully escorted about two hundred civilians—a few of the thousands who had sought refuge with us in Kigali, the capital of Rwanda—through many government- and militia-manned checkpoints to reach safety behind the Rwandese Patriotic Front (RPF) lines. We were seven weeks into the genocide, and the RPF, the disciplined rebel army (composed largely of the sons of Rwandan refugees who had lived over the border in camps in Uganda since being forced out of their homeland at independence), was making a curved sweep toward Kigali from the north, adding civil war to the chaos and butchery in the country.

Having delivered our precious cargo of innocent souls, we were headed back to Kigali in a white UN Land Cruiser with my force commander pennant on the front hood and the blue UN flag on a staff attached to the right rear. My Ghanaian sharpshooter, armed with a new Canadian C-7 rifle, rode behind me, and my new Senegalese aide-de-camp, Captain Ndiaye, sat to my right. We were driving a particularly dangerous stretch of road, open to sniper fire. Most of the people in the surrounding villages had been slaughtered, the few survivors escaping with little more than the clothes on their backs. In a few short weeks, it had become a lonely and forlorn place.

Suddenly up ahead we saw a child wandering across the road. I stopped the

413

vehicle close to the little boy, worried about scaring him off, but he was quite unfazed. He was about three years old, dressed in a filthy, torn T-shirt, the ragged remnants of underwear, little more than a loincloth, drooping from under his distended belly. he was caked in dirt, his hair white and matted with dust, and he was enveloped in a cloud of flies, which were greedily attacking the open sores that covered him. He stared at us silently, sucking on what I realized was a high-protein biscuit. Where had the boy found food in this wasteland?

I got out of the vehicle and walked toward him. Maybe it was the condition I was in, but to me this child had the face of an angel and eyes of pure innocence. I had seen so many children hacked to pieces that this small, whole, bewildered boy was a vision of hope. Surely, he could not have survived all on his own? I motioned for my aide-de-camp to honk the horn, hoping to summon up his parents, but the sound echoed over the empty landscape, startling a few birds and little else. The boy remained transfixed. He did not speak or cry, just stood sucking on his biscuit and staring up at us with his huge, solemn eyes. Still hoping that he wasn't all alone, I sent my aide-de-camp and the sharpshooter to look for signs of life.

We were in a ravine lush with banana trees and bamboo shoots, which created a dense canopy of foliage. A long straggle of deserted huts stood on either side of the road. As I stood alone with the boy, I felt an anxious knot in my stomach: this would be a perfect place to stage an ambush. My colleagues returned, having found no one. Then a rustling in the undergrowth made us jump. I grabbed the boy and held him firmly to my side as we instinctively took up defensive positions around the vehicle and in the ditch. The bushed parted to reveal a well-armed RPF soldier about fifteen years old. He recognized my uniform and gave me a smart salute and introduced himself. He was part of an advance observation post in the nearby hills. I asked him who the boy was and whether there was anyone left alive in the village who could take care of him. The soldier answered that the boy had no name and no family but that he and his buddies were looking after him. That explained the biscuit but did nothing to ally my concerns over the security and health of the boy. I protested that the child needed proper care and that I could give it to him: we were protecting and supporting orphanages in Kigali where he would be much better off. The soldier quietly insisted that the boy stay where he was, among his own people.

I continued to argue, but this child soldier was in no mood to discuss the situation and with haughty finality stated that his unit would care and provide for the child. I could feel my face flush with anger and frustration, but then noticed that the boy himself had slipped away while we had been arguing over him, and God only knew where he had gone. My aide-de-camp spotted him at the entrance to a hut a short distance away, clambering over a log that had fallen across the doorway. I ran after him, closely followed by my aide-de-camp and the RPF child soldier. By the time I had caught up to the boy, he had disappeared inside. The log in the doorway turned out to be the body of a man, obviously dead for some weeks, his flesh rotten with maggots and beginning to fall away from the bones.

As I stumbled over the body and into the hut, a swarm of flies invaded my nose and mouth. It was so dark inside that at first I smelled rather than saw the horror that lay before me. The hut was a two-room affair, one room serving as a kitchen and living room and the other as a communal bedroom; two rough windows had been cut into the mud-and-stick wall. Very little light penetrated the gloom, but as my eyes became accustomed to the dark, I saw strewn around the living room in a rough circle the decayed bodies of a man, a woman and two children, stark white bone poking through the desiccated, leather-like covering that had once been skin. The little boy was crouched beside what was left of his mother, still sucking on his biscuit. I made my way over to him as slowly and quietly as I could and, lifting him into my arms, carried him out of the hut.

The warmth of his tiny body snuggled against mine filled me with a peace and serenity that elevated me above the chaos. This child was alive yet terribly hungry, beautiful but covered in dirt, bewildered but not fearful. I made up my mind: this boy would be the fourth child in the Dallaire family. I couldn't save Rwanda, but I could save this child.

Before I had held this boy, I had agreed with the aid workers and representatives of both the warring armies that I would not permit any exporting of Rwandan orphans to foreign places. When confronted by such requests from humanitarian organizations, I would argue that the money to move a hundred kids by plane to France or Belgium could help build, staff and sustain Rwandan orphanages that could house three thousand children. This one boy eradicated all my arguments. I could see myself arriving at the terminal in Montreal like a latter-day St. Christopher* with the boy cradled in my arms, and my wife, Beth, there ready to embrace him.

That dream was abruptly destroyed when the young soldier, fast as a wolf, yanked the child from my arms and carried him directly into the bush. Not knowing how many members of his unit might already have their gunsights on us, we reluctantly climbed back into the Land Cruiser. As I slowly drove away, I had much on my mind.

By withdrawing, I had undoubtedly done the wise thing: I had avoided risking the lives of my two soldiers in what would have been a fruitless struggle over one small boy. But in that moment, it seemed to me that I had backed away from a fight for what was right, that this failure stood for all our failures in Rwanda.

Whatever happened to that beautiful child? Did he make it to an orphanage deep behind the RPF lines? Did he survive the following battles? Is he dead or is he now a child soldier himself, caught in the seemingly endless conflict that plagues his homeland?

That moment, when the boy, in the arms of a soldier young enough to be his brother, was swallowed whole by the forest, haunts me. It's a memory that never lets me forget how ineffective and irresponsible we were when we promised the Rwandans that we would establish an atmosphere of security that would allow them to achieve a lasting peace. It has been almost nine years since I left Rwanda, but as I write this, the sounds, smells and colours come flooding back in digital clarity. It's as if someone has sliced into my brain and grafted this horror called Rwanda frame by blood-soaked frame directly on my cortex. I could not forget even if I wanted to. For many of these years, I have yearned to return to Rwanda and disappear into the blue-green hills with my ghosts. A simple pilgrim seeking forgiveness and pardon.

---

*St. Christopher: a fearless martyr of the third century, patron saint of travellers.

But as I slowly begin to piece my life back together, I know the time has come for me to make a more difficult pilgrimage: to travel back through all those terrible memories and retrieve my soul.

I did try to write this story soon after I came back from Rwanda in September 1994, hoping to find some respite for myself in sorting out how my own role as Force Commander of UNAMIR interconnected with the international apathy, the complex political manoeuvres, the deep well of hatred and barbarity that resulted in genocide in which over 800,000 people lost their lives. Instead, I plunged into a disastrous mental health spiral that led me to suicide attempts, a medical release from the Armed Forces, the diagnosis of post-traumatic stress disorder, and dozens upon dozens of therapy sessions and extensive medication, which still have a place in my daily life.

It took me seven years to finally have the desire, the willpower and the stamina to begin to describe in detail the events of that year in Rwanda. To recount, from my insider's point of view, how a country moved from the promise of a certain peace to intrigue, the fomenting of racial hatred, assassinations, civil war and genocide. And how the international community, through an inept UN mandate and what can only be described as indifference, self-interest and racism, aided and abetted these crimes against humanity—how we all helped create the mess that has murdered and displaced millions and destabilized the whole central African region.

A growing library of books and articles is exploring the tragic events in Rwanda from many angles: eyewitness accounts, media analyses, assaults on the actions of the American administration at the time, condemnations of the UN's apparent ineptitude. But even in the international and national inquiries launched in the wake of the genocide, the blame somehow slides away from the individual member nations of the UN, and in particular those influential countries with permanent representatives on the Security Council, such as the United States, France and the United Kingdom, who sat back and watched it all happen, who pulled their troops or didn't offer any troops in the first place. A few Belgian officers were brought to court to pay for the sins of Rwanda. When my sector commander in Kigali, Colonel Luc Marchal, was court-martialled in Brussels, the charges against him were clearly designed to deflect any responsibility away from the Belgian government for the deaths of the ten Belgian peacekeepers under my command. The judge eventually threw out all the charges, accepting the fact that Marchal had performed his duties magnificently in a near-impossible situation. But the spotlight never turned to the reasons why he and the rest of the UNAMIR force were in such a dangerous situation in the first place.

It is time that I tell the story from where I stood—literally in the middle of the slaughter for weeks on end. A public account of my actions, my decisions and my failings during that most terrible year may be a crucial missing link for those attempting to understand the tragedy both intellectually and in their hearts. I know that I will never end my mourning for all those Rwandans who placed their faith in us, who thought the UN peacekeeping force was there to stop extremism, to stop the killings and help them through the perilous journey to a lasting peace. That mission, UNAMIR, failed. I know intimately the cost in human lives of the inflexible UN Security Council mandate, the pennypinching financial management of the mission, the UN red tape, the political manipulations and my own personal limitations. What I have come to realize as the root of it all, however, is the fundamental indifference of the world community to the plight of seven to eight million black Africans in a tiny country that had no strategic or resource value to any world power. An overpopulated little country that turned in on itself and destroyed its own people, as the world watched and yet could not manage to find the political will to intervene. Engraved still in my brain is the judgment of a small group of bureaucrats who came to "assess" the situation in the first weeks of the genocide: "We will recommend to our government not to intervene as the risks are high and all that is here are humans."

My story is not a strictly military account nor a clinical, academic study of the breakdown of Rwanda. It is not a simplistic indictment of the many failures of the UN as a force for peace in the world. It is not a story of heroes and villains, although such a work could easily be written. This book is a *cri de coeur* for the slaughtered thousands, a tribute to the souls hacked apart by machetes because of their supposed difference from those who sought to hang on to power. It is the story of a commander who, faced with a challenge that didn't fit the classic Cold War-era peacekeeper's rule book, failed to find an effective solution and witnessed, as if in punishment, the loss of some of his own troops, the attempted annihilation of an ethnicity, the butchery of children barely out of the womb, the stacking of severed limbs like cordwood, the mounds of decomposing bodies being eaten by the sun.

This book is nothing more nor less than the account of a few humans who were entrusted with the role of helping others taste the fruits of peace. Instead, we watched as the devil took control of paradise on earth and fed on the blood of the people we were supposed to protect.

PERSONAL RESPONSE

What feelings do you have when you read Dallaire's account of what happened? How would have you responded in his situation? Is your response to Dallaire coloured by your being a Canadian?

QUESTIONS FOR CLASS OR SMALL-GROUP DISCUSSION

1. What does Dallaire's desire to save the little boy reveal about him and about the real situation in Rwanda?

2. Discuss the various levels of failure, being haunted, and guilt in the piece and in what the piece suggests. Who or what has failed? Who or what is haunted, and by what? Who feels guilt, and why?

3. There are many terms and phrases to describe what happened in Rwanda: war, tribal war, civil war, mass murder, ethnic cleansing, and genocide. Discuss how these different terms make us look at the event differently. Which term do you think is most appropriate, and why?

4. In the writings by Dallaire and Stephen Lewis, the United Nations comes under strong criticism. Research how the UN functions, and offer constructive criticism of how it has handled any one of these issues: genocide, AIDS/HIV, or the environment.

A CENTURY OF CINEMA

SUSAN SONTAG

Susan Sontag, one of the twentieth century's pre-eminent thinkers and human rights activists, was born in New York City in 1933. She grew up in Tucson, Arizona, and attended high school in Los Angeles. She received her B.A. from the University of Chicago and did graduate work in philosophy, literature, and theology at Harvard University and Saint Anne's College, Oxford. Her books include four novels; a collection of short stories; several plays; and eight works of nonfiction, starting with Against Interpretation *and including* On Photography, Illness as Metaphor, Where the Stress Falls, *and* Regarding the Pain of Others. *She also wrote and directed four feature-length films. Her books have been translated into thirty-two languages. She died in 2004.*

Cinema's hundred years appear to have the shape of a life cycle: an inevitable birth, the steady accumulation of glories, and the onset in the last decade of an ignominious, irreversible decline. This doesn't mean that there won't be any more new films one can admire. But such films will not simply be exceptions; that's true of great achievement in any art. They will have to be heroic violations of the norms and practices which now govern moviemaking everywhere in the capitalist and would-be capitalist world—which is to say, everywhere. And ordinary films, films made purely for entertainment (that is, commercial) purposes, will continue to be astonishingly witless; already the vast majority fail resoundingly to appeal to their cynically targeted audiences. While the point of a great film is now, more than ever, to be a one-of-a-kind achievement, the commercial cinema has settled for a policy of bloated, derivative filmmaking, a brazen combinatory or re-combinatory art, in the hope of reproducing past successes. Every film that hopes to reach the largest possible audience is designed as some kind of remake. Cinema, once heralded as *the* art of the twentieth century, seems now, as the century closes numerically, to be a decadent art.

Perhaps it is not cinema which has ended but only cinephilia—the name of the distinctive kind of love that cinema inspired. Each art breeds its fanatics. The love movies aroused was more imperial. It was born of the conviction that cinema was an art unlike any other: quintessentially modern; distinctively accessible; poetic and mysterious and erotic and moral—all at the same time. Cinema had apostles (it was like religion). Cinema was a crusade. Cinema was a world view. Lovers of poetry or opera or dance don't think there is *only* poetry or opera or dance. But lovers of cinema could think there was only cinema. That the movies encapsulated everything—and they did. It was both the book of art and the book of life.

As many have noted, the start of moviemaking a hundred years ago was, conveniently, a double start. In that first year, 1895, two kinds of films were made, proposing two modes of what cinema could be: cinema as the transcription of real, unstaged life (the Lumière brothers) and cinema as invention, artifice, illusion, fantasy (Méliès). But this was never a true opposition. For those first audiences watching the Lumière brothers' *The Arrival of a Train at La Ciotat Station,* the camera's transmission of a banal sight was a fantastic experience. Cinema began in wonder, the wonder that reality can be transcribed with such magical immediacy. All of cinema is an attempt to perpetrate and to reinvent the sense of wonder.

Everything begins with that moment, one hundred years ago, when the train pulled into the station. People took movies into themselves, just as the public cried out with excitement, actually ducked, as the train seemed to move toward *them.* Until the advent of television emptied the movie theatres, it was from a weekly visit to the cinema that you learned (or tried to learn) how to strut, to smoke, to kiss, to fight, to grieve. Movies gave you tips about how to be attractive, such as . . . it looks good to wear a raincoat even when it isn't raining. But whatever you took home from the movies was only a part of the larger experience of losing yourself in faces, in lives that were *not* yours—which is the more inclusive form of desire embodied in the movie experience. The strongest experience was simply to surrender to, to be transported by, what was on the screen. You wanted to be kidnapped by the movie.

The prerequisite of being kidnapped was to be overwhelmed by the physical presence of the image. And the conditions of "going to the movies" secured that experience. To see a great film only on television isn't to have really seen that film. (This is equally true of those made for TV, like Fassbinder's *Berlin Alexanderplatz,* and the two *Heimat* films of Edgar Reitz.) It's not only the difference of dimensions: the superiority of the larger-than-you image in the theater to the little image on the box at home. The conditions of paying attention in a domestic space are radically disrespectful of film. Since film no longer has a standard size, home screens can be as big as living room or bedroom walls. But you are still in a living room or a bedroom, alone or with familiars. To be kidnapped, you have to be in a movie theater, seated in the dark among anonymous strangers.

No amount of mourning will revive the vanished rituals—erotic, ruminative—of the darkened theater. The reduction of cinema to assaultive images, and the unprincipled manipulation of images (faster and faster cutting) to be more attention-grabbing, have produced a disincarnated, lightweight cinema that doesn't demand anyone's full attention. Images now appear in any size and on a variety of surfaces: on a screen in a theater, on home screens as small as the palm of your hand or as big as a wall, on disco walls and mega-screens hanging above sports arenas and the outsides of tall public buildings. The sheer ubiquity of moving images has steadily undermined the standards people once had both for cinema as art at its most serious and for cinema as popular entertainment.

In the first years there was, essentially, no difference between cinema as art and cinema as entertainment. And *all* films of the silent era—from the masterpieces of Feuillade, D. W. Griffith, Dziga Vertov, Pabst, Murnau and King Vidor to the most formula-ridden melodramas and comedies—look, are, better than most what was to follow. With the coming of sound, the image-making lost much of its brilliance and poetry, and commercial standards tightened. This way of making movies—the Hollywood system—dominated filmmaking for about twenty-five years (roughly from 1930 to 1955). The most original directors, like Erich von Stroheim and Orson Welles, were defeated by the system and eventually went into artistic exile in Europe—where more or less the same quality-defeating system was in place with lower budgets; only in France were a large number of superb films produced throughout this period. Then, in the mid-1950s, vanguard ideas took hold again, rooted in the idea of cinema as a craft pioneered by the Italian films of the early postwar era. A dazzling number of original, passionate films of the highest seriousness got made with new actors and tiny crews, went to film festivals (of which there were more and more), and from there, garlanded with festival prizes, into movie theaters around the world. This golden age actually lasted as long as twenty years.

It was at this specific moment in the hundred-year history of cinema that going to movies, thinking about movies, talking about movies became a passion among university students and other young people. You fell in love not just with actors but with cinema itself. Cinephilia had first become visible in the 1950s in France: its forum was the legendary film magazine *Cahiers du Cinéma* (followed by similarly fervent magazines in Germany, Italy, Great Britain, Sweden, the United States and Canada). Its temples, as it spread throughout Europe and the Americas, were the cinematheques and film clubs specializing in films from the past and directors' retrospectives. The 1960s and early 1970s were the age of feverish moviegoing, with the full-time cinephile always hoping to find a seat as close as possible to the big screen, ideally the third row center. "One can't live without Rossellini," declares a character in Bertolucci's *Before the Revolution* (1964)—and means it.

Cinephilia—a source of exultation in the films of Godard and Truffaut and the early Bertolucci and Syberberg; a morose lament in the recent films of Nani Moretti—was mostly a Western European affair. The great directors of "the other Europe" (Zanussi in Poland, Angelopoulos in Greece, Tarkovsky and Sokurov in Russia, Jancsó and Tarr in Hungary) and the great Japanese directors (Ozu, Mizoguchi, Kurosawa, Naruse, Oshima, Imamura) have tended not to be cinephiles, perhaps because in Budapest or Moscow or Tokyo or Warsaw or Athens there wasn't a chance to get a cinematheque education. The distinctive thing about cinephile taste was that it embraced both "art" films and popular films. Thus, European cinephilia had a romantic relation to the films of certain directors of Hollywood at the apogee of the studio system: Godard for Howard Hawks, Fassbinder for Douglas Sirk. Of course, this moment—when cinephilia emerged—was also the moment when the Hollywood studio system was breaking up. It seemed that moviemaking had re-won the right to experiment; cinephiles could *afford* to be passionate (or sentimental) about the old Hollywood genre films. A host of new people came into cinema, including a generation of young film critics from *Cahiers du Cinéma;* the towering figure of that generation, indeed of several decades of filmmaking anywhere, was Jean-Luc Godard. A few writers turned out to be wildly talented filmmakers:

Alexander Kluge in Germany, Pier Paolo Pasolini in Italy. (The model for the writer who turns to filmmaking actually emerged earlier, in France, with Pagnol in the 1930s and Cocteau in the 1940s; but it was not until the 1960s that this seemed, at least in Europe, normal.) Cinema appeared to be reborn.

For some fifteen years there was a profusion of masterpieces, and one allowed oneself to imagine that this would go on forever. To be sure, there was always a conflict between cinema as an industry and cinema as an art, cinema as routine and cinema as experiment. But the conflict was not such as to make impossible the making of wonderful films, sometimes within and sometimes outside of mainstream cinema. Now the balance has tipped decisively in favor of cinema as an industry. The great cinema of the 1960s and 1970s has been thoroughly repudiated. Already in the 1970s Hollywood was plagiarizing and banalizing the innovations in narrative method and editing of successful new European and ever-marginal independent American films. Then came the catastrophic rise in production costs in the 1980s, which secured the worldwide reimposition of industry standards of making and distributing films on a far more coercive, this time truly global, scale. The result can be seen in the melancholy fate of some of the greatest directors of the last decades. What place is there today for a maverick like Hans Jürgen Syberberg, who has stopped making films altogether, or for the great Godard, who now makes films about the history of film on video? Consider some other cases. The internationalizing of financing and therefore of casts was a disaster for Andrei Tarkovsky in the last two films of his stupendous, tragically abbreviated career. And these conditions for making films have proved to be as much an artistic disaster for two of the most valuable directors still working: Krzysztof Zanussi (*The Structure of Crystals, Illumination, Spiral, Contract*) and Theo Angelopoulos (*Reconstruction, Days of '36, The Travelling Players*). And what will happen now to Béla Tarr (*Damnation, Satantango*)? And how will Aleksandr Sokurov (*Save and Protect, Days of Eclipse, The Second Circle, Stone, Whispering Pages*) find the money to go on making films, his sublime films, under the rude conditions of Russian capitalism?

Predictably, the love of cinema has waned. People still like going to the movies, and some people still care about and expect something special, necessary from a film. And wonderful films are still being made: Mike Leigh's *Naked*, Gianni Amelio's *Lamerica*, Hou Hsiao-hsien's *Goodbye South, Goodbye*, and Abbas Kiarostami's *Close-Up* and Koker trilogy. But one hardly finds anymore, at least among the young, the distinctive cinephilic love of movies, which is not simply love of but a certain *taste* in films (grounded in a vast appetite for seeing and reseeing as much as possible of cinema's glorious past). Cinephilia itself has come under attack, as something quaint, outmoded, snobbish. For cinephilia implies that films are unique, unrepeatable, magic experiences. Cinephilia tells us that the Hollywood remake of Godard's *Breathless* cannot be as good as the original. Cinephilia has no role in the era of hyperindustrial films. For by the very range and eclecticism of its passions, cinephilia cannot help but sponsor the idea of the film as, first of all, a poetic object; and cannot help but incite those outside the movie industry, like painters and writers, to want to make films, too. It is precisely this that must be defeated. That has been defeated.

If cinephilia is dead, then movies are dead . . . no matter how many movies, even very good ones, go on being made. If cinema can be resurrected, it will only be through the birth of a new kind of cine-love.

PERSONAL RESPONSE

What role does watching movies play in your life? Do you prefer to watch movies at home or in a darkened theatre surrounded by strangers? What are your three favourite movies of all time, and what kind of movies are they?

QUESTIONS FOR CLASS OR SMALL-GROUP DISCUSSION

1. Sontag says that cinema is an attempt to perpetuate or re-invent the sense of wonder that reality can be transcribed with magical immediacy. However, she also says that contemporary film is often "witless" and characterized by pointless rapid cutting between images. Name two contemporary films that illustrate her position. What is the effect of the quick cut on you, the viewer?

2. How have music videos affected commercial cinema?

3. Do you believe that commercial cinema has become a combinatory or re-combinatory art? What exactly does Sontag mean by "combinatory"?

4. Examine the relationship between cinema and capitalism and the effect of showcases such as the Sundance Film Festival on independent filmmaking. What, in your opinion, is the effect of the Toronto International Film Festival on moviegoers' tastes? In what ways does the Toronto festival differ from Cannes?

5. Agree or disagree with Sontag's contention that if cinema can be resurrected, it can only be through a new kind of cine-love.

6. In Sontag's essay, originally published in 1995, in the German newspaper *Frankfurter Rundschau,* she writes that cinema appears to be in an irreversible decline. Do you believe cinema is still declining? Can you give at least three examples that support your point of view?

AFRICA'S WORLD OF FORCED LABOR, IN A 6-YEAR-OLD'S EYES

Sharon LaFraniere

Sharon LaFraniere is an award-winning journalist for The New York Times. *In covering southern Africa for the* Times, *she has specialized in writing on the challenges facing the region's women and children. Reporting from both war zones and disaster areas, she has been praised for the way she looks at everyday life in ways that are both respectful and unflinching.*

KETE KRACHI, Ghana—Just before 5 a.m., with the sky still dark over Lake Volta, Mark Kwadwo was rousted from his spot on the damp dirt floor. It was time for work.

Shivering in the predawn chill, he helped paddle a canoe a mile out from shore. For five more hours, as his coworkers yanked up a fishing net, inch by inch, Mark bailed water to keep the canoe from swamping.

He last ate the day before. His broken wooden paddle was so heavy he could barely lift it. But he raptly followed each command from Kwadwo Takyi, the powerfully built 31-year-old in the back of the canoe who freely deals out beatings.

"I don't like it here," he whispered, out of Mr. Takyi's earshot.

Mark Kwadwo is 6 years old. About 30 pounds, dressed in a pair of blue and red underpants and a Little Mermaid T-shirt, he looks more like an oversized toddler than a boat hand. He is too little to understand why he has wound up in this fishing village, a two-day trek from his home.

But the three older boys who work with him know why. Like Mark, they are indentured servants, leased by their parents to Mr. Takyi for as little as $20 a year.

Until their servitude ends in three or four years, they are as trapped as the fish in their nets, forced to work up to 14 hours a day, seven days a week, in a trade that even adult fishermen here call punishing and, at times, dangerous.

Mr. Takyi's boys—conscripts in a miniature labor camp, deprived of schooling, basic necessities and freedom—are part of a vast traffic in children that supports West and Central African fisheries, quarries, cocoa and rice plantations and street markets. The girls are domestic servants, bread bakers, prostitutes. The boys are field workers, cart pushers, scavengers in abandoned gem and gold mines.

By no means is the child trafficking trade uniquely African. Children are forced to race camels in the Middle East, weave carpets in India, and fill brothels all over the developing world.

The International Labor Organization, a United Nations agency, estimates that 1.2 million are sold into servitude every year in an illicit trade that generates as much as $10 billion annually.

Studies show they are most vulnerable in Asia, Latin America and Africa.

Africa's children, the world's poorest, account for roughly one-sixth of the trade, according to the labor organization. Data is notoriously scarce, but it suggests victimization of African children on a huge scale.

A 2002 study supervised by the labor organization estimated that nearly 12,000 trafficked children toiled in the cocoa fields of Ivory Coast alone. The children, who had no relatives in the area, cleared fields with machetes, applied pesticides and sliced open cocoa pods for beans.

In an analysis in February, Unicef says child trafficking is growing in West and Central Africa, driven by huge profits and partly controlled by organized networks that transport children both within and between countries.

"We know it is a huge problem in Africa," said Pamela Shifman, a child protection officer at the New York headquarters of Unicef. "A lot of it is visible. You see the kids being exploited. You watch it happen. Somebody brought the kids to the place where they are. Somebody exploited their vulnerability."

Otherwise, she asked, "How did they get there?"

John R. Miller, the director of the State Department Office to Monitor and Combat Trafficking in Persons, said the term trafficking failed to convey the brutality of what was occurring.

"A child does not consent," he said. "The loss of choice, the deception, the use of frauds, the keeping of someone at work with little or no pay, the threats if they leave—it is slavery."

Some West African families see it more as a survival strategy. In a region where nearly two-thirds of the population lives on less than $1 a day, the compensation for the temporary loss of a child keeps the rest of the family from going hungry. Some parents argue that their children are better off learning a trade than starving at home.

Indeed, the notion that children should be in the care of their parents is not a given in much of African society.

Parents frequently hand off children to even distant relatives if it appears they will have a chance at education and more opportunity.

Only in the past six years or so has it become clear how traffickers take advantage of this custom to buy and sell children, sometimes with no more ceremony than a goat deal.

In 2001, 35 children, half of them under age 15, were discovered aboard a vessel in a Benin port. They said they were being shipped to Gabon to work.

In 2003, Nigerian police rescued 194 malnourished children from stone quarries north of Lagos. At least 13 other children had died and been buried near the pits, the police said.

Last year, Nigerian police stumbled upon 64 girls aged 14 and younger, packed inside a refrigerated truck built to haul frozen fish. They had traveled hundreds of miles from central Nigeria, the police said, and were destined for work as housemaids in Lagos.

In response to such reports, African nations have passed a raft of legislation against trafficking, adopting or strengthening a dozen laws last year alone.

There were nearly 200 prosecutions of traffickers on the continent last year, four times as many as in 2003, according to the State Department's trafficking office.

Some countries are encouraging villages to form their own surveillance committees. In Burkina Faso, the government reported, such committees, together with the police, freed 640 children from traffickers in 2003. Still, government officials in the region say, only a tiny fraction of victims are detected.

Ghana, an Oregon-size nation of 21 million people, has yet to prosecute anyone under the new antitrafficking law it adopted last December. But the government had taken other steps—including eliminating school fees that forced youngsters out of classrooms, increasing birth registrations so that children have legal identities and extending small loans to about 1,200 mothers to give them alternatives to leasing out their children.

The International Organization for Migration, an intergovernmental agency set up after World War II to help refugees, has also mounted a United States-financed program to rescue children from the fishing industry.

Since 2003, the organization says, 587 children have been freed from Ghana's Lake Volta region, taken to shelters for counseling and medical treatment, then reunited with parents or relatives.

"We sign a social contract with the fishermen," said Eric Peasah, the agency's Ghana field representative. "If they have 10 children, we say, 'Release four, and you can't get more, or you will be prosecuted.' Once they sign that, we come back and say we want to release more."

To reduce child trafficking significantly, said Marilyn Amponsah Annan, who is in charge of children's issues for the Ghanaian government, adults must be convinced that children have the right to be educated, to be protected, and to be spared adult burdens—in short, the right to a childhood.

"You see so many children with so many fishermen," she said. "Those little hands, those little bodies. It is always very sad, because this is the world of adults.

"We have to educate these communities because they do not know any other way of existence. They believe this is what they need to do to survive."

That is the fishermen's favorite defense in Kete Krachi, a day's drive through dense forests from Ghana's capital, Accra. For the area's roughly 9,000 residents, fishing is their lifeblood. Children keep it going.

Nearly every canoe here holds at least a few of them, some no older than 5 or 6, often supervised by a teenager. A dozen boys, interviewed in their canoes or as they sewed up ratty nets ashore, spoke of backbreaking toil, 100-hour workweeks and frequent beatings. They bore a pervasive fear of diving into the lake's murky waters to free a tangled net, and never resurfacing.

One 10-year-old said he was sometimes so exhausted that he fell asleep as he paddled. Asked when he rested, another boy paused from his net mending, seemingly confused. "This is what you see now," he said.

They never see the pittance they earn. The fishermen say they pay parents or relatives each December, typically on trips to the families' villages during the December holidays.

The children's sole comfort seems to be the shared nature of their misery, a camaraderie of lost boys who have not seen their families in years, have no say in their fate and, in some cases, were lured by false promises of schooling or a quick homecoming.

On Nkomi, a grassy island in the lake, Kwasi Tweranim, in his mid to late teens, and Kwadwo Seaako, perhaps 12 or 13, seemed united by fear and resentment of their boss. Both bear inchlong scars on their scalps where, they said, he struck them with a wooden paddle.

"I went down to disentangle the net, and when I came up, my master said that I had left part of it down there," Kwasi said. "Then I saw black, and woke up in another boat. Only the grace of God saved me."

Kwadwo, stammering badly, said he had been punished when the net rolled in the water.

Not every fisherman is so pitiless. Christian Lissah employs eight children under 13, mostly distant relatives. He said he knew many children who were treated no better than workhorses, and some who had drowned.

"In general, this is not a good practice because people mishandle the children," he said. Yet he said he could not imagine how he would fish profitably without child workers, and depends on friends and acquaintances to keep him supplied—for a commission.

"You must get people who are a very low background who need money," he said. "Some of them are eager to release their children."

Mark Kwadwo's parents, Joe Obrenu and his wife, Ama, were an easy sell. Mr. Obrenu fished the seas off Aboadzi, a hilly, sun-drenched town on the Gulf of Guinea, and his wife dried the catch for sale. But the two often ran short of food, said Mark's aunt, Adwoa Awotwe. Over the years, they sold five of their children into labor, she said, including Mark's 9-year-old sister Hagar, who performs domestic chores for Mr. Takyi.

Mr. Obrenu drummed up other recruits from neighbors, sometimes to their lasting regret. "It was hunger, to get a little money; the whole today, I have not eaten," said Efua Mansah, whose 7-year-old son, Kwabena, boarded a small blue bus with Mr. Takyi four years ago for the 250-mile trip to Kete Krachi.

She has seen him only twice since then. In all that time, Mr. Takyi has paid her $66, she said, a third of which she spent on buses and ferries to pick up the money.

In her one-room hut decorated with empty plastic bottles, she forced back tears. "I want to bring my son home," she said.

Mark also cried when his turn to leave came this year, his aunt said, so his mother told him that Mr. Takyi would take him to his father. Instead he was brought to Mr. Takyi's compound of caked mud huts, to a dark six-foot-square cubicle with a single tiny window. He shares it with five other children, buzzing flies and a few buckets of fish bait.

In two days, a smile never creased Mark's delicate features. He seldom offered more than a nod or a shake of the head, with a few telling exceptions: "I was beaten in the house. I can't remember what I did, but he caned me," he said of Mr. Takyi.

Mr. Takyi, who sleeps and works in the same gray T-shirt, is disarmingly frank about his household. He can afford to feed the children only twice a day, he said, and cannot clothe them adequately. He himself has been paddling the lake since age 8.

"I can understand how the children feel," he said. "Because I didn't go to school, this is work I must do. I also find it difficult."

Yet he does not hesitate to break a branch from the nearest tree to wake the boys for the midnight shift.

"Almost all the boys are very troublesome," he complained. "I want them to be humble children but they don't obey my orders."

One recent morning, his young crew, wrapped in thin bedsheets for warmth, hiked in the darkness down to the shore.

They paddled out in two leaky but stable canoes, searching the water for a piece of foam that marked where their net was snagged on submerged tree stumps. Kwabena, 11, stripped off his cutoff shorts and dived in with an 18-year-old to free it, yanking it at one point with his teeth.

Mark has not mastered the rhythm of paddling. Mr. Takyi said the boy cries when the water is rough or he is cold. He cannot swim a stroke. If the canoe capsizes, Mr. Takyi said, he will save him.

"I can't pay what is asked for older boys," Mr. Takyi said, as Mark bailed out the canoe with the sawed-off bottom of a plastic cooking oil container. "That is why I go for this. When I get money, I go to get another one."

In the other canoe, Kwame Akuban and Kofi Quarshie plucked fish from the net with the air of prisoners waiting for their terms to end.

Kofi, 10, said his mother had told him his earnings would feed their family. But he suspects another motive. "They didn't like me," he said softly.

Kwame, 12, said his parents had promised to retrieve him in a year's time and send him to school.

"I have been here three years and I am not going home, and I am not happy," he said quietly.

As if on cue, Mr. Takyi shouted: "Remove the fish faster, or I will cane you."

Running away is a common fantasy among the boys. Kofi Nyankom, who came from Mark's hometown three years ago, at age 9, was one of the few to actually try it.

Last December, he ran to town half-naked, his back a mass of bruises. He said Mr. Takyi had tied up him and whipped him.

George Achibra, a school district official, demanded that the police intervene, and Mr. Takyi was forced to let Kofi go.

But before many weeks passed, he had brought in a replacement—younger, more helpless, more submissive. It was Mark Kwadwo.

PERSONAL RESPONSE

How did you feel when you read about parents who, for a few dollars a year, give up their children to be indentured servants? What would you do about this if you were a federal politician in Canada or a United Nations official?

QUESTIONS FOR CLASS OR SMALL-GROUP DISCUSSION

1. According to this article, forced child labour is not unique to Africa. Children are forced to race camels in the Middle East, weave carpets in India, and fill brothels all over the developing world. Is it elitist for people in the West to want to change other cultures and eliminate these practices? Is it a just cause? Discuss.

2. The International Labor Organization, a United Nations agency, estimates that 1.2 million children are sold into servitude every year in an illicit trade that generates as much as $10 billion annually. Studies show that children are most vulnerable in Asia, Latin America, and Africa. Why doesn't LaFraniere begin her piece with these statistics—why does she begin and end her article with the example of a boy who must work as a deckhand?

3. Get a group of people together to watch the documentary *Born into Brothels* (2004) and relate it to this essay. Discuss your response to the film.

FOR FURTHER VIEWING: THE MARKETPLACE

Goin' Down the Road (1970); *Wall Street* (1987); *Roger and Me* (1989); *Enron: The Smartest Guys in the Room* (2005); *The Corporation* (2003); *Children Who Labor* (1912); *Supersize Me* (2004).

30 LITTLE TURTLES

Thomas L. Friedman

Thomas L. Friedman has written for the New York Times *since 1981. In 1995, he became the paper's foreign affairs columnist. Friedman was awarded the 1983 Pulitzer Prize for international reporting (from Lebanon) and the 1988 Pulitzer Prize for international reporting (from Israel). In 2002, he won the Pulitzer Prize for commentary. His book* From Beirut to Jerusalem *(1989) won the National Book Award for nonfiction in 1989.* The Lexus and the Olive Tree: Understanding Globalization *(2000) won the 2000 Overseas Press Club award for best nonfiction book on foreign policy and has been published in twenty languages. He is also author of* Longitudes and Attitudes: Exploring the World after September 11 *(2002) and* The World is Flat: A Brief History of the Twenty-first Century *(2005). This op-ed column was published in the February 29, 2004, issue of the* New York Times.

Indians are so hospitable. I got an ovation the other day from a roomful of Indian 20-year-olds just for reading perfectly the following paragraph: "A bottle of bottled water held 30 little turtles. It didn't matter that each turtle had to rattle a metal ladle in order to get a little bit of noodles, a total turtle delicacy. The problem was that there were many turtle battles for less than oodles of noodles."

I was sitting in on an "accent neutralization" class at the Indian call center 24/7 Customer. The instructor was teaching the would-be Indian call center operators to suppress their native Indian accents and speak with a Canadian one—she teaches British and U.S. accents as well, but these youths will be serving the Canadian market. Since I'm originally from Minnesota, near Canada, and still speak like someone out of the movie "Fargo," I gave these young Indians an authentic rendition of "30 Little Turtles," which is designed to teach them the proper Canadian pronunciations. Hence the rousing applause.

Watching these incredibly enthusiastic young Indians preparing for their call center jobs—earnestly trying to soften their t's and roll their r's—is an uplifting experience, especially when you hear from their friends already working these jobs how they have transformed their lives. Most of them still live at home and turn over part of their salaries to their parents, so the whole family benefits. Many have credit cards and have become real consumers, including of U.S. goods, for the first time. All of them seem to have gained self-confidence and self-worth.

4 A lot of these Indian young men and women have college degrees, but would never get a local job that starts at $200 to $300 a month were it not for the call centers. Some do "outbound" calls, selling things from credit cards to phone services to Americans and Europeans. Others deal with "inbound" calls—everything from tracing lost luggage for U.S. airline passengers to solving computer problems for U.S. customers. The calls are transferred here by satellite or fiber optic cable.

I was most taken by a young Indian engineer doing tech support for a U.S. software giant, who spoke with pride about how cool it is to tell his friends that he just spent the day helping Americans navigate their software. A majority of these call center workers are young women, who not only have been liberated by earning a decent local wage (and therefore have more choice in whom they marry), but are using the job to get M.B.A.'s and other degrees on the side.

I gathered a group together, and here's what they sound like: M. Dinesh, who does tech support, says his day is made when some American calls in with a problem and is actually happy to hear an Indian voice: "They say you people are really good at what you do. I am glad I reached an Indian." Kiran Menon, when asked who his role model was, shot back: "Bill Gates—I dream of starting my own company and making it that big." I asked C. M. Meghna what she got most out of the work: "Self-confidence," she said, "a lot of self-confidence, when people come to you with a problem and you can solve it—and having a lot of independence." Because the call center teams work through India's night—which corresponds to America's day— "your biological clock goes haywire," she added. "Besides that, it's great."

There is nothing more positive than the self-confidence, dignity and optimism that comes from a society knowing it is producing wealth by tapping its own brains—men's and women's—as opposed to one just tapping its own oil, let alone one that is so lost it can find dignity only through suicide and "martyrdom."

8 Indeed, listening to these Indian young people, I had a déjà vu. Five months ago, I was in Ramallah, on the West Bank, talking to three young Palestinian men, also in their 20's, one of whom was studying engineering. Their hero was Yasir Arafat. They talked about having no hope, no jobs and no dignity, and they each nodded when one of them said they were all "suicide bombers in waiting."

What am I saying here? That it's more important for young Indians to have jobs than Americans? Never. But I am saying that there is more to outsourcing than just economics. There's also geopolitics. It is inevitable in a networked world that our economy is going to shed certain low-wage, low-prestige jobs. To the extent that they go to places like India or Pakistan—where they are viewed as high-wage, high-prestige jobs—we make not only a more prosperous world, but a safer world for our own 20-year-olds.

PERSONAL RESPONSE

Are you sympathetic with Friedman's view of the young Indians that he describes in his essay?

QUESTIONS FOR CLASS OR SMALL-GROUP DISCUSSION

1. Do you think that Friedman anticipated an audience who would be supportive or critical of him? How can you tell?
2. Do you find the title effective? How does it relate to the essay?
3. How well do Friedman's examples of individual Indians help convey his view that being with them was an "uplifting experience" (paragraph 2)?
4. How adequately does Friedman make his case that "there is more to outsourcing than just economics" (paragraph 8)? Are you convinced?

○ PERSPECTIVES ON THE ECONOMIC IMPACT OF OUTSOURCING ○

Suggested Writing Topics

1. Write a response to Michael Mandel's "The Real Cost of Offshoring" by explaining whether you are convinced by his arguments of the importance of statistics in the overall assessment of the effects of offshoring.
2. Select one of the arguments in Daniel W. Drezner's "The Outsourcing Bogeyman" and explain whether you are convinced by what he says.
3. In response to Charles Fishman's "The Wal-Mart You Don't Know," defend Wal-Mart's business practices.
4. Write a critique of Thomas L. Friedman's "30 Little Turtles."
5. Describe your own buying habits in terms of whether you are socially conscious or not. Do you consciously buy only "fair trade" products, for instance? Do you boycott products of companies that employ sweatshop labor?
6. Select a statement from any of the essays in this chapter that you would like to respond to, elaborate on, or argue for or against.
7. Drawing on the readings in this chapter, compare and contrast the benefits of offshore outsourcing.
8. If you know someone who has lost a job because the company moved offshore, narrate that person's experience.

ROBERT L. HEILBRONER

Over a long and distinguished career, Robert L. Heilbroner (1919–) has sought to make the highly technical disciplines of social philosophy and economics understandable to intelligent general readers. In that regard, he is one of the vanishing breed of public intellectuals. For many years, he taught economics at the unconventional New School for Social Research in New York City. His books include The World Philosophers *(1954),* The Future as History *(1960), and* The Nature and Logic of Capitalism *(1985).*

Don't Let Stereotypes Warp Your Judgment

CONTEXT: *Most critiques of stereotyped and prejudicial thinking adopt a moralistic and judgmental tone, which tends to alienate the neutral or hostile reader. In "Don't Let Stereotypes Warp Your Judgment," which first appeared in* Reader's Digest, *Heilbroner shows how stereotypes can cause those who accept them to be less observant of the world in which they live. By employing a friendly and nonthreatening tone, the author himself avoids the tendency to stereotype as incorrigible bigots people who generalize.*

1 Is a girl called Gloria apt to be better-looking than one called Bertha? Are criminals more likely to be dark than blond? Can you tell a good deal about someone's personality from hearing his voice briefly over the phone? Can a person's nationality be pretty accurately guessed from his photograph? Does the fact that someone wears glasses imply that he is intelligent?

2 The answer to all these questions is obviously, "No."

3 Yet, from all the evidence at hand, most of us believe these things. Ask any college boy if he'd rather take his chances with a Gloria or a Bertha, or ask a college girl if she'd rather blind-date a Richard or a Cuthbert. In fact, you don't have to ask: college students in questionnaires have revealed that names conjure up the same images in their minds as they do in yours—and for as little reason.

4 Look into the favorite suspects of persons who report "suspicious characters" and you will find a large percentage of them to be "swarthy" or "dark and foreign-looking"—despite the testimony of criminologists that criminals do not tend to be dark, foreign or "wild-eyed." Delve into the main asset of a telephone stock swindler and you will find it to be a marvelously confidence-inspiring telephone "personality." And whereas we all think we know what an Italian or a Swede looks like, it is the sad fact that

when a group of Nebraska students sought to match faces and nationalities of 15 European countries, they were scored wrong in 93 percent of their identifications. Finally, for all the fact that horn-rimmed glasses have now become the standard television sign of an "intellectual," optometrists know that the main thing that distinguishes people with glasses is just bad eyes.

5   Stereotypes are a kind of gossip about the world, a gossip that makes us prejudge people before we ever lay eyes on them. Hence it is not surprising that stereotypes have something to do with the dark world of prejudice. Explore most prejudices (note that the word means prejudgment) and you will find a cruel stereotype at the core of each one.

6   For it is the extraordinary fact that once we have typecast the world, we tend to see people in terms of our standardized pictures. In another demonstration of the power of stereotypes to affect our vision, a number of Columbia and Barnard students were shown 30 photographs of pretty but unidentified girls, and asked to rate each in terms of "general liking," "intelligence," "beauty" and so on. Two months later, the same group were shown the same photographs, this time with fictitious Irish, Italian, Jewish and "American" names attached to the pictures. Right away the ratings changed. Faces which were now seen as representing a national group went down in looks and still farther down in likability, while the "American" girls suddenly looked decidedly prettier and nicer.

7   Why is it that we stereotype the world in such irrational and harmful fashion? In part, we begin to type-cast people in our childhood years. Early in life, as every parent whose child has watched a TV Western knows, we learn to spot the Good Guys from the Bad Guys. Some years ago, a social psychologist showed very clearly how powerful these stereotypes of childhood vision are. He secretly asked the most popular youngsters in an elementary school to make errors in their morning gym exercises. Afterwards, he asked the class if anyone had noticed any mistakes during gym period. Oh, yes, said the children. But it was the unpopular members of the class—the "bad guys"—they remembered as being out of step.

8   We not only grow up with standardized pictures forming inside of us, but as grown-ups we are constantly having them thrust upon us. Some of them, like the half-joking, half-serious stereotypes of mothers-in-law, or country yokels, or psychiatrists, are dinned into us by the stock jokes we hear and repeat. In fact, without such stereotypes, there would be a lot fewer jokes. Still other stereotypes are perpetuated by the advertisements we read, the movies we see, the books we read.

9   And finally, we tend to stereotype because it helps us make sense out of a highly confusing world, a world which William James once described as

"one great, blooming, buzzing confusion." It is a curious fact that if we don't know what we're looking at, we are often quite literally unable to see what we're looking at. People who recover their sight after a lifetime of blindness actually cannot at first tell a triangle from a square. A visitor to a factory sees only noisy chaos where the superintendent sees a perfectly synchronized flow of work. As Walter Lippmann has said, "For the most part we do not first see, and then define; we define first, and then we see."

10   Stereotypes are one way in which we "define" the world in order to see it. They classify the infinite variety of human beings into a convenient handful of "types" towards whom we learn to act in stereotyped fashion. Life would be a wearing process if we had to start from scratch with each and every human contact. Stereotypes economize on our mental effort by covering up the blooming, buzzing confusion with big recognizable cutouts. They save us the "trouble" of finding out what the world is like—they give it its accustomed look.

11   Thus the trouble is that stereotypes make us mentally lazy. As S. I. Hayakawa, the authority on semantics, has written: "The danger of stereotypes lies not in their existence, but in the fact that they become for all people some of the time, and for some people all the time, substitutes for observation." Worse yet, stereotypes get in the way of our judgment, even when we do observe the world. Someone who has formed rigid preconceptions of all Latins as "excitable," or all teenagers as "wild," doesn't alter his point of view when he meets a calm and deliberate Genoese, or a serious-minded high school student. He brushes them aside as "exceptions that proved the rule." And, of course, if he meets someone true to type, he stands triumphantly vindicated. "They're all like that," he proclaims, having encountered an excited Latin, an ill-behaved adolescent.

12   Hence, quite aside from the injustice which stereotypes do to others, they impoverish ourselves. A person who lumps the world into simple categories, who type-casts all labor leaders as "racketeers," all businessmen as "reactionaries," all Harvard men as "snobs," and all Frenchmen as "sexy," is in danger of becoming a stereotype himself. He loses his capacity to be himself—which is to say, to see the world in his own absolutely unique, inimitable and independent fashion.

13   Instead, he votes for the man who fits his standardized picture of what a candidate "should" look like or sound like, buys the goods that someone in his "situation" in life "should" own, lives the life that others define for him. The mark of the stereotype person is that he never surprises us, that we do indeed have him "typed." And no one fits this strait-jacket so perfectly as someone whose opinions about other people are fixed and inflexible.

14   Nor do we suddenly drop our standardized pictures for a blinding vision of the Truth. Sharp swings of ideas about people often just substitute one stereotype for another. The true process of change is a slow one that adds bits and pieces of reality to the pictures in our heads, until gradually they take on some of the blurriness of life itself. Little by little, we learn not that Jews and Negroes and Catholics and Puerto Ricans are "just like everybody else"—for that, too, is a stereotype—but that each and every one of them is unique, special, different and individual. Often we do not even know that we have let a stereotype lapse until we hear someone saying, "all so-and-so's are like such-and-such," and we hear ourselves saying, "Well—maybe."

15   Can we speed the process along? Of course we can.

16   First, we can become aware of the standardized pictures in our heads, in other people's heads, in the world around us.

17   Second, we can become suspicious of all judgments that we allow exceptions to "prove." There is no more chastening thought than that in the vast intellectual adventure of science, it takes but one tiny exception to topple a whole edifice of ideas.

18   Third, we can learn to be chary of generalizations about people. As F. Scott Fitzgerald once wrote: "Begin with an individual, and before you know it you have created a type; begin with a type, and you find you have created—nothing."

19   Most of the time, when we type-cast the world, we are not in fact generalizing about people at all. We are only revealing the embarrassing facts about the pictures that hang in the gallery of stereotypes in our own heads.

Understanding Meaning

1. What sort of examples does Heilbroner offer to prove that we tend to believe stereotypes?
2. What does Heilbroner mean when he states in paragraph 5 that "stereotypes are a kind of gossip about the world"?
3. According to Heilbroner, *why* do we stereotype the world?
4. How does stereotyping harm those who are guilty of it as well as those who are being stereotyped?
5. How does Heilbroner suggest that we break the habit of stereotyping others?
6. *CRITICAL THINKING.* Heilbroner's essay was written in 1961. Do you believe that Americans today are as guilty of stereotyping those different from them as they were at that time in our history? Explain.

Evaluating Strategy

1. In this essay, Heilbroner makes extensive use of rhetorical questions, or questions he does not really expect to have answered. How would you judge the effectiveness of this technique?
2. What does Heilbroner's purpose seem to be in paragraphs 3–6? How is his purpose different in paragraphs 7–10? Paragraphs 11–14?
3. *BLENDING THE MODES.* Heilbroner shifts to a different mode in paragraphs 15–18. What mode?

Appreciating Language

1. Heilbroner quotes Walter Lippmann: "For the most part we do not first see, and then define; we define first, and then we see." What does this quote mean?
2. Heilbroner also quotes William James, who refers to our world as "one great, blooming, buzzing confusion." Heilbroner contrasts that confusion and our tendency to save mental effort by seeing the world as "big recognizable cutouts." Explain how those terms suggest very different views of the world.
3. Heilbroner uses the terms "Good Guys" and "Bad Guys." What do those terms suggest about the problem with stereotypes?

Writing Suggestions

1. Write an essay in which you explain a stereotype you once accepted until you met a person or group who broke the stereotype.
2. Write an essay in which you analyze stereotypes of college students and explain how accurate or inaccurate you believe them to be.
3. Do you agree with Heilbroner that we tend to stereotype others because it is easier than drawing conclusions based on each individual? Explain in an essay.
4. *COLLABORATIVE WRITING.* Exchange your essay from Writing Suggestion #1, #2, or #3 above with a classmate and let that classmate evaluate the effectiveness of your use of examples.

BRUNO BETTELHEIM

If the psychoanalyst Bruno Bettelheim (1903–1990) did not have the historic impact of Sigmund Freud or Carl Jung, he was of the next level of importance. A native of Freud's Vienna, he was imprisoned by the Nazis in the Buchenwald and Dachau concentration camps. After he was freed, he taught at the University of Chicago from 1944 until 1973. His many books on child psychology include Love Is Not Enough *(1950),* Truants from Life *(1955),* The Children of the Dream *(1969), and his masterpiece* The Uses of Enchantment *(1976).*

The Holocaust

BEFORE YOU READ: *Virtually all Americans have heard of the Holocaust, the murder of millions of European Jews and other groups by Hitler's Nazis. It is almost incomprehensible, given the widespread media coverage of countless events worldwide today, that at the time the Holocaust was taking place, much of the world was unaware of it. The world was shaken by the images that were finally released after the survivors of the concentration camps were liberated. Only then was the magnitude of the crime revealed. Bettelheim speaks out as a survivor to object to the use of terms for the mass murder that decrease the emotional impact of the catastrophe.*

TIPS FOR READING: *This is an essay about word choices, so notice both what Bettelheim says about the terms used to refer to the murder of European Jews by the Nazis and the words that he himself chooses to use in referring to their murder.*

Words to Know:

hapless	unlucky, unfortunate
unmasterable	unable to be duplicated
circumlocution	a roundabout expression
Nuremberg	the site in Germany of trials of Nazi criminals
neologism	invented word
genocide	the deliberate and systematic extermination of a national, racial, political, or cultural group
abhorrence	extreme loathing
erudite	learned or scholarly
germane	relevant
connotations	associations made with a word that go beyond its primary meaning
delusional	holding false beliefs or opinions

embellishing	enhanced by some sort of additions
Warsaw ghetto	the Jewish quarter of the Polish city Warsaw

TIPS FOR WRITING: *A tried and true method of defining a term is to tell what it is* not. *When you need to define something, it may be useful to tell how it is different from things with which it might be confused.*

1   To begin with, it was not the hapless victims of the Nazis who named their incomprehensible and totally unmasterable fate the "holocaust." It was the Americans who applied this artificial and highly technical term to the Nazi extermination of the European Jews. But while the event when named as mass murder most foul evokes the most immediate, most powerful revulsion, when it is designated by a rare technical term, we must first in our minds translate it back into emotionally meaningful language. Using technical or specially created terms instead of words from our common vocabulary is one of the best-known and most widely used distancing devices, separating the intellectual from the emotional experience. Talking about "the holocaust" permits us to manage it intellectually where the raw facts, when given their ordinary names, would overwhelm us emotionally—because it was catastrophe beyond comprehension, beyond the limits of our imagination, unless we force ourselves against our desire to extend it to encompass these terrible events.

2   This linguistic circumlocution began while it all was only in the planning stage. Even the Nazis—usually given to grossness in language and action—shied away from facing openly what they were up to and called this vile mass murder "the final solution of the Jewish problem." After all, solving a problem can be made to appear like an honorable enterprise, as long as we are not forced to recognize that the solution we are about to embark on consists of the completely unprovoked, vicious murder of millions of helpless men, women, and children. The Nuremberg judges of these Nazi criminals followed their example of circumlocution by coining a neologism out of one Greek and one Latin root: genocide. These artificially created technical terms fail to connect with our strongest feelings. The horror of murder is part of our most common human heritage. From earliest infancy on, it arouses violent abhorrence in us. Therefore in whatever form it appears we should give such an act its true designation and not hide it behind polite, erudite terms created out of classical words.

3   To call this vile mass murder "the holocaust" is not to give it a special name emphasizing its uniqueness which would permit, over time, the word becoming invested with feelings germane to the event it refers to. The

correct definition of *holocaust* is "burnt offering." As such, it is part of the language of the psalmist, a meaningful word to all who have some acquaintance with the Bible, full of the richest emotional connotations. By using the term "holocaust," entirely false associations are established through conscious and unconscious connotations between the most vicious of mass murders and ancient rituals of a deeply religious nature.

4   Using a word with such strong unconscious religious connotations when speaking of the murder of millions of Jews robs the victims of this abominable mass murder of the only thing left to them: their uniqueness. Calling the most callous, most brutal, most horrid, most heinous mass murder a burnt offering is a sacrilege, a profanation of God and man.

5   Martyrdom is part of our religious heritage. A martyr, burned at the stake, is a burnt offering to his god. And it is true that after the Jews were asphyxiated, the victims' corpses were burned. But I believe we fool ourselves if we think we are honoring the victims of systematic murder by using this term, which has the highest moral connotations. By doing so, we connect for our own psychological reasons what happened in the extermination camps with historical events we deeply regret, but also greatly admire. We do so because this makes it easier for us to cope; only in doing so we cope with our distorted image of what happened, not with the events the way they did happen.

6   By calling the victims of the Nazis martyrs, we falsify their fate. The true meaning of *martyr* is: "One who voluntarily undergoes the penalty of death for refusing to renounce his faith" *(Oxford English Dictionary).* The Nazis made sure that nobody could mistakenly think that their victims were murdered for their religious beliefs. Renouncing their faith would have saved none of them. Those who had converted to Christianity were gassed, as were those who were atheists, and those who were deeply religious Jews. They did not die for any conviction, and certainly not out of choice.

7   Millions of Jews were systematically slaughtered, as were untold other "undesirables," not for any convictions of theirs, but only because they stood in the way of the realization of an illusion. They neither died for their convictions, nor were they slaughtered because of their convictions, but only in consequence of the Nazis' delusional belief about what was required to protect the purity of their assumed superior racial endowment, and what they thought necessary to guarantee them the living space they believed they needed and were entitled to. Thus while these millions were slaughtered for an idea, they did not die for one.

8   Millions—men, women, and children—were processed after they had been utterly brutalized, their humanity destroyed, their clothes torn from their bodies. Naked, they were sorted into those who were destined to be

murdered immediately, and those others who had a short-term usefulness as slave labor. But after a brief interval they, too, were to be herded into the same gas chambers into which the others were immediately piled, there to be asphyxiated so that, in their last moments, they could not prevent themselves from fighting each other in vain for a last breath of air.

9   To call these most wretched victims of a murderous delusion, of destructive drives run rampant, martyrs or a burnt offering is a distortion invented for our comfort, small as it may be. It pretends that this most vicious of mass murders had some deeper meaning; that in some fashion the victims either offered themselves or at least became sacrifices to a higher cause. It robs them of the last recognition which could be theirs, denies them the last dignity we could accord them: to face and accept what their death was all about, not embellishing it for the small psychological relief this may give us.

10   We could feel so much better if the victims had acted out of choice. For our emotional relief, therefore, we dwell on the tiny minority who did exercise some choice: the resistance fighters of the Warsaw ghetto, for example, and others like them. We are ready to overlook the fact that these people fought back only at a time when everything was lost, when the overwhelming majority of those who had been forced into the ghettos had already been exterminated without resisting. Certainly those few who finally fought for their survival and their convictions, risking and losing their lives in doing so, deserve our admiration; their deeds give us a moral lift. But the more we dwell on these few, the more unfair are we to the memory of the millions who were slaughtered—who gave in, did not fight back—because we deny them the only thing which up to the very end remained uniquely their own: their fate.

Understanding Meaning

1. Who was it that named the Nazi extermination of millions of Jews the Holocaust? Why do you think that name was chosen?
2. Why does Bettelheim, who was himself imprisoned by the Nazis, dislike the term *Holocaust* to represent the killing of so many Jews? What term would he prefer?
3. What did the Nazis themselves call the mass murder of European Jews? Why?
4. What technical term did the judges of the Nazi criminals use in referring to the deaths?
5. Why does Bettelheim not want the murder of Jews linked with a term that literally means "burnt offering"?

6. Why, according to Bettelheim, were the people who died in the concentration camps not martyrs?

7. Who were the very small number of Jews who resisted imprisonment, and why do we tend to dwell on them?

8. *CRITICAL THINKING.* Do you think that the term used in referring to what happened to European Jews detracts from the understanding people today have of the tragedy? Explain.

Evaluating Strategy

1. Even though the subject must have been a very painful one for Bettelheim personally, in the essay he builds a very careful and rational case for why he feels as he does about the term *holocaust*. In the first paragraph, he explains who chose the term and why they did. Analyze what point he makes in each of the other paragraphs as he builds his case.

2. For the most part, Bettelheim refers to the murder of the Jews without going into graphic details of the horror of their deaths. Where does he go into the most detail?

3. What point is Bettelheim trying to make in mentioning, at the end, the small minority who resisted imprisonment?

4. *CRITICAL THINKING.* One of the best known books about the Nazi treatment of the Jews, *The Diary of Anne Frank*, actually ends before Anne and her family were captured by the Nazis. Bettelheim's writings about the event have been widely read because they are the reports of a survivor. Why might a diary kept by a young girl *before* she was imprisoned have captured the attention of the world?

Appreciating Language

1. Bettelheim's essay is about language and why and how it is used. What terms that he himself uses have negative connotations that reveal his feelings toward the atrocities he is referring to? In other words, which words are charged with negative meaning?

2. *CRITICAL THINKING.* Have you yourself heard the events that Bettelheim is referring to called the Holocaust? Do you think you respond to the term in the way that he describes? Explain.

3. Why does Bettelheim object to the use of the term *genocide*?

4. What is the literal meaning of the term *holocaust*? Of *martyr*?

Writing Suggestions

1. *PREWRITING.* Mark in the text or list the words that Bettelheim uses to refer to the event that others refer to as the Holocaust.
2. *COLLABORATIVE WRITING.* Brainstorm with your group or class, making a list of what knowledge you have of the Holocaust and where you obtained it. Is most of your knowledge, for instance, from movies? Is the subject something you have studied in school?
3. Write a paragraph in which you summarize Bettelheim's objections to terms used to distance those who use them from the reality of the Holocaust.
4. Choose a movie about the Holocaust that you have seen and speculate in a paragraph how Bettelheim might respond to its portrayal of events.

JUDY MANN

During her career as a columnist for the Washington Post, *Judy Mann (1943–) has written extensively on the way in which traditional gender roles have affected the larger society. She is the author of* Difference: Growing Up Female in America *(1994).*

New World Daughters: How Parents Raise Boys and Girls Differently and Why It's Wrong

CONTEXT: *Judy Mann is an example of the single-issue reformer—someone who believes that changing one fundamental practice or belief will have a positive impact on a wide range of seemingly unrelated social problems. Her strategy in this essay is to suggest that much of the cost of poverty and welfare could be eliminated if girls were raised to be more self-assertive and independent. In other words, she is trying to make what might seem like a liberal attitude toward child rearing economically attractive to conservatives.*

1   When my daughter was 11, I realized that as much as I'd written about what happens to girls in schools, in their homes, and in the culture at large, I had no idea what I could do to help my own daughter. I have spent the last four years researching what happens to girls, and I have come to a number of conclusions that bear directly on today's welfare reform debate.

2   Perhaps most critically, I concluded that we will never change the outcome for girls until we change the way we raise boys. We need to break the false sense of entitlement—at the expense of girls—that boys have, and we need to break the equally destructive cycle in which we raise girls to be "nice," submissive and deferential.

3   This cycle of entitlement and submission plays a powerful role in a range of problems plaguing American society, including teenage violence, teenage pregnancy, wife battering and the costly sexual harassment suits that haunt the business community.

4   The irony for conservatives who have fought a rear-guard action for 20 years against women's rights is that the surest way out of the welfare state they rail against is to raise girls with the same range of opportunities and possibilities that boys have. This is the best inoculator against teenage pregnancy that we know of, the best vaccine against welfare dependency we have.

5   Though the hand-wringers would have you believe otherwise, teenagers are not all sex-crazed. In fact, it's more likely that the culture is sex-crazed and teenagers are trying to resist it. Almost universally, they tell researchers that they wish they had waited until they were older to have sex. In one study, nearly a quarter of the teenagers—boys as well as girls—said they believed in abstinence before marriage.

6   But the emphasis we place on feelings in girls, on their interpersonal skills and on their ability to care for others is precisely what sets them up to succumb to sexual overtures by boys. They usually regret it later.

7   Proof of this is found in a study by Marion Howard and Judith McCabe, who asked more than 1,000 sexually active girls 16 years of age or younger what topic they most wanted to have more information about. Abortion? Masturbation? AIDS prevention? None of the above. Instead, a whopping 84 percent of the girls checked this item: "How to say no without hurting the other person's feelings."

8   Parents can help their daughters through the messages they give about what they value in their families. If we stress the importance of boys and being popular, that tells our daughters that we value the social agenda. If we praise our daughters' school efforts, instead, that helps establish a different priority.

9   Parents can also help their daughters by coaching them to set boundaries. This means giving girls the sense that they are entitled to question boys' behavior and to say things such as, "Why do you think it's all right to do that?" Or, "How do you think that makes me feel when you do (say) that?" Or, "No, stop, it's not all right."

10   The goal is nothing short of changing the image in boys' minds of what is appropriate behavior toward girls and women and to make them more reflective about their own sexual desires. This is where mothers, who can remember very well what it is like to be a teenage girl, can make an important contribution by talking to their sons about the need to respect girls and women. Mothers need to tell their sons what it feels like to have to cope with the double standard in which boys who are sexually active are looked up to for being studs and girls are looked down on for being sluts.

11   There are some other things we can do to promote mutual respect between boys and girls and to encourage self-reliance in girls:

   • *Have boys do things for girls, such as getting them a drink or fetching a book.* The point is to have girls feel entitled to ask boys to do things for them and to develop in boys the capacity to do things for girls, as opposed to expecting girls to wait on them.

- *Encourage boys to be emotional and to be socially and interpersonally sensitive and responsive to others.* Men who cannot express their emotions can turn to violence.
- *Encourage boys and girls to be friends and to do things together, but keep a wary eye out for tendencies by both to fall back on stereotypical patterns of girls doing things for boys, such as cleaning up.*
- *Don't let boys get away with interrupting girls.* Encourage girls to talk and boys to listen. Tell girls to speak out if they feel no one is listening.
- *Don't cosset daughters.* Encourage them to be rough and ready and independent. Don't be too ready to help them. Encourage daughters to take risks, and let them learn to fail.
- *Praise girls for their talents and abilities, not just their hard work.* Instead of telling a girl, "you worked hard," tell her, "Gee, honey, you were great!" Learn to visualize her as a scientist, a college professor, a community leader.
- *Expect girls to do as well in math and science as boys, and encourage them to take the highest, hardest levels of math and science.* Stress to them the usefulness of these courses in gaining access to high-paying careers.
- *Encourage girls to form study groups with their pals and to take the challenging math and science courses with friends.* Daughters who are crossing gender lines into "male" territory in school need support just as we mothers did when we crossed gender lines in the workplace.
- *Encourage your schools to treat boys' and girls' athletic endeavors equally, by deglamorizing the macho sports and elevating the status of female athletes and girls' teams.*
- *Teach sons that promiscuity is equally debasing for boys and girls.* Don't wink or smirk at media reports of promiscuous sexual activity, whether it is high school athletes or adult celebrities.

12 The pattern in America has always been that boys' lives expand, while girls' lives are constrained. To break this pattern, girls should be given more freedom and opportunities in everything from athletic endeavors to schoolwork and to out-of-school activities such as summer camps that specialize in sports and computers. Encourage girls to take internships in nontraditional fields.

13 Girls who are centered rather than man-centered, who are valued for what they can do rather than how they look, who have a vision of a self-reliant and independent future rather than a life of domestic or welfare dependency will have the confidence to make choices that will promote their own success. If the choice comes down to hurting themselves or hurting someone else's feelings, girls who have practiced these skills and who have a clear eye about what is at stake will place their own welfare first. They will feel entitled to do that.

14   Welfare reform has to be viewed as a two-step process: what we should be doing with people who are on welfare now, and how to keep a new generation of teenage mothers and their babies from going on the rolls. No matter what Congress and the Clinton administration do to address the first stage, we will never succeed in creating long-term, systemic welfare reform until we raise girls to believe that their ticket to happiness, security and success is to be found in themselves, and not someone else. They need to understand that the main task of adolescence is to become the most competent and accomplished person they can be, with a full range of possibilities open to them of what life has to offer.

15   Self-reliance is not a conservative or a liberal value: It is one of the most cherished values in American culture. We need to nurture that quality in our daughters, just as we do in our sons.

Understanding Meaning

1.   What was Mann's purpose in writing the essay?
2.   What link does she forge between the way boys and girls are raised and welfare reform?
3.   What does she offer as one of the primary reasons that young girls give in to the pressure to have sex? What are some ways of helping them to avoid doing so?
4.   What are some of the specific ways that parents can teach their daughters self-reliance and self-respect?
5.   What do the boys need to be taught if the cycle of entitlement and submission is to be broken?
6.   *CRITICAL THINKING.* Among your peers, what are the primary forces at work to convince girls to have sex at a young age? Would any of Mann's suggestions help them resist the pressure to do so?

Evaluating Strategy

1.   Why do you think Mann might have chosen to mention her daughter in the first paragraph?
2.   Mann assumes that her readers will accept her claim that boys are raised to feel empowered and girls are raised to be "nice" and therefore submissive. What happens to the rest of her argument if her readers do not accept that?
3.   Mann presents her suggestions in the form of a bulleted list. Why is that a wise tactic, particularly in an article intended for publication in a newspaper?

4. Why might Mann have chosen to end her article with a reference to shared and cherished American values?
5. Why is Mann's essay classified as a comparison/contrast essay? What is being compared or contrasted?

Appreciating Language

1. Mann uses a number of "loaded" terms to emphasize the negative impact that current childrearing practices are having on our nation. She talks about boys' *false sense of empowerment*, the *destructive cycle* in which girls are raised to be submissive, and how our society is *plagued* and *haunted* by this cycle. Find other examples of loaded language that she uses.
2. What does she seem to be suggesting when she refers to seeking an *inoculator* against teen pregnancy and a *vaccine* against welfare dependency?

Writing Suggestions

1. *PREWRITING.* Write a paragraph in which you respond to Mann's article.
2. *COLLABORATIVE WRITING.* Share with your group the paragraph you wrote in Writing Suggestion #1 above. Do the various responses divide according to gender lines?
3. Write an essay in which you either agree or disagree with Mann's plan for changing the way America's children are raised.
4. Write an essay in which you explain whether or not your own observation of teenagers—male and female—supports Mann's claim about the cycle of entitlement and submission that controls male/female relations among America's young.

WILLIAM SEVERINI KOWINSKI

William Severini Kowinski is a writer, editor, speaker, and consultant who lives in northern California. He has served as an editor of the Boston Phoenix *newspaper. He has published articles on the arts, the environment, politics, and urban design. Many of his essays have appeared in* Smithsonian *magazine. His 1985 book* The Malling of America, *which analyzes the effects of shopping malls, was republished in 2002.*

Kids in the Mall: Growing Up Controlled

BEFORE YOU READ: *You may have seen large numbers of teenagers hanging out at the mall. You may even have been one of them. Kowinski looks at the reasons young people spend so much time at malls, and the consequences.*

TIPS FOR READING: *As you read, think in terms of causes and effects. What causes the teenagers to spend time at the mall? What causes their parents to need to let them? What are the effects on them and on the malls, positive and negative, of their being there so much?*

Words to Know:

viable	workable
resonance	echoing of sound
incursion	a hostile entrance into a place
inestimable	too valuable to be estimated
Valley Girls and Boys	a certain group of California teenagers in the late twentieth century with their own slang vocabulary and style of dress
mores	values
ramifications	consequences
plethora	overabundance
surrogate	a person who acts or stands in for another
denizens	people who regularly frequent a certain place
passivity	inactivity
impertinence	inappropriateness
inexorably	unyieldingly; in a manner not to be persuaded easily

Butch heaved himself up and loomed over the group. "Like it was different for me," he piped. "My folks used to drop me off at the shopping mall every morning and leave me all day. It was like a big free baby-sitter, you know? One night they never came back for me. Maybe they moved away. Maybe there's some kind of a Bureau of Missing Parents I could check with."

–Richard Peck

Secrets of the Shopping Mall,
a novel for teenagers

1   From his sister at Swarthmore, I'd heard about a kid in Florida whose mother picked him up after school every day, drove him straight to the mall, and left him there until it closed—all at his insistence. I'd heard about a boy in Washington who, when his family moved from one suburb to another, pedaled his bicycle five miles every day to get back to his old mall, where he once belonged.

2   These stories aren't unusual. The mall is a common experience for the majority of American youth; they have probably been going there all their lives. Some ran within their first large open space, saw their first fountain, bought their first toy, and read their first book in a mall. They may have smoked their first cigarette or first joint, or turned them down, had their first kiss or lost their virginity in the mall parking lot. Teenagers in America now spend more time in the mall than anywhere else but home and school. Mostly it is their choice, but some of that mall time is put in as the result of two-paycheck and single-parent households, and the lack of other viable alternatives. But are these kids being harmed by the mall?

3   I wondered first of all what difference it makes for adolescents to experience so many important moments in the mall. They are, after all, at play in the fields of its little world and they learn its ways; they adapt to it and make it adapt to them. It's here that these kids get their street sense, only it's mall sense. They are learning the ways of a large-scale, artificial environment; its subtleties and flexibilities, its particular pleasures and resonances, and the attitudes it fosters.

4   The presence of so many teenagers for so much time was not something mall developers planned on. In fact, it came as a big surprise. But kids became a fact of mall life very easily, and the International Council of Shopping Centers found it necessary to commission a study, which they published along with a guide to mall managers on how to handle the teenage incursion.

5   The study found that "teenagers in suburban centers are bored and come to the shopping centers mainly as a place to go. Teenagers in suburban centers spent more time fighting, drinking, littering and walking than did their urban counterparts, but presented fewer overall problems." The report observed that "adolescents congregated in groups of two to four and predominantly at locations selected by them rather than management." This probably had something to do with the decision to install game arcades, which allow management to channel these restless adolescents into naturally contained areas away from major traffic points of adult shoppers.

6   The guide concluded that mall management should tolerate and even encourage the teenage presence because, in the words of the report, "The vast majority support the same set of values as does shopping center management." *The same set of values* means simply that mall kids are already preprogrammed to be consumers and that the mall can put the finishing touches to them as hard-core, lifelong shoppers just like everybody else. That, after all, is what the mall is about. So it shouldn't be surprising that in spending a lot of time there, adolescents find little that challenges the assumption that the goal of life is to make money and buy products, or that just about everything else in life is to be used to serve those ends.

7   Growing up in a high-consumption society already adds inestimable pressure to kids' lives. Clothes consciousness has invaded the grade schools, and popularity is linked with having the best, newest clothes in the currently acceptable styles. Even what they read has been affected. "Miss [Nancy] Drew wasn't obsessed with her wardrobe," noted the *Wall Street Journal*. "But today the mystery in teen fiction for girls is what outfit the heroine will wear next." Shopping has become a survival skill and there is certainly no better place to learn it than the mall, where its importance is powerfully reinforced and certainly never questioned.

8   The mall as a university of suburban materialism, where Valley Girls and Boys from coast to coast are educated in consumption, has its other lessons in this era of change in family life and sexual mores and their economic and social ramifications. The plethora of products in the mall, plus the pressure on teens to buy them, may contribute to the phenomenon that psychologist David Elkind calls "the hurried child": kids who are exposed to too much of the adult world too quickly and must respond with a sophistication that belies their still-tender emotional development. Certainly the adult products marketed for children—form-fitting designer jeans, sexy tops for preteen girls—add to the social pressure to look like an adult, along with the home-grown need to understand adult finances (why mothers must work) and adult emotions (when parents divorce).

9   Kids spend so much time at the mall partly because their parents allow it and even encourage it. The mall is safe, doesn't seem to harbor any unsavory activities, and there is adult supervision; it is, after all, a controlled environment. So the temptation, especially for working parents, is to let the mall be their baby-sitter. At least the kids aren't watching TV. But the mall's role as a surrogate mother may be more extensive and more profound.

10   Karen Lansky, a writer living in Los Angeles, has looked into the subject, and she told me some of her conclusions about the effects on its teenaged denizens of the mall's controlled and controlling environment. "Structure is the dominant idea, since true 'mall rats' lack just that in their home lives," she said, "and adolescents about to make the big leap into growing up crave more structure than our modern society cares to acknowledge." Karen pointed out some of the elements malls supply that kids used to get from their families, like warmth (Strawberry Shortcake dolls and similar cute and cuddly merchandise), old-fashioned mothering ("We do it all for you," the fast-food slogan), and even home cooking (the "homemade" treats at the food court).

11   The problem in all this, as Karen Lansky sees it, is that while families nurture children by encouraging growth through the assumption of responsibility and then by letting them rest in the bosom of the family from the rigors of growing up, the mall as a structural mother encourages passivity and consumption, as long as the kid doesn't make trouble. Therefore all they learn about becoming adults is how to act and how to consume.

12   Kids are in the mall not only in the passive role of shoppers—they also work there, especially as fast-food outlets infiltrate the mall's enclosure. There they learn how to hold a job and take responsibility, but still within the same value context. When *CBS Reports* went to Oak Park Mall in suburban Kansas City, Kansas, to tape part of their hour-long consideration of malls, "After the Dream Comes True," they interviewed a teenaged girl who worked in a fast-food outlet there. In a sequence that didn't make the final program, she described the major goal of her present life, which was to perfect the curl on top of the ice-cream cones that were her store's specialty. If she could do that, she would be moved from the lowly soft-drink dispenser to the more prestigious ice-cream division, the curl on top of the status ladder at her restaurant. These are the achievements that are important at the mall.

13   Other benefits of such jobs may also be overrated, according to Laurence D. Steinberg of the University of California at Irvine's social ecology department, who did a study on teenage employment. Their jobs, he found, are generally simple, mindlessly repetitive and boring. They don't

450

really learn anything, and the jobs don't lead anywhere. Teenagers also work primarily with other teenagers; even their supervisors are often just a little older than they are. "Kids need to spend time with adults," Steinberg told me. "Although they get benefits from peer relationships, without parents and other adults it's one-side socialization. They hang out with each other, have age-segregated jobs, and watch TV."

14 Perhaps much of this is not so terrible or even so terribly different. Now that they have so much more to contend with in their lives, adolescents probably need more time to spend with other adolescents without adult impositions, just to sort things out. Though it is more concentrated in the mall (and therefore perhaps a clearer target), the value system there is really the dominant one of the whole society. Attitudes about curiosity, initiative, self-expression, empathy, and disinterested learning aren't necessarily made in the mall; they are mirrored there, perhaps a bit more intensely—as through a glass brightly.

15 Besides, the mall is not without its educational opportunities. There are bookstores, where there is at least a short shelf of classics at great prices, and other books from which it is possible to learn more than how to do sit-ups. There are tools, from hammers to VCRs, and products, from clothes to records, that can help the young find and express themselves. There are older people with stories, and places to be alone or to talk one-on-one with a kindred spirit. And there is always the passing show.

16 The mall itself may very well be an education about the future. I was struck with the realization, as early as my first forays into Greengate, that the mall is only one of a number of enclosed and controlled environments that are part of the lives of today's young. The mall is just an extension, say, of those large suburban schools—only there's Karmelkorn instead of chem lab, the ice rink instead of the gym: It's high school without the impertinence of classes.

17 Growing up, moving from home to school to the mall—from enclosure to enclosure, transported in cars—is a curiously continuous process, without much in the way of contrast or contact with unenclosed reality. Places must tend to blur into one another. But whatever differences and dangers there are in this, the skills these adolescents are learning may turn out to be useful in their later lives. For we seem to be moving inexorably into an age of pre-planned and regulated environments, and this is the world they will inherit.

18 Still, it might be better if they had more of a choice. One teenaged girl confessed to *CBS Reports* that she sometimes felt she was missing something by hanging out at the mall so much. "But I'm here," she said, "and this is what I have."

Understanding Meaning

1. What does Kowinski say are some of the reasons that teenagers spend so much time in malls?
2. What are some of the disadvantages to spending so much time in the malls, according to Kowinski? What lessons are teens learning there? What are they missing out on?
3. What does Kowinski cite as an example of how mall managers have responded to the presence of so many teenagers?
4. It might seem that having a job in a mall would have positive effects on the teenager. Why is that not necessarily true, according to Kowinski and his sources?
5. Near the end of the essay, Kowinski turns to some of the benefits of time spent in the mall. What are those benefits?
6. *CRITICAL THINKING.* Do you agree with Kowinski's analysis of the mall culture as it relates to teenagers? Are there reasons for their being there that he doesn't mention? Explain.

Evaluating Strategy

1. In his essay, Kowinski analyzes both causes and effects. Where in the essay does he analyze what causes the presence of teenagers in such large numbers in the malls of America? Which paragraphs most directly address the effects that hanging out at the mall has on the youth?
2. Which paragraphs address the effects on teenagers of having a job in a mall?
3. Mall managers did not originally foresee the extent to which teenagers would spend large amounts of time in malls. What decisions have they made in response to the situation?
4. Does Kowinski come across as a reasonable person, willing to consider both sides of a situation? Explain.

Appreciating Language

1. How does Kowinski establish from the first paragraph that he has chosen a fairly informal style for this piece?
2. Would you consider Kowinski's treatment of the mall culture objective or subjective? That is, does he keep his own personal opinion out of the piece (objective), or does he show his bias through his content and word choice (subjective)? Explain. Is the same true of the sources that Kowinski quotes?

Writing Suggestions

1. Whether you spend a great deal or hardly any time at all in malls, write a paragraph explaining why you go there.
2. *COLLABORATIVE WRITING.* Work with your group to brainstorm some of the types of people you tend to see in the average mall. Appoint one member of the group to make a list of the ideas the group generates.
3. Using the list from Writing Suggestion #2 above as a starting point, write an essay in which you categorize some of the types of people you see in the mall.
4. Write a paragraph in which you explain why you agree or disagree with Kowinski's points about why young people go to malls and what the effects are.

STEPHEN KING

Stephen King (1947–) is a phenomenally successful writer of horror fiction. His books have sold millions of copies, and several have been made into popular motion pictures. His novels include Carrie *(1974),* Salem's Lot *(1974),* The Shining *(1977),* Firestarter *(1980),* Cujo *(1981),* Christine *(1983), and* Misery *(1988).*

Why We Crave Horror Movies

BEFORE YOU READ: *King tells us that horror movies may appeal to the insanity and the potential for violence in all of us—and that could be a good thing.*

TIPS FOR READING: *Notice that early in the essay King presents a simple list of reasons why people go to horror movies. The analysis of causes gets more complicated, however, when he asks why viewers enjoy seeing others suffer. The answer has to do with the dangerous effects of not finding an outlet for negative emotions.*

Words to Know:

innately	arising naturally
reactionary	extremely conservative
voyeur	a person who derives enjoyment from observing
lynch	to be hung by a mob
penchant	a strong liking for something
sanctions	penalties
remonstrance	protest
anarchistic	promoting disorder or overthrow of government

TIPS FOR WRITING: *Don't oversimplify your explanation of causes or effects to try to fit an organizational plan. Let your content and your organization acknowledge the complexity of the situation.*

1 I think that we're all mentally ill; those of us outside the asylums only hide it a little better—and maybe not all that much better, after all. We've all known people who talk to themselves, people who sometimes squinch their faces into horrible grimaces when they believe no one is watching, people who have some hysterical fear—of snakes, the dark, the tight place, the long drop . . . and, of course, those final worms and grubs that are waiting so patiently underground.

---

2   When we pay our four or five bucks and seat ourselves at tenth-row center in a theater showing a horror movie, we are daring the nightmare.

3   Why? Some of the reasons are simple and obvious. To show that we can, that we are not afraid, that we can ride this roller coaster. Which is not to say that a really good horror movie may not surprise a scream out of us at some point, the way we may scream when the roller coaster twists through a complete 360 or plows through a lake at the bottom of the drop. And horror movies, like roller coasters, have always been the special province of the young; by the time one turns 40 or 50, one's appetite for double twists or 360-degree loops may be considerably depleted.

4   We also go to re-establish our feelings of essential normality; the horror movie is innately conservative, even reactionary. Freda Jackson as the horrible melting woman in *Die, Monster, Die!* confirms for us that no matter how far we may be removed from the beauty of a Robert Redford or a Diana Ross, we are still light-years from true ugliness.

5   And we go to have fun.

6   Ah, but this is where the ground starts to slope away, isn't it? Because this is a very peculiar sort of fun, indeed. The fun comes from seeing others menaced—sometimes killed. One critic has suggested that if pro football has become the voyeur's version of combat, then the horror film has become the modern version of the public lynching.

7   It is true that the mythic, "fairy-tale" horror film intends to take away the shades of gray. . . . It urges us to put away our more civilized and adult penchant for analysis and to become children again, seeing things in pure blacks and whites. It may be that horror movies provide psychic relief on this level because this invitation to lapse into simplicity, irrationality and even outright madness is extended so rarely. We are told we may allow our emotions a free rein . . . or no rein at all.

8   If we are all insane, then sanity becomes a matter of degree. If your insanity leads you to carve up women like Jack the Ripper or the Cleveland Torso Murderer, we clap you away in the funny farm (but neither of those two amateur-night surgeons was ever caught, heh-heh-heh); if, on the other hand, your insanity leads you only to talk to yourself when you're under stress or to pick your nose on your morning bus, then you are left alone to go about your business . . . though it is doubtful that you will ever be invited to the best parties.

9   The potential lyncher is in almost all of us (excluding saints, past and present; but then, most saints have been crazy in their own ways), and every now and then, he has to be let loose to scream and roll around in the grass. Our emotions and our fears form their own body, and we recognize that it

demands its own exercise to maintain proper muscle tone. Certain of these emotional muscles are accepted—even exalted—in civilized society; they are, of course, the emotions that tend to maintain the status quo of civilization itself. Love, friendship, loyalty, kindness—these are all the emotions that we applaud, emotions that have been immortalized in the couplets of Hallmark cards and in the verses (I don't dare call it poetry) of Leonard Nimoy.

10 When we exhibit these emotions, society showers us with positive reinforcement: we learn this even before we get out of diapers. When, as children, we hug our rotten little puke of a sister and give her a kiss, all the aunts and uncles smile and twit and cry, "Isn't he the sweetest little thing?" Such coveted treats as chocolate-covered graham crackers often follow. But if we deliberately slam the rotten little puke of a sister's fingers in the door, sanctions follow—angry remonstrance from parents, aunts and uncles; instead of a chocolate-covered graham cracker, a spanking.

11 But anticivilization emotions don't go away, and they demand periodic exercise. We have such "sick" jokes as, "What's the difference between a truckload of bowling balls and a truckload of dead babies?" (You can't unload a truckload of bowling balls with a pitchfork . . . a joke, by the way, that I heard originally from a ten-year-old). Such a joke may surprise a laugh or a grin out of us even as we recoil, a possibility that confirms the thesis: If we share a brotherhood of man, then we also share an insanity of man. None of which is intended as a defense of either the sick joke or insanity but merely as an explanation of why the best horror films, like the best fairy tales, manage to be reactionary, anarchistic, and revolutionary all at the same time.

12 The mythic horror movie, like the sick joke, has a dirty job to do. It deliberately appeals to all that is worst in us. It is morbidity unchained, our most base instincts let free, our nastiest fantasies realized . . . and it all happens, fittingly enough, in the dark. For those reasons, good liberals often shy away from horror films. For myself, I like to see the most aggressive of them—*Dawn of the Dead*, for instance—as lifting a trap door in the civilized forebrain and throwing a basket of raw meat to the hungry alligators swimming around in that subterranean river beneath.

13 Why bother? Because it keeps them from getting out, man. It keeps them down there and me up here. It was Lennon and McCartney who said that all you need is love, and I would agree with that.

14 As long as you keep the gators fed.

Understanding Meaning

1. King could have had a very simple five-paragraph essay if he had simply presented the three reasons people go to horror movies that he discusses in paragraphs 3–5. Why does he say, though, that after that, "the ground starts to slope away"?
2. What does King mean when he uses the term "the mythic 'fairy-tale' horror film"? How is a horror film like a fairy tale? What is the effect when a person watches such films?
3. Explain what King means by his statement that we need to exercise our emotional muscles, both those associated with positive and those associated with negative emotions? What does he say happens when the emotional muscles don't get any exercise? How do horror movies help them get the needed exercise?
4. According to King, how are horror films like "lifting a trap door in the civilized forebrain and throwing a basket of raw meat to the hungry alligators swimming around in that subterranean river beneath"?
5. *CRITICAL THINKING.* Does King's discussion of horror movies shed any light on why such movies appeal to teenagers in particular? Explain.

Evaluating Strategy

1. Explain why King's introduction and conclusion are effective.
2. Examine the different ways in which King makes use of cause-and-effect relationships in the essay.

Appreciating Language

1. In what specific ways does King make use of an informal style?
2. What fear is King referring to when he writes of "those final worms and grubs that are waiting so patiently underground" (paragraph 1)?
3. What does King mean when he says that when people attend horror movies, they are "daring the nightmare"?
4. Two metaphors are key to understanding King's analysis of why people like to see horror movies. Explain how, according to King, emotional muscles are like physical muscles. How is watching a horror movie like throwing raw meat to hungry alligators?

Writing Suggestions

1. *COLLABORATIVE WRITING.* Work with a group to make a quick list of horror movies that come to mind. If you can, narrow that list down to a short list of horror movies all members of the group have seen. Choose two or three of the movies, and decide if what King says about "fairy-tale" horror movies is true. Are good and bad presented in clear-cut terms? Consider, for example, what the victims or the villains have in common.

2. Write a paragraph in which you agree or disagree with what King says about "fairy-tale" horror movies. Use as examples movies from your group's list or other movies that you think of. Remember that movie titles are italicized.

3. Write a paragraph in which you agree or disagree with King's claim that it is good to see horror movies because they exercise the "muscles" associated with our negative emotions.

4. Write a paragraph in which you explain why you personally like or dislike horror movies.

LAURA FRASER

A freelance writer whose work has appeared in such leading magazines as Glamour, Vogue, *and* Mother Jones, *Laura Fraser (1961–) is a recovering bulimic who has published widely on American attitudes toward food. Her books include* Losing It: False Hopes and Fat Profits in the Diet Industry *(1997) and* An Italian Affair *(2001). Born in Denver, Colorado, Fraser graduated from Wesleyan University in 1982, has taught writing at Berkeley, and currently lives in San Francisco.*

Why I Stopped Being a Vegetarian

CONTEXT: *During Fraser's adolescence in the 1970s, she became a vegetarian as part of an alternative lifestyle. Over the years, however, she began to turn against the various moral arguments advanced on behalf of vegetarianism. She eventually concluded that a refusal to eat meat is itself morally suspect because it disregards humanity. Thus, her argument turns the tables on what she regards as the self-righteousness of many vegetarians. The essay was published on January 7, 2000, on the online magazine* Salon.

1 Until a few months ago, I had been a vegetarian for fifteen years. Like most people who call themselves vegetarians (somewhere between 4 and 10 percent of us, depending on the definition; only 1 percent of Americans are vegans, eating no animal products at all), I wasn't strict about it. I ate dairy products and eggs, as well as fish. That made me a pesco-ovo-lacto-vegetarian, which isn't a category you can choose for special meals on airlines.

2 About a year ago, in Italy, it dawned on me that a little pancetta was really good in pasta, too. After failing to convince myself that pancetta was a vegetable, I became a pesco-ovo-lacto-pancetta-vegetarian, with a "Don't Ask, Don't Tell" policy about chicken broth. It was a slippery slope from there.

3 Nevertheless, for most of those fifteen years, hardly a piece of animal flesh crossed my lips. Over the course of that time, many people asked me why I became a vegetarian. I came up with vague answers: my health, the environment, the impracticality and heartlessness of killing animals for food when we can survive perfectly well on soy burgers. It was political, it was emotional and it made me special, not to mention slightly morally superior to all those blood-thirsty carnivores out there.

4 The truth is, I became a vegetarian in college for two reasons. One was that meat was more expensive than lentils, and I was broke, or broke enough

"Why I Stopped Being a Vegetarian" by Laura Fraser from SALON.com, January 7, 2000.

to choose to spend my limited budget on other classes of ingestibles. The other was that I was not a lesbian.

5   This is not to say that all lesbians are carnivores; in fact, there's probably a higher percentage of vegetarians among lesbians than most other groups. But there was a fair amount of political pressure to be something in those days. Since, as a privileged white girl from suburban Denver, I couldn't really identify with any oppressed minority group, I was faced with becoming a lesbian in order to prove my political mettle. I had to decide between meat and men, and for better or worse, I became a vegetarian.

6   The identity stuck, even though the political imperative for my label faded. It wasn't an identity that ever really fit: My friends thought it odd that such an otherwise hedonistic woman should have that one ascetic streak. It was against my nature, they said. But by then, I'd started to believe the other arguments about vegetarianism.

7   First was health. There's a lot of evidence that vegetarians live longer, have lower cholesterol levels and are thinner than meat eaters. This is somewhat hard to believe, since for the first few years of not eating meat, I was basically a cheesetarian. Try leafing through some of those vegetarian recipe books from the early '80s: You added three cups of grated cheddar to everything but the granola. Then vegetarianism went through that mathematical phase where you had to figure out which proteins you had to combine with which in order to get a complete protein. Since many nutritionists will tell you people don't need that much protein anyway, I gave up, going for days and days without so much as contemplating beans or tofu.

8   For whatever haphazard combination of proteins I ate, being a vegetarian did seem to have a stunning effect on my cholesterol level. This, of course, could be genetic. But when I had a very involved physical exam once at the Cooper Institute for Aerobic Fitness in Dallas, my total cholesterol level was a super-low 135, and my ratio of HDL (good) cholesterol to LDL (evil) was so impressive that the doctor drawled, "Even if you had heart disease, you would be reversing it." This good news, far from reassuring me that I could well afford a few barbecued ribs now and then, spurred me on in my vegetarianism, mainly because my cholesterol numbers effectively inoculated me against the doctor's advice that I also needed to lose fifteen pounds.

9   "Why?" I asked. "Don't you lose weight to lower your cholesterol?"

10   He couldn't argue with that. Whether or not most vegetarians are leaner than carnivores, in my case I was happy to more than make up the calories with carbohydrates, which, perhaps not coincidentally, I always craved.

11   After the health rationale came the animal rights one. Like most vegetarians, I cracked Peter Singer's[1] philosophical treatise on animal rights, and
bought his utilitarian line that if you don't have to kill animals, and it
potentially causes suffering, you shouldn't do it. (Singer, now at Princeton,
has recently come under attack for saying that if a human being's incapaci-
tated life causes more suffering than good, it is OK to kill him.)

12   It's hard to know where to stop with utilitarianism. Do I need a cash-
mere sweater more than those little shorn goats need to be warm themselves? Do animals really suffer if they have happy, frolicking lives before a
quick and painless end? Won't free-range[2] do?

13   My animal rights philosophy had a lot of holes from the start. First of
all, I excluded fish from the animal kingdom—not only because fish taste
delicious grilled with a little butter and garlic, but also because they make
it a lot easier to be a vegetarian when you go out to restaurants. Now that's
utilitarian. Besides, as soon as you start spending your time fretting about
the arguments that crowd the inner pens of animal rights philosophy—do
fish think?—then you know you're experiencing a real protein deficiency.

14   I rationalized the fish thing by telling myself I would eat anything I
would kill myself. I had been fly-fishing with my dad and figured a few seconds of flopping around was outweighed by the merits of trout almondine.
(Notice that I, not the fish, was doing the figuring.) But who was I kidding?
If I were hungry enough, I'd kill a cow in a heartbeat. I'd practically kill a
cow just for a great pair of shoes.

15   Which brings me to the leather exception. As long as other people are
eating cow, I decided, I might as well recycle the byproducts and diminish
the harm by wearing leather jackets and shoes. When everyone stopped
eating meat, I'd stop buying leather jackets and shoes. In the meantime,
better stock up.

16   Then there's the environmental rationale. There is no doubt, as Frances
Moore Lappe first pointed out in her 1971 book *Food First*, that there is a
huge loss of protein resources going from grain to meat, and that some animals, especially cattle and Americans, use up piggish amounts of water, grain
and crop land.

17   But the problem really isn't meat, but too much meat—overgrazing, over-
fishing and overconsumption. If Americans just ate less meat—like driving cars

---

[1] Utilitarianism, as Singer defines it in "The Singer Solution to World Poverty" (p. 534), is a standard
that "judges whether acts are right or wrong by their consequences." Singer's book on animal rights is
Animal Liberation (1975).—EDS.

[2] Free-range animals are not penned up in a small space but are allowed to move about freely in ample
space.—EDS.

less often—the problem could be alleviated without giving up meat entirely. That approach has worked for centuries, and continues to work in Europe.

18   All my deep vegetarian questioning was silenced one day when a friend ordered roasted rosemary chicken for two. I thought I'd try "just a bite," and then I was ripping into it like a starving hyena. Roasted chicken, I realized, is wonderful. Meat is good.

19   From a culinary point of view, that's obvious. Consider that most vegetarians live in America and England, places tourists do not visit for the food. You don't find vegetarians in France, and rarely in Italy. Enough said.

20   As for health, if nutritionists are always telling you to "listen to your body," mine was definitely shouting for more meat. One roasted bird unleashed fifteen years' worth of cravings. All of a sudden I felt like I had a bass note playing in my body to balance out all those soprano carbohydrates. Forget about winning the low-cholesterol Olympics. For the first time in a long time, I felt satisfied.

21   As a vegetarian, not only had I denied myself something I truly enjoyed, I had been antisocial. How many times had I made a hostess uncomfortable by refusing the main course at a dinner party, lamely saying I'd "eat around it"? How often did my vegetarianism cause other people to go to extra trouble to make something special for me to eat, and why did it never occur to me that that was selfish? How about the time, in a small town in Italy, when the chef had presented me with a plate of very special local sausage, since I was the American guest—and I had refused it, to the mortification of my Italian friends? Or when a then-boyfriend, standing in the meat section of the grocery store, forlornly told a friend, "If only I had a girlfriend who ate meat"? If eating is a socially conscious act, you have to be conscious of the society of your fellow *Homo sapiens* along with the animals. And we humans, as it happens, are omnivores.

Understanding Meaning

1.   Fraser had a list of reasons she gave people when they asked why she was a vegetarian. What does she admit were the two real reasons? What do those two reasons suggest about how serious her commitment to vegetarianism was? What did it take to get her started eating meat again?

2.   In paragraph 6, Fraser says that she had "started to believe the other arguments about vegetarianism." What were those other arguments? Does she seem to believe very strongly in any of those arguments? Where does she make it pretty clear that these are simply reasons she is repeating, but not reasons that make vegetarianism a matter of principle for her?

3.   What effect does Fraser now think her vegetarianism had on other people?

Evaluating Strategy

1. What are some of the first hints that Fraser is going to take a humorous approach to her subject? What are some of the parts of the essay that you found humorous?
2. *BLENDING THE MODES.* Explain how Fraser makes use of cause/effect reasoning in the essay.
3. Why does it serve Fraser's purpose to emphasize her lack of commitment to vegetarianism?
4. Is she appealing primarily to the readers' emotions, logic, or ethics?

Appreciating Language

1. Does Fraser make use of a specialized vocabulary? Does the vocabulary seem appropriate for the audience for which it was written? What assumptions can you make about the audience for which she was writing?
2. Where does Fraser make use of biased language in order to get her point across? Notice, for example, that she speaks of meat eaters as "bloodthirsty."
3. Where in the essay does Fraser come across as most sincere?

Writing Suggestions

1. Write an essay in which you explain why fast-food restaurants suit the American lifestyle, for good or ill.
2. In the final paragraph, Fraser states that while she was a vegetarian, she was antisocial. Do you or your friends have different dietary requirements than other people? How should people with specific food needs be treated by others?
3. News reports tell us that we are rapidly becoming an obese nation. Even our children are increasingly at risk for developing such weight-related ailments as diabetes. What suggestions do you have for improving the situation?
4. *COLLABORATIVE WRITING.* Exchange the draft of your essay from Writing Suggestion #1, #2, or #3 above with a classmate. For your classmate's essay, do the following:
   - Underline the sentence you feel most clearly states the thesis of the essay.
   - Put in brackets sentences you feel best support the thesis.
   - Put a wavy line under the sentences you feel are unclear or need more support.

MARK LYNAS

Mark Lynas (1973–) was born in Fiji and grew up in Peru, Spain, and the United Kingdom. After graduating with honors from the University of Edinburgh, he joined OneWorld.net, an Internet portal dedicated to human rights and sustainable development issues. He is the author of High Tide: News from a Warming World *(2004).*

It's Later Than You Think

BEFORE YOU READ: *Mark Lynas concludes his article, published in the British magazine the* New Statesman *in 2003, by saying, "We must abandon the old mindset that demands an oil-based economy, not just because it sparks wars and terrorism, but because the future of life on earth depends on leaving it behind."*

TIPS FOR READING: *Lynas's organization is easy to follow. He opens by declaring that there is no longer any scientific dispute concerning global warming. He then describes in vivid narrative detail the effect of climate change on several areas of the world he has visited. He ends by explaining what he thinks must be done to head off a global disaster.*

Words to Know:	
unassailable	something that cannot be successfully denied
greenhouse gas	gases like carbon dioxide that are absorbed into the ozone in the Earth's atmosphere, resulting in a gradual increase in temperature of the atmosphere
emissions	a release
frontmen	apparently respectable people under whose cover secret or illegal activities are carried out
hostel	a supervised, inexpensive lodging for young travelers
Xanadu	an imaginary land described in fables and in a famous poem by Samuel Taylor Coleridge entitled "Kubla Khan"
cockerels	young roosters
superseded	replaced

This is taken from an article which first appeared in New Statesman. "It's Later Than You Think" by Mark Lynas from NEW STATESMAN, June 30, 2003. Reprinted by permission of New Statesman Ltd.

TIPS FOR WRITING: *One of the strengths of Lynas's writing is the detail with which he presents the changing conditions in different parts of the world. Instead of merely presenting statistics, he shows how individual villages and individual lives are being disrupted by climate change.*

1   Hardly anyone realises it, but the debate about climate change is over. Scientists around the world have now amassed an unassailable body of evidence to support the conclusion that a warming of our planet—caused principally by greenhouse gas emissions from burning fossil fuel—is under way.

2   The dwindling band of climate "sceptics," a rag-tag bunch of oil and coal industry frontmen, retired professors and semi-deranged obsessives, is now on the defensive. Although names such as Fred Singer, Philip Stott and Bjorn Lomborg still appear from time to time in the popular press here and in the United States, their views are notable by their absence from the expert literature.

3   Meanwhile the world as we once knew it is beginning to unravel. The signs are everywhere, even in Britain. Horse chestnut, oak and ash trees are coming into leaf more than a week earlier than two decades ago. The growing season now lasts almost all year round: in 2000 there were just 39 official days of winter.

4   Destructive winter floods are part of this warming trend, while in lowland England snow has become a thing of the past. Where I live in Oxford, six out of the past ten winters have been completely snowless—something that happened only twice during the whole 30-year period between 1960 and 1990. The rate of warming has now become so rapid that it is equivalent to your garden moving south by 20 metres every single day.

5   In other parts of the world, the signs of global warming are more dramatic. Over the past three years, researching a book on the subject, I have witnessed major climate-driven changes across five continents, changes that are leaving millions homeless, destitute and in danger.

6   In Alaska I spent a week in the Eskimo village of Shishmaref, on the state's remote western coast, just 70 miles from the eastern coast of Russia. While the midnight sun shone outside, I listened as the village elder, Clifford Weyiouanna, told me how the sea, which used to freeze in October, was now ice-free until Christmas. And even when the sea ice does eventually form, he explained, it is so thin that it is dangerous to walk and hunt on. The changing seasons are also affecting the animals: seals and walruses—still crucial elements of the Eskimo diet—are migrating earlier and are almost impossible to catch. The whole village caught only one walrus last year, after covering thousands of miles by boat.

7   Shishmaref lives in perpetual fear. The cliffs on which the 600-strong community sits are thawing, and during the last big storm 50 feet of ground was lost overnight. People battled 90mph winds to save their houses from the crashing waves.

8   I stood on the shoreline a year ago with Robert Iyatunguk, the co-ordinator of the Shishmaref Erosion Coalition, looking up at a house left hanging over the clifftop. "The wind is getting stronger, the water is getting higher, and it's noticeable to everybody in town," he told me. "It just kind of scares you inside your body and makes you wonder exactly when the big one is going to hit." In July 2002 the residents voted to abandon the site altogether—a narrow barrier island that has been continuously occupied by Eskimos for centuries—and move elsewhere.

9   In Fairbanks, Alaska's main town in the interior, everyone talks about warming. The manager of the hostel where I stayed, a keen hunter, told me how ducks had been swimming on the river in December (it's supposed to freeze over in autumn), how bears had become so confused they didn't know whether to hibernate or stay awake, and that winter temperatures, which used to plummet to 40 degrees below zero, now barely touched 25 below.

10   All around the town, roads are buckling and houses sagging as the permafrost underneath them thaws. In one house, the occupants, a cleaning lady and her daughter, showed me that to walk across the kitchen meant going uphill (the house was tilting sideways) and how shelves had to be rebalanced with bits of wood to stop everything falling off. Other dwellings have been abandoned. New ones are built on adjustable stilts.

11   Scientists have long predicted that global warming will lead in some places to intense flooding and drought. When I visited China in April last year, the country's northern provinces were in the grip of the worst drought in more than a century. Entire lakes had dried up, and in many places sand dunes were advancing across the farmers' fields.

12   One lakeside village in Gansu Province, just off the old Silk Road, was abandoned after the waters dried up—apart from one woman, who lives amid the ruins with a few chickens and a cow for company. "Of course I'm lonely!" she cried in answer to my rather insensitive question. "Can you imagine how boring this life is? I can't move; I can do nothing. I have no relatives, no friends and no money." She was tormented by memories of how it had once been, when neighbours had chatted and swapped stories late into the evenings, before the place became a ghost town.

13   Minutes after I had left, a dust storm blew in. These storms are getting more frequent, and even Beijing is now hit repeatedly every spring. During an earlier visit to a remote village in eastern Inner Mongolia,

not far from the ruins of Kubla Khan's fabled Xanadu, I experienced an even stronger storm. Day was turned into night as a blizzard of sand and dust scoured the mud-brick buildings. I cowered inside one house with a Mongolian peasant family, sharing rice wine and listening to tales of how the grass had once grown waist-high on the surrounding plains. Now the land is little more than arid desert, thanks to persistent drought and over-grazing. The storm raged for hours. When it eased in the late afternoon and the sun appeared again, the village cockerels crowed, thinking that morning had come early.

14   The drought in north-west China is partly caused by shrinking run-off from nearby mountains, which because of the rising temperatures are now capped with less snow and ice than before. Glacier shrinkage is a phenomenon repeated across the world's mountain ranges, and I also saw it at first hand in Peru, standing dizzy with altitude sickness in the high Andes 5,200 metres above the capital, Lima, where one of the main water-supplying glaciers has shrunk by more than a kilometre during the past century.

15   A senior manager of Lima's water authority told me later how melting ice is now a critical threat to future freshwater supplies: this city of seven million is the world's second-largest desert metropolis after Cairo, and the mountains supply all its water through coastal rivers that pour down from the ice fields far above. It is the snows that keep the rivers running all year round—once the glaciers are gone, the rivers will flow only in the wet season. The same problem afflicts the Indian subcontinent: overwhelmingly dependent on the mighty Ganges, Indus and Brahmaputra rivers that flow from the Himalayas, hundreds of millions of people will suffer water shortages as their source glaciers decline over the coming century.

16   Unless alternative water supplies can be secured, Lima will be left depopulated, its people scattered as environmental refugees. This is a category already familiar to the residents of Tuvalu, a group of nine coral atolls in the middle of the Pacific. Tuvalu, together with Kiribati, the Maldives and many other island nations, has made its plight well known to the world community, and an evacuation plan—shifting 75 people each year to New Zealand—is already under way.

17   I saw at first hand how the islands are already affected by the rising sea level, paddling in knee-deep floodwaters during last year's spring tides, which submerged much of Funafuti and almost surrounded the airstrip. Later that same evening the country's first post-independence prime minister, Toaripi Lauti, told me of his shock at finding his own crop of *pulaka* (a root vegetable like taro, grown in sunken pits) dying from saltwater intrusion. He recalled how everyone had awoken one morning a few years previously to

find that one of the islets on the atoll's rim had disappeared from the horizon, washed over by the waves, its coconut trees smashed and destroyed by the rising sea.

18 However severe these unfolding climate-change impacts seem, they are—like the canary in the coal mine—just the first whispers of the holocaust that lies ahead if nothing is done to reduce greenhouse gas emissions. Scientists meeting under the banner of the UN-sponsored Intergovernmental Panel on Climate Change (IPCC) have predicted a warming during this century alone of up to six degrees Celsius, which would take the earth into dangerous uncharted waters. A few weeks ago, scientists at the UK's Hadley Centre reported that the warming might be even greater because of the complexities of the carbon cycle.

19 The IPCC's worst-case forecast of six degrees could prove almost unimaginably catastrophic. It took only six degrees of warming to spark the end-Permian mass extinction 251 million years ago, the worst crisis ever to hit life on earth (expertly chronicled by Michael Benton in *When Life Nearly Died*) which led to the deaths of 95 per cent of all species alive at the time.

20 If humanity is to avoid a similar fate, global greenhouse gas emissions need to be brought down to between 60 and 80 per cent below current levels—precisely the reverse of emissions forecasts recently produced by the International Energy Agency. A good start would be the ratification and speedy implementation of the Kyoto Protocol, which should be superseded after the following decade by the "contraction and convergence" model proposed by the Global Commons Institute in London (www.gci.org.uk), allocating equal per-person emissions rights among all the world's nations.

21 In the meantime, a network of campaigning groups is currently mobilising under the banner of "No new oil," demanding an end to the exploration and development of new fossil fuel reserves, on the basis that current reserves alone include enough oil, coal and gas utterly to destabilise the world's climate. Searching for more is just as illogical as it is wasteful.

22 Avoiding dangerous climate change and other large-scale environmental crises will need to become the key organising principle around which societies evolve. All the signs are that few in power realise this—least of all the current US administration, which has committed itself to a policy of wanton destructiveness, with control and exploitation of oil supplies a central theme.

23 We must abandon the old mindset that demands an oil-based economy, not just because it sparks wars and terrorism, but because the future of life on earth depends on leaving it behind.

Understanding Meaning

1. Some scientists believe that the debate about global warming is not over. What is Lynas's attitude toward those scientists?
2. What are some examples that Lynas found close to home that convinced him that the Earth's temperature is changing?
3. What other arguments does he present to prove that he is right?
4. How serious could a six-degree increase in temperature be?
5. What does Lynas suggest be done?
6. *CRITICAL THINKING.* Lynas presents detailed anecdotal evidence that the temperature in some parts of the world is changing to the extent that it is affecting the quality of life of the people living there. Does he establish a link between the changes in the Earth's temperature and human activity? In other words, does he establish that humans have caused the change in temperature?

Evaluating Strategy

1. What effect was Lynas trying to achieve in the first sentence? If you have read or heard others' ideas on global warming, do you think they would agree with Lynas?
2. *BLENDING THE MODES.* What types of evidence does Lynas base his opinions on? How did he get this evidence? What are some specific examples?
3. Does his evidence convince you that change is occurring, and in some cases at least, affecting the quality of life of people in various parts of the world? What strategies did he use that convinced you, or how could he have changed his strategy to present a stronger case?

Appreciating Language

1. How does Lynas refer to those who disagree with him? What does that reveal about his attitude toward their theories? Have you read works by seemingly reliable sources that disagree with Lynas?
2. What are some specific words that Lynas uses that reflect the seriousness of the situation?

Writing Suggestions

1. Write a paragraph in which you analyze the strengths and the weaknesses of Lynas's argument.
2. Some of the examples that Lynas provides are very detailed. Write two to three paragraphs in which you make use of one or two well-developed examples to establish a need for an environmental change in your former high school or in your community.
3. *COLLABORATIVE WRITING.* Discuss Lynas' article with a group of students. Lynas argues that oil exploration should be stopped. Does that sound realistic? Would stopping oil exploration only make the West more dependent on Middle Eastern oil? Would it force industry to develop alternative fuels? Write a paragraph stating the views of your group. If students have differing opinions, draft opposing statements.

JOHN TAYLOR GATTO

John Taylor Gatto (1935–) taught in New York City public schools for twenty-five years and was named the city's Teacher of the Year three times. He has published several books about public education, including Dumbing Us Down *(1992),* The Exhausted School *(1993), and* A Different Kind of Teacher *(2002). Since leaving teaching, Gatto has become a public speaker, addressing audiences at the White House and the NASA-Goddard Space Center.*

Why Schools Don't Educate

BEFORE YOU READ: *What was your schooling like? Did you get a good education? Were your teachers inspiring? What attitudes did the students have toward education, their teachers, their studies? Were students motivated to learn? What could have made your schools or teachers better?*

TIPS FOR READING: *In this section of a speech Gatto presented after receiving an award, he outlines the effects television and schools have had on children. As you read his list, consider if there could be other causes for the symptoms he describes.*

Words to Know:

fortitude	strength
temperance	moderation
abstraction	concept, idea
mentors	people who guide or assist others
proscribed	limited
inevitable	predictable
cosmetic	superficial
initiate	start
accumulation	buying or getting things
pathologies	diseases
façade	something superficial
indifferent	uncaring
transitory	fleeting
inextricably	unable to be separated
predestined	determined by fate
candor	honesty
bravado	bravery, daring
vacuum	emptiness

"Why Schools Don't Educate" by John Taylor Gatto, former New York State Teacher of the Year; author, of DUMBING US DOWN and THE UNDERGROUND HISTORY OF AMERICAN EDUCATION. Reprinted by permission of the author.

1   Two institutions at present control our children's lives—television and schooling, in that order. Both of these reduce the real world of wisdom, fortitude, temperance, and justice to a never-ending, nonstop abstraction. In centuries past, the time of a child and adolescent would be occupied in real work, real charity, real adventures, and the real search for mentors who might teach what one really wanted to learn. A great deal of time was spent in community pursuits, practicing affection, meeting and studying every level of the community, learning how to make a home, and dozens of other tasks necessary to becoming a whole man or woman.

2   But here is the calculus of time the children I teach must deal with:

3   Out of the 168 hours in each week, my children must sleep fifty-six. That leaves them 112 hours a week out of which to fashion a self.

4   My children watch fifty-five hours of television a week, according to recent reports. That leaves them fifty-seven hours a week in which to grow up.

5   My children attend school thirty hours a week; use about eight hours getting ready, going, and coming home; and spend an average of seven hours a week in homework—a total of forty-five hours. During that time they are under constant surveillance, have no private time or private space, and are disciplined if they try to assert individuality in the use of time or space. That leaves twelve hours a week out of which to create a unique consciousness. Of course my kids eat, too, and that takes some time—not much, because we've lost the tradition of family dining. If we allot three hours a week to evening meals we arrive at a net amount of private time for each child of nine hours.

6   It's not enough. It's not enough, is it? The richer the kid, of course, the less television he watches, but the rich kid's time is just as narrowly proscribed by a broader catalogue of commercial entertainments and his inevitable assignment to a series of private lessons in areas seldom of his choice.

7   And these things are, oddly enough, just a more cosmetic way to create dependent human beings, unable to fill their own hours, unable to initiate lines of meaning to give substance and pleasure to their existence. It's a national disease, this dependency and aimlessness, and I think schooling and television and lessons—the entire Chautauqua idea—have a lot to do with it.

8   Think of the things that are killing us as a nation: drugs, brainless competition, recreational sex, the pornography of violence, gambling, alcohol, and the worst pornography of all—lives devoted to buying things—accumulation as a philosophy. All are addictions of dependent personalities and that is what our brand of schooling must inevitably produce.

9   I want to tell you what the effect is on children of taking all their time—time they need to grow up—and forcing them to spend it on abstractions. No reform that doesn't attack these specific pathologies will be anything more than a facade.

10   1.   The children I teach are indifferent to the adult world. This defies the experience of thousands of years. A close study of what big people were up to was always the most exciting occupation of youth, but nobody wants to grow up these days, and who can blame them. Toys are us.

11   2.   The children I teach have almost no curiosity, and what little they do have is transitory; they cannot concentrate for very long, even on things they choose to do. Can you see a connection between the bells ringing again and again to change classes, and this phenomenon of evanescent attention?

12   3.   The children I teach have a poor sense of the future, of how tomorrow is inextricably linked to today. They live in a continuous present; the exact moment they are in is the boundary of their consciousness.

13   4.   The children I teach are ahistorical; they have no sense of how the past has predestined their own present, limiting their choices, shaping their values and lives.

14   5.   The children I teach are cruel to each other; they lack compassion for misfortune, they laugh at weakness, they have contempt for people whose need for help shows too plainly.

15   6.   The children I teach are uneasy with intimacy or candor. They cannot deal with genuine intimacy because of a lifelong habit of preserving a secret self inside an outer personality made up of artificial bits and pieces, of behavior borrowed from television or acquired to manipulate teachers. Because they are not who they represent themselves to be, the disguise wears thin in the presence of intimacy, so intimate relationships have to be avoided.

16   7.   The children I teach are materialistic, following the lead of schoolteachers who materialistically "grade" everything—and television mentors who offer everything in the world for sale.

17   8.   The children I teach are dependent, passive, and timid in the presence of new challenges. This timidity is frequently masked by surface bravado or by anger or aggressiveness, but underneath is a vacuum without fortitude.

18   I could name a few other conditions that school reform will have to tackle if our national decline is to be arrested, but by now you will have grasped my thesis, whether you agree with it or not. Either schools, television, or both have caused these pathologies. It's a simple matter of arithmetic. Between schooling and television, all the time children have is eaten up. That's what has destroyed the American family; it no longer is a factor in the education of its own children.

Understanding Meaning

1. How, in Gatto's view, are television and schools linked in children's lives?
2. According to Gatto, how has television affected children's views of the world and others? How do children treat other children?
3. Gatto states that schoolchildren are "cruel" and "passive." Can one be both cruel and passive? What can be the effect of pent-up energy and stunted creativity?
4. Gatto observes that children are materialistic. How much of this do you feel is caused by television and how much by the values of their parents?
5. Do Gatto's observations explain why many people advocate school choice and homeschooling? Why or why not?
6. *CRITICAL THINKING.* Gatto remarks that "children live in a continuous present" without a sense of past and future. Is this a natural attribute of childhood or something induced by television? Doesn't television teach children something about history, even if simplified and distorted?

Evaluating Strategy

1. How effective is Gatto's use of numbered steps?
2. All of Gatto's eight points open with "The children I teach. . . ." This is repetition suited to a speech. Does it help hammer home his ideas to a listening audience? Does it seem less effective in print?
3. What risk does a writer take in criticizing children? How might parents respond?

Appreciating Language

1. Gatto uses the word *ahistorical.* How would you define this word?
2. Gatto calls "being devoted to buying things" the "worst pornography of all." Is "pornography" an effective word choice?

Writing Suggestions

1. Write a paragraph detailing the effects television has had on your generation or on your children. Do your observations match Gatto's?

2. Write a brief narrative about an elementary school experience that truly taught you something. Did it occur in the context of the traditional classroom?

3. *COLLABORATIVE WRITING.* Discuss Gatto's article with a group of students. Record their observations about school reform. Select the major ideas you come up with and write a letter to the school board suggesting ways to improve education.

NANCY KALISH

Nancy Kalish lives in New York City and has published articles about relationships and parenting in Self, Reader's Digest, Family Life, Redbook, *and* Parenting.

"My Son Doesn't Act Like a Boy": What It's Like to Have a Child Who Challenges Gender Stereotypes

BEFORE YOU READ: *In this article, published in* Family Life *in 2001, Kalish observes the way parents react when their small children adopt interests or characteristics associated with the opposite sex. If a girl plays with toy trucks or imitates a male superhero, she may be seen as breaking a stereotype. However, if a boy plays with dolls or imitates a female character, parents are more likely to suspect some kind of developmental problem and seek professional help.*

TIPS FOR READING: *Watch the headings that Kalish provides. They are an accurate guide to what she covers in each section of the essay and make her structure easy to follow.*

Words to Know:
burgeoning	**flourishing; growing or developing rapidly**
aberrant	**deviating from what is normal or typical**

TIPS FOR WRITING: *Your writing may not be long enough to need headings, but have a plan as clear as Kalish's so that your readers can see how the parts of your paragraph or essay fit together.*

1   From an early age, Robert Samuels,* now 8, has choreographed dance routines and performed them at home. When he was 4, he loved to wear red, sparkly shoes at school; he still enjoys playing with dolls. "In preschool, everyone accepted his behavior," says his mother, Annabeth Samuels,* of San Jose, California. "But at his next school, we were advised to talk to a psychologist about gender issues. Instead, my husband told me to really look at Robert—he's a happy, confident child—and realize that taking such a step may make him feel abnormal." Even though the parents vetoed professional help, they could still see that, in class, their son "was becoming a poster child for boys who were different," says Samuels.

"My Son Doesn't Act Like a Boy" by Nancy Kalish from FAMILY LIFE, April 1, 2001.

2 What does this type of behavior really mean—if anything? Parents, psychologists, and even kids themselves are struggling with this question. Through feminism and the burgeoning men's movement, we've blurred what used to be recognized as the line between male and female roles. Today, few adults would question a girl who would rather play with a soccer ball than with Barbie. But the issue isn't as simple for boys.

3 Because while we may cheer for the young hero of the film *Billy Elliot* in his struggle to become a ballet dancer, some of us wouldn't eagerly applaud our own sons if they chose such a traditionally feminine pursuit.

4 Listen in as parents share their feelings about raising boys in a society that is still shockingly hard on those who don't conform to stereotypes.

Where Gender Identity Starts

5 At age 3, Timmy Moore* refused to answer unless people called him Cinderella. "Even the pediatrician had to say, 'Okay, Cinderella, you're next,' or Timmy wouldn't go into the examination room," says his mom, Carol Moore,* of Seattle.

6 But "pretending to be a character of the opposite sex is not necessarily a sign of gender confusion," explains Gayle Peterson, Ph.D., a family therapist in Berkeley, California, and author of *Making Healthy Families.* To a child, Cinderella could represent kindness, nurturing, or just plain goodness—all qualities worth encouraging.

7 According to William S. Pollack, Ph.D., assistant clinical professor of psychiatry at Harvard Medical School and author of *Real Boys: Rescuing Our Sons from the Myths of Boyhood,* this type of exploration is healthy and even necessary—though that doesn't make it any less puzzling to parents.

8 While it's easy to say "boys will be boys," typical male (or female) behavior isn't as biologically determined as many of us think. Gender identity is far from fully formed at birth, and it continues to develop throughout early childhood.

9 Starting around age 5, most kids experience an intense period of identification with their own sex. "Boys usually become supermacho and girls superfeminine," explains Ellen Galinsky, author of *The Preschool Years.* "They can be very unforgiving of a child who hasn't reached that point."

When the Teasing Begins

10 It's when a kid doesn't conform and starts to be taunted that many parents first realize there's a problem. "Timmy came home crying because another

boy told him that only girls play with Barbies, and it was hard to know how to comfort him," says Moore. "My heart breaks because all he wants to do is be himself. I wish he wasn't into dolls, but I don't want him to think there's anything wrong with him. So I just said, 'Well, that's not true. You're a boy and you play with Barbies, and that's okay.'"

11   Sometimes it's not just classmates who pass harsh judgment, but other adults, which leads to more parental anxiety and confusion. "We thought the school psychologist wanted to talk about some adjustment issues Julian* was having," says Steve Shore,* a dad from West Hartford, Connecticut. "But when I called her, all she wanted to discuss was why Julian sometimes dressed up in girls' costumes during free playtime. When I admitted that my wife had just bought him a girl's costume to wear at home, the psychologist said that was a big mistake. She made me feel like we were encouraging aberrant behavior. I was upset—I felt ambushed by the school."

12   Criticism can also come from closer to home. "My father is very conservative and had tremendous difficulty accepting that Robert played with Barbies," says Samuels, who recalls that the turning point came when her son matter-of-factly explained to his grandfather that he played with dolls because he liked them. Being forthright with family while continuing to support the child is a smart approach, says Pollack. "To shame the grandparents for their feelings doesn't help. There needs to be less blaming and more listening to what the child really wants in order to move in a positive direction for change."

13   The Samuelses make a point of allowing Robert to pursue his interests. "What matters is that I haven't lost my connection with my son," explains his mom. She and his dad have also joined Supporting Our Sons (www.supportingoursons.org), a group dedicated to "helping boys break out of the gender straitjacket," according to Pollack, who is on the board of directors.

14   Lisen Stromberg, the organization's president, explains, "Girls can be anything they want to be, but we still need to expand the code of acceptable male behavior, whether it's allowing boys to be more emotional or to take up dance." Stromberg's crusade grew out of personal experience: When her son was 3, a favorite dress-up costume was a princess gown. "His choice raised eyebrows, but no one batted an eye when my daughter went through her truck phase," she says. "I'm glad for that, but it's a sad double standard."

How the Issue Intensifies

15 For older boys who enjoy pursuits labeled girlish, the situation gets tougher. Shame and fear of their parents' reactions can drive them to battle their tormentors on their own—sometimes with disastrous results. "Rich* has always preferred acting to sports," says his mom, Roberta Folkers,* of Gary, Indiana. Her son is active in local theater and school plays, and takes both voice and dance classes. "But football and basketball are big here," notes Folkers. "When Rich started middle school, the other kids got on his case for not playing. They wrote 'gay' on his locker and tripped him when he went to the blackboard."

16 A once-happy kid, Rich, then 11, became angry and combative. His worried parents had no idea why he was so upset—until the day he made a fake bomb threat on his home and tried to pin the blame on his abusers. This cry for help got everyone's attention. Still, the school's effort to stop the bullying only made the boys tease him more. Folkers homeschooled Rich for a time, then enrolled him in a private school where, fortunately, the kids seem more open-minded. But now that the tuition money has run out, he must return to his old public school next year. Says Folkers, "We can hardly bear to think about it."

Why Parents Really Worry

17 Even when the situation is not quite so desperate, raising a child who doesn't conform to gender stereotypes brings up all sorts of disturbing questions for parents. The first: Did I do something to confuse my child?

18 "When Aidan's* girlish behavior—dressing up and playing with dolls—didn't stop, I had to ask myself: Was I too smothering? Was my husband not home enough?" says Grace Shickler,* a mother of five from Boulder, Colorado, whose son is now 10. "The guilt was awful." A child psychologist reassured her that she wasn't responsible for Aidan's likes and dislikes, but that wasn't the end of it. "He wanted dolls for Christmas. If his sister asked for a baseball bat, we gave it to her. So I felt he should get what he wanted too. He did—and we've had to make this sort of decision over and over again."

19 Shickler did the right thing, says Peterson. "Playing with dolls won't have any effect on his masculinity beyond perhaps helping to make him a more sensitive, nurturing man," she explains. "Parents shouldn't attribute so much meaning to something so innocent and should support their child's needs. Otherwise, he may feel he has to choose between his gender and his natural

inclinations." The result: A boy who's macho on the outside but has low self-esteem and continues to display cross-gender behavior behind your back.

20   When a kid's being picked on, Pollack notes, reassurance is key. Say, "It's okay to be who you are and to make the choices you do. You are unique, and we love you." Then, assuming your child isn't in danger, work together to stop the teasing.

21   Still, there's another question that some parents are too uncomfortable to even voice: Does this mean my son will be gay? And am I truly open-minded and ready to make a stand for my child—or do I wish I didn't have to?

22   Even though her then 4-year-old son, William,* hadn't shown any interest in typical boy stuff, Isabelle McGinley,* a mom in Pittsburgh, was still thrown when he wanted to be Dorothy from *The Wizard of Oz* for Halloween. She felt this request crossed a line. "I worried that it meant he would be gay," she says. "My husband and I consider ourselves liberals, but it's still difficult to accept when this is your kid—we're concerned about our culture's prejudice. As awful as it is to say, I don't want to have to deal with it as a parent. Raising a straight kid is hard enough."

23   Still, McGinley allowed William to wear the costume. "I hoped this phase would pass, and it did," she explains. A few months later, William discovered Pokemon, and he quickly forged a bond with the other boys in his class. "Now he goes around growling all the time and being supermacho," reports McGinley. "And though I know it's no proof that he's straight, I'm embarrassed to say that I'm relieved."

24   Rich Folkers's mom has experienced some eye-opening personal growth. "My husband always said, 'Let Rich be who he is.' But I just couldn't. His younger sister is athletic and popular, and I wanted him to fit in that way, too, so he wouldn't be teased," says Folkers. "The reality is that he just doesn't, and I've had to consider that he might be gay. It's not what we concentrate on, but if he is, I'm going to have to accept it."

25   In fact, there are conflicting opinions as to whether cross-gender behavior in childhood means a kid will be homosexual. It's also possible for either a macho-acting 8-year-old boy or a superfeminine girl to grow up to be gay, says Pollack. "We need a broader view of what gender can be," he insists.

26   "The real challenge for me," says Samuels, "is to make sure Robert knows that—whatever he does—I'm going to support and love him. And that's not just about sexuality. It's about being a parent."

---

*Names have been changed to protect privacy.

Understanding Meaning

1. What are some of the different reactions that parents quoted in this article have when their sons don't act "like boys"?
2. According to Kalish, why do boys around the age of five start to be more critical of those among them who still act in ways considered feminine?
3. Why is it that parents really worry, according to Kalish? Are their concerns usually justified?
4. In the examples Kalish gives, how do the parents tend to react to behavior that is not typical "boy" behavior? How do other non-specialist adults tend to react? How do the psychologists and psychiatrists respond?
5. *CRITICAL THINKING.* How do you think you might have reacted in the place of Robert Samuels's parents, when they saw their son "was becoming a poster child for boys who were different"? Would you have reacted as his parents did?
6. *CRITICAL THINKING.* Why is it perceived as acceptable for a girl to engage in "male" activities while the opposite is seen as aberrant?

Evaluating Strategy

1. *BLENDING THE MODES.* Reread paragraph 4. What does that short paragraph tell us about how to expect the rest of the essay to be developed?
2. How helpful are the headings that introduce the various sections of the essay?
3. How successful is the use of examples as a primary type of support in this essay?

Appreciating Language

1. Does Kalish use a vocabulary that is easy for the average reader to understand? Are there any technical terms?
2. What difference does it make that we are able to hear some of the voices of individual parents who have had the problems being discussed?
3. Kalish does not use the real names of some of the boys and their parents. What does that in itself suggest about boys who prefer activities usually associated with girls?

Writing Suggestions

1. Write a paragraph in which you explain whether you agree or disagree with how Robert Samuels's parents handled his behavior.

2. Do you feel that parents can teach their sons to avoid behavior that will keep them from being teased without harming their individuality? Are boys harmed more, for instance, by being teased for not being "masculine" enough than they would be by having their parents simply say, "No, you cannot wear that to school" or "No, I am not letting you dress like a princess"? Write one or more paragraphs explaining your views.

3. Write a paragraph describing your own gender. Did you always know how a male or female should act? Did you experience any conflict growing up?

4. *COLLABORATIVE WRITING.* Discuss this essay with a group of students and create a list of suggestions you would give parents of a boy who engaged in "female" behavior. If students have conflicting advice, consider drafting opposing lists.

ELLEN GOODMAN

Ellen Goodman (1941–) was born in Massachusetts and graduated from Radcliffe College. She worked for Newsweek *and the* Detroit Free Press *before joining the* Boston Globe *in 1967. Her column "At Large" has been widely syndicated since 1976. As an essayist and television commentator, Goodman has discussed feminism, changes in family life, sexual harassment, and male and female relationships. Her essays have been collected in several books, including* Close to Home *(1979),* At Large *(1981), and* Turning Points *(1979).*

Girls Will Be Girls. Unfortunately.

BEFORE YOU READ: *In this nationally syndicated column, published in 2002, Goodman uses the term "really mean girls" to describe those who are adept at hurtful gossip and nasty conversation—usually meant to destroy the reputation of other girls or women. Goodman sees this often self-destructive hostility as a reaction to the general powerlessness women experience in a male-dominated culture.*

TIPS FOR READING: *Goodman is amazed that the meanness of adolescent girls is considered news, then considers how girls' meanness is different from boys'. She explains why meanness should not be accepted as being inevitable. Parents, in her view, should let young people know when their behavior is unacceptable, in spite of what they see in the media.*

Words to Know:

Zeitgeist	the spirit of the time
inundated	to cover with, as with a flood
Alpha	aggressive; leader
relational aggression	destructively hostile to others
dourly	sullenly
revisionist	a person who revises or favors the revision of some accepted theory
empathic	capacity to understand another's feelings
perpetrators	those who perform something, like a crime
constricting	making smaller or narrower; limiting
ruefully	sorrowfully
seminal	like a seed in having a potential for development

"Girls Will Be Girls. Unfortunately." by Ellen Goodman from NATIONAL POST, May 25, 2002.

1   You have to hand it to Ally McBeal. In with the Zeitgeist, out with the Zeitgeist—and without ever gaining an ounce.

2   Oooh, was that mean? Well, never mind. Meanness is the point.

3   In the final episode of the series, everybody's favourite neurotic was driven out of town by a pack of 10-year old girls. Ally gave up her job, her friends, her apartment to rescue her daughter Maddie—product of a college egg donation—who was being tormented by classmates otherwise known as the RMGs: the really mean girls.

4   Does this final twist of the plot sound like something lifted from the latest media mania? It should. For the past several months, mean girls have been everywhere. On best-seller lists, on talk shows, in magazines. We've been inundated with anxiety about Alpha females, queen bees, girl bullies and RMGs on a rampage of "relational aggression."

5   Three years ago, right after the Columbine killings, everyone seemed to be worried about the schoolboy culture. Now suddenly everyone seems to be in a panic about the schoolgirl culture.

6   The fact that girls can be mean to each other has been designated "news." The power of girls to harm each other has been dourly and duly described as "on the increase." Ted Koppel even put this revelation on *Nightline*, proclaiming, "I am just fascinated by this."

7   Frankly, I doubt that this is news to any woman past fourth grade. Margaret Atwood described this girl world first and best in her novel *Cat's Eye*. When Patricia O'Brien and I went to write about women's friendships in *I Know Just What You Mean*, we saw that "cliques are to girls as bullies are to boys." It's out there. But maybe there's a new, or at least revisionist, subtext to this bad-girl news. See, girls aren't all empathic, they're also vicious. See, girls aren't victims, they're perpetrators. See, girls don't lose their voice at adolescence; it just turns to whisper campaigns. See, it isn't just boys who are aggressive; so are girls. Girls just do it with words instead of their fists.

8   Bingo. Boys and girls are the same. They may be awful, but they're equally awful. Case closed.

9   I think it's useful to hold the adolescent culture up to the adult light. But it's also useful to keep a little perspective.

10 When Rachel Simmons, author of *Odd Girl Out*, told Oprah that being shunned was "meaner" than getting hit, I wanted a time out. Wasn't Columbine worse than a cruel instant message? More to the point, this isn't a contest. Sexism, if I remember Women's Studies 101, doesn't only affect women. Both genders are pushed into narrow, constricting roles. And bullies, of the male or female persuasion, are the gender police.

11   Marie Wilson, president of the Ms. Foundation, notes that girls turn on each other just as the boy-girl thing clicks in. They look at the world and find that their mothers and other women aren't really in charge. If they can't have power upward, she says ruefully, "they control downward." She adds, "It's the way boys are masculinized and the way girls are feminized that turns some of them into bullies."

12   Think of it as "informal initiation rites," says psychologist Carol Gilligan, who's done seminal work on girls. In her new book, *The Birth of Pleasure*, an elegant and powerful narrative that runs through mythology, memoir and literature, Gilligan observes that boys begin this initiation as young as five. "The cultural force driving this initiation surfaces in the often brutal teasing and shaming of boys who resist or do not fit cultural codes of masculinity."

13   At adolescence, she adds, girls "experience a similar initiation into womanhood . . . manifest in the often vicious games of inclusion and exclusion." Gilligan has compared adolescent girls to "sheepdogs." When one moves out of the pack, they herd her back in line. Girls are forced to toe the line, especially in sexual behaviour and appearance.

14   But why, she asks skeptically, has the old-girl culture come into the spotlight now? It's good to talk about what once felt shameful. But there's no proof that the old-girl culture is stronger today. The "mean girls" media mania, says Gilligan, "gives it a feeling of inevitability. I don't think it is inevitable."

15   As parents, we also have initiation rites when our children recycle our own experiences. It's only inevitable if we decide boys will be boys and girls will be girls. They will be unless we step in and create new ways for them to feel strong and safe.

16   Ally McBeal's law firm always did seem like a bad high school. Now she ends her run by giving up to the RMGs. Too bad for her—and for her daughter—that she didn't stand and fight.

Understanding Meaning

1. What is Goodman's purpose in the essay? How clear was that purpose as you read the essay?
2. What is the relationship between the television show *Ally McBeal* and her main point?
3. A few years after the school shootings in Columbine, Goodman saw a shift in focus away from "the schoolboy culture" to "the schoolgirl culture." Does she seem to agree that the meanness of girls and boys is really about the same?

4. According to this article, how does the meanness of boys and girls differ?
5. *CRITICAL THINKING.* Do you feel that the mean treatment of girls by other girls is worse because of all the attention it has gotten from the media? Explain.

Evaluating Strategy

1. How does Goodman make use of the once-popular series *Ally McBeal*? Why was she disappointed by the ending of the series?
2. How does she get across her idea that "Meanness is the point"?
3. Is Goodman's casual style appropriate, given her subject and audience? Why or why not?
4. Does Goodman really mean it at the end of paragraph 8 when she says, "Case closed"?

Appreciating Language

1. What is Goodman trying to suggest when she starts the second paragraph, "Oooh, was that mean?"
2. What is the effect of the parallel sentences at the end of paragraph 7 that all begin, "See . . . "?

Writing Suggestions

1. *COLLABORATIVE WRITING.* Discuss this essay in a small group. Have you seen depictions of RMGs—really mean girls—in movies and television shows? How have they been portrayed? Have they been used for humor or to expose a serious problem? Record comments by the group. Organize responses by division or classification.
2. Write a paragraph about how television influences the behavior of high school students.
3. Write a paragraph stating whether you agree or disagree with Goodman's view that boys and girls are mean in different ways.

GROWING UP NATIVE
Carol Geddes

1   I remember it was cold. We were walking through a swamp near our home in the Yukon bush. Maybe it was fall and moose-hunting season. I don't know. I think I was about four years old at the time. The muskeg was too springy to walk on, so people were taking turns carrying me—passing me from one set of arms to another. The details about where we were are vague, but the memory of those arms and the feeling of acceptance I had is one of the most vivid memories of my childhood. It didn't matter who was carrying me—there was security in every pair of arms. That response to children is typical of the native community. It's the first thing I think of when I cast my mind back to the Yukon bush, where I was born and lived with my family.

2   I was six years old when we moved out of the bush, first to Teslin, where I had a hint of the problems native people face, then to Whitehorse, where there was unimaginable racism. Eventually I moved to Ottawa and Montreal, where I further discovered that to grow up native in Canada is to feel the sting of humiliation and the boot of discrimination. But it is also to experience the enviable security of an extended family and to learn to appreciate the richness of the heritage and traditions of a culture most North Americans have never been lucky enough to know. As a film-maker, I have tried to explore these contradictions, and our triumph over them, for the half-million aboriginals who are part of the tide of swelling independence of the First Nations today.

3   But I'm getting ahead of myself. If I'm to tell the story of what it's like to grow up native in northern Canada, I have to go back to the bush where I was born, because there's more to my story than the hurtful stereotyping that depicts Indian people as drunken welfare cases. Our area was known as 12-mile (it was 12 miles from another tiny village). There were about 40 people living there—including 25 kids, eight of them my brothers and sisters—in a sort of family compound. Each family had its own timber plank house for sleeping, and there was one large common kitchen area with gravel on the ground and a tent frame over it. Everybody would go there and cook meals together. In summer, my grandmother always had a smudge fire going to smoke fish and tan moose hides. I can remember the cosy warmth of the fire, the smell of good food, and always having someone to talk to. We kids had built-in playmates and would spend hours running in the bush, picking berries, building rafts on the lake and playing in abandoned mink cages.

4   One of the people in my village tells a story about the day the old lifestyle began to change. He had been away hunting in the bush for about a month. On his way back, he heard a strange sound coming from far away. He ran up the crest of a hill, looked over the top of it and saw a bulldozer. He had never seen or heard of such a thing before and he couldn't imagine what it was. We didn't have magazines or newspapers in our village, and the people didn't know that the Alaska Highway was being built as a defence against a presumed Japanese invasion during the Second World War. That was the beginning of the end of the Teslin Tlingit people's way of life. From that moment on, nothing turned back to the way it was. Although there were employment opportunities for my father and uncles, who were young men at the time, the speed and force with which the Alaska Highway rammed through the wilderness caused tremendous upheaval for Yukon native people.

5   It wasn't as though we'd never experienced change before. The Tlingit Nation, which I belong to, arrived in the Yukon from the Alaskan coast around the turn of the century. They were the middlemen and women between the Russian traders and the Yukon inland Indians. The Tlingit gained power and prestige by trading European products such as metal goods and cloth for the rich and varied furs so much in fashion in Europe. The Tlingit controlled Yukon trading because they controlled the trading routes through the high mountain passes. When trading ceased to be an effective means of survival, my grandparents began raising wild mink in cages. Mink prices were really high before and during the war, but afterwards the prices went plunging down. So, although the mink pens were still there when I was a little girl, my father mainly worked on highway construction and hunted in the bush. The Yukon was then, and still is in some ways, in a transitional period—from living off the land to getting into a European wage-based economy.

6   As a young child, I didn't see the full extent of the upheaval. I remember a lot of togetherness, a lot of happiness while we lived in the bush. There's a very strong sense of family in the native community, and a fondness for children, especially young children. Even today, it's like a special form of entertainment if someone brings a baby to visit. That sense of family is the one thing that has survived all the incredible difficulties native people have had. Throughout a time of tremendous problems, the extended family system has somehow lasted, providing a strong circle for people to survive in. When parents were struggling with alcoholism or had to go away to find work, when one of the many epidemics swept through the community, or when a marriage broke up and one parent left, aunts, uncles, and grandparents would try to fill those roles. It's been very important to me in terms of emotional support to be able to rely on my extended family. There are still times when such support keeps me going.

7   Life was much simpler when we lived in the bush. Although we were poor and wore the same clothes all year, we were warm enough and had plenty to eat. But even as a youngster, I began to be aware of some of the problems we would face later on. Travelling missionaries would come and impose themselves on us, for example. They'd sit at our campfire and read the Bible to us and lecture us about how we had to live a Christian life. I remember being very frightened by stories we heard about parents sending their kids away to live with white people who didn't have any children. We thought those people were mean and that if we were bad, we'd be sent away too. Of course, that was when social workers were scooping up native children and adopting them out to white families in the south. The consequences were usually disastrous for the children who were taken away—alienation, alcoholism, and suicide, among other things. I knew some of those kids. The survivors are still struggling to recover.

8   The residential schools were another source of misery for the kids. Although I didn't have to go, my brothers and sisters were there. They told stories about having their hair cut off in case they were carrying head lice, and of being forced to do hard chores without enough food to eat. They were told that the Indian culture was evil, that Indian people were bad, that their only hope was to be Christian. They had to stand up and say things like "I've found the Lord," when a teacher told them to speak. Sexual abuse was rampant in the residential school system.

9   By the time we moved to Whitehorse, I was excited about the idea of living in what I thought of as a big town. I'd had a taste of the outside world from books at school in Teslin (a town of 250 people), and I was tremendously curious about what life was like. I was hungry for experiences such as going to the circus. In fact, for a while, I was obsessed with stories and pictures about the circus, but then when I was 12 and saw my first one, I was put off by the condition and treatment of the animals.

10   Going to school in Whitehorse was a shock. The clash of native and white values was confusing and frightening. Let me tell you a story. The older boys in our community were already accomplished hunters and fishermen, but since they had to trap beaver in the spring and hunt moose in the fall, and go out trapping in the winter as well, they missed a lot of school. We were all in one classroom and some of my very large teenage cousins had to sit squeezed into little desks. These guys couldn't read very well. We girls had been in school all along, so, of course, we were better readers. One day the teacher was trying to get one of the older boys to read. She was typical of the teachers at that time, insensitive and ignorant of cultural complexities. In an increasingly loud voice, she kept commanding him to "Read it, read it." He couldn't. He sat there completely still, but I could see that he was breaking

into a sweat. The teacher then said, "Look, she can read it," and she pointed to me, indicating that I should stand up and read. For a young child to try to show up an older boy is wrong and totally contrary to native cultural values, so I refused. She told me to stand up and I did. My hands were trembling as I held my reader. She yelled at me to read and when I didn't she smashed her pointing stick on the desk to frighten me. In terror, I wet my pants. As I stood there fighting my tears of shame, she said I was disgusting and sent me home. I remember feeling this tremendous confusion, on top of my humiliation. We were always told the white teachers knew best, and so we had to do whatever they said at school. And yet I had a really strong sense of receiving mixed messages about what I was supposed to do in the community and what I was supposed to do at school.

11   Pretty soon I hated school. Moving to a predominantly white high school was even worse. We weren't allowed to join anything the white kids started. We were the butt of jokes because of our secondhand clothes and moose meat sandwiches. We were constantly being rejected. The prevailing attitude was that Indians were stupid. When it was time to make course choices in class—between typing and science, for example—they didn't even ask the native kids, they just put us all in typing. You get a really bad image of yourself in a situation like that. I bought into it. I thought we were awful. The whole experience was terribly undermining. Once, my grandmother gave me a pretty little pencil box. I walked into the classroom one day to find the word "squaw" carved on it. That night I burned it in the wood stove. I joined the tough crowd and by the time I was 15 years old, I was more likely to be leaning against the school smoking a cigarette than trying to join in. I was burned out from trying to join the system. The principal told my father there was no point in sending me back to school so, with a Grade 9 education, I started to work at a series of menial jobs.

12   Seven years later something happened to me that would change my life forever. I had moved to Ottawa with a man and was working as a waitress in a restaurant. One day, a friend invited me to her place for coffee. While I was there, she told me she was going to university in the fall and showed me her reading list. I'll never forget the minutes that followed. I was feeling vaguely envious of her and once again, inferior. I remember taking the paper in my hand, seeing the books on it and realizing, Oh, my God, I've read these books! It hit me like a thunderclap. I was stunned that books I had read were being read in university. University was for white kids, not native kids. We were too stupid, we didn't have the kind of mind it took to do those things. My eyes moved down the list, and my heart started beating faster and faster as I suddenly realized I could go to university, too!

13   My partner at the time was a loving supportive man who helped me in every way. I applied to the university immediately as a mature student but

when I had to write Grade 9 on the application, I was sure they'd turn me down. They didn't. I graduated five years later, earning a Bachelor of Arts in English and philosophy (with distinction). . . .

14   Today, there's a glimmer of hope that more of us native people will overcome the obstacles that have tripped us up ever since we began sharing this land. Some say our cultures are going through a renaissance. Maybe that's true. Certainly there's a renewed interest in native dancing, acting, and singing, and in other cultural traditions. Even indigenous forms of government are becoming strong again. But we can't forget that the majority of native people live in urban areas and continue to suffer from alcohol and drug abuse and the plagues of a people who have lost their culture and have become lost themselves. And the welfare system is the insidious glue that holds together the machine of oppression of native people.

15   Too many non-native people have refused to try to understand the issues behind our land claims. They make complacent pronouncements such as "Go back to your bows and arrows and fish with spears if you want aboriginal rights. If not, give it up and assimilate into white Canadian culture." I don't agree with that. We need our culture, but there's no reason why we can't preserve it and have an automatic washing machine and a holiday in Mexico, as well.

16   The time has come for native people to make our own decisions. We need to have self-government. I have no illusions that it will be smooth sailing—there will be trial and error and further struggle. And if that means crawling before we can stand up and walk, so be it. We'll have to learn through experience.

17   While we're learning, we have a lot to teach and give to the world—a holistic philosophy, a way of living with the earth, not disposing of it. It is critical that we all learn from the elders that an individual is not more important than a forest; we know that we're here to live on and with the earth, not to subdue it.

18   The wheels are in motion for a revival, for change in the way native people are taking their place in Canada. I can see that we're equipped, we have the tools to do the work. We have an enormous number of smart, talented, moral Indian people. It's thrilling to be a part of this movement.

19   Someday, when I'm an elder, I'll tell the children the stories: about the bush, about the hard times, about the renaissance, and especially about the importance of knowing your place in your nation.

Geddes, Carol. "Growing Up Native." *Canadian Content.* Ed. Sarah Norton and Nell Waldman. 4th ed. Toronto: Harcourt, 2000. 41–46.

Questions for Discussion

1. What is the author's purpose in this essay? Which paragraphs most clearly state that purpose?
2. This narrative is filled with specific detail. Choose one paragraph and identify the details the author has included to help the reader form a vivid mental picture.
3. Look at paragraph 10. What does the anecdote in that paragraph tell you about the author? About her teacher? Find another anecdote in the essay that also illustrates the clash between two cultures.
4. A good narrative introduces the scene and major character(s) in the opening paragraph. Consider Geddes' first paragraph. Do you think it is effective? Why?
5. How does the concluding paragraph contribute to the unity of the piece?

APPENDIX:

APA Format

APA Format and Documentation[1]

Formatting an APA-Style Research Paper

TITLE PAGE

In APA style, a research paper or essay requires a separate title page. On the title page (and all other pages) include a running header consisting of an abbreviated version of your title and the page number. Leave 1.25 cm of space between the title abbreviation and the numeral. Choose a concise title that identifies the subject of your paper, and then shorten it for the running header. Capitalize main words, but don't underline, italicize, or put quotation marks around your title. Centre the title in the upper half of the page (quadruple-space it from the top of the page). If the title is more than one line, double-space between the lines.

After the title, centre your name, the course you are preparing the paper for, the professor's name, and the date of submission; double-space between each of these elements. A sample APA-style title page follows. The italicized words to the left of the page identify the components of the title page.

---

[1]The information in Appendix B has been adapted from Centennial College's *Revised Style Sheet: A Guide to Format and Documentation.* Permission is gratefully acknowledged.

Multigenerational Families   1

Title

Conflict in Multigenerational Families

Name

Wendy Garriques

Course number

CS 101

Professor's name

Professor Xiu

Date submitted

April 27, 2005

HEADER, PAGE NUMBERS, AND SPACING

Number your pages consecutively throughout the paper, beginning with the title page and ending with the last page of the References list. Use the right header function of your word processor and key in the abbreviated title and the page number. Include only your abbreviated title + 1.25 cm space + the numeral—no punctuation or *p*.

Double-space between all lines of your paper, including the title page, abstract, headings (if any), pages of the text itself, quotations, and References list. Indent all paragraphs 1.25 cm.

ABSTRACT

Some assignments require you to provide an abstract—a short summary of the contents of your whole paper. It should give the purpose of your paper and the key ideas; that is, it should give your reader a preview of your paper. An abstract is usually one paragraph long. It must be well organized and carefully written.

Type the abstract on a separate page that includes the running header and the page number (2). Centre the word "Abstract" at the top of the page. Type the abstract paragraph itself in block format (without indentation).

FIRST PAGE OF TEXT

On page 3 (following the title page and abstract), centre the full title of your research paper. Double-space, and begin the text of your essay.

Parenthetical Reference Citations

Parenthetical reference citations serve two functions: (1) they tell your reader that this material comes from somewhere else, and (2) they point the reader to full information about sources in the References list at the end of your paper.

To cite an author's work, name the author of the source in your own sentence and include the date of publication in parentheses immediately after the author's name. If you do not name the author in your sentence, put author's surname + comma + date in parentheses right after your quotation, summary, or paraphrase. (See the examples below.)

If you are quoting from a source, you must include in your parenthetical citation the page number(s) on which the quotation appears, using the abbreviation *p.* (page) or *pp.* (pages). Do not give page numbers if you are summarizing or paraphrasing, however. (See the examples below.)

Electronic sources (discussed below) do not follow the author/date-based citation method because they often do not have an identifiable author and rarely include page numbers.

EXAMPLES OF PARENTHETICAL CITATIONS: TRADITIONAL PRINT SOURCES

- **Author's name given in your paragraph**

Kevin Patterson (2000) writes about his sailing journey from British Columbia to the South Pacific and back: "Suffused with optimism and rum, I told Peter I wanted to sail to Tahiti" (p. 6).

For the entry for this source, see item 7 in the sample References list on page 511.

- **Author's name not given in your paragraph**

  Long voyages by sea, especially in small boats, present clear dangers depending on the ocean and the season of crossing: "The North Pacific is cold and volatile in the autumn and anyone who knew enough about the sea to consider sailing to Canada knew that much" (Patterson, 2000, p. 249).

- **No author named in source**

  Legislation to reduce the amount of pollution generated by large-scale vehicles has been on the federal agenda for some time: "Canada has said it will toughen pollution-emission rules for all new vehicles, ending a loophole that allowed less stringent standards for popular sport-utility vehicles and minivans" (Canada to toughen, 2002, p. A6).

When no author is named, as in the example above, give the first words of the title. For the entry for this source, see item 2 in the sample References list.

- **Source with two authors**

Name both in the order in which their names appear on the work.

  Norton and Green (2005) observe that inexperienced writers achieved superior results when they spent half the allotted time on planning and drafting, and the other half on revising.

If you do not name the authors in your own sentence, use an ampersand (&) instead of *and* in the parenthetical reference.

  One approach to writing recommends that students divide the process of revising into three steps or stages (Norton & Green, 2005).

- **Classical works**

The first time you quote or paraphrase from a classical work of literature (such as Shakespeare) or the Bible, identify in parentheses the version or edition you are using, and give the book, chapter, canto, act, scene, verse, and/or line numbers. Do not include this kind of source in your References list. The lines of such works are numbered systematically in all editions.

  In the Bible, it is clear that people who have suffered exile from their land are not allowed to subjugate others because they themselves have suffered and understand the suffering of the oppressed: "Also thou shalt not

oppress a stranger, seeing ye were strangers in the land of Egypt" Exodus
23:8 (King James Version).

Further information on APA parenthetical citations (e.g., two or more
books by the same author, a work in an edited anthology, a work cited in a
secondary source) can be found on the APA website (http://www.apa.org).

EXAMPLES OF PARENTHETICAL CITATIONS: ELECTRONIC SOURCES

If the electronic source lists an author, give the surname and the publication date in your reference citation. This is all the information your reader
needs in order to find the full bibliographical data in your References list.
Example:

> Planespotting is a popular hobby, even an obsession, for growing num-
> bers of people who are fascinated with aviation: "Some spotters take pho-
> tographs. Others make videotapes. But the majority flock to airports
> around the world, equipped with scanners and notepads with one goal
> in mind—recording the registration numbers painted on airplane tails"
> (Bourette, 2002).

The quotation in the example above comes from *Shift*, an online magazine.
(See item 1 in the sample References list.)

If the electronic source does not list an author, use the document title
(or a shortened version of the title) instead of the author's name.

> Statistics Canada calculates that the nation's infant mortality rate in 1997
> was 5.5 for every 1,000 live births (Statistics Canada, 2002).

The information in the example above comes from the Statistics Canada
website. (See item 9 in the sample References list.)

Electronic sources don't usually include page numbers or other naviga-
tion devices. If there are page, paragraph, or section numbers that could
guide your reader to the specific material being quoted, include them. Your
parenthetical reference should include the author's name (unless you've
mentioned it in your own paragraph), followed by a comma, the date, and
the sections or paragraph numbers, abbreviated as *par.* or *pars.* For example:

> In the short story "The Necklace," Mme. Loisel undergoes a dramatic
> change after she loses her friend's jewels:

The frightful debt must be paid. She would pay it. They dismissed the servant; they changed their rooms; they took an attic under the roof.

She learned the rough work of the household, the odious labors of the kitchen. She washed the dishes, wearing out her pink nails on the greasy pots and the bottoms of the pans. (Maupassant, 1907, pars. 98–99)

The quotation in the example above comes from an online edition of Guy de Maupassant's story "The Necklace."

If a source does not give page, paragraph, or section numbers that you can use to identify a quotation, give the author's name or the title in parentheses. If no publication date is given, use the date that you accessed the material in day-month-year format. If a reader needs to locate the source, Web browser search engines can help find it using keywords or phrases.

More information on the treatment of electronic sources can be found on the APA website (http://www.apa.org).

APA List of References

A page headed *References* is included at the end of your paper (see the sample References list). It gives detailed bibliographical information for all sources that you have quoted, summarized, or paraphrased in your essay.

The References list enables your reader to assess the extent of your research and to locate every source. In other documentation styles, this list is called Bibliography or Works Cited, but APA format prescribes *References* as the list heading.

Begin the References list on a new page. Two spaces below your header (abbreviated title + 1.25 cm space + page number), centre the word "References" on the page. Leave a double space between the title and the first entry, and double-space the entire document.

Begin each entry at the left margin. If the entry runs more than a single line—and most do—indent the second and subsequent lines 1.25 cm. (Use the five-space tab that you use for paragraph indentation.) This format is called a "hanging indent" and can be found in most word-processing packages.

Arrange the entries in your References list alphabetically, beginning with the first word in the entry (usually the surname of the author). If no author is listed, alphabetize by the first main word in the title, ignoring *A, An*, or *The*. For example, *The Canadian Encyclopedia* would be alphabetized under C, for Canadian. Do *not* number the entries.

BOOKS AND OTHER NONPERIODICAL WORKS

Below is the basic model for a book entry. (Note the capitalization, punctuation, and order of the information.) Leave one space between initials in author' names as well as after commas, colons, semicolons, and periods that separate parts of the reference citation. Give the author's surname, a comma, and initials only. Then, in parentheses, give the year the book was copyrighted. Only proper names and the first word of the title (and subtitle, if any) are capitalized, and the title/subtitle is italicized (or underlined). Use the first city if several cities are listed. Shorten the publisher's name (e.g., Alfred A. Knopf, Inc. to Knopf).

> Last name of author, Initials. (Year of Publication). *Title of book: Subtitle.* City: Publisher.

If you are citing an essay or chapter within a larger book, capitalize only the first word of the title (as above), but do not italicize the title or place in quotation marks.

> Turner, L. J. (2001). Truth or consequences. In S. Norton & B. Green, *The bare essentials, form A* (pp. 303–304). Toronto: Harcourt.

- **Book by one author**

> Patterson, K. (2000). *The water in between: A journey at sea.* Toronto: Vintage Canada.

> Turner, C. (2004). *Planet Simpson: How a cartoon masterpiece defined a generation.* Cambridge, MA: Da Capo.

- **Book by two authors**

> Leakey, R., & Lewin, R. (1992). *Origins reconsidered: In search of what makes us human.* New York: Doubleday.

- **Selection from an anthology or collection (with an editor)**

> Mistry, R. (2001). Journey to Dharmsala. In C. Meyer & B. Meyer (Eds.), *The reader: Contemporary essays and writing strategies* (pp. 38–51). Toronto: Prentice.

- Unidentified author

Roget's Thesaurus. (3rd ed.). (1998). New York: Random House.

PERIODICALS

Periodicals are publications that appear regularly at fixed intervals such as newspapers, magazines, and academic journals.

Begin your entry with the author's name (if available)—surname first followed by a comma—and initials. Then add the date in parentheses. For magazines and newspapers, give the year, followed by a comma and then the month and day. (For a magazine published once a month, give the month.) Do not abbreviate names of months. Reference entries for a newspaper include its name as it appears on the masthead (e.g., *The Globe and Mail*). Titles of periodicals are capitalized in the normal way.

Give page numbers for each article in your list. Cite all of the page numbers. For example, if the article begins on page 27 and concludes on page 29, follow the title with a comma and the span of pages (e.g., *Saturday Night,* 27–29). If the article is not printed on consecutive pages (if it begins, let's say, on pages 27 to 29 and concludes on page 40), provide all page numbers separated with commas: 27–29, 40.

In newspapers, the sections are usually paginated separately, so include the section number as well as the page number (e.g., *The Vancouver Sun,* pp. B1–2).

Note the order, punctuation, and capitalization in the model below.

> Author's last name, Initials. (Year, quarter, month, or month + day).
> Title of article. *Title of Periodical,* page numbers.

- Article in a scholarly journal

> Forrester, S., & Beggs, B. (2005, Winter). Gender and self-esteem in intramural sports. *Physical and Health Education Journal, 70*(4), 12–19.

> Lemire, J. A. (2001). Preparing nurse leaders: A leadership model. *Nursing Leadership Forum, 6*(2), 39–44.

In the examples above, note that the volume number is italicized as if it were part of the title, while the issue number (enclosed in parentheses) is not.

- **Article in a monthly magazine**

  Reece, E. (2005, April). Death of a mountain: Radical strip mining and the leveling of Appalachia. *Harper's,* 41–60.

- **Article in a weekly magazine**

  Hawaleshka, D. (2005, February 28). Power hungry. *Maclean's,* 22–23.

- **Article in a newspaper**

  Canada to toughen auto-emissions rules. (2002, April 5). *The Wall Street Journal,* p. A6.

Note that APA style requires you to include *p.* or *pp.* for page number(s) in newspaper entries, but not in entries for magazines or journals.

- **Review**

  Houpt, S. (2005, March 19). Spamalot a spoof to end all spoofs [Review of the play *Monty Python's Spamalot.*] *The Globe and Mail,* p. R7.

AUDIOVISUAL SOURCES

- **Movie or video recording**

  Moore, M. (Writer, Producer, Director). (2002). *Bowling for Columbine* [Motion picture]. Canada. Alliance Atlantis.

- **Television show**

  Neilson, L. (Performer). (2002, March 5). *Rock stars: The world of curling.* [Television Broadcast]. Toronto: Canadian Broadcasting Company. CBLT.

- **Radio show**

  Hallway Confidential. (2005, March 23). *Outfront* [Radio broadcast]. Toronto: CBC Radio One. Toronto.

ELECTRONIC SOURCES

Entries for electronic sources should identify the source and provide enough information to enable a reader to locate the material (e.g., author, title, publication information, and date). Be sure to include the URL (Uniform Resource Locator)—the sequence of words, abbreviations, numbers, and characters that identifies the source's location in cyberspace. You should also download and print the material you're using for your paper so that you can verify it if it is revised, unavailable, or inaccessible at a later date.

Do not use a hyphen to divide a URL over two lines, even if it is very long, because it introduces a symbol that will invalidate the URL. Put the URL on a single line, or break it only after a slash or before a period, even if doing so results in uneven lines. You can prevent your typed URLs from turning into hyperlinks (which don't print). In *Word 2000* and *Word 2003*, go into "Tools," choose "AutoCorrect," click on "AutoFormat As You Type," and delete the check mark in front of "Internet and network paths with hyperlinks."

Along with the URL, you must provide two dates: (1) the date of the publication of the material (if available) and (2) the date that you, as the researcher, located the information. The date of publication goes at the end of the entry and is placed in parentheses. Your access date follows the title and is introduced by the word "Retrieved."

Below is a basic model for online source entries in a References list:

> Author's Last Name, and Initials [if known]. (Date of publication if known). Title of document. *Title of complete work or site.* Retrieved month day, year, from Protocol and URL address

"Protocol" refers to a particular set of rules for performing tasks on the Internet such as Hypertext Transfer Protocol (HTTP), File Transfer Protocol (FTP), and telnet.

- **Online information database or scholarly project**

> Goofs browser. (1997–2002). *The Internet movie database.* Retrieved March 7, 2002, from http://us.imdb.com/Sections/Goofs

> Vassanji, M. G. (1997, August 8). *Canadian literature research service.* Retrieved April 28, 2005, from http://collection.nlc-bnc.ca/100/201/301/lecture/vassanji.htm

- **Personal or professional website**

  Shark byte. (1997–2002). *Jump the shark: The turning point of television programming.* Retrieved March 30, 2002, from http://www.jumptheshark.com/page.htm

  Shakespeare: Chill with Will. Retrieved May 22, 2005, from http://library.thinkquest.org/19539/front.htm

- **Online book or literary work**

  Maupassant, G. (1907). The necklace. *Bartleby.com: Great books online.* Retrieved March 7, 2005, from http://www.bartleby.com/195/20/html

  Service, R. (February 23, 2002). The cremation of Sam McGee. *The Robert W. Service home page.* Retrieved June 5, 2005, from http://www.ude.net/verse/cremation.html

- **Article in an online periodical**

  Bourette, S. (2002, March). Planespotting. *Shift.* Retrieved March 14, 2005, from http://www.shift.com/content/10.1/53/1.html

  Wahl, A. (2005, February 28). Emission impossible. *Canadian Business,* 24. Retrieved March 21, 2005, from eLibrary Canada database.

- **Online encyclopedia**

  Art Deco. *Encyclopaedia Britannica.* Retrieved April 22, 2005, from Encyclopaedia Britannica Online.

  Charter comes into effect. *The Canadian Encyclopedia 2001.* Retrieved March 14, 2005, from http://tceplus.com/Timeline/charter_frame.htm

- **Online government publication**

  Canada. Health Canada. Health Products and Food Branch. (2003, June). *Natural health products in Canada: A history.* Retrieved April 4, 2005, from http://www.hc-sc.gc.ca/hpfb-dgpsa/nhpd-dpsn/history_e.html#top

- **Newspaper article from an online (library subscription) database**

  Deutsch, C. H. (2005, February 27). Are women responsible for their own low pay? *New York Times*. Retrieved March 22, 2005, from National Newspaper Abstracts, ProQuest database.

- **CD-ROM**

  Canadian encyclopedia world edition. (1999). (Version 5). Toronto: McClelland & Stewart.

- **Online news service**

  MSNBC News Services. (2005, February 10). Images show wide rifts in tsunami seabed. Retrieved March 1, 2005, from the MSN.Com website: http://www.msnbc.msn.com/id/6946276/

- **Online posting, discussion group, or listserv**

  Fox, F. (2004, March 12). Nanotech—The next controversy alike GM? Message posted to http://www.euroscience.net/article6.html

- **Personal communications (electronic)**

E-mail, electronic bulletin board messages, and the like (along with non-electronic personal communications such as letters, memos, and telephone conversations) do not provide recoverable data and therefore are not included in the References list. Cite personal communications, including electronic communications, in your paper only. Give the surname and initials of the communicator along with the date. E.g.,

  (J. K. Smith, personal communication, June 13, 2005)

Never provide your source's e-mail address or telephone number.

SAMPLE REFERENCES LIST

Note that entries in a References list are arranged alphabetically according to the first word in the entry. Entries in a References list are *not* numbered. (The numbers listed to the right of the sample page are included only to help you find the entry format for some of the reference citations given earlier in Appendix B.)

The sample References list below includes the following sources:

1. Article in an online periodical
2. Article in a newspaper
3. Book by three authors
4. Article in a scholarly journal
5. Selection from an anthology
6. Movie
7. Book by one author
8. Article in a monthly magazine
9. Online government publication
10. Online database
11. Magazine article from an online (library subscription) database

References

Bourette, S. (2002, March). Planespotting. *Shift*. Retrieved March 14, 2005, from http://www.shift.com/content/10.1/53/1.html   1.

Canada to toughen auto-emissions rules. (2002, April 5). *The Wall Street Journal*, p. A6.   2.

France, H., Rodriguez, M., & Hett, G. (2004). *Diversity, culture and counselling: A Canadian perspective.* Calgary: Detselig.   3.

Helson, R., & Pals, J. (2000). Creative potential, creative achievement, and personal growth. *Journal of Personality, 68*(2), 39–44.   4.

Mistry, R. (2001). Journey to Dharmsala. In C. Meyer & B. Meyer (Eds.), *The reader: Contemporary essays and writing strategies.* (pp. 38–51). Toronto: Prentice.   5.

Moore, M. (Writer, Producer, Director). (2002). *Bowling for Columbine* [Motion picture]. Canada: Alliance Atlantis.   6.

Patterson, K. (2000). *The water in between: A journey at sea.* Toronto: Vintage Canada.   7.

Sreenivasan, A. (2002, February). Keeping up with the cones. *Natural History*, 40–46.   8.

Statistics Canada. (2002, October 11). Infant mortality rates. Retrieved October 12, 2005, from http://www.statcan.ca/english/Pgdb/health21.htm   9.

Vassanji, M. G. (1997, August 8). *Canadian literature research service.* Retrieved April 28, 2005, from http://collection.nlc-bnc.ca/100/201/301/lecture/vassanji.htm   10.

Wahl, A. (2005, February 28). Emission impossible. *Canadian Business*, 24. Retrieved March 21, 2005, from eLibrary Canada database.   11.

Copyright Acknowledgements